A LITTLE THING CALLED
LIFE

*On Loving Elvis Presley,
Bruce Jenner, and
Songs in Between*

LINDA THOMPSON

DEY ST.
AN IMPRINT OF WILLIAM MORROW *PUBLISHERS*

All photos courtesy of the author unless otherwise indicated.

HarperCollins books may be purchased for educational, business, or sales promotional use. For information, please email the Special Markets Department at SPsales@harpercollins.com.

A hardcover edition of this book was published in 2016 by Dey Street Books, an imprint of William Morrow Publishers.

FIRST DEY STREET BOOKS PAPERBACK EDITION PUBLISHED 2017.

Designed by Paula Russell Szafranski

Library of Congress Cataloging-in-Publication Data has been applied for.

ISBN 978-0-06-246975-5

17 18 19 20 21 DIX/LSC 10 9 8 7 6 5 4 3 2 1

A LITTLE THING CALLED LIFE

To Brandon and Brody—

I dedicate not only this memoir, but my very life to you.
You are my reason for being, and the greatest source of inspiration
for every beat of my heart and every breath that I take.
Thank you for teaching me how to love unconditionally.
Life has presented more than your fair share of challenges and
circumstances that you have had to accept and understand. That you
have had the capacity to reach deep into your being to excavate noble
displays of forgiveness, tolerance, strength, humility, fearlessness, loyalty,
love, and integrity, inspires me every day to try to be a better human being.
Enjoying the privilege and honor of being your mother
and watching you grow into the incredible men you
are today has been my life's greatest blessing.
I love you immeasurably—to infinity—and back again . . .

To Mama and Daddy—

I pray that wherever you are in the great ethereal unknown, you will
feel the love and gratitude I send out to you for being the best parents
you knew how to be. I think of you every day, and I acknowledge and
thank you for helping to nurture and mold me into the person I am. I am
grateful for the sacrifices you both made so that Sam and I could have a
better life than you did. I write my life's history in part because I want
Brandon and Brody to have questions answered that I never got to ask
you. I hope they will ask about anything unanswered on these pages.
Mama and Daddy, you were the genesis of my life, and it's only with
time and experience I now understand you were the truest hearts
who would never turn away from me—loving me unconditionally
as I now love my sons. That is a gift I could never repay, I can only
pass it on and be grateful for your devotion. I love you eternally.

Contents

Introduction

I originally began writing this book over ten years ago, but after completing about four chapters, I realized I could not reveal my whole truth without compromising or infringing on another's. So I put my book on the shelf until Caitlyn Jenner emerged, freeing me to share my journey.

I can't say it has been easy to dig down deep to excavate old, emotion-eliciting memories that I had long ago dealt with and compartmentalized. It has been furthermore challenging to relive the moments, feel the emotions again, and articulate them sensitively and effectively. But in navigating those personal, internal, meandering rivers of thought, I hold firm to the belief our experiences in life are meant to be shared with one another.

In many ways, the origins of this book go back even further than ten years. I was first approached to tell my story in a book almost forty years ago when Elvis died. I didn't accept because I never wanted to be thought of as someone who exploited my relationship with Elvis. There was already an abundance of those opportunistic individuals. I wanted to stand apart as someone who had been there for the right reason. It has always meant more to me than riches to know that as he lay dying, the last thought Elvis would have had of me was the certainty that he had been loved purely by me. That knowledge offers a soul satisfaction that money cannot buy. I simply loved him and I felt an obligation to protect the memory of the time I'd shared with him.

I knew, eventually, it would be important to discuss my time with him, to detail the man I knew for fans and cultural historians alike. I knew that by waiting until I had carved out my own way in the world and lived my life more fully, my inclusion of the Elvis years would carry more dignity and credibility. There was a sense of responsibility to Elvis's memory and his legions of fans I felt then, and still feel to this day, to portray him as I knew him. As the adage goes, "You don't really know someone unless you live with them." Only two women ever actually lived with Elvis. I was one of the two.

Trust is a critical component in every relationship. Elvis trusted me so completely that he allowed me to see him at his most vulnerable. He shared his deepest fears, sorrows, joys, memories, and aspirations with me. Elvis was a beautifully complex figure. All the passing years have allowed for many books and accounts of his life, his loves, his demise, and his subsequent purported sightings. So many of these have struggled to capture the paradoxical nature of the man I knew, and it was with no small sense of obligation that I knew my job was to do justice to the divergent sides of his personality—the good and the bad, the laughter and the rage, the levity and the depth.

His paradoxical nature was demonstrated in every facet of his life. There is no question that Elvis had his dark side. And that dark side, like everything else about Elvis, was larger than life. I'm sure it comes as no surprise that Elvis was not a perfect man. After all is said and done, he was, and we should always allow him to be, remarkably human. It would be a disservice to his memory and disingenuous on my part to portray Elvis as anything but that. My honesty takes nothing away from his absolute greatness. Undoubtedly, Elvis Presley changed my life forever, and after nearly forty years of harboring his special words and deeds to myself, I now feel compelled to share Elvis with those who love him still.

And yet I've always known that there would be more that I had to share. My poetry writing, which began when I was only nine years old, transformed into a career as a song lyricist not long after Elvis's death. Of course, Elvis was an extremely influential and important part of my history, but the hopeful thing about life was that it kept going even after Elvis "left the building." Never was that more true than in my case.

In the years since my time with Elvis, the story of my life has become a richer, more complicated version than I ever could have imagined. After Elvis's death, I met a man who would be my next great love, a man I was convinced would be with me for the rest of my life—Bruce Jenner, the father of my two sons, Brandon and Brody.

Bruce and I were together for six amazing years, building a perfect family and living a life as close to idyllic as I could have imagined. But in the same vein of sharing the truth and trying to live a life of integrity, I would not have been able to write an honest portrayal of my marriage to Bruce Jenner and the real reason we divorced, until now. Bruce confessed to me more than thirty years ago that he had gender dysphoria, and I kept his secret for all that time, not even telling our sons until three years ago. I would have never been the one to "out Bruce." I have respectfully kept these secrets private and would have taken these confidences to my grave had Bruce not publicly announced her transition to Caitlyn. It has always remained of crucial importance to me that Bruce be allowed to reveal his own truth on HER own terms. As Caitlyn, she is doing that. (Forgive the mixed use of pronouns when referring to Bruce, now Caitlyn. I will refer to Bruce as him before the transition because that's who I knew and fell in love with. No disrespect intended toward her, Caitlyn—I hope you will understand the complexity of my position.)

Caitlyn's story, and her struggle, is uniquely hers; my experiences with Bruce from almost three decades ago are, commensurately, uniquely my own. I was devastated when Bruce confided to me his gender dysphoria and his plans to transition. My fairy tale unraveled concurrently with my confidence in my own judgment, sexuality, femininity, the future for my two baby sons, and everything of which I thought I was certain. As destabilizing as my new truth was, and as brokenhearted as I was, my very spirit ached for the pain and disassociation that Bruce had felt for all of his life. As much as this is about Bruce and Caitlyn, it's not all about her. Every perspective has at least two sides, and this is the story of what I went through as a wife and a mother during a time when the cultural understanding of transgender was far less progressive than it is today.

If Bruce had told me earlier of his gender issues, I would not have married him. I am so thankful to him, the universe, God, and any powers that be that he didn't confide that truth because as difficult a time as that was, my marriage to Bruce gave me the two greatest joys of my life, my sons Brandon and Brody. They are the most important facets of my very existence. No matter what else I may have done or accomplished, no matter how many titles or awards I have received, no matter who I have loved—they will always be that part of my life of which I am most proud, and who I most love. They have inspired so many song lyrics that I have written, and I wish to share some of that inspiration with you. I have included some of those song lyrics here between each chapter of my life.

I have been fortunate to enjoy a very successful career as a lyricist that includes an Academy Award nomination for best song in a motion picture for "I Have Nothing" by Whitney Houston from *The Bodyguard*. There have been Grammy nominations, songs written for various philanthropic purposes, and an Emmy win.

And it was through my second marriage to mad musical genius David Foster that my songwriting career blossomed like never before, amid the backdrop of our sometimes difficult marriage. We were together for nineteen years, and shared a deep love for each other, for the art of making music, attempts at responsible parenting, and so much more. I will always be grateful for our time together, and I appreciate all that David has meant through the years to me and to my sons.

Life is nothing if not unpredictably strange. And yet, every breath we inhale and exhale is a gift not to be taken for granted. Despite the unpredictable ride that I've been on, I continue to practice the art of forgiveness. Forgiveness is a gift we give ourselves. We can only keep our side of the street clean. What our neighbor does or doesn't do is up to them. We cannot control other people. Time tempers all judgment, reveals all truth, and carves a deeper understanding of life and the human condition into our beings. I wouldn't allow the impulse to have a "knee jerk response" to circumstances in the story of my life dictate that I write my memoir before its time had come. Now I feel the time is right.

All of the events and experiences I share herein have been faithfully rendered as I recall them to the very best of my ability. In some cases, names have been changed to protect the privacy of those individuals. Though conversations stem from my keen recollection of them, and in some cases notes taken through the years, they are not meant to represent word for word documentation in every instance. I have painstakingly retold them in a manner that evokes the true meaning and feeling of what was said.

I have often declared that the girlfriend, wife, or ex of a celebrated person must be twice as good to be taken half as seriously at anything. I truly feel that I've been blessed with a life filled with its own set of successes, failures, heartaches, joys, and emotional explorations. In sharing it, my hope is that it may provide inspiration, comfort, humor, understanding, enlightenment, entertainment, and even a sense of belonging to another soul in search. Although I feel that everyone has a story worth telling, and that every life holds the same worth, let's be honest, some individual existences become "literary lives," simply in the process of living them fully as time presents them. Some of us have found ourselves woven into extraordinary tapestries, pages and chapters of life that become natural fodder for a memoir. Such is the life I have lived thus far.

The whole purpose of my career, and of my very existence, has been to connect with others on an emotional level. After all, the more we endeavor to understand and empathize with another human being's life, the more we unravel the mystery of our own, this extraordinary gift we've been given, A LITTLE THING CALLED LIFE.

"A Little Thing Called Life"

Somewhere near, a baby cries
Somewhere far, someone dies
And everywhere you'd swear
There were a pair of hidden eyes
When the moon sets, the sun will
  rise

Without a doubt, the rain will fall
And then the sky, reclaims it all
It's just a simple cycle
That happens someplace everyday
It's just a little thing called life

We'll never fully understand it
And we can't always command it
The truth is not always plain to see
Never ever underrate it
We should always celebrate it
Every day's a miracle for me

There'll be smiles along with tears
And you'll be strong to mask your
  fears
And people everywhere must share
  the ocean and the sky
It's just a little thing called life

Extraordinary people live each day
  as you and I
It's just a little thing called life

We'll never fully understand it
And we can't always command it
The truth is not always plain to see
Never ever underrate it
We should always celebrate it
Every day's a miracle for me

The planet turns and love unfolds
Passion burns, then turns cold
But every day's a new day
Another chance to get it right
It's just a little thing . . .
It's just a little thing called life

Lyric: Linda Thompson

Chapter One

The King Is Gone

"Linda! It's Lisa!" a breathlessly excited nine-year-old Lisa Marie Presley urgently gasped into the phone.

An immediate smile crossed my face upon hearing the voice of the little girl I had grown to love deeply over the past several years. It was not uncommon for Lisa to telephone me in a playful mood just to say, "Hi," and that she missed me, as she was doing now from Graceland in Memphis. Her father, Elvis, and I had broken up eight months before this August 16 phone call, after having lived together for almost five years. She had reached me in my apartment in Los Angeles, where her father had stayed with me on several occasions.

"Hey—you little goobernickle!" I jokingly answered. *Goobernickle* was a term of endearment Elvis and I had come up with for his little offspring. "I know who this is. You don't have to tell me!"

"Linda! My daddy's dead! My daddy's dead!"

"No! No!" I automatically responded, instantly frozen by a dread of acknowledging the truth. "He can't be. He's not, honey."

"Yes, he is! He is! They told me. He smothered in the carpet!"

Numbly, I threw the phone across the room. I stood there, catatonic, gazing at the receiver. *He smothered in the carpet*, repeatedly raced through my stinging mind. Those gravity-filled words sank my heart

1

with the reality that Elvis Presley was in all probability dead. On too many occasions to count, during my years of loving and caring for him, I had found and attended to him in deathly, compromising circumstances like the one Lisa had just described.

I stared at the phone for as long as it took me to gather my senses enough to realize that this incredibly bright and sensitive nine-year-old child had had the presence of mind to pick up the phone to share this devastating occurrence with me. *She needs me*, I thought, as I reached for the cold, hard, plastic transmitter that held my connection to the biggest part of Elvis's heart, his little girl.

"Oh, Lisa, are you sure, sweetheart?" I asked. "Are you sure he didn't just go to the hospital like when I was with him before? Remember, he was just sick, but he got better?"

"No, he's gone. That's what they said! Nobody knows yet! I called you first! Nobody knows but us! He's dead!"

Hearing the pain and disbelief in her too-young-to-lose-her-daddy voice, I knew I needed to say something to comfort Lisa.

"Oh, Yisa Marisa," I said, using another pet name Elvis and I had for her. "Your daddy loves you so much. Please always remember that. And, sweetheart, love never dies. You'll always have that. You'll always be his little Goobernickle, the one he's loved the most. What he's most proud of. It'll be okay, honey. You'll always feel his love with you."

I babbled on and on, hoping something I said might resonate with comfort and reassurance. I could just picture the diminutive, blond-haired, now fatherless Lisa Marie, her tiny hand clutching the phone, standing alone on unsteady little legs.

"Who's with you, baby?" I asked.

Before I had more time to dwell on the lonely, imagined scenario playing out in my mind, I heard a familiar, calm, and deep-voiced, Southern drawl take over the phone.

"Linda, you need to come home right away," said my brother, Sam, who had been working for Elvis as a bodyguard for the past few years. Even though Elvis and I were no longer together, he had kept Sam on as a trusted employee.

"Oh my God, Sam," I said. "Is he really gone? Is Elvis really dead? Could Lisa be mistaken?"

"You need to come home to Memphis as soon as you can get here," Sam answered, seemingly unable to articulate the doom-filled words that would in fact confirm my desperate query.

"Sam, is he dead? Please tell me the truth!" I pleaded.

A pause, a sigh, then a resigned and defeated, "Elvis is gone. You need to come home."

The words escaping from Sam's tight throat broke the last piece of my heart, still clinging to the hope that Elvis might somehow be alive.

"Sam, stay with Lisa," I said. "Take care of her. Let me speak to her again, please."

I rambled to the little girl, who was no doubt reeling, reassuring her as best as I could, and telling her I would be there soon to "mug her noggin."

"C'mere, you, get over here and let me mug your noggin!" Elvis would growl through grinding teeth when he was overwhelmed with his need to show affection for Lisa Marie or me. He would grab the backs of our necks, look deeply into our eyes with those otherworldly eyes of his, then press his forehead, hard, onto ours. He would then close his eyes tightly, grit his teeth together, and forehead to forehead, press and roll slightly to "mug noggins." It was apparently something his beloved mama did with him when he was just a "little shaver."

Elvis couldn't resist baby talk. He spoke it fluently, received it hungrily. I understood both the intensity and the silliness of the gibberish, since my own family communicated with each other in the same loving fashion. It was always the tone in which Elvis and I spoke to each other. If he addressed me as Linda, I knew our conversation would be serious. He always called me by pet names, such as Ariadne, in homage to Ariadne Pennington, a little three-year-old girl character in one of his movies, or more commonly, Mommy. Looking back now, these both seem a little odd to me, but at the time, they felt quite natural.

I hung up the phone. Silence. Time to grieve. No one to comfort, no one to comfort me. I was hesitant to call anyone, because Lisa had told me that nobody knew. I certainly didn't want to alert the media. I sat there in my quiet apartment, in my grief and disbelief, and began to cry.

If there had ever been any notion of reconciliation, any chance that Elvis and I might have gotten back together, it was now dashed;

between Elvis and me, there were no more maybes. The finality of this knowledge sank into my heart and deepened my grief. I would never again hear that voice I'd loved so much, except on the radio. I would never again feel his touch. I would never again have the chance to say anything I had left unsaid.

I turned on the television, hoping the news would break and I'd be free to call someone. Finally, it did. It was confirmed: "Elvis Presley died today at his Graceland mansion in Memphis, Tennessee." The voice droned on, and then something inexplicable happened: The anchor moved on to other news. *How could that be?* I thought, my irrational mind full of grief. *There is no other news. There is nothing else.* Suddenly I was confronted with a difficult truth to absorb—life does indeed go on, and we must roll along with it. But for those of us who are shocked into stricken grief, we must be gentle with ourselves, and others, and allow for that time of mourning. And looking around my apartment, I came to see just how difficult this would be for me.

The space of my apartment was still filled with Elvis's energy. I was sitting on an army green sofa he had given me from his Beverly Hills home, on which he and I had sat and lounged together. On my walls were the paintings he had also given me from his home. The bed I lay down on was a bed he and I had shared together. When I retreated to the bathroom to look in the mirror at my tear-swollen face, it was a mirror that he had looked into and seen his own reflection in. When I sat down to have a cup of tea, I was seated at the glass-topped table at which he'd also sat. Looking at the four white wicker fan-backed chairs, I recalled him sitting across from me, and still saw his face lingering there.

I stood and washed my cup in the sink, realizing that nowhere was safe in that little apartment because he had been in all of those rooms with me. From the living room, the sound of the news drifted in, as the channel I had turned on earlier was revisiting the story of his passing with expanded and repeated coverage, and I could hear him singing, "Are You Lonesome Tonight?" Hearing his voice, and those words, of all words, of course, I just lost it. So many feelings, rushing me, stirring my memories. I could still feel him there with me, his presence and the history we'd shared together, and even to this day, I can recall vividly, viscerally, the essence of who and what Elvis Presley was in my life. He had breathed that same air I was breathing, and now, he would breathe no more. I started crying again, and this time I couldn't stop.

Elvis had now more than left the building. His soul had "slipped the surly bonds of earth and winged and soared where eagles dare not fly." Elvis loved the Blue Angels' creed, that lovely prose he quoted often. In so many ways, he was not of this earth. He felt a strong connection to the spirit world and to the ethereal, that he was merely "passing through" this world.

Maybe Elvis is home at last, I thought.

As word spread, some of my friends began calling to check on me. Between calls, I started the process of packing, with memories of Elvis still flooding my thoughts. How he used to come in through the back sliding glass door that led out to my little patio and the alley beyond, because he couldn't just walk in the front door. How he used to baby-talk my dog, a little Maltese he had given me.

Sometime shortly after I began to pack, all the power went off in my apartment. Not long after that, my next-door neighbor knocked on my door and stuck her head in.

"Can I get you anything?" she asked. "Can I do anything for you? We heard the news about Elvis, and we know he was a big part of your life. We used to see him slipping in the back door here."

"Thank you so much," I said. "But, no, I have everything I need. Oh, is your power off?"

"No, ours is fine," she said. "Let me know if you do need anything."

I smiled and nodded as she closed the door behind her. As the day darkened into night, I began to light candles to better navigate around my apartment. A few friends came by, including my workout buddy, Deborah.

"Oh, how sweet, you're lighting candles for Elvis," she said.

"Well, not really," I said. "I have to see to get ready to fly out of here, and there's no power in my apartment."

I was not unaware of the strangeness of the situation. It was downright eerie. As the night wore on, and the power remained inexplicably out in my apartment only, I began to consider all the candles for Elvis after all. It was his first candlelight vigil, a tradition his fans have carried out every anniversary of his passing since that day.

And so, with candles lighting the way, I put one thing after another in the suitcase, until I was confronted with a question:

What would he want me to wear to his funeral?

Even though I went through the motions of going to my closet to survey the many dresses Elvis had gotten made for me in Las Vegas by the dressmaker-to-the-stars, Suzy Creamcheese, I knew immediately what I would wear to his funeral. Still, I paused at a really pretty black backless dress I'd bought at Giorgio's on Rodeo Drive, when Elvis sent me on a shopping spree there toward the end of our relationship. I knew that wasn't what he'd want me to wear, and besides, it wouldn't be appropriate to wear a backless dress to a funeral in Memphis, a Southern Baptist capital. Knowing how Elvis had been deeply influenced by colors and numbers, and their spiritual significance, I chose the dress I'd always known I'd wear, a lavender silk dress, not the traditional black outfit. Elvis believed that all shades of purple emitted the highest spiritual vibrations and considered the color to be the most closely connected to the purity and power of God. That was enough of a fashion endorsement for me.

I didn't care if eyebrows would be raised because I wasn't wearing traditional black at a funeral in the conservative South. I only wanted to honor Elvis's sweet soul and his deepest beliefs. Coincidentally, I'd been wearing a skirted bodysuit with lavender flowers on it the night we met, and so it was the perfect symbol of our union. Quite honestly, I felt a little smug that I knew him so very well, and could nearly channel his thoughts and feelings. Wearing a lavender dress in a sea of dark mourners would be my way of communicating with Elvis's spirit.

It was between him and me, and I knew he would have heartily approved.

"To Where You Are"

Who can say for certain
Maybe you're still here
I feel you all around me
Your memory's so clear
Deep in the stillness
I can hear you speak
You're still an inspiration
Can it be
That you are my
Forever love
And you are watching me from up
  above

Fly me up to where you are
Beyond each distant star
I wish upon tonight
To see you smile
If only for a while
To know you're there
A breath away's not far
To where you are

Are you gently sleeping
Here inside my dream
And isn't faith believing
All power can't be seen
As my heart holds you
Just one beat away
I cherish all you gave me every day

'Cause you are my
Forever love
Watching me
From up above
And I believe
That angels breathe
And that love
Will live on
And never leave

Fly me up to where you ae
Beyond each distant star
I wish upon tonight
To see you smile
If only for a while
To know you're there
A breath away's not far
To where you are
A breath away's not far
To where you are

LYRIC: LINDA THOMPSON

Chapter Two

Made in Memphis

My love for Elvis began long ago in my little Memphis girl's heart. In my mind, it seemed perfectly logical that I would grow up to marry the man everyone in the Mississippi Delta talked about and swooned over, and whose music was rocking the world. *Why not aim high?*

"Y'all know what, Mama and Daddy?" I declared at the breakfast table one humid Memphis morning. "When I grow up, I'm gonna marry Elvis Presley!"

My parents smiled indulgently.

"Well, now honey child, by the time you grow up, Elvis will be too old for you," they said.

"I don't care, he'll still be singing 'Hound Dog'!" I retorted, undeterred.

And so he was.

My family was "country"—Southern to the core, as was Elvis's. *Country* connotes much more than a musical genre. It indicates strong familial ties, a particular preference for "soul food"—country fried, refried, chicken fried *anything*, double dipped, extra creamy and thickened gravy (*not* on the side). In fact, just fry any food group. If it's fried, it'll always taste good. Add some overcooked vegetables, preferably turnip greens steeped in ham hocks or salt pork for flavoring, and finish it off with hearty corn bread baked in the oven in a cast iron skillet. Of course, the unique musical mélange of the region is so much a part of life in the South that it was a form of sustenance for us, too. It certainly was for Elvis. Southern gospel, country, blues, rock, and the amalgamation of all those genres engendered his redefinition of music as we know it today. Although Elvis drew on familiar Southern musical forms, he was a true original, and he created a sound that was his alone.

My mother, Margie White Thompson, was five feet ten inches and 126 pounds of dark-haired beauty when she married my father, Sanford Able Thompson, a six-foot-tall, 165-pound handsome young man. He had just returned from two and a half years of service fighting in Germany, Belgium, France, and England during World War II. The first time my father saw my mother, he turned to his army buddy in the restaurant.

"You see that woman over there?" he declared. "I'm going to marry her."

For him, it was truly love at first sight. They knew each other for only six months before they married, and their marriage lasted for forty-five years, until my mother died. My father never remarried. She was the one love of his life.

Even with their deep love, theirs was not an easy life. They both had their own privations growing up in the Depression-era South, and these shaped much of their adult lives. My mother had been one of five sisters born to a poor tenant farmer and his housewife. She had to quit school before graduating to help her father work in the fields, picking cotton, sawing logs, and plowing rows with a team of mules. Her statuesque height, fitness, strength, and determination came in handy for the hard work she had to do.

Her long legs couldn't move fast enough when she decided to get married at only eighteen, just to get away from her difficult life, and in the process she said "yes" to a man who would prove to be abusive. She soon became pregnant, which only made things harder. Mama told us the story of when she decided to leave her philandering new husband. It seems she was eight months along when hubby pulled into their driveway *with a date*, who waited in his car while he changed shirts. I don't believe he escaped with that new shirt intact, and that was the end of that ill-fated union.

My mother's first child was a boy, and she named him Donald Joseph. She readily took to mothering and brought her newborn treasure home to live with her parents. Donald Joseph was a gorgeous baby, Mama said, with perfect little features, long eyelashes, olive skin, and a head full of dark hair. Sadly he died in my mother's arms when he was only weeks old. Mama said when she went to his crib to gather him in her arms, a beautiful blue light mysteriously moved across his bed. She knew then something was wrong. My mother was left devastatingly alone with the love only a mother knows lingering in her aching heart.

Years later, when my brother, Sam, and I were born to Mama and Daddy, she became obsessed with protecting us and made certain we never doubted how deeply she was devoted to us. We would come to understand that her overprotective nature was the result of her tragic loss so many years before, a loss she never overcame. Her deep sadness over Donald Joseph stayed with her until she left this earth.

My father graduated from high school in Monette, Arkansas, a place he liked to refer to as "God's country." It was anything but. Oh sure, it had its own charm, as do most quaint, small towns. But as in many of the small Southern communities of the day, there was a heavy pathos to go along with the oppressive humidity.

Like Elvis's father, my daddy worked very hard, picking cotton, plowing fields, milking cows, and doing all the chores that come with country life. He would revel in telling Sam and me stories about when he was a little boy, our favorite being about how he and his brothers took turns riding their milk cow, Susie. It all seemed so Tom Sawyeresque that I guess we idealized our daddy's childhood, imagining it was more fun than it was in reality.

My mama and daddy helped to create and mold the person I still am today. Their hardships growing up, their successes and losses, their absolute selflessness in regard to their children, and their complicated relationship with each other still flow through my mind and memory, becoming an intrinsic part of who I am.

My relationship with my mother, however, was a complicated one. We lived in dread of her anger and frustration, for her sake as much as our own. When she lost control of her sensibilities, things started flying.

My poor father was usually the brunt of her rage. When Mama was having one of her tantrums, she would say unthinkably unkind things to Daddy and throw anything from ashtrays to full coffeepots at him, without thought of the damage she might be doing to her children's psyche, much less to my father's flesh and bones. I felt protective of him, yet helpless in my ability to deflect her anger toward him, so I quickly became a "daddy's girl."

Making things harder was the fact that we were poor, and we knew it. God bless my mother, she didn't have the "tools" we all refer to now to keep her from hysteria when the bills came due that we were unable to pay. She went into panic-and-blame mode. My security was threatened every time (and there were many) I heard my mother becoming hysterical about the conditions under which we lived. She would have to balance our family budget down to the last nickel, and didn't quit her calculations until our meager books were balanced. Still, there was often not enough money to pay our rent, and then Mama would embark on her passionate tangents about how she was going to leave "big M" (Memphis), take us with her, and divorce Daddy.

Because of all this, my childhood was not an easy one. As a matter of fact, I'm now certain that as a child, I effectively learned how to "walk on eggshells" to avoid inciting anger and contentious confrontation, an instinct that would later carry over to my relationship with a volatile Elvis, and perhaps others. As a little girl I vowed to never treat my man with less than total respect and kindness. In a way, I unconsciously prepared myself to put up with more indignation and potential mistreatment, although I only became aware of this later in life.

Living through someone's tirades was never a comfortable experience, but it was a familiar one. I learned how to compartmentalize the variable behaviors of those I loved. My mother, like Elvis, was inordinately affectionate and loving, and I never doubted her devotion to me, but that intensity could turn on a dime and become highly reactive, unbridled anger. Very unsettling, but familiar nonetheless. When you don't crumble at repeated verbal lashings, you eventually don't feel as threatened by them. However, let me state here and now as an older, wiser, more experienced being, that verbal abuse—and abuse of any kind—should never be tolerated. Sometimes we tend to make excuses for those we love, but that's not our responsibility. We all should own our actions.

But growing up wasn't all bad. When Mama was not on a tirade, she was quite kindhearted. She taught me many valuable lessons, the most important being about a parent's unconditional love for their child. My parents gave me that glorious gift, devoting their hearts, souls, and lives to my brother, Sam, and me. I believe they did the best they could under the circumstances.

Along with all of her shortcomings, my mother was beautiful, bright, talented, and had a wonderful sense of humor, but she seldom got to let any of those attributes fully flower. With a rich, alto voice that could sing any harmony, she seemed at her best and happiest when she was singing or playing piano. She was also incredibly kind toward animals, instructing me early on that animals were "at the mercy of the world." I'm sure my animal advocacy began early and that I was influenced by her tender teachings. Of course, even my mama thought I sometimes went too far. I rescued every creature I could, from a cat I named Tabby, who was eventually hit by a car, necessitating a proper funeral, to a broken-winged bird I nursed with a Popsicle stick splint.

"What are you dragging into this house now, for God's sake?" she used to say.

Her speech was peppered with colloquialisms like "You can't make a silk purse out of a sow's ear," but she was never hesitant to throw in a fairly generous dose of expletives as well. She was all Southern lady, with every contradiction, complexity, and fascination that term embodies.

Beyond my parents, my family was large and Southern in many senses of the word. I called my mother's mother Ninny, and her father, Pappaw, and together with them, Mama and Daddy, aunts, uncles, and cousins . . . thirteen of us grandchildren, we all got together at Christmas, Thanksgiving, birthdays, and other holidays. It was usually a pot-luck affair with everyone bringing a covered dish. There was always singing. We gathered in a circle and sang hymns mostly. My aunts would blend together in perfect harmonies, and we would earnestly emote until we all collapsed in laughter over some silly moment. There was great kinship, closeness, kindness, music, laughter, and deep love shared by my family in those formative years of mine.

In many ways, mine was a fairly typical childhood in the South. As a little girl growing up in Memphis, I loved it when my daddy took me on Saturdays to the Strand theater, where they showed Elvis movies. I grew up on those movies, and they colored my notions of romance, music, and cinema. My best friend as a little girl was a pretty blond girl named Teresa, who lived across the street from me on Queensbury Circle. Sometimes she and I rode the bus downtown to go see a movie and have our photos taken at Blue Light Studios.

Though I was young, I was aware from an early age of the problems facing the South. There was, and still is today to a degree, a pathos indigenous to "Dixie," and the poverty and the prejudice that were woven into its history. I remember as a very young child going to a park with Mama and Daddy and wanting a drink of water. I headed toward a water fountain but Mama stopped me.

"Not that one, honey . . ." she said. "You have to drink from this one that says 'Whites Only.' "

"Why?!" I asked. "Why can't I just drink water from this one, Mama?"

I wanted to know. Mama was at a real loss for an explanation because the very heart of the concept was so ridiculous.

"I don't know why, to tell you the truth, hon," she stammered. "That's just the way it is, and I don't want anybody giving us any trouble over a drink of water today."

I often heard my mother speak of the plight of blacks striving for equality, and she and my father both were sympathetic to the struggle. I remember that occasion vividly because I couldn't understand what the big deal was. *People are just people and water is just water*, I thought. It didn't make sense to me then, and makes even less today.

When I was nine, I was baptized at Graham Heights Baptist Church. I always felt that God's gift to me when I was baptized was to anoint me with the ability to write poetry. I started writing poetry when I was nine years old, and wrote fairly prolifically for birthdays, Mother's Day, Father's Day, special occasions, and just to express myself and my feelings. It never occurred to me that I would one day make a good living at writing lyrics for songs. I would then, and will still now, write purely for my own self-expression without any commercial consideration (though those royalty checks are nice).

We grew up believing that cleanliness is next to godliness, and that our bodies are our temples and we have a responsibility to take care of our health and well-being. My mama also always made a point to instill in me the belief that being poor is nothing to be ashamed of, that you should always carry yourself with dignity and pride no matter your circumstance in life. There are certain things that one can help and things that one cannot help. Regarding those things of which we have no control, we should never have to apologize or be embarrassed.

More than anything, these early years shaped me into the woman with whom Elvis Presley would fall in love. To Elvis, all of these aspects of my Southern upbringing—from my family to my church to the aphorisms I heard—were familiar. Growing up in the South with poor but protective parents, experiencing Southern culture, the religious fervor, the familial ties, and hearing and dancing to the music that emanated from that region, those are all ingredients that my life shared with Elvis's. Elvis and I would often discuss how similarly our parents were raised, and how they raised us. Even our deeply idiosyncratic mothers seemed to share the same temperament. Elvis's mother was very much like mine, according to him: fiercely protective, undisciplined in her temper, inordinately affectionate, and loyal.

Elvis told me stories of when he was a little boy in Tupelo, Mississippi. Elvis's mother, Gladys Love Presley, doted on her only child. Elvis absolutely adored her. When speaking about her even years after her own untimely death at forty-six years of age, he grew teary-eyed and wistful. He was the ultimate mama's boy, in the very best sense of the term. He slept in the same bed as his mama and daddy until he was nine years old, he said. He grew up in the Pentacostal Church, where he said he'd run down the aisles singing "Adawoochie" because he was too little to pronounce "Hallelujah." He "got saved" while he and his family were living in a predominantly black neighborhood, according to him. Elvis said he was suddenly "filled with the Holy Spirit," inspiring him to gather his most treasured possessions, his comic book collection, run out into the streets, and give away these cherished comics to the neighborhood kids. In that moment of religious-fervor-fueled giving, Elvis's legendary spirit of generosity was born.

I believe it was there and then in the heart of the Delta, in the loving arms of his mother, with an acute sense of God, humanity, and humility, electrified with black gospel choirs singing traditional hymns in an untraditional way, that Elvis Presley developed such a huge capacity to feel for others, and to channel his God-given gift of song for the world to enjoy.

Elvis's father, Vernon Presley, told me that when Elvis was born on January 8, 1935, in a little "shotgun" house in Tupelo, he had an identical twin, Jessie Garon, who was stillborn. Mr. Presley said he always felt that Jessie Garon's soul became a part of Elvis's being, doubling his capability, charisma, and talents. He felt that perhaps Jessie's influence was even the reason for Elvis's paradoxical, dichotomous nature.

Mr. Presley went on to say that in that little nondescript house where legend was born, there were two identical glass bottles sitting decoratively, side by side, on a shelf. When the twins were born, as Elvis cried, and Jessie Garon lay still, one of those bottles inexplicably, spontaneously burst. Mr. Presley told me that he always perceived that as a sign from the heavens that one baby was destined to live for two, to survive to do great things. He felt there was a mystical quality to Elvis's very birth. In both mine and Elvis's families, there were convictions held that not everything in life has or needs an explanation. I believe that's called faith. Faith would always play a big part in my life and in Elvis's life.

In the end, all these similarities spoke to things Elvis loved in a woman and helped to make us feel as if we knew each other before we met. We were kindred spirits, sharing very much the same backstory and understanding each other's deepest thoughts.

It wasn't until junior high that I realized boys were paying more attention to me than they used to. I'd really never worn much makeup and had dressed fairly simply since we had no extra money for exceptional clothing. I always did take pride, however, in good grooming habits— my mother and I would sit at the kitchen table some evenings and do our nails together. But still, I was surprised when some of the boys in junior high nicknamed me "Hot Body." I must not have been very self-aware, because I had no idea that my body was changing shape into something that might be appealing to the opposite sex. I was embarrassed by the nickname, and yet strangely pleased.

I carved out a happy and memorable junior high and high school experience for myself. I made decent grades, had a lot of friends, and always seemed to have a boyfriend. I was one of those Goody Two-shoes who never smoked or drank, never did drugs, or had sex. Interestingly enough, even with all those self-imposed prohibitions, I still managed to accumulate a lot of friends, and be accepted into the "popular crowd." I was voted by my classmates Most Hilarious, Campus Leader, and even Homecoming Queen. I was also lucky enough to find a teacher, Nancy Crick, who continued to inspire my writing and develop my deep love of the English language and literature, and a fascination for words in general.

My senior year, I decided to crank it up a bit and made straight As, bringing up my grade point average enough for college. Even though I honestly felt I would be married with children before I ever finished a degree, my daddy made me promise I would go to college, convincing me to hold off on marriage until I gave college a try. At the time, I had been dating a high school football star who was going on to Arkansas State College in Jonesboro, and I planned to marry him and traipse along with him. We had an engagement ring on layaway—yes, layaway—but I called it off to follow my father's wishes.

I lived at home with my parents and commuted to Memphis State University, where I studied for four years, majoring in English and theater. I loved learning, growing, meeting new people, and feeling a sense of accomplishment, but, of course, I had to work to pay my own tuition and to have spending money. In fact, from the time I was fourteen, I worked various jobs ranging from hair styling for neighbors, to babysitting, to handling claims at the Tennessee Department of Employment Security Claims Division.

Around the time that I began at Memphis State, when I was eighteen, I was recruited by the organizers of a pageant that was a precursor to the Miss Tennessee America pageant. I was asked to enter the

Miss Shelby County pageant. I guess many of the pageant organizers at that time would peruse high school beauty queens and solicit their entry into pageants. Preliminary pageants leading up to Miss America involved a swimsuit competition, evening gown competition, and talent competition. I remember wondering what I would wear for the evening gown competition in the Shelby County pageant that year. My mother and I went out shopping and found a lovely white lace evening gown for less than thirty dollars. I went on to win the evening gown competition as well as Miss Congeniality and the title of Miss Shelby County. I felt I was onto something.

Around that same time I also won the title of Miss Mid-South. That was a particularly fun pageant to have won because it meant I was queen of the Mid-South Fair. As such, I got to go to the fairgrounds every day while the fair was going on, ride all the rides I wanted, and make appearances, but I also won a thousand-dollar wardrobe, luggage, and a small scholarship for school. I then won another scholarship by winning the pageant for the West Tennessee Okra Festival, a preliminary pageant that qualified me for Miss Tennessee America. Yes, I *was* onto something. This "pageant thing" could be a pretty good deal for a young girl looking to get ahead in life, as well as a ticket out of Memphis.

In the late 1960s and into the early '70s, there wasn't the stigma attached to the world of beauty pageants that we have now—if there was, I wasn't aware of it in my sheltered world. I did, however, find myself somewhat apologetic for being so successful in that arena. I continued my "career" of beauty pageant wins throughout my college years. One year, in fact, I held *seven* concurrent titles. I never thought I was the prettiest, smartest, or most outstanding contestant at any of the pageants I was in, but pageants represented opportunities on many levels, so I made the most out of them. I was personally awarded thousands of dollars in scholarship money, which I used to put myself through college. I won the use of a Pontiac Grand Prix for a year, and drove it to Fort Lauderdale, Florida, with five friends for spring break that year. I wore new clothes on the trip I had also won. I packed those new clothes in my new luggage, also bounty from the win. As Miss Liberty Bowl, I won a brand-new Chevrolet Vega that I eventually drove up to my new life at Graceland, where a bemused and smitten Elvis Presley goaded me about driving a Vega, handing me the keys to a new Continental Mark IV. I got to meet famous people like Bob Hope, Danny Thomas, and others. Yes, those pageants paid off handsomely.

I also met some lovely women in the various pageants in which I competed; some were incredibly talented, and some phenomenally gorgeous. Some were career pageant girls—one girl had entered more than ninety beauty contests and never won. Finally, one year, she was crowned Miss Fire Prevention, and it happened to be the same year she set a fireman's shirt ablaze while gesticulating and smoking a cigarette. Thankfully no firemen or beauty queens were actually harmed in the process. You can't make that up.

I didn't just win Miss Tennessee Universe. I also made a lifelong friend in the form of Tennessee pageant director Pat Kerr, a former Miss Tennessee Universe, who helped me with my wardrobe and confidence. I then went on to San Juan, Puerto Rico, to compete in the Miss USA pageant as Miss Tennessee Universe 1972. Each girl was assigned a roommate and mine was a busty, bawdy girl named Jeanne LeMay, representing Rhode Island. Jeanne liked to declare that she was from the smallest state but had the biggest boobs of any girl that year. And she did. She also had a darling, chatty, funny, profane personality and we became fast friends. We had so much fun together, and bonded so well, we couldn't care less about winning the pageant.

In the end, Miss Hawaii won the title of Miss USA that year. Jeanne and I booked a hotel room for the next two weeks, and we stayed on in Puerto Rico to extend our time together and vacation on that balmy island.

By the time I finished my pageant career I had accumulated about a dozen crowns and titles and participated in close to twenty contests. I had memorized more show tunes than I care to recall. I felt I was walking away a winner as I got closer to a hot summer July night that would change my life forever.

"God Bless the Heartaches"

Many times in a lifetime
A heart knows despair
And you wonder why some souls
  must bleed
And sometimes I question just who
  would be there
In my last hour of need

Life can be so uncertain
With pain all around
And heartache is so hard to face
For everything lost there's another
  found
And love seeks its own sacred space

God bless the heartaches
That reshape the soul in return
God keep our memories
God bless the lessons we learn

It is out of the shadows
We find warm sunlight
And we wouldn't know joy without
  sorrow
And there'd be no morning without
  the darkest night
That's just how life seems to go

So God bless the heartaches
That reshape the soul in return
God keep our memories
God bless the lessons we learn

So God bless the heartaches
That reshape the soul in return
God keep our memories
God bless the heartaches
God bless the tough breaks
God bless the lessons we learn

LYRIC: LINDA THOMPSON

Chapter Three

Love at First Sight

I've had more than a few days that changed my life forever, but none more than July 6, 1972. Not that I knew it at the time, of course. That's the thing about life-changing events—they have a way of appearing out of nowhere to alter your destiny.

On this sweltering summer day, I was walking down Madison Avenue in midtown Memphis with Miss Rhode Island, Jeanne LeMay, who, following our time in Puerto Rico, had moved to Memphis a few weeks earlier and started living with me at my aunt Betty Sue's house. I was a twenty-two-year-old theater and English major at Memphis State. I'd acted in some plays at school, and my dream was to move to Los Angeles and have a variety show like *The Carol Burnett Show*, with sketches, music, and musical comedy. Jeanne and I had talked about moving to New York so we could model and earn money being stewardesses for Eastern Airlines, which was based there. I guess you could say that was our Plan B, until we were able to facilitate our move to L.A. Regardless of L.A. or New York, I knew it would be up to me to make my way in the world, but I felt like I was on the right path. And having Jeanne, an upbeat friend who brought out the best in me, at my side was definitely one of the reasons.

"I'm hungry," Jeanne said. "There's a T.G.I. Friday's. Let's go eat."

"Oh, we can't go in there," I said.

"Why not?" she said.

"We can't go in there as unescorted ladies, because they serve alcohol in that establishment, and we'll look like pickups," I said, in full-on Southern Baptist mode.

"Put down your Bible and come on," she said, pushing through the door.

"What are you doing?" I asked, nervously, but just a step behind her.

"Let's live a little," she said. "Move your ass. We're going to get a hamburger."

"All right," I said. "But we're going to look like pickups. I'm telling you."

As we stood in the doorway, waiting for a table, I saw my friend Bill Browder, better known by his stage name, T. G. Sheppard, who had a big hit called "Devil in the Bottle."

When he saw me, he waved in my direction, a big grin on his face.

"Linda, come over," he said. "We'll buy you lunch."

"See, we're getting picked up," I said. "I told you we'd look like pickups."

Jeanne was used to how proper I was, and so she just rolled her eyes and headed right for the guys. We sat down at their table and ordered lunch.

"Hey, you girls want to meet Elvis tonight?" T.G. asked.

"Yes, absolutely," Jeanne said without taking a breath.

"Well, he rents out the Memphian Theater after midnight when he's in town," T.G. said. "He screens movies. I'd love to introduce you to Elvis."

"Oh, we'd love to, but we have to work tonight," I said, thinking of the modeling gig we were committed to as Miss Tennessee Universe and Miss Rhode Island Universe.

"Forget it," Jeanne said. "We're getting substitutes. We'll be there."

Just before midnight we drove down to the Memphian Theater in my little Chevy Vega. It didn't have any air-conditioning, and the heat was oppressive. We had the windows down, hoping for any breeze that might trickle in. As a longtime Elvis fan, it was hard to control my nerves, and on that hot summer night, the air enveloped us like a moving blanket of warmth and anticipation. Figuring we'd be immune to a ticket at midnight, I found an illegal parking space just outside the theater's front door. I had reasons for wanting my car close by.

"We're going to park right in the front here," I said. "Just in case things aren't on the up-and-up, we can make a quick getaway."

"Oh my God, you're so stuffy," Jeanne said, laughing.

As we walked up to the theater, I smoothed down my short silk skirt, which was fitted at the waist and flouncy. I was wearing it with a matching cream-colored bodysuit printed with lavender flowers, and lavender suede high-heeled sandals. I was, after all, beauty pageant material then, so I had a tiny little waist. Tanned from the Puerto Rican sun, I was wearing a push-up bra, enhancing the appearance of my Sally Average–sized breasts. *False advertising*, I thought to myself with a chuckle, as we knocked on the door and were admitted to the theater. Not that I was trying to dress attractively for Elvis. As far as I knew, he was a married man—he'd been with his wife Priscilla since 1967—and therefore absolutely off-limits. But I took my role as Miss Tennessee Universe just seriously enough that I felt I should look the part when meeting the King of Rock and Roll.

As we entered the theater lobby, I observed what looked to be a sizable entourage present, including Elvis's stepbrother, David Stanley, deejay George Klein, and a bunch of his friends. I was being introduced around as Miss Tennessee Universe; I smiled demurely, wondering what would happen next.

All of a sudden, a loud banging sound came from the direction of the side door. Somebody went over and opened it. In swooped Elvis, looking 100 percent Elvis, in a black suede cape with red satin lining, black pants with a flared leg and red satin piping, black stage boots, and big sunglasses, even at midnight—because when you're that cool, the sun shines on you twenty-four hours a day.

"Who the hell locked this door?" he yelled. He was carrying a two-foot-long black flashlight and started shining the light around the room in an aggressive manner.

"Oh, sorry boss," one of his entourage members said, squinting into the light.

Elvis flicked the light onto one of the other guys.

"Sorry, boss," that guy said. "We thought you were coming in the front door."

"I told somebody I was coming in the side door," he said. "I won't have that happen again."

Then he flashed the light on me. As soon as he saw my face, he dropped the light.

"Oh, excuse me," he said, his tone changing immediately to pure Southern gentleman. "Hello, honey."

Elvis strode right over to me, and I immediately felt the extraordinary presence he exuded, his natural charisma, a force field of pure energy and charm that radiated out of him.

"Hey, boss, this is Miss Tennessee Universe, Linda Thompson," said David Stanley.

"Oh, you're Miss Tennessee," Elvis said, his voice like honey.

Oh my God! When he smiles, his lip really does curl slightly, I mused.

"And this is Miss Rhode Island, Jeanne LeMay."

Jeanne, of course, was batting her eyelashes at him and smiling that blinding smile of hers from ear to ear.

But he already seemed smitten with me, as he had from the first moment he'd held the light on my face.

"Aren't you hot?" I teased him. "It's so hot and humid outside."

"No, honey, I just came out of the air-conditioned car into an air-conditioned building," he said, laughing uncertainly, as if unused to being questioned about his choice of wardrobe or anything else he did.

"We're kind of dressed a little like Dracula tonight, aren't we?" I said, still teasing.

Now he laughed openly, that wonderful, joyous laugh of his, catching on to the edge intrinsic to my sense of humor, and seeming to appreciate the fact that he'd found a sweet Southern belle who dared to joke and spar with him. One who would even venture to call him out for wearing a black suede cape in the middle of summer in hot, humid, Memphis, Tennessee.

We made a little small talk about the pageant, but it was as if he and I were already speaking a familiar language, born of our common upbringings yet personal to the two of us. We couldn't take our eyes off each other. Finally, he looked around the crowded lobby, everyone half-watching him, but pretending not to be. Everyone always watched Elvis when he was in the room.

"Let's get this movie started," he said.

Elvis swept into the theater first, and we all trailed behind him, as if he were the Pied Piper. A TV tray was set up by one of the seats midway down the theater, and right smack in the middle of the row. That was his designated seat and nobody sat in front of him. Ever. On his tray were a big Coca-Cola, a Mountain Valley Mineral Water, and his Tiparillo cigars.

After he took his seat, we all left an empty row behind him and then settled into the seats in the next few rows. George Klein, a locally famous deejay on the most popular station, WHBQ, and host of a weekly dance party in Memphis, came in and sat down next to me. I'd been a guest several times on his talk show, which was devoted to promoting local events and happenings. He'd had me on when I won Miss Memphis State University, Miss Liberty Bowl, and Miss Mid-South, and he'd taken to referring to me as "Miss Everything," as in "Here she is, again, ladies and gentlemen: Miss Everything."

During the lull before the movie started, Elvis turned around and smiled that gorgeous smile at me. He asked me a few questions, and I remembered to blurt out, "By the way, my aunt Marie went to high school with you at Humes High School, and she said to be sure to say hello to you if I met you tonight."

That seemed to amuse him.

"Oh, Aunt Marie," he said, as if he knew her, when of course he didn't.

As he turned back around, I felt slightly embarrassed that I'd blurted out such a random comment. I figured the movie would start any minute and conceal my shame.

But, no, Elvis turned around again. This time he held up his watch, which featured a lightning bolt design, all done in diamonds.

"You like this watch, honey?" he asked.

"Yeah, it's really pretty," I said. "It's beautiful."

He smiled and nodded, as if he agreed, and then turned around again.

He's trying to keep making small talk with me, I couldn't help but notice.

"Roll the movie," he said, in a voice meant to travel, waving his arm as if giving a royal command.

Just like that, the movie started. That was my first observation, how with the snap of his fingers, Elvis got the world to do what he wanted.

Not long into the movie, Elvis stood up. Of course, all eyes in the theater were on him, not on the screen, but we all pretended like we were still watching the movie. Elvis walked toward the back of the the-ater, pausing in the aisle by George, who was seated next to me. Elvis tapped George on the shoulder and beckoned him out to the lobby.

"Excuse me, Linda," George said.

"Sure," I said.

A few minutes later, I felt someone sit down next to me, and I assumed it was George again. But when I turned around to look, Elvis was there in the seat beside me.

"Oh, to what do we owe this honor?" I asked, rather impertinently.

"Well, I, I, I just . . ." he said, stumbling over his words a bit in a way that was boyish and very endearing. "I wanted to sit here, honey, and get to know you better."

On my other side, Jeanne jabbed her elbow into my ribs so sharply, she just about broke the bone, and I could hear her whispering under her breath.

"Oh my God, I can't believe he's sitting next to you," she said.

He's still married, I thought. *I definitely don't date married men. And, besides, he's probably just being polite because I'm Miss Tennessee. I repre-sent his state.*

With that in mind, I was gracious to him, but not overly friendly, as we talked a little bit more. During all of this, Elvis's high school friend turned bodyguard, Red West, came and sat next to Jeanne. She leaned over.

"Great, you get Elvis Presley, and who's this guy sitting next to me?" she whispered in my ear. "Red fucking West. What's wrong with this picture?"

"Relax, he's married," I whispered back. "Everything's fine. Elvis is married."

And then, he started to pull the old yawn and put his arm on the seat behind me trick, and started hugging me up. Now Jeanne, of course, was really breaking my ribs with her elbow. While Elvis was attempting to get cozier and friendlier with me, I was very resistant, pulling back from him as far as I could in my seat. Finally, I turned to Jeanne.

"I think we should go," I said to Jeanne.

Elvis leaned around and toward me to get my attention.

Looking me intently in the eyes, he said, "Honey, you know I'm not married anymore."

"No," I said, totally shocked. "I had no idea."

"Well, we haven't released it to the press yet, but I've been separated since last December," he said. "I'm officially separated. We're going to get a divorce. She left me for someone else."

"Oh, I'm really sorry to hear that," I said. "But you know, you should have married a Southern girl."

He seemed a little taken aback that I would speak so bluntly to him, and about something so personal, but then he smiled at me.

"Yeah, you know, you're absolutely right," he said.

And that, right there, was the beginning of Elvis and me. In the years that followed, he would always remind me that one of the wisest and most memorable things I'd ever said to him was right in our first meeting, when I told him that he should have married a Southern girl.

"You were one hundred percent right," he always said. "It's like you and I knew each other before we knew each other, because you grew up the same way I did. I know you. I know your spirit. I know how you think and how you feel."

And I felt the same way about him. I knew who Elvis Presley was, of course, because he was famous, and so I knew trivial things about him that I'd read in magazines. But beyond that, on a visceral level, I knew what was important to him, because it was also what was important to me.

Elvis leaned in and kissed me, and the fullness, tenderness, and sweetness of his absolutely perfect lips were like kissing marshmallows. Seriously, if you want to know what it was like to kiss Elvis, get the biggest, puffiest marshmallows you can find and press a few of them against your lips, because his lips really were that sweet and soft. He was the most mesmerizing kisser, so very sensual and intense. So, yeah, it was a pretty staggering first kiss, intoxicating to the point that neither of us seemed to mind that we were surrounded by people in the theater. We were oblivious to everything and everyone. And all my pious propriety as Miss Tennessee Universe went out the side door of that theater and up in smoke.

Those first kisses went on and on, and then he started nuzzling me, and kissing me on the neck, and whispering sweet everythings to me, like, "Where have you been all my life?"

To which I answered: "Umm, growing up, I'd have to say."

He laughed out loud.

"I've been looking for someone like you, honey," he continued.

In fact, I have no idea what movie we saw. It was a double feature, and yet it wasn't nearly long enough for me. I never wanted that night to end. I'm sure the movie was something about karate, or maybe a Blaxploitation film, because Elvis loved movies like that, movies like *Across 110th Street* with Anthony Quinn and Yaphet Kotto, which was released later that year. And as I soon came to find out, when Elvis was in the building, we always did what Elvis loved.

Eventually the movies were both over and the lights came on. With Elvis kissing me for several hours, I had been dimly aware of a ripple of interest in the theater around us, as everyone there seemed to notice that Elvis had met a girl, and it looked like it was getting kind of serious. Now in the light, I knew they were all staring at me. I smoothed down my clothes and pressed my palms against my cheeks and chin, trying to cool the heat of the whisker burn I thought had to be apparent on my face. He and I both giggled at the awkwardness of the moment. For the first time in hours, I was self-conscious and shy about the total abandon Elvis and I had displayed during the movies.

We both stood, and even though other people were gathering their things around us and starting to make their way out of the theater, Elvis seemed hesitant to make any move away from me.

"Honey, I don't know where you've been all my life, but I'm really happy I met you, and I want to see you again," he said. "I want you to come to Graceland tomorrow night and meet my daddy."

Is this really happening? This is really happening!

"Oh, we're going on vacation tomorrow night with my aunt and uncle," I said, my heart sinking at the thought of going away from him, "But I can come for a while anyway."

"Yeah, I want to show you Graceland," he said. "I want you to meet my daddy. What's your number?"

"Well, I don't have a pen or a piece of paper," I said in a playfully resistant tone.

What? I've probably been making out with him for four hours in a movie theater full of people, and now I'm playing coy? Well, I can't make it too easy for him.

Elvis called his longtime friend and road manager Joe Esposito over and asked him for a piece of paper and a pen. Joe had a book of matches, so Elvis took it and a pen from him and wrote down the number himself. On a book of matches, what a cliché. But that's exactly how it happened. As I would soon learn, this was a big deal, because Elvis didn't do *anything* for himself, really. That's what Joe was there for; he was always the guy who wrote things down and made calls for Elvis. But in this instance, Elvis took down my number for himself.

"I'll call you," he said.

"Okay, we'll come over tomorrow night," I said.

He pulled me into him and gave me another kiss, held me for a minute, and asked where I was parked. Like the gentleman he was, he escorted me to my car, opened the door for me, and leaned in for one more kiss as I settled into my little Vega.

I waved goodbye as Jeanne climbed in next to me, and I drove us down the deserted street on my way back to Aunt Betty's house. And reality.

"What's the matter with me?" I chided myself out loud. "Why did I make him write down my number? He probably didn't even write the number correctly. Why was I being so cool and coy? I should have written it myself. At least I'd know he has it!"

"I know," Jeanne said. "I couldn't believe that you didn't just write it down for him in the biggest block letters."

"I probably won't hear from him again," I wailed. "Oh my God, I can't believe I played that hard to get."

When we got back to my aunt Betty Sue's house, I could hardly believe it was four o'clock in the morning. Elvis and I had been kissing for almost four hours. Even though it was so late, almost morning, Betty Sue was waiting up for us. She was excited that we'd gotten to meet Elvis Presley that night, and she wanted to hear all about it.

"Well, was he there?" she said to begin. "Did you get to meet him?"

"Not only did she get to meet him," Jeanne said, "he kissed her. He's crazy about her."

Aunt Betty Sue could tell by the look on my face, and quite possibly the telltale beard-burn flush, that all of this was true.

We sat at the kitchen table, going over the evening in every wonderful detail, when the phone rang. By this point, it was around four thirty.

Betty Sue looked at me questioningly as she answered the phone.

"Hello," she drawled in her sweet Southern accent. "Why, yes, oh, well, it's *lovely* to speak to you, Elvis. Yes, she's here. Just one moment, please. Let me get her for you. Nice talking to you. Bye-bye."

Putting her hand over the phone receiver, she raised her eyebrows in exaggerated surprise.

"Oh my God, it's him! It's Elvis Presley on my phone. On my phone!!" she exclaimed.

"Ssshhh," I said, not wanting him to hear her, as I stood to take the call.

"Hi," I said, trying to sound as casual as possible.

"Hey, honey, I just wanted to tell you one more time . . ." he said, noticeably slurring, his voice groggy and trailing off at the end of words. "I can't tell you how happy I am to have met you. You're everything I've been looking for. I don't know where you've been all my life, but I'm so happy I met you, and I want to be with you." He repeated the same sweet things he had said to me in the theater.

"Well, I'm just glad you didn't write down my number wrong, and you called," I said. "Have you been drinking? You sound very sleepy, or something."

"Ahhh, nnnooo, honey," he drawled. "I'm just tired. I, uh, I really want you to come over tomorrow."

"Okay," I said, surmising that was perhaps simply Elvis's unique way of speaking when he was super-tired, his own cadence, with his kind of sexy, slurred mumbling. Anyway, I bought his explanation. I didn't have any experience with drinking or drugs to make me think otherwise.

"I'm going to get Joe Esposito to call you tomorrow, and he's going to give you all the instructions," Elvis said.

The next day, amid packing and other preparations for our departure for our family vacation that night, Joe Esposito really did call and give me the information I needed to gain access to Graceland that evening. At 6 P.M., as instructed, I pulled up to the gates of Graceland in my little non-air-conditioned Vega, with Jeanne in the passenger seat. As we stopped at the guard shack, I thought back to when I was a ten-year-old Elvis fan who'd seen all his movies and knew the words to all his songs, and I'd gone to the Graceland gate with an Elvis calendar, hoping for an autograph. Back then, his uncle Vester watched over the gate, and when he saw me staring through the bars, he came over to me.

"Honey, do you want this autographed?" he asked me.

"Yes, please," I said, sticking it through the bars. "Is Elvis home?"

"He is home," he said. "I'll just take this up to him and get him to sign it for you."

"Oh, wow, that's great, thank you, sir," I said, amazed that *the* Elvis Presley was really in there.

Vester took my calendar up to the house while I waited excitedly at the gate. Of course, now I'd make an educated guess he probably got Elvis's cousin, Patsy, to sign the thing for me. But when he brought it back down to me, I was convinced I had the one and only Elvis Presley's signature in my possession, and it became a treasure. And now, unbelievably, the gates of Graceland were opening to me, and we were driving up that long, winding driveway into this fantasyland that I had grown up only observing from outside those famous guarded gates.

The front door opened to reveal a tall, handsome man with a full head of white, wavy hair and a rather terse smile.

"Hello there, Miss Tennessee, I presume?" Vernon Presley said. "I'm Vernon, Elvis's daddy. Y'all come on in."

We walked right in, even though it felt a little like a dream to do so.

"It's nice to meet you, sir," I said, appropriate to my Southern upbringing.

We were led back to what is now known as the Jungle Room, but what was then the TV Room, before Elvis and I redecorated it into

Elvis's wild jungle fantasy. Elvis was sitting there, his leg shaking rhyth-mically, as it always did, his body forever in motion. He sprang up and gave me a big hug, and I was enveloped in his sweet, sexy scent, which was already becoming familiar to me.

"Let's go for a golf cart ride," Elvis said.

At the time I didn't know what a golf cart ride might entail, but I was game for *almost* anything Elvis might suggest. Elvis climbed into the driver's seat of a golf cart that was parked behind the house, and I climbed up front next to him, while Red West and Jeanne climbed into the backseat. Elvis started driving fast, laughing when he saw me holding on as tightly as I could, and steered us toward a field where corn had once been grown. The earth was still furrowed in rows, and he bounced us over the bumpy earth, laughing the whole way. And even though he kept nearly turning the cart over, and I was slipping and sliding around on my seat, nearly falling off with every big bump we hit, for some reason I always felt so safe with Elvis, like if anything happened to me, he'd take care of it. If I got broken, he'd fix me. He could do anything, and would do it for me, because that's who he was.

After our wild ride, Elvis showed us all through his beloved home, Graceland, pointing out special features and telling us stories about things that had happened there.

"I sometimes play the piano in this room, so I call it the music room," he laughed.

"Sounds reasonable," I offered supportively.

We both laughed.

"We don't use the living room much," he said. "I think that's true in most houses. I like a less formal room where you can kick back, put your feet up, and relax."

He seemed so proud of his famous home. He was like a little kid showing me through his playhouse he had built himself.

"Through there is Dodger's room. That's my grandmother, but I call her Dodger. I used to play games, throwing small things at her when I was a little boy, and she would dodge them. My aunt Delta takes care of her and stays in that room over there."

When we were all standing together back in the TV Room, he turned to the others.

"Jeanne and Red, excuse us, I want to show Linda my upstairs," he said. "I'm going to show her my bedroom."

I'd had boyfriends before, and obviously had even been proposed to by my football player high school sweetheart, but like the good Southern Baptist girl I was, I was a virgin. And Elvis, well, he was Elvis. And we were about to be alone together in his bedroom, but somehow I felt perfectly comfortable about all of this. Of course, Jeanne, being my best friend, knew my virginal status, and she wasn't so sure about me climbing the stairs up to Elvis Presley's bedroom, where God knows what had taken place through the years, or what might happen to her innocent friend.

"Oh, I don't know if that's such a good idea," she said, like she was my bodyguard.

"Don't worry, I'm going to take care of your friend," he said. "I'm a gentleman."

"Relax, it's fine, Jeanne," I said. "I'll be all right. I'm a big girl."

We went upstairs, and just as he'd promised, Elvis was a gentleman. While showing me his dressing area, the lady's dressing area, the office, with its piano organ, and Lisa Marie's room, he was absolutely respectful of me. Finally, we were alone in his bedroom, with its huge, nine-foot-by-nine-foot bed.

"Wow, that's the biggest bed I've ever seen," I said.

"Yeah, honey, I had it custom made," he said. "I like to have plenty of room when I sleep."

A gold-plated phone sat on the table on one side of the bed, with a regular phone on the other side, and there were guns everywhere, including on the nightstand.

"Are those loaded?" I asked.

"Oh, absolutely," he said. "Why would I have them if they weren't?"

We sat down together on the edge of the bed and talked and kissed. We talked and kissed some more. Even though it was only our second night together, we were already very comfortable, cuddling and talking baby talk to each other.

"Your skin is so soft, smooth, and pretty," he effused. "Like a baby. You're my baby, aren't you?"

Dreaming, I must be dreaming.

This man I grew up watching in movies, listening to on the radio and records, fantasizing about with my young girlfriends, was now holding me in his arms and kissing me like he never wanted to let me go. Every so often, we'd stop kissing, and he'd show me some detail of his room. He had books on philosophy and spirituality stacked all around, including the Bible, of course, but also Paramahansa Yogananda's *Autobiography of a Yogi*, and even books by Karl Marx, who had famously said, "Religion is the opium of the people." As Elvis shared with me about his reading and his studies on the subject, it was clear that he had done his research and was delving into every aspect of spirituality. Not only what God meant to him, but also what God meant to others all over the world. Having been raised with a deep faith of my own, I found it fascinating and wonderful that here was a man who was sitting on the pinnacle of success, and he still wanted to know what it all meant, and where he fit in, and what good he could do in the world.

"I think about it all the time," he said. "What God wants me to do. I can't help but wonder why God put me here. Why he gave me the talent to sing and entertain people. Why me, Lord? 'For those to whom much has been given, much is expected.' Have you heard that, honey? I know I am supposed to give all that I humanly can to repay my maker and for blessing me with all that he has."

As I was learning, that's how Elvis thought every day of his life, and how he functioned. And then, we kissed and snuggled close together some more, until before I knew it, it was three o'clock in the morning.

"Oh, I've got to go," I said, like I was Cinderella.

"Why?" he said, sounding surprised and disappointed. "I want you to stay here with me."

"Oh, I can't, and I wouldn't," I said. "Even if I could, I wouldn't stay with you tonight, only just having met you last night. It would be too soon to sleep over."

"Well, I respect that," he said. "But just know that I don't like to be alone, and I want you to be with me. I really want you to be with me. Be with me."

"Okay, okay," I said, flattered, but not fully understanding the desperate level of his need. "But my aunt Betty Sue, uncle Steve, my cousins, and I are all leaving at four in the morning to drive down to Gulf Shores, Alabama, for two weeks. And I'm still here. I've got to go."

"All right, I'll let you go," he said. "Just promise me I'll see you again."

"Of course I want to see you again, too," I assured him.

He walked me downstairs, where we found Red and Jeanne in the TV room, and then he walked Jeanne and me out to my car. Elvis and I were standing there, kissing and saying goodbye, when Jeanne broke into our moment.

"I can't take it anymore," she said. "I just have to be able to tell my friends back in Rhode Island that I kissed Elvis Presley. Can I just have one kiss?"

Elvis looked at me with a wry little smile crossing his perfect lips, as if to ask permission.

"It's okay with me if it's okay with you," I said.

"That's fine," he said. "How many girls have I kissed in my life? Yeah, it's fine."

He gave her a little kiss on the lips, and she nearly swooned right then and there.

"Ahhh, oh my God," she said.

"I know," I said, laughing. "Marshmallows, right?"

"Yes, I'm good for life now," she said, climbing into the car to wait for me.

Elvis and I continued to kiss and hold each other, and I could tell he didn't want to let go of me, didn't want me to go at all.

"I have to go because my aunt's going to be waiting for us," I said once more. "I'd feel terrible if I kept them waiting. This has been planned for a while. Their car is all loaded. We're driving to Gulf Shores, and we'll all be gone for two weeks."

We said one more goodbye and shared one more kiss before I finally pulled myself out of his arms and in a state of slight delirium drove down the driveway. When I got back to Aunt Betty Sue's house, they were all waiting for us. As we all piled into the car and finally got on the road, my aunt popped in an Elvis eight-track.

As I listened to Elvis croon his way through "Until It's Time for You to Go," "I Just Can't Help Believing," and all of those beautiful songs,

I sat in the backseat, reliving actually being in the presence of that voice, *his* voice.

It didn't take long for me to start second-guessing everything I'd been through in the last forty-eight hours. "Do you think I'll ever hear from him again?" I asked. "It's Elvis Presley. Why did I believe he wants to be with me? He's been with Ann-Margret. He's been with every beautiful movie star, and he could be with any model."

I spent the better part of the ten-hour drive to Gulf Shores, and all through the next two weeks, bemoaning my fate. We didn't have a phone in our little rental cottage. I didn't have his number anyway. And it's not like one just picks up the phone and calls *Elvis Presley*. The vacation was everything a great big family trip should be. We slept out on the screened-in porch, walked on the beach, talked about life, cooked out, showered outside, had family sing-alongs, and got suntans. But the whole time, I was awash with wonder and the thrill of my newly made memories with the King of Rock and Roll. My Elvis.

"A Love That Will Last"

I want a little
Something more

I don't want the middle
Or the one before
I don't desire
A complicated past
I want a love that will last

Say that you love me
Say I'm the one
Don't kiss and hug me
And then try to run
I don't do drama
My tears don't fall fast
I want a love that will last

I don't want just a memory
Give me forever
Don't even think about
Saying goodbye
'Cause I just want one love
To be enough
And remain in my heart
Till I die . . . so . . .

Call me romantic
I guess that's so
There's something more that
You ought to know
I'd never leave you
So don't even ask
I want a love that will last . . .
     forever . . .
I want a love that will last

I don't want just a memory
Give me forever
Don't even think about
Saying goodbye
'Cause I just want one love
To be enough
And remain in my heart
Till I die . . .

LYRIC: LINDA THOMPSON

Chapter Four

A Vegas Fairy Tale

By the time we got back to Memphis, we were all road weary. The primary thought going through my mind was how wonderful a soft pillow was going to feel against my cheek. As we ambled, dragging our luggage into my aunt's house at the end of our ten-hour drive, it was around ten o'clock at night and the phone was ringing.

"Wow, who could that be this late at night?" Aunt Betty Sue asked, picking up the phone.

My heart raced at the thought it might be Elvis. *Get a grip on yourself*, I thought. *You just walked through the door after two weeks away. Just because your mind has been utterly consumed with Elvis doesn't mean he has given you equal time in his consciousness. He's a little busy, being Elvis, after all.* My silent self-admonishment came to an abrupt halt when, with a big grin on her face, Aunt Betty turned to me and rather ceremoniously plunked the receiver into my hand.

"It's for you," she said, beaming.

"Hello?" I asked.

"Oh my God, is this Linda?" said the man on the other end of the line.

"Yes, this is she," I said, politely and cautiously.

"Linda Thompson! This is Joe Esposito, Elvis's road manager," he said. "I've dialed your number so many times in the last two weeks I've memorized it."

He recited the number to me, as if offering proof.

"Elvis has been trying to reach you nonstop for two weeks," he said.

"Oh, I'm sorry I've been unavailable. I told him I was going to be out of town," I said. "I was in Gulf Shores, Alabama."

"Hold on, hold on," Joe said. "He's grabbing the phone. He's grabbing the phone away from me."

"Honey, where the hell have you been?" Elvis said.

"I told you I was going to be on vacation for two weeks with my aunt and uncle," I said.

"Sweetheart, you told me you were going on vacation," he said. "You didn't tell me you were going to drop off the face of the earth for two weeks. I've been going crazy trying to get a hold of you. Who do you think I am? Who the hell do you think I am? What do you think I meant when I said I want to be with you? I meant every word I said to you! I want to be with you."

"Well, I'm sorry," I said, flustered. "I thought you understood that I'd be gone for a couple of—"

"I want you on a plane in the morning," he said, interrupting me.

"Oh, but honey, I just got in," I said. "I'm not even unpacked from the beach. I may still have sand between my toes."

Elvis chuckled. "You won't need anything," he said. "Just get on the plane tomorrow morning. I've got to go to Vegas for rehearsals. I'm opening in Vegas, and I want you to fly into Los Angeles, see my house here, and then we'll fly into Vegas together."

"I don't have any . . . I don't . . ." I said, trying to catch up with what he was telling me.

"No, no ifs or buts," he said. "You're on that plane in the morning."

"Okay, okay then," I said. "If you insist."

"Oh, I insist," he said, very powerfully yet tenderly summing up the purpose of his phone call. "I can't wait to see you, baby. You are all I've been able to concentrate on. Don't ever leave me again like that."

I hung up the phone and turned to Jeanne and Aunt Betty Sue's expectant faces.

"Oh my God, I only have my little college clothes, and Elvis wants me to go to Las Vegas with him," I said. "What am I going to do? What kind of clothes do I take? What am I talking about? What kind of clothes do I even own appropriate to Vegas?!"

We immediately started going through my meager wardrobe.

"Well, let's just fix this dress up," Betty Sue said. "Let's fix that dress up."

While I had a few beauty pageant dresses and some long ones leftover from the evening gown competitions, I'd never been to Vegas. But I wasn't just going to Las Vegas: I was going to be on the arm of Elvis Presley, the man who ruled that town. Aunt Betty and my cousins Lori and Brenda and I put some things together as quickly and painstakingly as we could, folded them in a suitcase, and, oh yeah, tried to get a little sleep before the next morning, when I found myself flying, first class, to Los Angeles.

A long, black Mercedes limousine picked me up at the airport. Let's just pause for a moment to savor the scene: The limo was Elvis Presley's personal one and had lush fox fur carpeting. *What?!* I was expected to put my shoes on that gorgeous fur on the floor? I was familiar with the term "four on the floor," but c'mon, "fur on the floor"?

When I walked into Elvis's home on Hillcrest Road in the Trousdale Estates section of Beverly Hills, it was around eleven o'clock in the morning, and there was Elvis, waiting with open arms to greet me and welcome me personally to his home. Of course, at that early stage of our relationship, I had no idea what a big deal it was for him to be awake and dressed before late afternoon, or even the evening. But there he was, in all his regal splendor. As soon as I walked in, he reached out for me, commanding, "Come here, you," and held on to me for the longest time.

"Oh my God, where have you been?" he said. "When I tell you I want to be with you, that's what I mean. I want to be with you. I've been going crazy trying to find you."

"I'm sorry," I said. "I just thought you knew that I was going to be gone for two weeks."

Elvis gently pushed back from me and stood there with his hands on my shoulders, looking lovingly and deeply into my eyes, seeming to just absorb me. I had dressed very carefully for our reunion, in a little sleeveless emerald green dress with a scoop neck and a ruffle at the neckline. It was a body-skimming, slightly above the knee, feminine, sexy, but classy dress. I had even used what I thought to be a subtle amount of precisely matching green eye shadow to complement my dress.

"Honey, couldn't you find any green eye shadow to match that green dress?" he asked.

"Oh yes, can't you see?" I said, closing my eyes so he could get a better look at my artistry. "Look, see, it's exactly the same color." I was a little too pleased with myself.

He started laughing his wonderful, contagious laugh.

"Honey, I was joking," he said, pulling me into him to hug me tighter than ever.

"Oh, is it that obvious?" I said, finally catching on to his teasing sarcasm. I started laughing, too.

We held on to each other, laughing together, and just like that, my nerves dissolved, as if we were children finding something to giggle about.

He showed me around his house, and explained that this would be the last time he would be in it. It had been sold, and he had bought a house in Holmby Hills on Monovale Drive that he would be moving into at the end of his upcoming engagement in Las Vegas. He explained to me that soon after finishing decorating and preparing for the move into the Monovale estate, Priscilla had given him the news that she had fallen in love with another man, Mike Stone, their karate instructor, and she would be moving to Marina del Rey in Los Angeles to live with Mike.

"I'm hoping you will come with me and stay with me in Holmby Hills after we are finished in Vegas," Elvis said. "I don't want you to even think of leaving, not even for a day."

He pulled me into his arms and held me close.

"I've got you now," he teased.

I was a willing, smitten subject already.

We ended up in the kitchen, where the housekeeper had prepared lunch for us.

"Honey, we're going to take a Learjet to Vegas in a little bit," he said. "Do you mind small planes?"

"Uh, yeah, not so much. Are you kidding me? I've barely flown in a big plane, never flown privately, never been to Las Vegas, so yeah, I'm all good!" I said, full of joy at the very thought of all that lay before me.

Before I knew it, it was time for the limousine to roll back around and take us to the airport, where we crowded on the five-seater Lear-jet that was fired up and waiting for us on the tarmac. Seated between Elvis and Red West on the tiny back row of seats in the plane, I could hardly believe I was on my way to Las Vegas, where Elvis was due to start rehearsals for his Hilton International engagement. And yet, it all somehow felt totally natural, as if I was exactly where I was meant to be.

When we arrived at the Hilton, we were swept up to the Presidential Suite, using the service elevators and meandering through the kitchen, back doors, and what I would come to call the "garbage route." We were then, and always, surrounded by the thirteen guys—known as the Memphis Mafia—who were part of the original rock star entourage, some working as valets or bodyguards, one or two as court jesters, or any combination, according to Elvis's needs or wants. The guys had gone into the suite before him and gotten it all set up for us. I walked into the bedroom behind Elvis, looking around to survey the sleeping arrangements.

"This is so beautiful!" I remarked. "It's even more spectacular than I imagined!"

Then, the reality of his plans for our arrangement began to dawn on me.

"So where's my room?" I tentatively asked.

"Well, you're going to stay with me," he said, nodding the guys out. "I said I want to be with you, remember? How many times do I have to say I want to be with you?"

"Yes, but I'm not comfortable sharing a room this early in our relationship."

He surprised me then.

"Honey, I know you're a virgin," he said, drawing close to me. "And I'm not going to touch you until you're ready for me to touch you, and I just want you to know that. I want you to trust me. Do you trust me?"

"I do," I said, feeling like I was safely living in the pages of a fairy tale.

"You can sleep right here with me, and we will only go as far as you want to go, as quickly or as slowly as you want to get there. I want to preserve you for as long as you need." He actually used that word, *preserve*, like the perfect Southern gentleman he could be, just one of the many sides of his gloriously complex personality.

He pulled my body into his, and we lay on the bed kissing and holding each other. "I respect you, honey, and I'm willing to wait," he assured me once again. He held me down, looked at me for a long moment, and said with more than a twinkle in his eyes, "And you really believe all that shit, don't you?!" He laughed so hard he cried at his own silly joke. We both rolled around laughing at his ambush humor, which I was about to get very accustomed to.

"Oh, you're funny!" I said, leaning into his kiss. We eventually pulled apart, and I looked around the room.

In addition to several guns on what would become his side of the bed, I noticed an assortment of at least a dozen prescription medicine bottles.

"Have you been sick?" I asked.

"No, why?" he said. "Why do you ask that?"

"Well, what are all those prescription medicine bottles then?"

He looked around, so used to seeing the bottles, he apparently didn't even notice them anymore, and he had to stare at them for a moment before he formulated an answer.

"Oh, yeah, yeah, I had a little respiratory thing, but I'm fine now," he said. "It's just leftover medicine from when I was sick."

"Oh, I'm sorry to hear that you were sick," I said.

I believed him, because, at that point, I had no reason not to. I'd grown up in a household where my parents didn't even have any alcohol in the house, not even beer. My parents both smoked cigarettes, which I hated, but that was it. I didn't even know that people abused prescription drugs. And so, of course, I didn't doubt his explanation.

I don't remember him taking a sleeping pill that night at bedtime, although I suppose he must have, as he would every other time we went to sleep together. But, of course, I remember the feeling of lying down next to him, as you remember so distinctly the first time you fall asleep with someone you love. What made the moment even more notable was the fact that I'd never lived with a man before, and so this was all new for me. Although I'd hardly slept at all the night before, and I'd had more than a full day with Elvis, and I found myself exhausted, I was not quite ready to give myself over to my dreams. There was too much to experience, the sensation of him spooning me, and then as he drifted off, his breath brushing the back of my neck, making me feel very aware of the fact of another entity there with me. I'd already been struck during our first hours together how affectionate he was, and now, even as he slept, he made me feel so cherished, holding me as tightly as he could all through the night. *He really does need me*, I thought, as I curled into the curve of his body. When I did finally doze off to a fitful sleep, I was awakened by his slightest movement.

Those first few days with Elvis were sublime—everything was new—and yet, it all felt surprisingly familiar. True to his word, Elvis cuddled and kissed and spooned with me, but he didn't take our physical relationship any further than that, or put any pressure on me to do so. Instead, he was incredibly romantic, tender, thoughtful, and loving. Any surprises were of the magical, sweep-you-off-your-feet variety.

During my second or third day in our over-the-top suite, Elvis told me he was going to go out for a little bit. He was only gone for about an hour, and when he returned, I had just gotten out of the shower. I was wearing the cozy white hotel robe with a matching white towel wrapped around my head, turban-style, and was getting ready to dry my long, dark hair when I looked up and saw him.

He was resplendent in a white high-collared suit, with white pants and flared inserts in the pant legs. He was slim, sporty, perfect, with his "Elvis sideburns," his trademark sunglasses, and his skin glowing with a great tan. Elvis Presley at his finest.

I was so struck by his overwhelming presence in that moment that I actually lost my breath, the air all leaving me at once.

"Honey, I went out and ran a little errand," he said. "I got you something."

He held out a beautiful, big curved ring, almost in the shape of the infinity sign, encrusted with diamonds and emeralds mounted on high spirals. It wasn't lost on Elvis that emeralds are my birthstone. The ring was beautiful and far more extravagant than anything I'd ever owned, or even dreamed of owning. And then he pulled out a second yellow gold ring, also set with diamonds and emeralds.

"What the—why?" I said, unable to hide my surprise. As if his presence alone were not enough to thrill me without end.

"Because you are you," he said. "You are beautiful, and you deserve to have beautiful things."

"I don't even know what to say. You really don't have to do things like this. You are enough just your own self for me." I stammered in an attempt to explain my feelings. "My gosh, thank you. This is unbelievable. *You* are unbelievable."

"Get used to it," he breathed into my ear as he held me close.

I kissed him as he slid each ring onto a finger they fit. He then said something I would hear him repeat during our years together as often as I witnessed such shows of his incredible generosity. It's advice to which I still try to adhere:

"An object is not beautiful if nobody sees it. Wear the pretty things you have."

Those would be the first of so many pieces of jewelry, and gifts, he gave me over the years.

From our first moments together, our relationship was all-encompassing. In addition to our bond formed through our backgrounds, we both thrilled at a slightly sharp, sarcastic sense of humor that was just the slightest bit wicked, especially when the jokes were coming from Elvis, who could be quite profane and adored the chance to shock unsuspecting listeners. But also because we both understood the same manner of love, which was given purely and unabashedly, and often expressed through baby talk. We'd both been raised on it—my mother had baby-talked me, while petting me, just as his mother had petted and baby-talked him.

Without ever pausing to speak our intentions aloud in advance, or establish any proper rules for our communication, as if we'd always known each other and the words had always existed between us, we talked baby talk almost instantly. Elvis especially liked something he called "iddytream," which you non–baby talkers might know as ice cream. "Butch" was our word for milk, and "butter butch" was buttermilk. But these words could also be special terms of endearment, as I sometimes called him "Butch" or "Butter Butch."

It was our own private language, and we were living in our own special world. I never called him Elvis. My other baby names for him included Gullion and Buntyn, like baby bunting, although I pronounced it more like "Buntyn" ("button"). On reflection, with the babies I birthed and baby-talked now grown men themselves, I know all of this might sound a little odd, but at the time it felt completely natural. And he had his own names for me. Besides calling me Mommy and Ariadne (or Ari), he called me other sweet nicknames, including "darling," "honey," and "baby." As he spoke these words to me, the sound of his incomparable, sexy, melodic drawl, infused with childish whimsy, was unlike anything I'd ever heard, nor have since then.

Elvis had a pet name or nickname for just about everything and everyone, it seemed. During the first few months I was with him, while he was still getting to know me and discovering my physical features, as well as my disposition and personality, I caught him staring at my bare feet while we were comfortably lounging on our bed at Graceland. He picked up the phone by his side of the bed and called downstairs and requested that Charlie Hodge, who accompanied Elvis on stage, playing guitar and handing Elvis water and scarves, come up. I had no idea why Charlie was being summoned, but thought maybe it was a song idea Elvis wanted to share or something like that.

"Hey boss, what's up? You need something?" Charlie queried.

"Yeah, I do, Charlie," Elvis said. "I need you to come over here and look at Linda's pretty feet. Aren't those the prettiest 'sooties' you've ever seen?"

Charlie laughed out loud at the reason he had been called upstairs, and after ensuring there was nothing more required of him, excused himself. But Elvis wasn't done with him.

"Look how well groomed her feet are, Charlie, and how her 'yittle' toes just line up perfectly," Elvis had remarked.

"Honey, I don't miss anything on a woman's body," Elvis said after Charlie left the room. "If your 'sooties' are well groomed, then it stands to reason you take pride in your appearance. Call it a foot fetish if you want; that's just the way I am. I don't like to look down from a pretty face and see calloused-up, dirty feet." I should note that Elvis was a leg and butt man and didn't care at all for big breasts. He often said, "If I want big tits in my face, I'll throw a freaking cow in the bed with me." Whew!

The more highly evolved, independent, experienced woman I am today would more than likely take exception to being so closely scrutinized by anyone. But then, it was Elvis, I was naïvely in love, and he was a baby-talking, one-of-a-kind charmer.

From our first days together, Elvis also shared with me his profound and abiding spirituality, and his lifelong quest to understand his place in the world through his religious explorations, delving deeper into the conversation that we'd begun at Graceland, when he'd discussed all the books on his shelves. Often when Elvis spent time with new people, as I would learn, he was hungry to speak with them about his faith and question them on their own beliefs. After his passion for music, this was the most profound way in which he connected with others. Elvis grew up Christian, and he held an amalgamation of different Christian faiths, with the overriding one being Pentecostal. He believed in the laying on of hands, and faith healing, and he believed in the Holy Spirit.

I think at the core of his being, and at the core of his belief, Elvis was a Christian, and he took Jesus as his king. Since he was the King of Rock and Roll, fans used to sometimes pass Elvis crowns onstage when he was performing.

"You're the king, you're the king," they said.

"There is only one king, and that's God," Elvis sometimes replied. "That's Jesus. I'm not the king."

Elvis was very humble about his place in the cosmos and had an abiding faith in Jesus. At the same time, he was never judgmental about the beliefs of others and didn't feel everyone in the whole world had to be Christian. He and I often discussed this point. We agreed that the God we knew and loved, which was all-encompassing, did not hold the belief that if you're raised with Hinduism, or Buddhism, or any other non-Christian faith, you're doomed to hell. That's not the God we recognized.

We discussed our spiritual leanings a great deal. Fundamental to both of us was the idea that there is an energy and spirit that endures into the afterlife. In the Bible, it says, "In my father's house are many mansions. If it were not true, I would have told you so." Our interpretation of this idea was that these "mansions" could have meant anything: heaven, reincarnation, or even that our energy is dispersed to different planets after death. We didn't discount any possibility. "With God, all things are possible" it states in the Bible.

Yes, Elvis did believe in Christ, and he believed in all of Christ's teachings. He also believed in Paramahansa Yogananda, and metaphysical meditation, and was completely nonjudgmental about nearly all other forms of worship. He respected anybody who was looking up to a higher good and trying to be a better human. Around his neck Elvis wore a crucifix, as well as a Star of David, a lamb, an Egyptian ankh, and even a little crescent moon and star, to represent Islam. In other words, he wore every religious symbol there was on a chain. I once saw someone ask about this.

"Hey, Elvis, are you confused?" the guy asked.

"No, man, I just don't want to miss heaven on a technicality," Elvis said.

In the summer of 1972, when I met him, Elvis was in his prime. He was thirty-seven years old, six foot one, and on the slender side for him, probably weighing about 165 or 170 pounds. He had an incredible physique, a noticeable physicality, a great bone structure, even. It was as if it wasn't just his build and his features that were perfectly crafted, but also his skeletal structure. Before then, and later on, of course, he famously battled his weight, which always fluctuated at least ten pounds. His mother had had problems with her weight. And he loved to eat. But for this moment in time, he was perfection incarnate.

He was so magnificent that after he'd fallen asleep I used to lie awake with my face drawn up close to his and use the opportunity to study and memorize every pore. From the curvature of his lips, to his eyebrows, to his eyelashes, he was a physically incomparably beautiful man. I often woke up before he did and enjoyed the feeling of just being there with him.

From the start, my life revolved around him and his schedule, and making him happy, which along with his laughter became the greatest source of my own happiness. The only time I have since known a love so deep and complete was when I gave birth to my sons and felt the unconditional, powerful force of a mother's love. But at this moment of my life's journey, all of my love was reserved for Elvis. When he woke up in the late afternoon or early evening, my day, too, could begin. At the Hilton, this meant a room service breakfast, which was laid out at the foot of our king-sized mattress so we could sit in bed together and dine.

As I immediately came to realize, this was a grandiose life, a life of being catered to, of presidential suites and private planes. He *was* "the King," so people treated him accordingly. That took some getting used to for a girl from modest means like me, but when the fairy dust settled, I began to adjust to it as my new reality.

While we did everything together in those first days, he did send me out shopping for a whole new wardrobe. At the time, the height of Las Vegas fashion and fabulousness was the high-end couture dreamed up by Suzy Creamcheese, whose labels were emblazoned with the memorable tagline "Suzy Creamcheese Loves You!" Her boutique was frequented by the likes of Cher, Ann-Margret, Dionne Warwick, and, a few years later, Stevie Nicks. She had made stage costumes and every-day clothes for Elvis, not that there was all that much difference when it came to the glitz and drama of the clothes he wore onstage and in his day-to-day life. He sent me shopping as an expression of his generosity, as he knew I would never have been able to afford such clothes in my old life as a college student. He also wanted me to represent him well by looking glamorous and beautiful. So I bought these stunning, sleek jersey dresses that fit me like a second skin, and would peer at myself in the mirror with wonderment at my good fortune.

Elvis didn't spend a substantial amount of time rehearsing, which left us with ample hours to enjoy each other's company and get to know each other better. It was during my first few weeks in Vegas with Elvis that he decided to take me to dinner downstairs at the Hilton's steak house. We never went anywhere alone, and so, as always, his entourage of thirteen guys surrounded us, a full convoy with bodyguards both leading and following behind. Although we were, of course, given the full star treatment and impeccable service by the restaurant staff, it didn't take long for the whole adventure to go awry.

We'd been seated at a table in front of one of the windows that looked out onto the casino floor, and almost instantly, a stunned passerby stopped short at the sight of us, and then so did another. Their thoughts were written clearly on their startled faces: *Wait? Is that Elvis Presley? It can't be. But it is!* As the crowd swelled in size, and with it, the palpable excitement of everyone assembled, it became clear that the onlookers were not going to disperse anytime soon. And who could blame them? It was just too remarkable an occurrence. People were not accustomed to seeing Elvis Presley out and about. By that time, his fame was so enormous that he had become an almost total recluse, and this moment right here was a clear example of why. It was as if he were magnetized. There were soon a hundred people gathered around, peering in the window at us, some of them even banging on the glass. It quickly became more than a little scary. He could have gotten hurt, the instinct to touch him was so strong in his fans. We decided to make a quick exit back to our room, and our usual room service dinner, using the garbage route, by now familiar to me. And *that* was the only time he ever tried to take me on a dinner date during regular dining hours.

About two weeks into our time together in Las Vegas, we decided to sunbathe in the late afternoon. I changed into my bikini and went to find Elvis in our bedroom. He was shaking a few pills from a bottle into his open palm.

"Do you want to take this?" he asked.

"What is it?" I asked, surprised, as he knew I didn't take drugs.

"It's just a little pill for tanning that promotes melanin," he said.

"No, I tan just perfectly, thank you," I said, trying not to let myself worry about what it meant that he even had a pill for tanning.

We stretched out together side by side, working on our tans, on two chaise longues on the balcony that extended from our suite at the Hilton. (Since we couldn't go outside anywhere that was within view of the public, we had to find ways to bring the outside to us. We had multiple Las Vegas stays during which we literally did not leave the hotel once in several weeks, and such private havens kept us from feeling completely enclosed by the property. Later, I would find the grounds at Graceland were also a much-needed sanctuary for us.) I had that dozy, heat-drenched sensation after time spent in the blazing hot August Las Vegas sun, and I was fully relaxed, enjoying the feeling of his hand holding mine. I had by now grown accustomed to his physical demonstrativeness, which was near constant. Such visible displays of affection felt very comfortable for me, as I had grown up that way, with an incredible amount of physical closeness and love in my household. And so being with him felt like a homecoming of sorts. Without any apparent cause, he squeezed my hand in his strong grip, and I could sense that he was about to speak.

"You know what we've done, don't you?" he said.

"What?" I said.

"We fooled around and fell in love," he said.

"We have?" I said, my heart pounding with the truth of his words. "We did?"

He opened his eyes and looked at me; those impossibly long lashes, those deep, soulful pools of blue. The depth and intensity of the blue in Elvis's eyes was intoxicating. His eyes were often described as bedroom eyes. I rather think they escaped the bedroom, though and circumnavigated the globe, gathering beauty along the way. Elvis's eyes told his story and could be as mercurial as his personality, from the serenity of the blue Caribbean to the raging depths of the North Atlantic. They could twinkle with mischief, glare cold with anger, fill with tears of tenderness, and pierce your heart with the pain they sometimes mirrored from his soul. They were beautiful, and in this moment, they were telegraphing pure love right into me.

"Well, at least I have," he said, pausing dramatically, always the master of timing, looking at me *imploringly*. "I love you. I'm in love with you." I think I was a little shocked because we had only been together for about two weeks.

"I love you, too," I said. "I do, I love you."

He leaned across the few inches of space between us and kissed me, and we kissed and kissed, expressing the full depth of our feelings for each other and the great humbling grace of the divine power that had brought us together. *We are in love.* I let the reality roll around in my psyche and unleash butterflies in my stomach. *We are in love.* Elvis Presley and I are in love with each other.

After that, he told me every day, in so many ways that he loved me, with his many terms of endearment, and his kisses and caresses, and his generous gifts, and even with his practical jokes, which were how his playful, boyish side showed affection. He needed to receive a wealth of adoration, but he had a need to give just as much love in return, which made for a wonderfully passionate environment, most of the time.

As I'd come to learn, under the best of circumstances, he was more than a little needy, but especially in that first year, I was honored to be there for this man I loved so completely, and this legend who was loved by so many. I could tell he was deeply wounded, and more than a little insecure, in the wake of his divorce. He didn't speak of it much in our initial days together, but I could tell from the little he did say that he'd been hurt immensely by Priscilla, because she'd left him for another man. Regardless of whether his own behavior or expectations of her had been fair or realistic, he hadn't wanted his marriage to end, or his family to be broken apart. Still in pain over the dissolution of his home life, he needed me to reassure him and be the loving foundation on which he could build himself back up.

Because I knew he'd been married, I felt it was important for me to be honest with him about my own romantic history.

"I know about your past relationships," I said. "I know you dated Anita Wood. I know you were married. I know you dated Ann-Margret and almost married her, and that you were in love with her. Do you want to know anything about any of my boyfriends?"

"Oh no, oh hell no," he said, almost physically recoiling at the thought. "Don't go any further. Don't say another word. I don't ever want to hear about anybody that you ever dated, anybody that you ever kissed, anybody that you ever liked. I don't want to know. Don't ever, ever, ever tell me about a guy that you think is handsome. Don't ever mention a guy that you think is good looking, or a guy that you dated in high school or college. I don't want to know anything about it. I'm a really jealous motherfucker. I don't ever want to see you looking at another man. I don't ever want to see you talk about another man. I want to know you're mine and all mine."

I was happy to reassure him, and yet, at the same time, I couldn't help but be amazed by his reaction. *Gosh, to be the greatest sex symbol in the world, the man that every woman wants to be with, and yet he's so insecure he can't stand to hear about anybody I ever dated.* But the more I got to know Elvis, the more I came to understand that this was just one more aspect of his complex nature.

The first year of the four and half years we would share, we were together twenty-four hours a day, seven days a week, other than a few short trips he took to Thunderbird Jewelers in Las Vegas to buy presents for me, which he did frequently.

One day, he gave me a ring with a big, beautiful blue diamond surrounded by other, smaller white diamonds.

"Honey, I got this for you," he said.

"Why?" I asked. "It's not my birthday. It's not Valentine's Day. It's not anything."

"It's Tuesday, and I love you," he said.

That's the kind of romantic guy he was, generous with compliments, always making me feel appreciated and loved.

If he was in the shower, he had me talk to him from outside the curtain as the steam wafted the scent of his Neutrogena soap into the bathroom around me. We slept, woke, ate, read, laughed, and loved together, as if we were all either of us needed in the whole wide world.

Once his run of shows began, our day's activities shifted to accommodate his needs as a performer. When we got up in the afternoon, he began getting ready for his shows with a routine he'd perfected by this point in his career. This meant steps to care for his voice, including a saltwater nasal douche to clear out his nasal passages, followed by all of these god-awful sounds, and spewing and spitting. It wasn't the most romantic or attractive thing in the world, but he applied himself to his preparations with special attention. He also sometimes took shots to dry up mucus, and in Vegas, we slept with a humidifier. Elvis felt that he had been graced with a God-given talent; that God had imbued him with his incredible, incomparable gift, and he felt a great responsibility to maintain what he had been given, caring for his voice in a way that he did not employ with his body.

He also took steps to enhance his appearance, including his application of a touch of eyebrow pencil because his eyebrows were not as dark as one might have thought. And then Charlie Hodge usually came in to comb and spray his hair for him. Once Elvis was all dressed and fully done up, we went downstairs together, with his entourage, through the belly of the hotel, to the backstage area. One of the bodyguards escorted me up to my regular seat, which was a center booth in the show room.

When the lights went down before the show, there was a hum of excitement in the room. Many of these loyal fans had saved their hard-earned money, managed to purchase tickets for Elvis's engagement in Las Vegas, and traveled from far and wide just to witness the King in all his glory. Their focus on the stage was intense, and with good reason. The way he charged onto the stage, the way he carried himself was absolutely electric. To this day, he's the best entertainer I've ever seen. He put everything into it. And he was never more purely himself than when he was onstage. Not even the tiniest nuance was contrived or studied—it all came very naturally to him. That really was the way he talked. That really was the way he smiled, with the curl on one side of his lip. That really was the cocky way he stood, his confidence on display as he strutted and prowled the stage.

From the electrifying theme from *2001: A Space Odyssey* that announced his onstage arrival, to the moment he threw his final scarf to the last hyperventilating, awestruck fan and sauntered off the side of the stage, Elvis was the world's most famous rock star. And now he was my first and truest love.

"I Have Nothing"

Share my life; take me for what I am;
'Cause I'll never change all my
  colors for you.
Take my love; I'll never ask for too
  much . . .
Just all that you are, and everything
  that you do

I don't really need to look
Very much farther. I don't want to
  have to go
Where you don't follow.
I can't hold it back again—
This passion inside.
I can't run from myself
There's nowhere to hide.

Don't make me close one more door.
I don't want to hurt anymore.
Stay in my arms, if you dare
Or must I imagine you there?
Don't walk away from me,
I have nothing—nothing—
  nothing . . . if I don't have you.

You see through—right to the heart
  of me.
You break down my walls
With the strength of your love.
I never knew love, like I've known it
  with you.

Will a memory survive? . . . One
  I can hold on to?

I don't really need to look
Very much farther.
I don't want to have to go,
Where you don't follow.
I can't hold it back again—
This passion inside,
I can't run from myself
There's nowhere to hide
Your love—I'll remember—forever.

Don't make me close one more door.
I don't want to hurt anymore.
Stay in my arms, if you dare
Or must I imagine you there?
Don't walk away from me,
I have nothing—nothing—
  nothing . . . if I don't have you.

LYRIC: LINDA THOMPSON

Chapter Five

The Other Elvis

As captivating as his stage shows were, it didn't take long for me to see the toll that they could take on Elvis, often bringing out the neediest parts of him. As soon as he came off the stage and then finished the meet-and-greet portion of the evening, which happened in his dressing room downstairs before carrying the party upstairs to our suite, he reverted to being my baby. Safe in the personal oasis he created for us and carefully guarded from intruders, we curled together on our big king-sized bed. Once alone together, he clutched me close, as if wanting as little space between us as possible.

"Mommy, Buntyn's really pitiful tonight," he often said, his voice babyish and ravenous with need. "Buntyn really needs extra love tonight."

Whenever this needy Elvis surfaced when we were alone together, I knew he genuinely did require extra love from me just then. I gladly opened up and showered him with all the feeling in my heart. Not only because I did love him so unreservedly, but also because it was just so endearing. Here was this musical idol up on the marquee, this incredibly powerful, iconic sex symbol who could sing like nobody else, move like nobody else, entertain like nobody else, while holding an enraptured audience in the palm of his hand, even make people laugh like nobody else. And yet, when he came offstage, he peeled back the godlike layers to reveal the sweet babe he was deep down inside. In fact, this tender core that needed to be cuddled and cared for in private was the part of Elvis that I came to love the most. And these were among the moments I cherished the most, because he seemed so vulnerable, and I felt so needed.

Ours was a complete relationship—when the need arose, we got to be everything to each other. He was almost sixteen years older than I, and so it was natural for me to sometimes be the little girl, with him playing the daddy. More often that not, though, I was the mommy, and he was the baby. Sometimes we were lovers. Sometimes we were brother and sister. Sometimes we were best friends. We were all things to each other at one time or another. And Elvis was always, always *everything* to me.

Of course, Elvis being Elvis, and me being the malleable young girl devoted to pleasing and caring for him, on any given day he almost always chose the dynamic between us. There were times when I wanted to be the little girl, and I wanted to be stroked, and petted, and comforted.

"No, no, no, you can't be the little girl right now," he said. "I need to be the baby. You have to be the grown-up, and I'm the baby right now."

And I always capitulated to his needs, so willingly selfless in my total devotion. I was very aware of the fact that I was not just taking care of him in these tender moments; I was also keeping him going for all of his legions of fans, to whom I felt a growing responsibility, because of how much they gave to him. For the first few years, at least, I was more than happy to put his needs above my own. After all, he was Elvis Presley.

One day when we were sitting together in bed, as we usually were when we were relaxing, he told me a secret that made me love the little boy he'd been, the little boy who got bullied at school, the little boy who grew up in the Memphis version of the ghetto.

"Mommy, you know these high-collared outfits, and shirts and suits that I wear?"

"Yes, honey," I said.

"Before I was able to have those kinds of clothes made for me, I would always turn my collar up."

"Yes, I remember," I said, thinking back to the mesmerizing photos of him early in his career, which I'd admired in fan magazines long before he'd become my love.

"Everybody thinks I did that because I think I'm cool," he said. "It's really because when I was a little shaver, and I was sitting at the kitchen table, my mama and daddy used to come by and say, 'Look at that little chicken neck. Look at that little scrawny neck.' "

"Aw, honey," I said, putting my arms around him, even as I couldn't help but giggle compassionately.

"So I was always self-conscious about my neck," he said. "I thought I had a skinny little chicken neck, because my mama and daddy said that to me when I was little, sitting at the kitchen table. That's why I've always worn my collar turned up. It's not because I think I'm cool, or I'm trying to be cool. It's because I'm trying to hide my little chicken neck. The people don't understand that. But you know because I'm telling you."

"My poor little Gullion," I said, kissing his neck and thinking how incredible it was that he'd started the international fad of turning your collar up, to look sharp, and be cool, all because he'd been trying to hide what he thought of as his most embarrassing feature.

Of course, this only made me love him more. As did another deeply personal story, this time not about an aspect of his iconic dress, but about one of his most beloved songs, "In the Ghetto." As Elvis told me, when his good friend Sammy Davis Jr. was given that song by its writer, Mac Davis, he turned it down.

"In all authenticity, I can't do this song, because I never lived this," Sammy said. "But I'll tell you who did. Elvis Presley."

So Mac Davis gave the song to Elvis. And while Sammy would go on to cover it, the definitive version was, of course, recorded by Elvis, who could sing it with such authority and feeling because he had lived in the ghetto. He'd experienced firsthand the desperation and injustice of that kind of life. Anyone who knows the song only has to think of the recurring line, "And his mama cried," to be reminded of the powerful love he had for his mother.

There was a simple goodness to Elvis's mother that kept him humble, no matter the stratospheres of fame and wealth he achieved. He always remained aware of the greater worth of people like Gladys and the values they lived by. Elvis told me his mother could not read or write, and that when people asked her for her autograph after he became famous, she could have only signed with an "X," but she didn't want to do that.

"Let me just take this to the back room," she said to cover for herself. Once out of sight, she had someone write her name for her.

That's how it was in the Depression era.

He talked about his mother a lot, always referring back to their nicknames for each other—he called her Satnin—and the wise advice she'd given him. He occasionally called me Satnin, too.

"My mama always said I should marry a brown-eyed girl," he told me early on.

"Really?" I asked.

"Yeah, when I saw your brown eyes, I thought that's the girl that my mama would've wanted me to be with," he said. "You have kindness in your eyes. Mama said never trust a blue-eyed woman. You've got to marry a brown-eyed girl. She'll be more down-to-earth. She'll care for you more. She'll be there for you. She won't be disloyal to you. She won't be unfaithful." Of course I think Elvis's mother having brown eyes herself might have had something to do with her admonition.

Elvis was the original mama's boy. And I don't attach an ounce of derogatory meaning to the term, either. I've always encouraged my girlfriends and any young women I meet to look for a man who loves his mother, because that makes a big difference in the way he perceives women. Anyone could mask a darker side, of course. But I think if men love their mothers, they're innately going to have a basic respect and love for women, as well as a desire to protect them.

During our first month together, Elvis showed this respect for me in many ways, but perhaps the clearest display was how he remained true to his word and never put any pressure on me to have sex with him until I was ready. Not that he didn't continue to enjoy teasing me on the subject, which was his way with *most* subjects, no matter how serious or silly. A couple of weeks after we'd first said, "I love you," we were in our suite at the Hilton together. As we kissed and caressed each other, he came to be lying on top of me on the bed. He pulled back a little and looked into my face.

"Honey, are you nervous?" he asked. "You feel like you're kind of nervous."

"Well, a little a bit," I said.

"Sweetheart, you know I promised you when we first met," he said. "I know you're a virgin. I respect that. I'm glad you're a virgin, and I want you to wait until you're absolutely ready, and you can absolutely trust me to wait until you're ready."

"Oh, I know that," I said, smiling with appreciation.

"And you really do believe all that shit, don't you?" he joked, laughing uproariously, as he had when he'd made a similar remark during our first night together in Las Vegas, which, although only a month earlier, now felt like lifetimes ago, and in a way, it was.

"No, I'm just kidding, honey," he said. "Of course we'll wait."

So we didn't have sex that night. We rolled around on the bed, and kissed, and laughed while he tickled me, and as always, we had a lot of fun with each other.

And then, it was early September, after we'd been living together for nearly two months, in our Presidential Suite on the thirtieth floor of the Las Vegas Hilton. We were in our king-sized bed on a pedestal, with a mirrored ceiling above us, reflecting Elvis and me tangled in a loving entwinement of arms, legs, kisses, and deeply felt intimacy. And let's just say if you're not ready then, you're never going to be ready in your whole entire lifetime. It was time to go big or go home. It was all so unbelievably romantic, and perfect, and heartfelt, and I knew I was ready to make love with this man I absolutely adored with all of my heart and soul.

He was so sweet and tender with me, and yet I was overcome by emotion, and I began to cry softly. I believe I had attached so much significance to losing my virginity I needed to shed a few tears over the moment. Looking back, I realize how antiquated my perception of the entire scene was, but remember, Elvis was an old-fashioned guy who appreciated the heck out of my innocence.

Elvis held me close, comforting me.

"Honey, don't cry," he said. "Please don't cry."

I don't want to give the impression that I was a drama queen in any way—there were just a few teardrops quietly moistening my flushed cheeks. For a long moment, Elvis and I held each other's gaze, and then he rethought his directive.

"No, go ahead," he said. "You go ahead. You cry. That's what you need to do right now. You do anything you want to do. If you want to cry, you cry, sweetheart."

In that moment, as in so many others, he was such a loving, kind, compassionate partner. *That's why he got away with so much*, I think now, with a knowing laugh, when I look back on our time together. But I also view him with so much appreciation and gratitude, because he was a genuine love of a person, and that's why I was compelled to give him everything that I was, with every fiber of my being.

And perhaps it was because we'd become so close that Elvis felt comfortable letting me into the most guarded part of his world. In early September, Elvis finished up in Las Vegas, and he took me back to Los Angeles, where we would now be staying in his new estate on Monovale Drive in Holmby Hills. His daughter, Lisa Marie, who had been splitting her time between Priscilla and Elvis since they'd separated earlier in the year, would be joining us there.

I've always loved children, and of course I knew how much Elvis cherished his little girl, and so I was excited to meet her. Elvis didn't give me any special instructions about how to talk to her or behave around her; he trusted me with her, which of course meant the world to me.

When we arrived at the house, Elvis gave me a tour, and afterward we lay together on side-by-side chaise longues next to the pool, holding hands, as was our way, with our faces turned up to the sun. A member of Elvis's entourage came down the driveway toward us to let Elvis know that Lisa Marie had arrived. Elvis went up and got Lisa and brought her down to the pool. As they approached, I sat up and smiled at her. She was so cute, looking like a miniature Marilyn Monroe. She definitely had her daddy's sleepy eyes, and her blond hair was slightly disheveled. She was a part of Elvis, and so I'd loved her before I even met her.

"This is Daddy's new girlfriend, Linda," he said. "She's from Memphis."

Lisa was only four and a half years old at the time, and of course she was very shy about meeting someone new, and so she stayed close by her daddy's leg.

"Hi," she said, tentatively.

"Hey, I've heard a lot about you," I said. "Your daddy's told me so many nice things about you. I'm really happy to meet you."

Elvis stretched out again on the chair next to me, our hands instantly finding each other. Lisa began to play around the side of the pool, with both of us keeping a careful watch over her, to make sure she was safe and having a good time.

I had really long hair that fell down past my waist, and because it was a hot afternoon, I had it hanging over the back of my chair to keep it off my shoulders. After Lisa had a chance to get her bearings, she rambled up to me and ran her fingers along the edges of my hair, playing with it as it cascaded behind me. And then, she just kept moving along, like a skittish animal, continuing to play around the pool. This happened several times, with Elvis and me smiling at her, and at each other, every time she approached.

And then she came up to me and paused in front of me, more confident now.

"Excuse me, Linda," she said.

"What, honey?"

"Do you mind if I brush your hair?"

"No, that would be great," I said, trying to contain how thrilled I was.

"Daddy, can I go up to the house and get a brush?"

"Of course, honey," he said.

Because the property was gated, and there were employees everywhere on the grounds, we knew it was safe for her to walk back to the house by herself. As we watched her run away, Elvis beamed at me again. I could tell he was very pleased that Lisa Marie and I had connected right away.

"Oh, your hair is so pretty and so long," she said when she returned with her brush.

"Well, thank you," I said.

She was so careful and gentle with me that she didn't catch a tangle or anything. She was very serious about doing a good job, and she stood there for probably ten minutes, brushing my hair. We were close from that moment on.

I think it made Elvis feel good to know just how much I loved Lisa Marie, and that he could leave her in my charge. I believe he trusted that I would always keep an eye on her and look out for her best interests by caring for her and nurturing her growth. He didn't ever give me any parameters with Lisa Marie, and I was really pleased that he had faith in my instincts as much as he did. I think that, because I nurtured him so completely, he understood that would carry over to Lisa as well.

The more time I spent with Elvis, the more I understood that he was an extremely paradoxical person. As I had already witnessed, he could be the sweetest man, one just too good for this earth. As I came to see soon enough, though, he could also flip that switch with a temper so vicious and uncontrolled it seemed he'd never calm down again. In times of reflection and repose, I know he struggled with this aspect of his personality, but given that everything about his life was exaggerated—his looks, his talent, his fame, his generosity, and his passion—so was his anger. When he let go of all self-control, he morphed from an angel descended from heaven to the devil incarnate, and the sparks could really fly. With time, I came to learn what would set him off, but in the beginning, I was shocked by how quickly he could change from light to shadow.

The first time I saw it happen was in our first month together. We were having a general conversation about our day-to-day life, and he was talking about the guys who worked for him. I was still trying to get everybody straight, being as there were thirteen central guys in the Memphis Mafia, plus assorted members of his entourage.

"Red, I know," I said. "Then there's Sonny. And Lamar Fike. Jerry Schilling is your friend that comes to support sometimes. Charlie Hodge works onstage with you."

"Well, Sonny West is Red West's cousin," he said.

"Sonny is the good-looking guy, right?"

"What?"

"Sonny, he's the good-looking guy," I said.

"Oh you think Sonny's good looking?" he said, the volume and tone of his voice rapidly escalating. "Oh really? Oh you think he's good looking? I think I told you before, don't you *ever* tell me that another guy is good looking. He works for me. I don't want that in my head that you think he's good looking. He works for *me*."

"I didn't mean anything except trying to differentiate who's who," I said, shocked.

It wasn't like I'd said that I found him really attractive. I'd simply observed that he happened to be a nice-looking guy. And just like that, my sweet little Buntyn flipped out on me. Once a little time had passed, Elvis's anger subsided. It was almost as if he emerged from the center of a hurricane of his own creation and came blinking into the light. I made a mental note not to do *that* again.

There were also moments when I saw that Elvis's boyish impulsiveness could have some potentially dire consequences, and not just for him, but also for those around him. And even with so many constant companions in his orbit, there wasn't necessarily anyone present to be the voice of reason. With all of those pills readily available all of the time, Elvis wasn't the only one who indulged. And some of the guys would sometimes laugh and tell stories about how they'd all been obliterated on one night or another. This left the job of being responsible to fall on me, and made me feel even more like his mommy than when he called me such as a term of endearment.

During one of our first few stays together at the Las Vegas Hilton, I had just gotten out of the shower and still had a towel wrapped around my head, and another around my body. Having just walked past the toilet area, I was standing in front of the mirror, about to remove my towel turban to comb out my long wet hair. I felt a rush of air behind me, against my lower legs. There were a couple of loud pings, and the glass mirror on the bathroom door shattered with a dramatic cascade of broken glass.

I stood frozen in shock, my arms still reaching up toward the towel on my head, my heart thundering in my chest, afraid to move or step any closer to the shattered glass. There was a loud pounding on the other side of the door.

"Linda, Linda, are you all right?" said one of Elvis's guys.

"Yeah, what was that?" I asked. "What happened?"

"Elvis was just having a little target practice out here, and the bullet went through the wall."

"What?" I asked, opening the door to see that the bullet had also broken a glass-mirrored closet door in the adjacent room.

I turned and looked back into the bathroom, where my eye was drawn to the toilet paper holder, a few inches from where I'd passed by only seconds before. It was made of metal, which was flared out from the bullet's impact. So the bullet had apparently passed through the wall from the room where Elvis was playing with one of his guns, gone through the toilet paper holder, past my legs, out through the bathroom door, breaking the mirror as it did so, and then hit the glass doors in the room outside my bathroom, also fracturing them. If I had been sitting on the toilet, the bullet would have hit my thighs, possibly going straight through them. You get the picture. It was an extremely close call and could have been devastating. I had no idea what caliber gun he'd fired, but clearly it was powerful, if it had managed to travel that far and do that much damage along the way.

I threw on my robe, the towel still on my head, and rushed into our suite's living room, where I found Elvis lying on the sofa. He was ghost white and clearly shaken up, but trying to appear calm. Against the far wall, which was directly behind my bathroom, was a big poster with a bull's-eye target on it, which they put up all over Vegas at the time, advertising Elvis's engagement. Perhaps he was bored, but for some reason he'd had the notion to take a shot. He hadn't thought about the fact that my bathroom was behind the wall, and I was in the bathroom at that exact moment.

"What the hell are you doing?" I yelled. "And what were you thinking? You could have killed me."

Now, remember, I didn't swear at all back then, so these were strong words.

His face was ashen, and he had abruptly sat up, his leg jiggling nervously.

"Honey, I just didn't think," he said. "I didn't realize you were in the bathroom, and I didn't think the bullet would go through the wall."

"It went through two walls and the toilet paper holder. If I had been sitting on the toilet, it would have gone through both of my thighs. You could have killed me."

"Well, honey, I'm sorry," he said. "I didn't know."

"You're sorry, really?" I asked, too scared and mad to accept his first apology.

"Well, what the hell do you want me to say?" he said, getting defensive. "You just want to go back to Memphis?"

"Yeah, at least I won't get shot at there," I said, storming away to my dressing room.

He followed close behind me, taking me in his arms and holding me for a long time, until we both recovered from what had happened and the even greater terror of what might have been.

"Oh my God, I'm so sorry," he said again and again. "I just wasn't thinking."

"Don't be so crazy with those guns," I said. "They are not toys. You could kill somebody."

Elvis may have been my life's first adventure into loving unconditionally, but he tested that love more than a few times. Most of the time in our first year or two, such incidents were few and far between, and I was fortunate enough to only see his temper flare up against the guys in his entourage. But even then, I hated being around when Elvis went over to his own personal dark side.

There was a man who worked for Elvis as a general valet, or more accurately, something of a gofer. The boys in Elvis's crew had given him a nickname related to the fact that he seemed to be continually fetching things for Elvis and the others. Let's just call him Fetchit. I actually liked him and felt rather sorry for him, as he was slightly delusional, fancying himself to be an insider in Elvis's world and a bit of a gangster. We all found it amusing the way Fetchit would posture, arching his eyebrow to his hairline as if he were a real villain. Although I thought he was harmless, Elvis found him annoying, and then began to be suspicious of him, and finally fired him. We were in Vegas at the time, so Fetchit went to the airport to return to Memphis. It was then that Elvis discovered that some compromising private photos and a ring had gone missing. He gathered his troops and charged off to the airport to commandeer the perpetrator from his flight.

Elvis actually managed to stop the plane he believed to be carrying Fetchit on the tarmac by flashing the federal narcotics badge President Nixon had given him. Fetchit was not on the plane, though, and I can only imagine the passengers' shock when Elvis Presley roared up and down the aisles in search of his betrayer. Back in the airport, a couple of the bodyguards had found Fetchit before he could board his plane, whisking him back to the Hilton, where he was met in the Presidential Suite by a livid Elvis.

I don't believe Elvis cared about the ring he found in Fetchit's possession so much as he did the Polaroids, which were of a very personal nature, showing one of his former loves engaged in a simulated sex act with another woman. The image was fairly explicit and both women's faces were visible and recognizable. Elvis had shown me the photos, which he'd taken, explaining to me that the women had posed to please and excite him. The women were by no means lesbians, but the photos would seem to indicate otherwise. So the chivalrous side of Elvis's personality, dedicated to protecting a woman's honor and reputation, was provoked into an incredibly angry, violent reaction. With several members of his entourage and me watching, Elvis slapped and punched poor Fetchit senseless. We all knew how dangerous Elvis's rage could be and Fetchit was rightly terrified. It was horrible to behold, and I began to cry.

"Please don't!" I yelled. "Please!"

Fetchit was, after all, a simple man who'd made a terrible mistake. I couldn't bear to see him brutalized and humiliated by Elvis in his wrathful state.

Elvis was too consumed by his anger to hear me. He threw a glass Mountain Valley mineral water bottle at Fetchit's head, and then another and another, grazing his brow and drawing blood.

"Please, please stop!" I pleaded. "Just let him go back to Memphis. You have your photos and your ring back! Please, I'm begging you, don't hit him anymore!"

I hate violence and can't stand to see someone else hurt. Even if Fetchit had been wrong to do what he did, the punishment had not fit the crime in my estimation, and I was a wreck by this point. Finally, Elvis realized how upset I was, and he stopped and grew still. Fetchit sat cowering and shaking on the floor, and Elvis visibly softened toward him. Once the heat of his anger had cooled, he clearly felt sorry for what he had done to poor Fetchit.

"Here, let me help you out," he said, indicating that one of the guys should give Fetchit the money to cover his plane ticket back to Memphis.

"I'm sorry," Fetchit whimpered, still recovering from his frightening ordeal.

"It's okay," Elvis said, accepting his apology. "Good luck to you."

By the time Fetchit was escorted out into the hall, Elvis had returned to his normal, jovial self. But the rest of us were still very aware of the chill that had just passed over the room in the form of Elvis's blind rage.

As disturbing as episodes like this were, it was often easy—perhaps a bit too easy in retrospect—to forgive them, or at least forget them, because he was who he was. His stature, along with my love for him, made it possible to adjust to all kinds of behavior, even when it came to his problems with pills.

While we were in Los Angeles, he asked me to accompany him on an errand—to the dentist—and because he and I were inseparable during that time, I didn't think anything of it. I piled into the car with Elvis and Charlie Hodge, and both of us even accompanied Elvis into the room where he had a quick filling done. Then, as if they had some kind of a wink-and-a-nod agreement, the dentist left the room and Elvis immediately opened the cabinet under the sink and took out a gigantic jar of pills. Without hesitation, he began taking handfuls of pills and stuffing them into random pockets.

Clearly, this was not the first time he had been to this dentist to procure the pills he needed. He might have been acting like all of this was totally natural, but I couldn't believe what I was seeing.

"What are you doing?" I said.

"Oh, he knows I'm doing this," Elvis said. "It's fine. This is just Seconal. It's sleeping medication. It's just so tough to get prescriptions from doctors all of the time."

"Well, that's going to last you a lifetime, I would think," I said.

Having lived with him for more than a month, I knew he had to take sleeping pills to go to sleep, and something else to wake up, as well as oftentimes something to pep him up to go onstage. Elvis claimed he'd first been given Dexedrine when he was in the army to keep him awake on his post overnight. He'd never been without pills since then, but he believed prescription drugs were perfectly healthy and saw no reason to stop taking them or to more carefully monitor his intake. And I knew it to be true that he had always suffered from insomnia, since he had spoken often about it, and also about his sleepwalking when he was a teenager.

I was still very naïve about what it really meant for someone to take such quantities of "medication" every day. I knew about Judy Garland, and Marilyn Monroe, and a few other people I'd read about, but this was before there was as much transparency around prescription drug abuse as there is now, and so I had no idea what I was really witnessing. *Maybe that's just showbiz*, I thought.

Another aspect of show business I'd quickly had to become familiar with was the entourage. Anytime Elvis and I weren't alone in our bedroom, we were around the same thirteen men who formed the entourage we rolled with, and we all traveled everywhere together. Before Elvis bought his own airplane, he would either charter a plane or take over the whole first-class section of a commercial flight. And I was usually the only woman in the mix. The other guys couldn't always bring a girlfriend or wife along, but Elvis always had me with him, at least in the beginning.

The guys quickly came to think of me as one of them, and I saw things, including the occasional mistress or affair. Of course, this made it extremely uncomfortable for me when I'd meet a girlfriend, and then the wife came around, especially because I was very green at first. In fact, early on, I once came right out and asked Elvis about one of his entourage members.

"Isn't he married?" I said.

"Honey, I'm really not sure," Elvis said.

Oh really? I thought. *This guy's worked for you for how many years, and you don't know if he's married or not?*

They all kind of covered for each other, as I learned over time, which I guess was all a part of the rock-and-roll reality. I will say this, though: While their first loyalty was of course to Elvis, they showed me a great deal of compassion and kindness through the years. Elvis expected them to cover for him with me, but they didn't always keep me completely in the dark about what was really going on, and I appreciated it.

Although I was comfortable with the guys, I did sometimes feel somewhat self-conscious about living out my private life in front of them, which Elvis was completely accustomed to by now. During one dinner at the Monovale house, there were about eight of the guys there, including Red and Pat West, and Jerry Schilling, as well as his wife at the time, Sandy, and Lisa Marie. Elvis was at the head of the table, and I was at his left. As the housekeeper served us, we were all talking and socializing. Out of nowhere, I felt this searing stare, coming from my right.

I looked up at Elvis, and he was staring at me with heated intensity. I saw *the* look in his eye, the one he would call "that lean and hungry look." Without a word, he reached for me under the table, took my hand, and led me upstairs, leaving everybody behind at the table. He didn't excuse himself, and I didn't know what to say, so I didn't, either. Everybody sat hushed, and just kind of watched us get up from the table. But I think they'd probably seen the way he'd been staring at me while we were talking, and noticed the look in his eye, too. When the moment hit, his passion overtook him, and there was no denying him what he wanted. He rushed us upstairs to our bedroom, but we never made it to the bed.

The way Elvis kissed was also the way he made love, with his whole being, giving the experience, and his partner, his absolute undivided attention. He was in the moment, and he got lost in our connection in the deepest, most incredible way.

Obviously, he was much more experienced than I, but he found it very endearing that I had so much catching up to do. He was fond of mirrors in the bedroom. If I looked like Elvis Presley, I'd be fond of mirrors, too. He also had a few porn movies, including *The Devil in Miss Jones* and *Behind the Green Door*.

"Honey, have you ever seen a porn?" he asked me, early in our relationship.

"You mean a pornographic movie?" I asked. "No, of course not."

"Well, would you watch one with me?"

"I don't know. Is it sexy?"

"Yes, it's very sexy."

So he put on *The Devil in Miss Jones*, and we settled in to watch.

I was so innocent and naïve that it didn't take long for me to be shocked.

"She doesn't have any clothes on!" I said. "Oh my God. You can see her . . . You can see everything! Look! Oh! Oh my God! You can practically see all the way up to her tonsils! Is this legal for people to get naked, and do things on camera like that? Can't they be arrested for this? That's gotta be illegal, isn't it?"

Elvis was laughing so hard, he was crying. This was not a sexy moment. It was a hysterical moment, and it definitely dampened our foray into the world of watching porn. I guess I was too much of a Goody Two-shoes at the time to get into it like Elvis may have hoped I would.

Elvis was uninhibited in pretty much all areas, except for one. At the beginning of our relationship, I came out of my dressing room one night wearing a see-through negligee and glided over to where he was lying on the bed.

"You going to wear that to bed?" he said.

"Yeah, I though it was sexy," I said.

"Yeah, it's sexy as hell," he said. "But what if there's a fire, and we have to leave the premises? You need to wear something a little more modest, just in case we have to dart out of the house quickly. I wouldn't want anyone else to see you in a negligee!"

I looked at him and noticed he was wearing a set of men's silk pajamas, as usual.

"I'm not gonna be naked," he said. "I don't want you naked. I don't want you in that sexy lingerie. Let's just go to bed pretending there's going to be a fire, so we will be dressed for it."

I went and changed as I'd been ordered.

Of course, in any new relationship, there's an adjustment period during which both partners get used to each other's quirks, particularly when you live together and are in each other's company 24/7 almost immediately. In our case, the adjustment period was helped by the fact that I made it a point to be accommodating of nearly all of Elvis's desires (if not porn) in every moment. I was that Southern belle who lived for her man and catered to his every whim. I was pretty much a perfect fit for him "right off the rack"—few alterations necessary.

• • •

We'd been splitting our time between Las Vegas and Los Angeles for nearly six weeks before we finally returned to Graceland. It was the longest I'd ever been away from home at one stretch, and so I was excited to see my family and Jeanne again. But I didn't want to be separated from Elvis, and he clearly felt the same way about me.

"I think I'll go see my mama and daddy today," I said one morning.

"Well, I'll come with you," he said.

I felt relief knowing he wouldn't be alone while I was gone. Not only did I always want to be near him, but even at this early stage, I'd become aware that the quantities and variety of medication he took could endanger his health. During those initial weeks together, I'd seen him so incapacitated by sleeping pills as to cause me alarm. I was so protective of him that I always wanted to be there to make sure he was breathing okay or not in danger of hurting himself.

While I was excited for my family to spend time with Elvis, I was a little embarrassed about the fact that he and I were living together—and sleeping together—without being married, not because it bothered me, but because I'd been raised in a very proper, religious household. I worried my mama might be upset by this arrangement. It was a relief to find that she wasn't judgmental. However, she was very protective of me. It didn't matter that he was the King of Rock and Roll, as far as she was concerned. I was her daughter, and she was a very strong-willed woman, and she wanted to make sure he was treating me well.

When we went over to their house, and she and I went into the kitchen together to bring out iced tea for everyone, she pulled me aside.

"Are you happy?" she asked.

"I've never been so happy, Mama," I said. "I love him so much, and he really loves me, too."

My mother could tell I was genuinely loved and cared for, and this alleviated her anxiety somewhat. Elvis was always on his best behavior with my parents and came to sincerely care for my family.

Having my family so close to Graceland made it that much more magical for me. Graceland was simple. Life there was simple.

Elvis's sanctuary was upstairs in the private suite that included his bedroom, his bathroom, my bathroom and dressing area, and the office where we often sat at the piano, playing and singing. We harmonized together and, always the gentleman, he let me sing lead because I can't sing harmony. We also listened to a lot of music at Graceland, spending hours playing old records, listening to them closely, and talking about the lyrics. We listened to a lot of gospel music—he loved the Singing Rambos—but we also listened to country and old groups like the Harmonizing Four, which he loved. Sometimes we'd even hear recorded speeches by Martin Luther King. In particular, our discussions about lyrics definitely found their way into the poetry I'd been writing and helped me with my increasing mastery of verse.

As we settled into our domestic routine at Graceland, we spent much of our time in the master bedroom, stretched out on his big nine-by-nine bed, watching TV. As Elvis had informed me when he'd first brought me upstairs to his bedroom, he'd had it specially made. As he later told me, he hated four-poster beds and refused to sleep in one. This was because, a few years earlier, he'd been staggering from his sleeping pills, and he fell against one of the posts and had to get stitches in his forehead. Of course, he couldn't give up the pills, so he gave up the bed.

In those days, we didn't have a remote control for the television. We only had me.

"Honey, would you turn the TV up?" Elvis asked.

Without even questioning his request, I crossed the room and raised the volume.

"Is that enough?" I asked. "You want more?"

Once we had the volume where he wanted it, I got back into bed.

"I'm tired of this channel," he said a few minutes later. "Put it on channel four. Let's go to NBC."

And so I got up again and changed the channel. While looking back I'd never do this again (thankfully we also have remotes now), at the time I reveled in the satisfaction of the feeling that this incredible man needed me in every way. I think we had a rather symbiotic relationship in that respect. At least that's pretty much how I viewed my acquiescence to his needs at this point in our time together—Elvis Presley needed me, and I loved being needed by him. I was enraptured by the delirious swoon of my first love. I may have been a twenty-two-year-old college student, but I was innocent enough in matters of the heart to possess the fervor of a teenage girl without any of the perspective or self-preservation of a woman of my age. Having stepped through the looking glass into the greatest romance imaginable, I also may have relished such signs of my usefulness. They proved to me, and Elvis, I was indispensable to him. As such, I would be welcome to stay in this paradise with him forever, as I never wanted to leave or lose this feeling.

While we watched a lot of different things on TV in the bedroom, we watched hour upon hour of the British comedy show *Monty Python's Flying Circus*, and I quickly came to see that, as his favorite comedy troupe, Monty Python spoke to Elvis's deeply irreverent and inventive sense of humor. We would act out our favorite scenes from some of our own well-rehearsed takes on Monty Python sketches, and howl with laughter at their inane insensibility and our own silliness. I think one of the reasons Elvis loved Monty Python is that, like him, they were original. Their humor was offbeat and ridiculous. Similarly, Elvis watched the variety show *Hee Haw* religiously, in part because it spoke to a different side of Elvis's humor—his "down home" country side.

Elvis was forever surprising me with his unpredictable humor. On an otherwise quiet night at Graceland, Elvis might come out of his bathroom, all stooped over, with his pajama bottoms pulled up to just below his nipples, and shuffle over to my side of the bed, where he'd pause dramatically and look down at me slyly.

"Honey, I'm ready for bed," he'd say in the rusty voice of an old, feeble man. "Are you ready to have a little hot sex?"

Our ability to make each other laugh always brought us together, and as someone who adored being silly, I was far from afraid of making an ugly face in order to amuse him. When he got tickled, laughter erupted out of him with tremendous force. It was a joy to watch him laugh, but it was best when I was the cause of his riotous response.

On another occasion, he lost the porcelain crown he'd long worn on one of his front teeth, leaving a gaping black hole in his otherwise immaculate mouth. Instead of being uncomfortable over this dental emergency, or being embarrassed about how he might appear to others, he got right into this new part he was suddenly ordained to play.

"Come here, honey, give me some love," he said, talking like a full-on hillbilly. "Give ol' toothless Elvis some sugar. I like being toothless. I want to see if you really love me. If you love me looking like this."

There was no question—I did. He made a face that showed off his gap in a quite dramatic fashion, and of course, I started laughing again. He could be wonderfully self-deprecating, especially for such a huge star.

We enjoyed a lot of alone time in that bedroom. He always wanted me with him, and he often sequestered himself there, with the door closed and nobody allowed up there without ringing first. Nobody, and I mean nobody, came in without Elvis's permission.

This was true even with meals. When Elvis would ask one of the four housekeepers to prepare us some food, after a little while, the phone would ring.

"Is it okay if Lottie brings your food up now?" one of the guys would ask.

Lottie, Pauline, Mary, and Nancy were the four housekeepers. They had all been there for many years, and along with the guys, who were always wandering in and out of the house, and Elvis's family members who lived at Graceland—Aunt Delta and Dodger—they were constants. They were wonderful, and I loved them all and still think of them fondly. Those four women all had families outside the house, but they devoted a lot of time to Elvis, and they kept the household going. Mary was the cook, and she kind of tiptoed around Elvis. Lottie was the fiery one, who would kind of speak her mind. Pauline was the really quiet one who had a lot of kids. One time I saw her vacuuming, and she was asleep standing up, that's how tired she was. God bless her. Nancy was kind of the comical one, and sweet. They all had designated areas to care for, and Nancy cleaned my dressing area, so she was probably the one I was the closest to. I still get a Christmas card from her every year—she's the last living housekeeper of Elvis's Graceland.

We spent much of that fall at Graceland, settling into our domestic rhythm and learning what life was like away from the lights of Vegas and L.A. Before we knew it, Christmas was upon us, and as I soon discovered, Christmas was a magical experience at Graceland.

One of the most beautiful aspects about Elvis was how deeply he enjoyed Christmas. It was his favorite time of year, and his passion for Christmas went back to his memories from when he was a little kid. Even though they'd had nothing, his mom and dad loved Christmas, too, and they always made it special for him. He loved the religious significance of the birth of Christ, which brought with it new hope for the world, and a communal aspiration toward a higher good. He loved the lights, so he decorated Graceland beautifully, inside and out, a tradition that continues today.

And then there was the music. He recorded several Christmas carols over the years, including "If Every Day Were Like Christmas," which Red West wrote. Little did I know back then that I'd go on to write the song "Grownup Christmas List," which has become something of a Christmas classic. And I can't help but wish that I'd written it many, many years ago, so that Elvis could have recorded it, because I know it's a song he would have really loved. Although phenomenal singers like Barbra Streisand, Natalie Cole, Kelly Clarkson, Michael Bublé, and many others have recorded my song, Elvis could have brought every word to life with his magical vocals.

But more than the memories or the music, Elvis relished the giving. Those who were close to him used to even jokingly call him Santa Claus, because there was no one who embodied the spirit of St. Nick quite like he did, or who derived more joy from giving. During his lifetime, Elvis gave away nearly everything he had, and when he died he had very little left. It wasn't something he did for show, either. He really derived great pleasure from his generosity. Generous to a fault, he loved to lavish gifts on people that he cared for, going so far as to send out spies with special instructions: "Find out what she wants. Find out what he wants." Before there was Oprah giving to her studio audience, there was Elvis buying everyone a new car at Christmas and throughout the year. Some years, Elvis would think: *Everybody needs a new car. Let's just buy everybody a new car.* He bought his cook Mary a new house. One time while he was looking at cars at a Cadillac dealership, he bought a new car for an African-American woman and her college-age daughter who happened to there, dreaming of owning a Cadillac. That's just how he was.

What he didn't like was when people blatantly, and with an attitude of entitlement, asked him for something. Giving was a natural expression of his spirit of goodness and generosity but never because people expected it of him. He felt that expectation diminished the joy intrinsic in the act of giving. One of his phrases to live by was that of the Christmas spirit: "There is greater joy derived from the act of giving than that of receiving."

Our first Christmas we were together Elvis bought me a beautiful, floor-length muskrat coat that looked like mink and had a big fox hood. From the knee down, it was red fox, which zipped off, so you could make it into a three-quarter-length coat with a fox stole. It was the first fur I'd ever owned, and as Elvis stood eagerly watching my reaction. I pulled the coat tight around me and did a spin, and then I put my hands in the pockets, testing the fit. As I did, Elvis's eyes began to sparkle in that mischievous way I'd come to know so well.

In both pockets, my hands brushed against smaller gifts, and I pulled them out to examine them. In one pocket was $2,500 in hundred-dollar bills (which allowed me to get him as a gift whatever I could afford with it). In the other pocket was a beautiful ballerina diamond ring set in platinum.

"Honey, one day this will be our engagement ring," he said. "For right now, you can wear it on any finger you want. We won't be officially engaged right now, but one day we'll make the announcement, and this will be your beautiful engagement ring."

He'd designed it himself and had it made for me, taking the center stone, which was about six carats, from one of his rings, so that it would be a part of him, and put it in the center of my ring. Then he had it surrounded by round-cut diamonds, which were then encircled by baguettes, and it was all mounted up high, which was why it was called a ballerina ring.

"Thank you," I said, recovering enough to kiss him. "I love it."

Although he wasn't officially divorced yet, in those days he talked often about marrying me. Of course, I was up for it. I loved him. I'd made love to him. I lived with him. He already felt like my husband. And now, I had my pre-engagement ring as a symbol of all that we felt for each other and all we'd already shared. And we were only just beginning.

"Grown-Up Christmas List"

Do you remember me?
I sat upon your knee
I wrote to you
With childhood fantasies
Well I'm all grown up now
Can you still help somehow?
I'm not a child
But my heart still can dream
So here's my lifelong wish
My grown-up Christmas list
Not for myself, but for a world
   in need

No more lives torn apart
That wars would never start
And time would heal all hearts
Every man would have a friend
And right would always win
And love would never end ·
This is my grown-up Christmas list

What is this illusion called
The innocence of youth
Maybe only in that blind belief
Can we ever find the truth

No more lives torn apart
And wars would never start
And time would heal all hearts
Every man would have a friend
And right would always win
And love would never end
This is my grown-up Christmas list
This is my only lifelong wish
This is my grown-up Christmas list

LYRIC: LINDA THOMPSON

Chapter Six

TCB with TLC

When we are under the influence of new love's first blush, we tend to put our best self forward as much as possible. Looking back with the full knowledge of what was to come, I now understand that Elvis was probably at his healthiest and most conscientious during the first year of our romance.

This was perhaps clearest during the run-up to the taping of his *Aloha from Hawaii via Satellite* special, scheduled for January 14, 1973. He very much wanted to be his best self for his fans. The previous November, we had gone to Hawaii to do some preparation for the production, and after our idyllic first Christmas together back at Graceland, Elvis went back into show preparation mode. He wanted to look and feel his finest, ideally at what he considered his fighting weight of about 160 pounds. And so he went on an extreme diet in the two weeks before we flew to Hawaii to tape the special, only allowing himself 500 calories per day, with all of his food delivered to him in precise, prepackaged quantities. Although he had a tendency to indulge his every whim the rest of the time, when he put his mind and his heart to a task, he could be incredibly disciplined, as was the case now. He didn't cheat at all—none of his beloved meat loaf, mashed potatoes, crowder peas, or "iddytream." When he was watching his weight, if he craved a snack, he would have an apple and butter butch (buttermilk), or his favorite—honeydew melon—or the sugar-free Jell-O we'd make special for him.

Sticking to his diet with complete focus, he lost between eight and ten pounds in early January. If he'd been looking sexy and handsome when I met him six months earlier, he was a sculpted God now. In retrospect, having learned so much about nutrition and fitness during my marriage to a former decathlete, I'm amazed Elvis had the stamina to put on such a demanding show, given how few calories he was consuming at the time. But of course, singing and performing was what Elvis was born to do, and so he was ready when it was time for him to shine his brightest.

There was a mood of excitement as we landed in Hawaii in the days before the concert and prepared the show's final touches. This was to be the first-ever satellite television broadcast, and the first use of a split screen on a television show. The production had a $2.5 million budget, which was the most expensive such special at that time, and it would ultimately go out to an estimated 1 to 1.5 billion fans in more than forty countries around the globe. No doubt most of them would otherwise never have been able to see him perform.

With such an ambitious undertaking and sense of obligation to his fans, Elvis put a great deal of pressure on himself to give the performance of a lifetime. He wanted to look perfect, sound perfect, put on a perfect show, and not disappoint anyone involved or anyone watching at home. In the days before the show, there was plenty of tension, but we were also having a wonderful time. Elvis loved Hawaii more than anywhere else in the world that he'd been. And so he took great pleasure in the fact that he was in his favorite place, doing what he most loved—I'd go so far as to say his spirit was rather Zen leading up to that enormous concert.

On the big day, I sat in the audience. By this point in our relationship, I had seen Elvis perform dozens of times, but this was clearly different. I knew what this opportunity meant to my Elvis, my little Buntyn. He looked stunning in his white American eagle jumpsuit, and the dramatic white cape, which he so famously threw into the audience at the end of the show. All of his dieting and careful living had paid off in an amazing show for fans the world over. Of course, he delivered, and then some.

During the months since I'd met her, I had spent quite a bit of time with Lisa Marie, including a wonderful experience of playing Santa Claus to her for the first time when she came to Graceland during the Christmas holidays. After the Hawaii special, we returned to Las Vegas for Elvis's next run of appearances, but equally important was the celebration of Lisa Marie's fifth birthday on February 1.

This birthday party would be held in a style benefiting the King's pride, but would be only the second time I'd meet Priscilla. Though the perception has been that we all were very close during the years following their divorce, that wasn't exactly the case. When it was time for Lisa Marie to visit us, the bodyguards traveled with her between her mom's home and wherever Elvis and I were staying at the time. I simply didn't have that much exposure to Priscilla, and I didn't know her very well.

My first encounter with Priscilla had been the previous fall, not long after I'd had my initial meeting with Lisa Marie by the pool at the Monovale Drive house. During this same stay in Los Angeles, Lisa Marie had a parents' conference at her school that was supposed to be attended by both parents. Elvis wanted me to accompany him but wait in the car, and so I agreed. It was then that Elvis told me I might meet Priscilla. And while Elvis had never felt the need to prep me for my time with Lisa Marie, he had a few instructional words for me before we interacted with Priscilla.

"Honey, do me a favor," he said. "You're probably going to meet Priscilla. Don't wear all the rings and other jewelry I've given you because I never gave Priscilla that much jewelry. I gave her things, sure, but not nearly like I've showered you with gifts. I don't want to make her feel bad."

As we spoke, I looked down at my fingers—well, at least what I could see of them, because they were covered in gold and jewels. *Hmmm, I get his point*, I thought. Because Elvis always used to admonish me to wear the jewelry he gave me, I often wore several diamond rings at once, much to his delight. But the last thing I would have wanted was to upset her.

On that particular day, I again found myself in the limousine with the fox fur floorboards, but this time I wasn't just a college girl going to meet her destiny. I knew I might meet Priscilla, so I'd been sure to dress nicely, carefully choosing my outfit for the occasion, a white jersey dress. And I was judicious about showing restraint in my accessories, as he'd requested, wearing only one ring, not wanting to create any discord for him or hurt anyone else's feelings.

When we arrived at Lisa Marie's school, Elvis gave me a hug and a kiss, and then he climbed out of the limo and went inside the school to attend Lisa Marie's parent-teacher conference. God bless him, he was a good daddy. The meeting didn't last long, and he soon returned to the car, this time with Priscilla walking beside him.

"Priscilla wanted to meet you," he said.

"It's very nice to meet you," she said to me.

"And I'm so happy to meet you as well," I answered.

"I know you'll be around Lisa, so I just wanted to say it's nice to meet you and thank you for looking out for her," she said.

I appreciated the level of cordiality we were able to create between all of us. I wanted her to feel comfortable and confident I would be a good influence on her little girl.

Because I absolutely adored Lisa, I was thrilled a few months later to find myself cohosting her birthday party in our suite at the Las Vegas Hilton. It had been Priscilla's idea to celebrate Lisa Marie's birthday in Las Vegas, but when Elvis had spoken to me in advance to make sure I was okay with this arrangement, I'd been happy to help create a dream birthday for her. I was always respectful of their coparenting relationship and did everything in my power to support his special bond with Lisa Marie.

Even this early on, I felt quite comfortable in my role as Elvis's partner because we were nearly inseparable. And he made me feel very much like the lady of the house, no matter where we were staying. So I was at ease on this particular evening as I welcomed guests to our suite for the celebration. I could tell a few people were looking at us a bit askance; this was an era when divorce was not nearly as common as it is now. Some people present seemed to find it slightly unusual that Elvis had his new girlfriend and his ex-wife in the same room. (Situations like this, of course, have pretty much become the norm today.)

I didn't care what anyone thought; I just focused on doing my best to take care of Lisa Marie and Elvis while making everyone else feel as relaxed as possible. We had food, and birthday cake, and spent several hours commemorating Lisa Marie's special day. Besides being the evening's hostess, and making sure Priscilla had everything she needed to enjoy herself, I didn't spend much time with her. And that was probably the most time I ever spent with her during my years with Elvis.

However, I did have at least one amusingly awkward experience you'd have to file under the category of "children say the darnedest things." During Lisa Marie's stay with us in Las Vegas, I gave her a beautiful blue satin dress and matching cape that I'd had Suzy Creamcheese make especially for her.

"I got you a cape like your daddy might wear," I said when I gave it to Lisa Marie.

She loved this thought, and her gift, and she wanted to try it on right away. We went into my dressing area together to get her changed, and she stood there, as proud and as cute as could be, looking at her reflection in the mirror while fixing her shiny little cape.

"I look pretty in this, don't I?" She preened and posed, gazing at her adorable reflection.

"Yes! You do indeed," I enthusiastically agreed.

"My mommy doesn't like you very much," she said.

"Oh, I'm sorry to hear that," I said, striving to keep my cool so Lisa Marie would always feel safe knowing she could say anything to me. "I'm not sure why."

"Well, my mommy says it's because when she was married to my daddy, he didn't take her anywhere, but my daddy takes you everywhere. You are always with my daddy, and my mommy never got to be with my daddy. So that's why."

"Oh, well, I understand that," I said. "I'm sure that would hurt my feelings, too. I'm really glad that your daddy does want me to go everywhere with him because I want to be here to take good care of your daddy, and make sure he's happy. But I understand how your mommy feels. I like your mommy, and hopefully her feelings will smooth out a little."

Lisa Marie nodded her head and scampered back into the suite, already onto something new, as kids always seem to be. Rather than be offended, I actually felt bad for Priscilla in that moment because I knew the situation Lisa had described was quite true. I went everywhere with Elvis, even to the bathroom, in the early days of our romance. He had told me that the wives didn't go on tour, and that they usually only got to go to the Vegas engagements for the opening and/or the closing shows. His classic line was, "You don't take your wife to work with you." So the wives stayed home, but the girlfriends got to travel. That routine was quite obviously not conducive to healthy marriages, and Elvis's wasn't the only one that fell apart as a result. My note to self back then: *Perhaps I'd be happier remaining a girlfriend with traveling privileges, if as a wife, I'd be tucked away at home in the "wife penalty box."*

My experience of Priscilla during these years was mostly through what I heard from Elvis about her. In the first months of our relationship, he was still in the process of recovering from his perceived betrayal by her, and he sometimes struggled to forgive her. As he was able to finally begin to salve his wounded pride in the wake of their separation, he set out to let go of any lasting animosity he might have had toward Priscilla.

I saw this most clearly one time when he asked me to write down a list of intentions for him. As something of an all-around girl Friday for Elvis, I often took dictation for him, writing everything from short lists of things he wanted to remember, to the breakdown for a karate movie he planned to write, which I'm sure would have been wonderful, given his fervent passion for karate and his fertile imagination. One day he had me take down a list of his intentions on his own personally embossed stationery, with his TCB (for "Taking Care of Business") logo with the lightning bolt, and "Elvis," printed at the top. As he spoke, it quickly became clear that he had something much more serious on his mind than the usual flitting fancies he wanted me to capture in writing. Instead, he narrated a series of resolves he swore to keep.

The first: "To love the Lord thy God with all my heart, soul, and body as best I can," he said.

And then, after pausing again to think partway through the list, he said something that surprised me.

"To wish happiness for Priscilla and Mike Stone," he said.

I couldn't help but glance up from my handiwork. He'd been so angry and hurt when they'd first separated that, as has been well documented, he'd once expressed a desire to take a hit out on Mike Stone. And our early conversations about Priscilla had resonated with his pain and frustration. So this intention on his part to do better, which was almost spoken like a prayer, was telling about the honorable man he strove to be.

"To love and appreciate Linda with all my heart and body," he said, continuing to enumerate items on his list. By the time he was done, he'd pledged to take care of nearly everyone in his orbit. After he'd concluded, he had me sign the paper, "EP," suggesting his resolve to follow through.

Knowing that Elvis was actively healing from the dissolution of his first marriage made our conversations about the possibility of getting married seem even more layered with significance. And yet, despite the pre-engagement ring he'd given me and my enthusiasm to marry him and possibly have a child with him, he did express a few opinions related to matrimony and family that gave me pause. One night, we were talking in bed in the blue light of the TV when the subject of motherhood came up.

"It's different when a woman has a baby," he said. "She's a different person. It's just not as much fun to make love to a woman who's had a baby."

"What does that mean?" I asked, thinking about how I'd always known I wanted to be a mother someday, and how, more recently, I'd thought about having his child.

"They're a mother," he said. "They've given birth. They've had a child. You just feel like you don't want to violate that."

It was almost as if having a baby pass through her made a woman's body somehow sacred, and he didn't want to defile that preciousness. And so, I do acknowledge there is some truth to the reports I've read that Elvis had something of a Madonna complex. But for that moment, at least, I didn't think too much about how his beliefs might impact our future life together someday. I was too busy basking in the joy and promise of our love. And in so many ways, I continued to feel as if I was already his wife, especially when we were enjoying the quieter existence that was more common during our time together at Graceland, as we were that winter and spring.

Fun as the road was, at Graceland we could totally relax and be ourselves, without any outside distractions. When were lounging in our bedroom, watching television in the evening, it was common for Elvis to look over at me beseechingly.

"Honey, Gullion's a little hungry," he said. "Will you go downstairs and make me some food?"

Now, of course, we had four housekeepers at Graceland, who all cooked. And so, before I knew better, my first instinct was that any one of them could probably create a much finer feast for the lord of the manor than the few dishes I knew how to make.

"Honey, do you want me to get Lottie to make it for you, or Pauline?" I asked.

"No, Mommy, it tastes better when you make it because you make it with TLC," he said. "You make it with love."

"Okay, honey, what do you want?" I asked.

"I want to have some bacon and eggs," he said.

While I was down in the kitchen, at least one of the housekeepers would always come out to offer their services to me. And I always had to turn them down because sometimes Elvis would actually stand at the top of the stairs, peering down into the kitchen to make sure I was really doing the cooking myself, putting in plenty of TLC.

The first few times I cooked for him, without thinking there was any reason to do otherwise, I made a single portion—two or three pieces of bacon, a couple of scrambled eggs, and two pieces of toast—and carried it up to him in bed on his usual tray.

"What is this?" he asked, looking down at the plate. "Ariadne, I need more food than this."

"No, that's a good amount of food," I said.

"Mommy, I need more food than this," he said. "I grew up poor. I had to be rationed when I was a kid. Now I don't. I want to see a feast in front of me, even if I don't eat it all."

After that, I quickly learned my lesson. From then on, whenever he asked me to cook for him, I made sure to prepare a pound of bacon, a six-egg omelet, and five or six pieces of toast. It was like cooking for an army. When I took the enormous portion up to him on his tray and put it in front of him, as he'd predicted, he didn't ever eat all of it. So, no, he didn't eat oversize portions every night. But sometimes he did eat too much, especially in the wake of *Aloha from Hawaii*, when he was recovering from the deprivation of that 500-calorie-a-day diet. He just wanted to know that he could have more than he could consume, whenever he wanted to, proving that he had pulled himself out from under the grinding deprivations of poverty. That mindset bled over to his fashion choices. He would never, ever wear another pair of blue jeans, he decisively declared, because when he was dirt poor that's all they could afford. So blue jeans, to him, represented a time when he and his family were impoverished. He would have no more of that.

On other nights, what he craved was his now famous peanut butter and banana sandwiches. If they were not made exactly the way he required, he would not eat them, and he had no hesitation about sending them back.

"Make it the way I want it," he would say to whoever had brought up the food.

Elvis was well aware that I knew exactly how to make his PB&B sandwiches to his liking, and so he more often than not sent me down to the kitchen to do just that. Now, I know that this is a very famous and much-discussed sandwich, with a great deal of folklore surrounding it, so I think it's well worth including the recipe here, as it was taught to me by Elvis himself.

The first, secret and crucial, step is to mash up the bananas, and mash up the peanut butter, and then blend them all together and put the mixture on the bread. Then put the sandwich together by placing the other slice of bread on top. Melt one stick of butter. That's right, one whole stick of butter. Saturate one side of the sandwich completely in the butter, and then saturate the other side, cooking the bread like a grilled cheese sandwich, until all of the butter is absorbed. And then cut it in half, and serve. I have to be honest, I tried to cut back on the butter as much as I could without incurring Elvis's wrath, but he never let me eliminate too much.

When I brought Elvis in something that he really loved to eat, he was adorable, sitting up against the pillows, cross-legged in his men's pajamas. He had this cute little dance he did in bed, where he rocked from side to side, sometimes with his eyes closed, with this beatific smile on his face, almost like Stevie Wonder. That's how much he loved his favorite foods. It tasted so good to him and made him so supremely content. I can still see him rocking left to right in bliss, enjoying his food.

I made every effort to help steer Elvis away from overindulging in unhealthy food, and tried to live the example of eating well and exercising. To this day, I eat basically a Mediterranean diet with a lot of fish and vegetables. My preferred diet suffered during those years because Elvis would never allow fish to be cooked at Graceland or anywhere we were. He hated the smell of fish. I did the best I could to influence him to eat more healthfully, but stubborn as he was, it was often a losing battle.

On some nights after dinner, he'd ask me to go downstairs and get him some "iddytream." He loved all of the flavors, but I'd say that vanilla and chocolate were his absolute favorites. Sometimes strawberry. What he really adored were ice cream sandwiches, and especially Eskimo Pies, the ones with the crispy chocolate coating encasing a square of vanilla ice cream. Sometimes he ate a whole box at once, with me bringing the treats to him one at a time.

That was his personality type, and it applied to food as well as to drugs. As I was beginning to learn, these tendencies could cause tension between Elvis and me if I tried to curtail his indulgences, and for those in his inner circle who were trying to look out for his best interests and keep him healthy.

One time when we were staying at the Monovale house, Elvis sent me down the back stairs to the kitchen to get him a snack. When I got there I met up with Charlie Hodge.

"Hey, Linda," he said. "What are you doing?"

"He wants another ice cream bar," I said.

"Well, don't take it to him," he said.

"You go up and tell him you're not going to take it to him," I said.

"Well, he's gaining weight," he said.

"I know, but what am I going to do?" I said. "I tell him but he doesn't listen."

Elvis overheard this conversation, and he went ballistic on Charlie.

"Don't you ever tell her what to do or not to do in my house!" he screamed. "This is my house and she's doing this for me. She's tries to tell me, but it's up to me what I'm eating and not eating. If she doesn't get me what I want when I want it, goddamnit, then I'll just get pissed, and I'll go down and get it myself. So just shut the fuck up!"

At his core, Elvis was an extremely sensitive person, which made his self-destructive behavior even more painful to be around. He knew every molecule of his being was subjected to the most intense—and potentially harsh—scrutiny, and he could be very hard on himself, which was excruciating to witness. Elvis had long since stopped reading any and every review of his shows. He did not have thick skin, and when a critic had negative things to say about him personally or his performances, it cut him deeply.

One night in the months after *Aloha from Hawaii*, when Elvis was battling his weight and clearly losing the battle, we were at Graceland and Lisa Marie was visiting us. He was standing in front of the mirror in our bedroom, and he just kind of relaxed his whole posture and bearing, not making any more effort to suck it in. As a result, his belly bulged over the waist of his pants.

"Oh God, I'm so fucking fat," he said.

"Don't say that in front of her," I said, nodding toward Lisa Marie.

But before the words were even fully out of my mouth, she chimed in with her sweet little girl's voice: "Daddy, you're not fucking fat."

"You can't say that in front of her," I said, through the laughter I couldn't contain.

He started laughing, too, and the whole mood of the room immediately lightened. She brought so much levity to our lives, even when Elvis was struggling against his personal demons.

He adored Lisa. We both did. She was my first experience at caring for a little child, something I always felt I was meant to do. It fit me naturally, though looking back now, I grow alarmed when I realize how many loaded guns were around her at all times when she was at Graceland and our other homes. Thinking about the accessibility of firearms when any child is around makes my blood run cold. It was grossly irresponsible to have those guns just lying about in the home.

Thankfully, she had been taught repeatedly to never touch them and knew better than to ever play with them.

I loved being with Lisa Marie when she visited us, but it didn't take long for me to become exhausted. Most days, I'd be off, chasing after Lisa Marie as she ran off on some new adventure. She had a lot of energy, and so this made for some very long days. In the late afternoon or evening, Elvis woke up and joined us in our playtime and was with us for the few hours until it was Lisa's bedtime. And then he was up all night, and my primary undertaking was to be there for Elvis, who often would be awake until around the time Lisa Marie was getting up again. Even if I managed to sneak in a few hours of sleep between the two, it was exhausting.

Blissful as our time with Lisa Marie was, as Elvis and I approached the first anniversary of our meeting, it was impossible to deny that his moods were growing more erratic and that prescription drugs were playing a larger role. At times, he'd show visible signs of impairment, and while I kept careful watch over him to make sure he didn't do any harm to himself or others, he was never an easy man to control.

One day when we were staying at the Monovale house, there was no doubt that he was mildly under the influence of some drug. But, quite honestly, that could very well describe his demeanor nearly every day.

"Honey, you know I'm a fifth-degree black belt in karate," he said, the words coming out slowly, so that I had to focus to follow the sentence to completion. "I've got swords," he said. "I mean I'm pretty much an expert Samurai swordsman as well."

"Really, honey?" I said, humoring him, as was my way. "That's wonderful."

"Yeah, do you trust me?" he asked.

"Well, to an extent," I said, trying to keep my tone light and playful.

"Let me show you what I can do," he said, pointing. "Lean against that wall and remain motionless."

Now, I had ridden with Elvis on the back of his motorcycle, neither of us wearing a helmet. And I'd ridden with him in his car, with no seat belts on, as he'd sped through the streets of Memphis. And during these adventures, I'd had nothing more to protect me than my prayers and my faith in Elvis. But this time, for some reason, I hesitated. Maybe it was the way his eyes were hanging half-mast like they were, or something about the full implications of the word *sword*.

"I'm really not that strong-hearted, honey," I said. "You know that. I don't even watch scary movies."

"Honey, trust me," he said. "I would never do anything to jeopardize your life or your beauty. You know I love you. I would never do anything to put you at risk. Trust me."

And I did. I trusted him, as I always had before, loving him in such an adoring, almost otherworldly way that I believed in him entirely. *He can fix anything,* I thought. *Whatever gets broken, he can fix it. Even me.*

"Just lean against that wall," he said. "Stay pressed against the wall and remain motionless, with your arms at your side."

"Okay, honey," I said, standing as he'd instructed.

He pulled two swords out of their sheaths and then chose one that looked like a machete. It was long and tapered to a point.

"What are you doing?" I asked.

"Honey, just stay motionless," he said.

He began swishing the sword around my body, and my face, showing me the different moves of a Samurai swordsman. I don't think I breathed at all for at least sixty seconds, knowing as I did that his capabilities were impaired because of the drugs. But he was as good as his word, and he didn't so much as scratch me, or even touch me.

Finally, he put his sword down at his side, and I took a deep, hungry breath.

"Okay, that was incredible," I said. "But, oh my God, no more, because I think my luck's run out."

Lucky as I was to survive that—and I truly was lucky—it didn't mask a more troubling reality: In the months following the *Aloha from Hawaii* special, it wasn't just his more voracious eating habits and slight weight gain that became noticeable and increasingly troubling. He was visibly impaired more frequently, it seemed to me, both when he was attempting to sleep, and during our waking hours. And yet he didn't seem to notice any difference in his own behavior or acumen. The guys clearly did, covering for him as they were used to doing, while acting like nothing was out of the ordinary. All of this caused me great concern. Either he was on so many drugs so much of the time that he could no longer distinguish how they impacted him, or he was purposely taking excessive amounts of drugs, not just for their prescribed benefits, but because he enjoyed the feeling. Either way, he was fallible because of them, and it was clearly a problem I began to recognize as the stardust in my eyes began to fade away and tears for this man I loved took its place.

This man, I now understood, needed a lot of care, and so I grew more resistant to always accepting his version of our reality. Maybe I was the one who could see clearly, even though I had the submissive role in our relationship. I didn't fear for my safety, trusting Elvis implicitly as I did. But I did begin to fear for my sanity, as I understood more and more how I was living a version of "the emperor has no clothes."

One day, he asked me to come into his bathroom at Graceland.

"Honey, can you give me a vitamin B shot?" he asked, holding out the syringe in my direction.

"What do you mean?" I asked. "I can't give shots. I'm not a nurse. And besides, I'm needle-phobic."

"There's nothing to it," he said. "The doctor left it for me—vitamin B is good for you. Here, just pull down my pants."

After I did so and I drew close to take the needle from him, I noticed that his buttocks were scarred. I had never inspected his naked posterior that closely before in the bright light of the bathroom, and I was admittedly taken aback.

"Oh my God, what happened to your butt, baby? You have scars and lumps."

For the first time in our relationship, Elvis seemed embarrassed.

"It's just a little scar tissue, honey, from B_{12} shots and stuff like that, you know."

The sight was disturbing to me, as clearly these types of injections were something he'd been doing for a long time, long enough to give him scar tissue that had formed into hard knots. I knew enough by this point to understand that he hadn't always been getting injected with vitamins. In fact, while I did squeamishly give him the B_{12} shot that day, as he'd requested, when he would subsequently ask me to give him shots of other medications, I simply refused.

I had never done any kind of drug and found it difficult to understand why someone would basically mutilate himself that way. Despite their prevalence in our house, taking drugs never occurred to me, honestly—they didn't seem like fun. To witness someone become incapacitated and even rendered unconscious: That didn't seem like something I'd want to get into. Let me tell you, watching him destroy his health with prescription drugs was the best deterrent. If I had ever needed one to keep me from doing them myself, that was it. So I led a squeaky-clean, drug-free existence and hoped it would make it easier for him to do the same, but my efforts were mostly futile.

Of course, those scars, like some of his emotional ones, Elvis kept hidden. And even though Elvis and I had many blissful days still in front of us, the troubled moments would become more frequent. Whatever struggles he was going through were only going to get worse.

"I'm Only Here for a While"

I ask myself what's lasting
What will go with time
Everything I touch while I'm here
It all seems to be mine

But life slips through our fingers
Just like grains of sand
The world revolves without our help
It's all part of God's plan

When this world and I must part
My legacy will be my heart
I'll try to leave some love behind
To ease a troubled mind

I'm only here for a while
What will I leave behind me?
I'm only here for a while
Shouldn't I act kindly . . .
With love and tenderness . . .
Over and over again
The same stars shine on every man
If I'm only here for a while
Why not help someone else's heart
   to smile?

It only takes a minute
To look up at the sky
And reaching out you might touch
   a soul
Or at least say you tried

I'm only here for a while
What will I leave behind me?
I'm only here for a while
Shouldn't I act kindly . . .
With love and tenderness . . .
Over and over again
The same stars shine on every man
If I'm only here for a while
Why not help someone else's heart
   to smile?

Searching for answers together
Leaving this world a little better
I know we'll find all the answers
Look inside your heart

I'm only here for a while
What will I leave behind me?
I'm only here for a while
Shouldn't I act kindly . . .
With love and tenderness . . .
Over and over again
The same stars shine on every man
If I'm only here for a while
Why not help someone else's heart
   to smile?

Lyric: Linda Thompson

Chapter Seven

A Little Breathing Room

In October, Elvis traveled to Los Angeles, and for the first time since our relationship had begun more than a year before, he didn't ask me to accompany him. While I felt slightly uneasy about not being there to take care of him, a part of me was worn down from the more pronounced nursing duties I'd been taking on of late. I was exhausted.

When Elvis and I reunited, my joy at seeing him was tempered by my now-constant concerns about his health. I was perpetually listening to Elvis's breathing patterns and making sure he didn't get up while under the strong influence of sleeping medication and perhaps fall and hurt himself. In fact, I felt as if I were caring for a newborn baby, and I began to sleep very lightly.

One morning that autumn, when we were back together at Graceland, we were still in bed. It was around 7 A.M. I woke up and could just feel that something wasn't right. Elvis's breathing as he slept sounded shallow and labored, as if he was struggling to catch a deep breath. I became so concerned I shook him awake.

"Honey, are you okay?" I said, unable to keep the concern out of my voice. "Your breathing sounds labored."

"I can't get my breath!" he said, sounding fragile and frightened.

I called his daddy and summoned a nurse we had on call with an explanation of what was happening, and she brought over some oxygen. That wasn't enough. Elvis's father and I agreed we should call for an ambulance, and so we had to rush him to the hospital. During the ride there, my mind was racing—struggling to understand how this could be happening. But in truth, I knew exactly how, and why. All I could do was hope that this terrifying moment would be enough to inspire him to stop abusing prescription drugs.

When we got to Baptist Memorial, Elvis was diagnosed with pneumonia and admitted immediately. Since we did everything together, I essentially checked into the hospital, too, even though I was twenty-three years old and in perfect health. He insisted that I be near him at all times, so they brought in my own hospital bed and he had them push it right up against his. I'm sure we broke every protocol there was, but this was Elvis Presley. And if he was the King all around the world, this was doubly so in his hometown of Memphis.

I suppose most anything can become normal after a time, and so it wasn't long before we'd established our own routine. It actually wasn't that much different from our life at Graceland, but with a few special touches. When Elvis raised and lowered his hospital bed, he expected me to raise and lower my own bed in sync with his, so we were always totally level with each other. Later, when he lowered his bed, he looked over at me.

"Okay, sweetheart, you've got to lower your bed now," he said, glancing at his control. "We're at forty-five degrees; now we're going to be down at thirty-three degrees."

Of course, looking back, all of this seems *just a little* beyond the type of sustainable, balanced relationship that allows both partners to thrive and grow (and sit up at the angle that's most comfortable for them in bed). But I must have been somewhat flattered by the notion that he needed me this completely, and I was willing to defer to Elvis in most matters, at least for a time. Still, there's something telling about the fact that he demanded such togetherness and total submissiveness that it even extended to the position of our beds. While at the time it didn't bother me to cater to his tastes and moods, looking back it's clear that it became harder for me to acquiesce in such situations, the more I grew up. At a certain point, I would have to become my own person. But for the time, I actually found it sweet that he wanted to be so connected to me.

Despite the ridiculousness about the hospital beds, there were ways in which the hospitalization was actually a relief—with Elvis's pill consumption monitored by the nurses, I no longer had to keep such a close watch on him. I was able to relax more than I had in months. Elvis hated hospital food, so we had all of our meals prepared by the housekeepers at Graceland and brought over by the guys. When we were lying side by side, eating Mary's soul food and watching TV, it really was almost like home. And always, we were just happy to be together, even under extraordinary circumstances.

We had two rooms at the end of the hall. Elvis and I stayed together in his hospital room and used the sitting room across the way for the guys. From there they could run out and procure anything Elvis might need, or come over to provide him with their usual jocular distractions. Mostly Elvis and I relaxed and watched TV alone together. When the programming went off at midnight, we contemplated the image of an Indian on the screen, which the station left up all night until the first show of the day resumed again in the morning. And then, every night we switched over to the nursery channel and watched the babies, picking out the ones we thought looked like they could be ours when we had a baby together someday. He wanted a son, so we tried to find a little boy for him.

"I like the name John."

"I know you do, Gullion," I said, well aware that John was his pseudonym when he checked into hotels on the road or otherwise needed to obscure his identity.

Elvis rolled over on his side and brought his focus to my eyes.

"If we ever had a baby, it would probably just be one big eyelash," he said. "We might have to name it Eyelash. Yours and my eyelashes are so long, and it's the same for everybody in your family. Yep, I'd say our baby is going to be one big eyelash, between yours and mine."

Listening to Elvis joke about babies, it was hard to deny the improvement in his health and well-being. He seemed so much clearer and more himself, although I'm sure he was never completely off sleeping pills.

Still, I faced a troubling reality: Elvis's drug abuse had landed him in the hospital. No matter how much Elvis wanted to deny it, prescription drugs, as we now are more aware, are every bit as addictive as street drugs. The distinction he made for "legal" drugs that a doctor had prescribed allowed him to not think of himself as an addict. Indeed, there was a stigma attached to drug addiction that Elvis would have been very embarrassed by. Making things harder was that, during this time, there was not the plethora of rehab centers found today. Addiction was a shameful thing to be dealt with in private, if at all. Whenever news got out of one of Elvis's hospitalizations, the official reason was stated as pneumonia, or exhaustion, or another innocuous ailment.

That silence about addiction held for me as well. I certainly would never have spoken about it with anyone else in our entourage or even with my own family. I was already good at keeping Elvis's secrets, deepening my desire to protect him, often from himself. The scenario that landed him in the hospital was exactly the kind of thing that kept me lying awake listening to his every breath, and it highlighted a problem that was growing worse. Drug addiction is not pretty for anyone, but when it came to Elvis, the pressure was on me to try to maintain a semblance of normalcy.

This first hospital stay was eye-opening, but as we prepared to leave the hospital after a little over two weeks, my impression was that he was taking fewer and milder sedatives, and they were enough to help him sleep and leave him well rested, without incapacitating him in any way. For this alone, I felt like it had been time well spent—something of a detox, before that term existed—and I hoped that the rejuvenating power of Graceland would only add to this.

There was always something magically soothing as Elvis and I walked through the doors into Graceland and returned to the cozy homestead he'd created. Even though we had wonderful adventures when we were in Las Vegas and Los Angeles, Graceland truly felt like home—especially during the holidays, which were rapidly approaching.

After that crazy year of 1973, I wasn't sure what I was going to do about giving him a Christmas gift. I wanted to get him something special to show him how much I loved him and appreciated his generosity to me. But the only money I had was the American Express card Elvis had given me, and of course, Mr. Presley paid the bill on Elvis's behalf. Even though it didn't have any spending limit attached to it, I never wanted to take advantage of our relationship.

More and more throughout the previous year, I had taken to expressing my love and devotion to Elvis by writing him love poems. I'd always written a great deal of poetry, and now, of course, I had the perfect muse. Having Elvis respond with enthusiasm was a wonderful feeling.

"Honey, this is beautiful," he said, reading the latest verses I had composed for him. "Let me have someone put this to music, and I'll record this."

"No, no, it's private," I said. "This is my little love sonnet to you."

In my ignorance and naïveté, I believed it was better to have these lines exist only between us. Looking back as someone who went on to have a three-decade songwriting career, and counting, I wish I had known then about royalties. Not to mention that it would have been incredibly poignant to have had him sing my lyrics. Just to have that for posterity. But at the time I felt I was protecting our privacy. Such praise encouraged my sense of my own prowess and effectiveness as a writer then, and it probably carried over to my future songwriting career. Having this seasoned icon of word delivery love my poetry enough to want to record some of it certainly gave me confidence about my way with words. But I never had an ulterior motive—I just wanted to express my love poetically. I suppose this made him love me more, at least knowing I had no agenda and was truly writing these love poems just for him. I can honestly say I was always there for the right reason.

With Christmas that year being an extra-special occasion, I couldn't simply write him a poem like I did any other day of the year. I puzzled over what to get him until I sat down and painstakingly sketched out a beautiful Maltese cross, which I chose because Elvis loved crosses, and because it exemplified Christmas. My design specified that the cross would be covered in pavé diamonds, and in the center would be a yellow gold eternity band, within which would be two sideways hearts, one done in emeralds, which is my birthstone, and the other done in garnets, which was his birthstone. The two hearts were connected at the tip with a diamond. The piece was to be inscribed, "Love Linda."

I brought my design to Elvis's personal jeweler, Lowell Hays.

"I want to give this to Elvis for Christmas," I said. "How much will it cost?"

"Well, I can do this for you for eight thousand dollars," he said.

So I formulated a plan, and I went back to Graceland, where I found Elvis relaxing in our bedroom.

"Honey, I have a great idea for a Christmas present for you," I said.

"Aw, Ari, you know how I feel about that," he said. "I already have everything I want, and if I saw something I didn't have and wanted it, I could buy it for myself. Besides, you know just having you with me is my gift. Your presence is my present."

But I wasn't letting go that easily. I persisted, explaining that it was an expensive gift that I would have to put on my American Express card.

"How expensive are you talking about?"

"It's twenty-five thousand dollars," I said.

"What? Twenty-five thousand dollars?" He gasped, his eyes widening.

"Now, doesn't eight thousand dollars sound a lot better?" I asked, smiling broadly at him.

He started laughing his wonderful, infectious laugh.

"What is it, honey, twenty-five thousand or eight thousand?"

"It's only eight thousand. What a bargain," I said.

By this point, he was just rolling with laughter.

"Oh that was clever," he said. "That was clever. Yeah. Eight thousand sounds just fine, sweetheart. If you want to spend eight thousand dollars on your Buntyn, on your little Gullion, you go ahead. I'm just a little fella, so I could use a nice big gift like that."

Lowell Hays made the cross for Elvis, and it turned out even more beautiful than I'd envisioned, a fitting symbol of all that I felt for Elvis. When I gave it to him at Christmas, he just sat there for a long moment, staring at the cross, taking in all the details I had planned out with such emotion and care.

"This is the best gift I've ever gotten at Christmas," he finally said, his voice full of feeling. "In fact, it may even be the best gift I've ever gotten. It means so much on so many levels."

I have no idea if that cross really was Elvis's best gift ever, but it didn't matter. Elvis deserved to have many "favorite gifts."

The cross was such a prominent piece that he tended to wear it for shows more than out and about on a daily basis (not that the size or ostentatiousness of a piece of jewelry or item of clothing ever deterred him from wearing it, obviously). It became an iconic piece that has traveled as part of exhibitions devoted to him and is currently on display at Graceland.

As 1974 dawned, we returned to Las Vegas for another engagement. Elvis had obviously benefited from his hospital stay, and for a time, he appeared healthier and clearer than I'd seen him in some time. However, as he submitted himself to the grueling schedule of his Vegas run, which included two performances a night, I began to notice his pill usage increasing again, even if not to the excessive levels it had been at before. I was beginning to become accustomed to the cycle of our life and how it alternated between the quieter, homey time spent with family and old friends at Graceland, and the fast-paced, glitzy aura of our existence on The Strip.

Elvis had breathed new life into Las Vegas with his multiyear run of shows, accelerating the city's evolution into the grown-up playground of today. Many of the fascinating people I met during my years with Elvis were in Vegas. Elvis was never overly interested in celebrities, though. He was the largest icon, the biggest innovator, the most notable trendsetter of his time. The celebrated people who were in his orbit in Vegas were often more in awe of and curious about him than he was about them. Everyone from Raquel Welch, to Barbra Streisand, to Bob Hope to Muhammad Ali came backstage after Elvis's performances at the Las Vegas Hilton. Many more would come up to the thirtieth-floor Presidential Suite for the after party that usually went on until past dawn. We enjoyed sing-a-long gospel sessions with Mama Cass and the Imperials, visits from Bobbie Gentry, Ann-Margret, and too many others to name.

We also loved going to see Tom Jones. Elvis was in awe of his voice and a true fan. He also liked Tom personally. The first time Elvis took me to meet Tom and attend his performance, we had been living together less than a year. He wanted me to wear the sexiest dress I owned.

"Honey, I want you to wear that white crocheted see-through dress from Suzi Creamcheese I just bought you," Elvis said. "That dress and your body is gonna blow Tom's mind! I can't wait to show off my new love to him. He's gonna eat his heart out!"

I thought that was funny that these two grown men, superstar performers, had such a boyish, even puerile show-off competition going. But I wore the dress and elicited the reaction Elvis had wanted. It was a very different story a mere year and a half later, when Elvis and I were going to see Tom perform again. I broke out one of my sexiest dresses and came out all set to leave.

"Honey, what the hell are you wearing?" Elvis said.

"What do you mean?" I asked. "The last time we went to see Tom you were anxious to show me off and asked me to wear my sexiest dress."

"Well, that's when you were my new girlfriend—now you're my woman! You're the woman I love and live with, and I don't want Tom, or Dick, or Harry, or anyone else looking at you with lust in their eyes. You're mine. Go change into something that won't cause eyes to bug out."

Funny how just a little passage of time, and growing closer to one another, made Elvis so much more possessive and protective of his woman.

While he enjoyed musicians of any kind, he identified more with regular people than he did with the biggest stars, something that he and I shared. He never felt like he was better than anyone. He felt a commitment to, and a bond with, his legions of admirers. This could be especially challenging when it came to his female fans. Being the girlfriend of one of the world's biggest heartthrobs definitely had its challenges, which were particularly apparent during our times in Vegas.

One night, when I was watching Elvis perform, I happened to notice this young woman who was sitting at a ringside table. She caught my eye because she was very beautiful, and because she was staring at him in a noticeably crazed way. I'd seen plenty of women stare at him intensely, of course, but this was another level of fervor. Finally, she jumped up during the middle of his show, reached up to the stage, and grabbed Elvis around his neck. The bodyguards had to pull her off, which was no easy feat, as she had a death grip on him. That quick action would leave him with a neck sprain. As they finally hooked her under her arms and dragged her away from the stage, her dress lifted, and it was clear for everyone to see that she wasn't wearing any underwear. She must have thrown them at Elvis earlier in the show. People sure went crazy around him, or more accurately, he brought out the crazy in people. Or, even more accurately, he brought out the crazy in *women*.

As he was famous for doing, he always bent down from the stage and kissed some of the ladies in the front rows and gave them scarves during his closing number, "Can't Help Falling in Love with You." Well, of course they wanted a real kiss from Elvis Presley, and so they kissed him on the lips. I understood this was part of his special relationship with his fans, but I had my limits. Being a bit of a germaphobe, when I went back to his dressing room after his show, I always made him brush his teeth, gargle, and sanitize his lips before I'd give him a kiss.

Elvis and I sometimes talked about how it would be nice to embark on a more normal life. But of course he was mostly living his dream, and it was hard to argue with the perks.

"You know, how can I possibly complain?" he said. "I have people paying me to do what I love to do. I have people doing things for me. And the cost is that you lose some of your individual freedom."

And yet, while he definitely appreciated all life had afforded him, at the same time he often experienced a sense of isolation.

"I feel an intense loneliness in my heart," Elvis sometimes said to me.

"But, honey, people love you," I'd say, pointing at the monitors in our bedroom that revealed the fans clustered outside Graceland. "Look at the gate. Look at all those people down there that just want to get a glimpse of you. They love you. They're so devoted to you."

"But they love Elvis Presley," he said. "They don't know Buntyn. They don't know little Gullion. It's an impersonal love. It makes me feel really lonely to know that not many people know me, the real me. But you do, Ariadne. You know who I am, and you love me, and one day maybe you'll write a book about me. About the man, not the myth."

His loneliness was an extreme, influential part of his complex self—that's why he so loved that song "Do You Know Who I Am?" which he released in 1969, and why, I think, his fans have always responded to it. Elvis definitely had that desire and the corresponding fear that if people knew the real, flawed him they might revoke their love.

To be fair, Elvis had always felt some degree of that feeling of isolation. From the time he was a little boy, he'd had this heightened sensitivity to life, and to other people, at least some of which came from growing up in the South. There's a great deal of emotion in that landscape, and I think being an impressionable young boy, Elvis felt that. And I do believe it was a huge part of his unique and matchless gift as well. When you listen to him sing, it's like it truly came from his soul. There was this kind of hollowed-out feeling, a true depth of pathos and humanity, that he was able to express in his music.

I think that's one of the reasons he was so glad to have found a companion in me. I could understand and sympathize with his deepest, darkest moods, and not only keep him company during the sleepless nights when he once again greeted the dawn, but also meet him in the silly humorous place that allowed him, for a time, to forget the pressures and expectations that went along with his wonderful, rarefied position. One night, after his second performance, Elvis went to his dressing room, and I went to mine. Having both changed, we came out hand in hand to where the stairs went down to the main part of our suite. We stood there for a beat, and then descended in step with each other.

Immediately, the whispers rose up: "Oh my God, there he is."

"Oh my God, isn't he gorgeous?"

"Oh, man, that's his girlfriend. She's pretty."

"No, I think she's too skinny."

"No, I think she's pretty."

All of these little rumblings were audible as we cruised down the stairs together. When we were sure all of our guests were looking up at us, we smiled in unison, revealing that both of us had blacked out our two front teeth with eyebrow pencil.

As if nothing out of the ordinary was happening, we glided up to the first group of guests and shook hands all around with the widest grins plastered on our faces.

"So nice to meet you," we said, natural as could be, trying to keep from laughing as we watched them do a double take but try to keep their cool in front of us.

They weren't sure if, because we were from Tennessee, that's how we did it, taking our teeth out when it was time to relax. It was so funny to see people's reactions, and so we really played it up, walking around the room and meeting everyone.

"This is my girlfriend," Elvis said.

"Hi, I was Miss Tennessee," I said, smiling, blacked-out teeth on full display.

Some people laughed, but others were afraid to laugh, which was even funnier.

As much fun as we had during that Vegas stay in early 1974, I could sense something was changing between us that would mark the beginning of a new and unwelcome chapter in our relationship. At first I just noticed a few almost imperceptible changes here and there—moments when Elvis seemed less attentive, distracted even. While his ongoing drug abuse was certainly part of the problem, there was something else going on as well.

Elvis was not monogamous by nature. Even if he had been, I can't imagine the amount of discipline it would have required to routinely look away from the available, willing women who regularly threw themselves at him. When we returned to Graceland after our Vegas run in February, Elvis decided he wanted me to stay there while he went out to California on his own. And having spent nearly eighteen months together with me, pretty much nonstop, Elvis was beginning to grow restless for his previous lifestyle. As important as this was to him, he was quite candid about his struggle.

"I've broken my fidelity record for all time," he said. "I've never been this faithful to anyone for this long in my entire life."

Sometimes we find ourselves believing what we want to believe. But I was certain he'd been completely faithful to me for the first year, at least, as he'd set up our life together so that he was never out of my sight, unless he was behind a closed door in the bathroom.

"But honey, I think we need to have a little breathing room for a few days," he said. "Like our favorite book, *The Prophet*, says about marriage, 'Let there be spaces in your togetherness, stand together yet not too near together: For the pillars of the temple stand apart.' Sweetheart, you know by now how much I love you and you should feel absolutely secure in that. That is not going to change. I love you."

Elvis was smooth when he needed to be, and he had a quote for just about every occasion or circumstance. He was surprisingly well read.

While I always appreciated his honesty, I was understandably conflicted about this in ways that went far beyond just the thought of him being with another woman. Though I couldn't deny how hurt I was by that prospect, the caretaker in me was concerned most urgently that whoever he was with wouldn't be able to watch out for him appropriately. I was already losing sleep over his prescription drug habits and that was when I was in the bed right next to him. Whoever the women sharing his bed would be, they wouldn't be attuned to his needs, or to possible changes in his breathing. This was not a simple matter of being jealous that he might have sex with another woman. I knew no one else would be as accustomed to his propensities, weaknesses, and needs as I was, and I worried about what that might mean. Would they know enough to send him to the hospital as I had? Probably not.

But beyond his well-being, there was the toll that this shift in our relationship would take on my feelings as well. I felt threatened, territorial, and angry. My heart and my soul were crying out: *That's my man. That's the man I saved my virginity for? That's the man I love. Why does he need to do this?*

As I weighed the different sides of this, there was a part of me that wanted to be unselfish about the possibility of him spending the night with someone new. This may sound like a crazy, almost delusional rationalization, but I was well aware that a private tête-à-tête with Elvis would more than likely consist of delving into his books on spirituality, and there would need to be a connection on that level for a physical one to ensue. And sometimes I would half-admit to myself that he was almost too fascinating, too much a bigger-than-life, one-of-a-kind phenomenon, not to be shared with others on a more personal level. I knew better than anyone how he was trapped by his own fame, and I didn't want to make his life more restrictive than it already was. I wanted him to be able to experience other people, if that's what he needed to be happy and feel inspired and fulfilled.

And so, after eighteen months of the most passionate, all-encompassing love I'd known, I had to decide if the possibility of infidelity on his part was going to be a deal breaker. For the time being, at least, I determined it wasn't. However, no matter how I tried to talk myself into understanding and accepting this new situation, the foundation of our love affair began a slow corrosion that would permanently alter our relationship.

While he was away in Los Angeles that first time, I found myself restless in our bedroom at Graceland, unable to stop myself from worrying: *I'm sure he's with another woman, even if it's just to fill the time, or to fill the empty space in the bed. And while I know he's not necessarily having sex with her, he's most likely sharing emotional intimacy. She looks at him and sees the King; she doesn't know how much help he needs to take care of himself.*

It was a difficult few days for me, but when Elvis returned to Graceland, he had clearly missed me, no matter what he'd been up to, or with whom, while he was gone. And if our process of coming back together wasn't seamless and instantaneous, it was relatively easy to act like nothing out of the ordinary had happened. And so we did just that.

That March, in 1974, Elvis entrusted me with a project that would consume much of my energy and creativity right through to July. It gave me a focus when he was away without me, which began to happen more, as I had anticipated it would, usually only for a few days at a time. During this time, many of the decisions I made, some based on Elvis's instructions, helped create what has become the iconic interior design of Graceland that so many people know today.

In particular, Elvis had big plans for a simple space that had begun as a screened-in porch before being enclosed.

"Honey, I want this to look like you're in the jungle," he said. "And we're going to put green carpet up the wall."

"Really, honey, you want to put it up the wall?" I asked, not quite picturing it.

"Yeah, I want green carpet to climb the wall like moss is climbing the wall," he said.

He and I actually went to Pier 1 Imports and bought the oversize fake fur chairs and some of the other wilder decorations. His taste was unique, to say the least, but it was his own.

It was his home, and so I was happy to help him make it over to his specifications. He had great taste in some ways, but then again, let's be honest, he could also lean toward the garish. His bedroom was all done in red and black with touches of gold, and so now he wanted the dining room and living room to be red and black as well. We had these enormous, high-backed, studded, red fabric chairs made for the dining room. Everything was exaggerated, and over the top. It looked like a bordello—it truly did. It wouldn't have been my taste, but it was totally Elvis.

After he passed away, Graceland restored these two rooms to their original white design. No disrespect to them, but I think this decision might have been a mistake on their part. Of course, it's a much classier, prettier place done all in white, and honestly more to my own taste. But he'd had such a strong impulse to redecorate as we did in 1974, and so I feel like something that was a real part of his vision was destroyed.

I'm glad they left the Jungle Room. Think about it. Some of these rooms are so renowned they've been mentioned in songs. I've always loved the line from Marc Cohn's wonderful "Walking in Memphis," where he sings: "there's a pretty little thing waiting for the King and she's down in the Jungle Room." When I first heard that, I thought, *Hey, I was that pretty little thing.*

The downstairs basement rooms were fun to decorate with the assistance of a man named Bill, who was quite a talented decorator. We did the pool room with a tentlike feel, gathering fabric for the ceiling and the walls. The TV room had three TVs, so one could watch CBS, NBC, and ABC at the same time. Remember, those and PBS were the only main networks back then. I designed the TCB and lightning bolt zinging through clouds on the back wall, and wanted mirrors on the ceiling to make that room appear higher and more open. I bought cute ceramic monkeys to place around and lighten the atmosphere as well.

I also planted gladiolas and a beautiful bush with gold- and orange-toned leaves, a coleus, in the meditation garden, so we could all enjoy seeing the gladiolas bloom. One time, I was outside the door at Graceland, in that front area of the lawn, planting some daffodil bulbs to come up in the spring. I was wearing coveralls, and I had my hair pulled back. A tour bus stopped down below the house, and I could hear the fans talking as they took pictures through the gate.

"Oh, does she work here?" one asked. "Is that the landscape person?"

I never wanted to turn around and have them see me looking like that. Instead, I was happy to have them think I was a worker bee, which, in a way, I was.

Though the redecoration of Graceland was very much Elvis's vision, it also affirmed my role in his life and my place in his heart—this was my home, too. Despite the new, unspoken reality that Elvis was probably straying during times when we were apart, he still made me feel like the lady of the manor in ways that really mattered to me, reinforcing that I was his only love.

Still, my heart broke a little bit every time I suspected him of spending time with another woman. And yet, I stayed. I stayed because I loved him. I stayed because I couldn't imagine my life without him. I stayed because the devil you know is better than the one you don't. And most of all, I stayed because I knew how much he needed me—whether he always knew it or not.

"And When She Danced"

Can you go back in time
To a place in your mind
To the one who knew
A part of you
That you just couldn't find.

If you asked me to choose
Between a memory or two
When it's said and done
I'd take the one
Whose love I had to lose.

'Cause when she danced
I lost my innocence.
I loved her then
I always will
She left with me
A burning memory.
She took with her
A part of me.

If I could get back where I've been
Feel the passion I felt then
I'd be there right now
And yet somehow
It never comes again.

She had nothing to gain
But a way out of pain
With her song and dance
She lost romance
The world had gone insane.

'Cause when she danced
I lost my innocence
I loved her then
I always will
She left with me
A burning memory
She took with her
A part of me.

Looking back I'm not sure
If I won or lost the war
But when she danced with me
Our hearts were free
As far as I could see.

And when she danced with me
Our hearts were free
As far as I could see.

LYRIC: LINDA THOMPSON

Chapter Eight

You'll Always Be Safe with Me

While our life together had taken on this new and sometimes painful dimension, it was still very much a life together. I continued to be Elvis's near-constant companion. In the spring and summer of 1974, this meant going on the road with him a great deal, as he took a six-month break from Las Vegas in order to bring his music and magic to fans elsewhere in America.

Our touring crew generally included most of his entourage and the same musicians and backup singers from his Vegas show, with one noticeable addition: Colonel Tom Parker, Elvis's longtime manager. These trips on the road were among the few times I saw the Colonel, as he accompanied us for at least part of every tour. But though I would sometimes cross paths with him at a venue, I did not interact with him much. We did not go out to dinner with him or socialize with him in any way—their relationship was strictly business, all based on a handshake, as has become legendary.

However, I got the distinct impression that the Colonel might have held Elvis back in later years. And I think Elvis was aware of this, whether or not he wanted to admit it. For one thing, Elvis very much wanted to tour Europe and Asia, and Colonel Parker always declined, claiming he couldn't provide appropriate security for Elvis overseas. But, as has become public knowledge in later years, some people believe the Colonel, who was born in the Netherlands, did not have legal citizenship in the United States, or at least he wasn't sure he did. It has been rumored that, because he was not sure he would have been able to secure a passport to travel with Elvis, he therefore put off any arrangements for international travel with any excuse he could fabricate.

Whatever the truth may be, Elvis also felt stymied because he wanted to do more movies and did not always feel that the Colonel was fully supporting his cinematic aspirations. Elvis had a tremendous talent for acting, and I believe he thought of himself as more of a Marlon Brando type and would have relished an opportunity to show off his greater depth as an actor. But it was very difficult for him to move beyond his image and be given opportunities to grow as a serious actor.

Indeed, there may have been some truth to the idea that the Colonel held Elvis's acting back. The following year, Elvis received a backstage visit from Barbra Streisand and her boyfriend, Jon Peters. They wanted to talk to Elvis about a film they were producing, *A Star Is Born*, and hoped that Elvis might be interested in starring opposite Barbra. They described how the film would be a remake of two earlier movies, updated to tell the story of an up-and-coming singer-songwriter who falls for a self-destructive rock star, only to find that her career is soon eclipsing his. Elvis thought it was a great project and really wanted the male part. A formal offer was presented to him, and he was thrilled at the prospect of finally having the opportunity to really immerse himself in a role and reveal new dimensions of his acting talent.

Unfortunately, even with Elvis's clear enthusiasm for the project, the Colonel made a negative assessment of its potential. According to what Elvis told me, the Colonel thought it was a bad idea for Elvis to play a character that might be viewed by some as a loser, saying that Elvis had an image to uphold. When the Colonel made his counteroffer later that month, it was rejected, and the role of course ultimately went to Kris Kristofferson.

Not being given the opportunity to display his acting ability opposite the incomparable Barbra Streisand was a real disappointment to Elvis. Having later become friends with Barbra, I think it's a shame they never got to work together. I'm sure they would have challenged each other in productive ways, as they were both strongly opinionated people, and she would be the first to admit that she's a perfectionist. Perhaps Elvis would have had his moments during which he wanted to have the final say, but I think he would have appreciated her perfectionism and compromised. Barbra is very savvy, too, and beneath her exterior strength, she's a very feminine, sensitive, vulnerable person, so I think she and Elvis would have enjoyed the process.

While this opportunity ostensibly fell apart over money, acting was never about money for Elvis. He never questioned how much commission the Colonel took on his acting roles, but he did resent that the Colonel would farm him out to do three movies a year for a million dollars a movie, with absolutely no script approval.

"Do you have any idea how hard it was for me to sing to a fucking bull or a wall?" Elvis said. "I hated those fucking movies . . . almost all of them. The best one by far was *King Creole*. I was damn good in that one! That was the most satisfying of all my acting roles."

Of course, I protested that as a little girl growing up on Elvis movies, no matter how inane the script, I was certainly entertained. And in an innocent fashion, I might add. Elvis loved that I had total recall of some of his more obscure movie songs, so he would have me sing tunes like "The Walls Have Ears" for him. On many occasions, I used such artful segues to distract Elvis when he was in a foul temper about the Colonel or other unsatisfactory aspects of his career, but there was only so much I could do when his anger and frustration finally boiled over.

All of this had come to a head the previous September, during one of our stints in Las Vegas. I was never clear on exactly what set Elvis off, but he seemed highly dissatisfied with Colonel Parker and maybe even slightly betrayed by him, like he wasn't being forthcoming about all aspects of their working relationship. Elvis soon wound himself up into one of his epic tirades. As he paced the room, all of his pent-up fury, possibly fueled by whatever amphetamines he had taken that day, seemed ready to break free.

"I want to fire him," Elvis fumed. "I'm going to get new management. I'm done with him. He's holding me back."

My role in such moments was to be a calming influence. I had learned how to identify and track the storm as it began to brew, the anger visibly rising within him. His eyes, which were usually blue and gorgeous and tender, would darken and grow cold. As he disappeared into the maelstrom of his wrath, he became almost unreachable. It was as if he lost his mind temporarily, which meant it took some time for him to calm down. However, once he'd rid himself of his dark temper, he would quickly settle back down. In the peaceful moments that followed he'd apologized profusely to me if we had argued, although I never heard him apologize to anyone else.

As angry as Elvis had been with the Colonel at this time, they were eventually able to patch things up and continue working together. I think they had their say, then let it go without much more ado.

Most of the time Elvis's rage would flare at other people, or even inanimate objects, but in mid-1974, a few months after he began taking his trips away from me, I brought out that wrath. We were at his home in Palm Springs, California, when I decided to confront him about another woman he had been seen with in my absence. Ever since his infidelities had begun, I'd been trying, with difficulty, to conceal the effect they were having on me. But this time it was hard for me to ignore it. It was brought to my attention via the grapevine that Elvis had spontaneously bought some random girl a car. Hurt and angry as I was, I was only able to be slightly passive-aggressive in discussing his indiscretion. I remember sort of needling him and intimating that I knew something, without coming out and openly declaring it. Instead I just insinuated deep dissatisfaction and suspicion until he lost it.

We were sitting in bed, eating spaghetti and salad, and watching television as I continued my string of insinuations. All of a sudden, Elvis jumped out of bed, picked up his plate of spaghetti, and threw it hard against the wall.

"Just shut up!" he screamed. "I know what you're talking about! It meant nothing . . . she meant nothing! No other woman means anything to me! It was just a diversion . . . a distraction . . . Don't you understand that? I'm around the same people all the fucking time! Once in a while I just need a little different stimulation! Different company . . . that's all! That doesn't mean I'm having sex with anybody else! That doesn't mean I'm falling in love with anybody else! That doesn't mean jack shit! I start feeling stifled when I can't have a little interaction in the outside world!"

Elvis went on with his verbal tirade, and I went to the bathroom to escape it. Of course, he followed me into the small space, where there was no escape. He was lashing out in frustration and anger. He took his open palm and pushed against my shoulders, causing me to lurch backward. He continued to scream at me as I stood there crying.

"Okay, okay, okay," I said meekly.

Elvis retreated to the bedroom, where he took his sleeping pills and dozed off. I gathered a few things, went out into the living area, and summoned Joe Esposito to arrange a plane for me back to Los Angeles. I felt violated and hurt—Elvis had added insult to injury by lashing out at me instead of reassuring me lovingly. I determined then and there that though I might have been hopelessly, helplessly in love with Elvis Presley, I would not allow him or anyone else to treat me that way.

As much as it tore at my heart to leave him peacefully sleeping there in our bed in Palm Springs, I got on that Learjet and flew back to Los Angeles. I retreated to the Monovale Drive house, where we were staying until he had sold it. A few hours later, I got a call from Elvis.

"Ariadne, why did you leave me?" he implored in his little baby-talk voice. "Where are you . . . why did you go? Baby Gullion woke up this morning and Mommy was gone. Baby Buntyn misses his mommy. I don't know why you left. Why did you leave me?"

That was typical Elvis. He would display great anger and then be over it in a matter of hours, if not minutes.

"Honey, don't you remember how badly you treated me before I left this morning?" I asked. "You were yelling at me. You threw your plate of spaghetti against the wall, and you pushed me in the bathroom when I was just trying to get away from you and give you time to cool off."

Elvis was quiet for a minute.

"Ariadne, you know I didn't mean any of that," he said. "I'm so sorry, baby. Please come back. Please, please, I need you. I need you so badly. Please come back and be with me."

Try to reserve judgment—as I have learned to do for the most part. Unless you've walked in that person's shoes, you don't know what you would do in any given circumstance. I was too desperately, devotedly, blindly in love to say no and move on. I understand better now why some people stay on in relationships that might not be healthy or fulfilling. There are so many things that keep you there, not the least of which is the deep, abiding love you feel for that person, the history you share, and the hope that things will get better. Today I am far more realistic, seasoned, and decidedly stronger and more independent, and I would never stay in a relationship that caused me such pain again.

But back then, I went flying back to Elvis's arms just as soon as I could get on a plane and get there.

For every time Elvis caused me to doubt our relationship and future, he made just as many overtures that reassured me. I suppose that's both the challenge and the gift of being with someone who has little fear of being candid.

"When I'm with somebody else, it's ultimately a disappointment," Elvis said to me on the few occasions he was caught having an affair. "I always think back on you. You are my ideal girl. I don't love anybody else. Every time I'm with someone else it just makes me realize how much I love you and how much I appreciate you and all you mean to me."

He also expounded on his theory about how women and men differed when it came to the affairs of the heart. It was an opinion I believe many men would second.

"A man can have an affair, and it means nothing. When you hear that I'm going out with somebody else, most of the time I'm not even having sex. Most of the time I'm reading religious books to them, and they're very disappointed. But on the rare occasion that I have sex with someone else, it doesn't mean anything. It's just me rubbing up against somebody, breathing hard. It doesn't mean I'm falling in love with her. But women aren't built like that. When a woman has an affair, she falls in love. That's why it's so important for women to be much more careful about having affairs: because women have a tendency to fall in love."

His philosophy didn't do away with my fears, or appeal to my reason, but being naïve and blinded by love—a term they use for very good reason—I ultimately believed what I wanted to believe. I listened to his words, which supported the uniqueness of our love, instead of his actions, which didn't.

In the end, though, none of his words could make up for the fact that I was deeply hurt by his need to be with other women. In many ways, our life was the same as it had always been, and I was almost always by Elvis's side. But increasingly it was clear that, as long as we remained together, his cheating would be a constant as well. Elvis was never going to get that aspect of his personality out of his system. If we had gotten married, he still would have had affairs—it certainly hadn't changed his behavior when he was with Priscilla. That's just who he was. There's right, there's wrong, there's black, there's white, and then, there's Elvis Presley.

The confrontation in Palm Springs showed me the stakes of trying to change his behavior, and as 1974 stretched on, I became increasingly uncertain if I could live with the reality of who Elvis was. As much as I loved him, I began thinking about breaking up with him, but I could never quite muster the determination to act. Instead, I talked myself down with reminders about how little of the world I knew. I didn't know what relationships or life were really like, beyond what I had known with Elvis. All I'd previously seen were examples from my own family—my grandparents had been married for fifty-six years; my parents had been married for forty years; my brother was happily married and faithful to his wife. I had been a very sheltered sorority girl before Elvis had swooped me up into his rarefied realm. Other than what I saw with him, I had active proof that people really can stay married forever.

And yet, the day-to-day life I now witnessed around me didn't resemble such stability at all. When I saw people in Elvis's inner circle committing adultery, saw Elvis's own dichotomous nature, I thought: *Maybe my idea of marriage is antiquated or unrealistic. Maybe this is the real world. Maybe this is what guys do.* When I followed the line of thinking that Elvis was just behaving as other men did, there was no advantage to ending things with him. As far as I could tell, I could break up with him and date a shoe salesman, plumber, or a Southern Baptist preacher, and any of them might be unfaithful, too.

I knew I had a lot of learning to do. I had to sift through all of these new experiences and do my best to figure out what was normal for the real adult world and what was distorted by the anything-goes ethos of rock and roll. While much of my process of trying to discern what was normal, real, and important was confusing and painful, looking back now, I can see that all of this was a distinct coming of age for me. I was growing a great deal at the time, becoming incrementally stronger, but not so strong that I was ready to fly the love nest we'd created for each other, at least not yet. I wasn't sure I could live with this uncertainty or emotional upheaval forever, but for now, I couldn't bring myself to leave. It's not that his other women didn't hurt or threaten me. My eyes were beginning to open to a possibly different future than the one I had hoped for with Elvis, as my heart began to drift slightly away from my total devotion to him, for its own preservation. However, for the time being at least, I chose not to let the other women, or my own doubts, undo me, or us.

And, looking back, I know that he made the exact same decision about wanting and needing me above any other—even if his heart was occasionally distracted. He never asked me or seemed to want me to leave. I lived at Graceland for as long as I wanted to be there with him because that was his choice. He wanted me to stay.

Even with all this emotional turmoil, life with Elvis was still life with Elvis, and that, as much as anything, kept me with him because it meant life could be as surprising and fun as only he could dream up.

One night we went into a pet store in Memphis after it had closed, and as was customary, they were happy to open up after hours to accommodate Elvis Presley. We discovered more than a dozen of the cutest puppies we'd ever seen, all in need of a good home. Of course, Elvis had to buy every single one. Riding home in the car was hilarious, like having momentarily joined a circus peopled entirely by puppies. Sweet puppy breath and kisses abounded, as well as wagging tails and barking. When we got home, we began distributing them to pretty much everyone we knew. My mother and father, Aunt Delta, and of course I kept one for myself, a little white Maltese. Elvis named him Foxhugh, because he thought it was hilarious to hear people call the dog and inadvertently say, "Fuck you." This harked back to a movie he'd done years earlier in which the director named one of the characters Mr. Foxhugh. Every time Elvis had to say the man's name, he stumbled.

"You bastard, you did that on purpose," Elvis said.

"Yup, I did," the director admitted.

Sure enough, my little niece, Jennifer, used to fall for the setup, much to Elvis's delight.

"Aunt Linda, where Fuck You at, where Fuck You at?" she asked.

"Foxhugh is over there," I said, trying to resist joining Elvis's laughter.

Such trips out and about in Memphis were a rarity, and we did get stir crazy. Elvis would sometimes want to just get in the car and take a drive. Even when we didn't have a particular destination in mind, and we weren't necessarily going to see anyone along the way, he usually took the time to dress himself like the Elvis Presley his fans admired. Whenever I tried to convince him he might enjoy his life more if he could find ways to be incognito and have greater freedom of movement, he would disagree.

"Honey, what if somebody does recognize me?" he said. "Then they're going to be disappointed that I'm dressed like a slob."

When Elvis did want to go out and be among friends, he rented the Memphian Theater for midnight screenings, just like the night we met. One night, Elvis and I were walking from our car to the Memphian when we crossed paths with a couple who happened to be walking down the street at the same time.

"Oh my God, you look just like Elvis Presley," the girl said. "You look like Elvis."

Elvis stopped short. I was standing right behind him.

"Well, honey, I am," he said.

"Oh my God, no," she said. "That's impossible. No, you can't be."

She was just incredulous, so he turned to me.

"Honey, tell this girl who I am," he said. "Honey, tell her. Tell her."

"You're not pulling that Elvis Presley crap again are you, Charlie?" I said to him.

I stepped up and spoke to the girl.

"This is Charlie," I said. "He gets that Elvis Presley thing all the time. Come on, Charlie. Let's go."

"No, no, I want her to know it's me," Elvis said. "Tell her . . ."

Then he started laughing, and I started laughing, and we finally came clean.

"Yeah, it is Elvis," I admitted to the girl.

We were all laughing as hard as we could by that point.

Elvis always loved that I dared to prank him in such ways, and he often told that story to others, laughing just as hard as when it happened.

Another night, after going to the Memphian Theater, this time with the full entourage, he looked at Sonny and Red with a devilish twinkle in his eye.

"Let's go to the Memphis Funeral Home," he said.

"I'm not going in," I said.

"You don't have to, but I'm going to go in," he said.

Now, this was something I knew he'd done before, even though I couldn't figure out what had motivated him to do such a thing.

"I've walked through there and there's these bodies just laid out in there," he'd said.

"Ew, why would you do that?" I'd asked him.

He could never give me a reason why, but I knew that he'd always had this fascination with death, and with dying, and with corpses. I don't know where that came from, but maybe he liked the dark thrill of it, like living out a bad dream. Not me. I don't even watch scary movies. *The Exorcist* was literally the last scary movie I saw.

And so, while Elvis and the guys went in, I sat in the car in the parking lot of the Memphis Funeral Home, and even that was enough to give me the heebie-jeebies.

Oh, God, what are they doing in there? I thought. *Why do they have to do this?*

There's no way in heaven or hell you'll find me in a funeral home, unless a loved one, or me, myself, and I have passed on.

Thankfully most of our adventures were not nearly as morbid. When my sister-in-law, Louise, gave birth to my darling niece, Jennifer, just after midnight on September 19th, Elvis was excited to accompany me to the hospital to see the baby. We were allowed through the side entrance at four in the morning, even though visiting hours were long over. I was very moved by this show of tenderness and love from him. Of course he created quite a stir in the maternity ward, with one woman in labor remarking she was hallucinating that she was seeing Elvis Presley. Another woman in labor forgot her pain long enough to get Elvis to autograph her pregnant belly, asking him to lay his hands on her tummy to bless her baby. That's the effect Elvis had on women even when he wasn't on stage gyrating. Louise's roommate in the hospital remarked the next morning that she'd had the best dream that

Elvis Presley had been visiting them in their room. Louise assured her it was not a dream.

On another occasion, in early fall 1974, he came racing upstairs to find me, as excited as he could be.

"Honey, look what I got you," he said. "Come outside. It was just delivered."

I went downstairs with him, where a bright yellow 1971 Ford Pantera, which very much resembled a race car, was parked in the driveway. He knew I loved the color yellow.

"Oh my God," I said. "Oh, wow, honey, it's beautiful. That looks like a fast race car."

"Yeah, it is beautiful," he said. "It's sleek. It looks like you."

"Thank you, sweetheart," I said.

"I'm just going to take it around the block with the boys," he said. "I want to see how it drives, and then I'll come back and let you drive it."

He took it out and drove it, and when he came back, he had a different perspective.

"Honey, I'm not going to be able to give you this car," he said.

"That's fine," I said. "I didn't ask for this car. I don't need a car. I've got a car."

"It's too fast, and I'm afraid you'll get killed if you try to drive it. I know how to drive it, but I'm afraid you won't. It's too squirrely. You can consider it yours, but you can't drive it."

"That's fine, honey," I said. "Let it be yours."

He drove it a few times after that. And then one night, we were getting ready to go out to the movies at midnight, and we climbed into the Pantera. He was driving, of course, and I was sitting in the passenger seat. Well, the car wouldn't start. He tried it again and again, until he'd tried to start it about five times in all, but still, nothing.

"Son of a bitch," he said.

"Honey, let's just take another car," I said.

"Hell no," he said, and he tried to start it again. "This son-of-a-bitch piece-of-shit motherfucker."

"It's not worth it," I said. "Don't be upset. Let's just take another car. We'll get it checked out tomorrow."

"Hell no," he said, clearly in one of his moods. "This son-of-a-bitching car is not cooperating with me. Honey, step out of the car."

He started pulling the gun he always carried out of the waistband of his pants.

"No, come on," I said.

"Honey, step out of the car and step away from it," he said.

"Buntyn, please don't," I said. "Please let's just take another car."

"I'm going to tell you one last time, step out of the car and step away from it."

"Okay," I said, resigned to the impending fate of that beautiful car.

I got out of the car, and then he did, too. I stepped away from the vehicle, and once he saw that I was safely out of range, he shot that car five times. All the guys had come out of the house and their caravan of cars in the driveway, and were circling us by this point.

"No, boss, no!" they shouted.

They all loved that car. It was beautiful. *Thank God he didn't hit the gas tank,* I thought. Well, I guess maybe he knew what he was doing after all, because he didn't cause it to explode, but he did put five bullet holes in his Pantera.

The rest of us all looked at each other and shrugged. *Okay, fine,* we thought. *He's in one of those moods. He's just going to shoot something up.*

A guy who worked for him got into the car, turned the key, and it started right up. It was like the car knew: *All right, boss. All right, I got the message. I'm going to start now.*

We all died laughing. The car is in a museum now, with the bullet holes still in it.

Elvis had a penchant for shooting things up, and that never changed. Another time we were at Graceland, watching the console television in our bedroom. This is another story that's gone around and transmuted through the years, but this is how it really happened. Robert Goulet was singing "Camelot," or "If Ever I Would Leave You," or something like that, in this operatic way that was a little affected. It's not that Elvis didn't like Robert Goulet or his singing. It was just his particular mood on this particular night; he was not in the mood to hear Goulet's voice.

"I can't stand to hear that son of a bitch sing that song right now," he said. "It sounds like he's trying too hard. Stiff. I just can't stand watching this. In fact, honey, step out of the room."

As he spoke, he was already pulling out his gun.

"Honey, don't do that," I said. "What are you doing?"

"Sweetheart, step out of the room," he said. "Close the door behind you."

"Buntyn, put the gun away," I said. "Don't be ridiculous. That's just silly. We'll just change the channel. I can change the channel. We have that technology."

"Step out of the room," he said. "I'm not going to tell you again."

Okay, I don't want flying glass to come at me, I thought. I stepped outside and closed the doors to our room, which were padded in thick black Naugahyde.

Boom, boom, boom, I heard through the doors.

"Okay, honey, you can come back in now!" he shouted.

I opened the door, stepped inside, and found that the television was shot to hell.

"Now get somebody to come up here and get this piece-of-shit TV out of here and get me a new one," he said.

"Okay," I said, reaching for the phone to call the guys downstairs.

"Elvis has shot the TV," I said into the receiver. "This one's dead. We need to get a live one."

That was Elvis for the most part: unapologetic and more than a little impetuous . . . even dangerous at times. There's a reason he wore an ID bracelet with "Elvis" spelled out in diamonds on one side and "crazy" inscribed on the back. I used to think that if he'd ever gone to a psychologist, they would have had a field day with him. Of course, looking back, I can see moments like these were most likely fueled by his drug use. When he was on a stimulant, he was more irritable and irate, and he was more prone to do something wild like shooting out a TV set. When he was on downers, he was more prone to give things away.

"You like this ring?" he might say, his voice relaxed. "Here, you can have it."

Sometimes simply being with Elvis meant death-defying excitement. One night at the Hilton in Las Vegas, he and I got into the elevator with thirteen of his guys, including Lamar Fike, who weighed more than three hundred pounds. Between the twenty-ninth and thirtieth floors, the elevator got stuck. Remaining calm, Elvis pulled out a little book, ironically titled *The Way Out*, and read quietly while the guys tried to attract attention to our predicament. Thirty minutes later, understandably panicked, Red West and Ricky Stanley broke open the doors, revealing a roughly three-foot space at the top, between the twenty-ninth and thirtieth floors. It was decided the guys would lift me up to climb out. My two concerns were that I was wearing a long, formfitting white jersey dress, which had caused me to leave off my underwear. And more alarmingly, that the elevator might suddenly start, crushing me. Thankfully, I was able to climb out, followed by one of the guys, and we were all soon laughing about our ordeal, comfortably ensconced in the Presidential Suite on the thirtieth floor.

There were few dull moments with Elvis, but in the unusual times when they arose, his family was often there to fill in the blanks. I think that presence of his family, whom he continued to feel a great responsibility for, was a huge part of keeping Elvis from getting lost in his fame. Even though our life at Graceland was quieter than it was in Las Vegas or on tour, it was certainly never boring.

His aunt Delta was a cantankerous, vocal presence at Graceland, though she softened in the years after Elvis's death. Aunt Delta always had a little bottle tucked away, which is probably a part of the reason she had such a loose tongue. Then there was Elvis's grandmother, Minnie Mae Presley, or Dodger, as we called her. She'd lived with him most of his life, and he always took care of her from the time that he was able. Dodger dipped snuff and had a little can by her chair that she would gingerly lift up to spit in, and then admonish herself.

"Ain't that awful?" she would say.

And of course, there was his father, Mr. Presley, who was not an easy man to win over, and who doggedly did everything in his power to protect his son. Until the end of his life, Mr. Presley took care of Elvis's finances, even though he only had a fifth-grade education. I give Mr. Presley a great deal of credit for trying as hard as he could to keep Elvis in good shape financially. But his lack of a more nuanced understanding of money definitely contributed to the fact that Elvis had a fairly down-home approach to his income, no matter how rich and famous he became. For one thing, he paid 50 percent of his income as taxes, straight across the board, without taking a single deduction. He was patriotic and felt grateful to live in this country he loved so deeply and to be as successful as he was, and so believed it was his duty to help contribute.

"I never want to have a problem with the IRS," he said on more than one occasion. Elvis really tried to be law-abiding. As much as he harmed his own body with the drugs he took, they were all legally . . . well, mostly legally, prescribed to him by doctors and dentists. Similarly, he didn't ever want to get in trouble with the IRS. "I'm an American. I'll pay my taxes. If I make a million dollars, Uncle Sam can have five hundred thousand of it."

At the same time, he did not feel it was his place to be political. While so many entertainers use their celebrity as a platform for good, which is commendable, he didn't think that would be the right move for him.

"I want to remain apolitical, because I don't think it's right for me to use my celebrity and my fame to persuade other people to think like I do," he said. "I think everybody should make their own decisions about how they vote. They shouldn't need me to tell them how to vote."

While Mr. Presley may have limited Elvis's financial fortunes somewhat, there was no one who could have protected Elvis's interests with more fierce determination. He had come across as a rather formidable figure of authority to me. He had an air of feigned arrogance at times, I believed, to mask his insecurities about the world into which the fame of his only child had thrust him. People used to call him a tough old bird, and I could see why. He didn't trust anybody, and he was not someone who would go out of his way to make you feel at ease. I had always called Vernon "Mr. Presley," and he was nice to me, but some of the guys didn't like him because they thought he was cranky and caustic.

Mr. Presley handled Elvis's money, but he couldn't handle Elvis, not really. Elvis was going to do what he wanted to do. Occasionally, Mr. Presley might try to reason with him.

"Son, you're spending too much money," he would say.

"Daddy, I work my ass off," Elvis would reply. "If I want to spend every dime I make, that's my business, not yours."

Elvis delegated most of the responsibility to other people. Sometimes his dad or Joe Esposito would come in and give him an update about something, and of course, Elvis always had the final say. If there was a matter he really took exception to, he made that known. For the most part, though, he let them make the decisions. They were expected to Take Care of Business. Thus his logo of "TCB"—"Taking Care of Business."

Tough as he was, Mr. Presley always made me feel like a part of the family, even if he wasn't overly demonstrative about it. And the rest of Elvis's kin did, too. It was a colorful time with a colorful cast of characters, and with the outside world out of reach at times, we needed all of them.

Around the end of 1974, one of his doctors suggested marijuana to relieve his eye pressure from secondary glaucoma, which he'd been diagnosed with sometime before we'd met. Of course, there was no legal, medicinal marijuana back then. Nor any rhyme or reason to why or when Elvis did something. All he needed to hear was that a doctor had recommended it, and he was all for it, getting some from his own source. I'm sure it wasn't the first time he'd used marijuana, but it was the first time he wanted to use it with me.

"Yeah, but it's not legal, honey," I said.

"I know that, but if it keeps me from going blind . . ." he said.

He smoked marijuana for about three months. Of course, I was completely straight during that time, but one night we were sitting in our bedroom at Graceland and he tried to get me to take a hit. Of course I told him I wasn't interested, but he was persuasive.

"It's just relaxing," he said. "It will just relax you."

I resisted, but he'd touched a nerve. For more than a year now, as I'd struggled with his infidelity and the anxiety it produced in me, I didn't have any kind of meditation practice or other relaxation techniques. And so I had nothing to help me relieve the pressure inside me, and frankly, the thought of relaxing was appealing. After about forty-five minutes of his constant badgering, the temptation finally wore me down. I relented, hoping *something* could soothe me and silence my inner worries.

He instructed me on how to inhale and hold the smoke in my lungs.

Apparently I did it correctly because we were suddenly both very silly, laughing outrageously and finding humor in every stupid little thing either one of us did. I collapsed beside him on the bed, where we lay side by side.

Then, all of the sudden, I panicked, sitting up abruptly. *Why do I feel so out of control, crazy like this?* I thought. *I'm out of control.* My heart was racing, and I felt like the blood had all rushed to my face and my neck. I retreated to my dressing area, flung open the window, and in my own version of Scarlett O'Hara's dramatic moment from *Gone with the Wind*, proclaimed, "God, I know you're punishing me for smoking marijuana. And if you'll just let my brain come back to me, I'll never do that I again. Do you hear me, God? Never again."

I've been offered pot many times since then but have always refused, answering, "I promised God I wouldn't, and you can't renegotiate with God."

I went back into the bedroom, where I told Elvis what was going on and he held me and rubbed my back and neck, attempting to comfort me.

"Honey, I'm right here," he said. "I love you. You're just fine. You're safe. You're with me. You'll always be safe with me."

For a moment it subsided. Then the panic rose within me again. Once more he held me and tried to quiet me. It went on like this for a while, until finally he convinced me to take a sleeping pill so that I could sleep it off.

The next day I woke up and I was okay. It was later revealed to me that I had actually smoked Colombian hashish, which apparently is stronger than marijuana. To this day, I've never touched marijuana or hashish again.

I was better in the short term, but for almost a year after that, I had random panic attacks. I never went to therapy or received any treatment for them, but I did self-analyze and get as much information about what had happened to me as I could. I read up on cannabis and learned how some people, especially if they don't drink or do anything else mood or mind altering, and they're not used to being out of control, suddenly feel like their consciousness is out of their own control and suffer ongoing panic attacks. That's exactly what happened to me.

In truth though, the lingering side effects of that night were far greater than periodic anxiety or anything physical. The incident marked a turning point in my hopes and dreams regarding a future life with Elvis. The lasting impact of that night was that for the first time I fully understood how little control I had over my own life. With my inhibitions eroded from the hash, I faced the oppressive reality of my situation with great clarity. Every nerve in my body was wound tighter than I had even realized. I was so consumed with trying to take care of Elvis, keep the peace, and accommodate his every emotion and need, while at the same time remaining vigilant to prevent him from accidentally overdosing and dying, that I had neglected to take care of my own needs. While he came and went as he pleased, free to sleep with any number of other women, I walked on eggshells to try to please and care for him. I didn't fully realize the damage it was doing to my being until all my walls and defenses literally went up in smoke that night. Living like that came with a tremendous amount of pressure under which to breathe and survive. Not only was it unsustainable; it was becoming unbearable.

Once this hard truth about my reality came to the surface, I could no longer pretend to myself that everything was fine in our relationship. I could no longer continue blindly hoping that one day down the line all the issues I had with him—his drug use, his infidelities, his need for total control and devotion to him—would suddenly resolve themselves. Something had to change and I knew that it wouldn't be him.

In the days following my first panic attack, I realized how desperately I needed to take back control of my life and my decision making. I could no longer hand over my complete heart, my identity, and relinquish my fate to someone else for safekeeping. Not even to Elvis Presley. From then on I started to pull away, slowly but surely, from my life with Elvis. I knew that it wouldn't happen overnight and that my resolve would be tested repeatedly, but in my heart I knew it was necessary. I needed to reclaim what was intrinsically mine, and in the process find the strength to one day leave, even if that meant leaving part of my heart forever behind me.

Chapter Nine

Our Hospital Home

Entering the third year of our love affair, as I began to consider the changes I needed to make in my life, I quickly came to see how difficult the process was going to be. Before I could gather my resolve, I was always called back into his arms and his whims, especially in his hours of need.

When Elvis turned forty on January 8, 1975, he experienced a bit of what you might call a midlife crisis, becoming obsessed with the idea that he must undergo a facelift, immediately. My admonitions that he didn't need anything done fell on deaf ears, and he began to spend long moments standing in front of the mirror, staring at himself with concern while pulling the skin at his jawline tauter and tauter. Any resulting difference was absolutely imperceptible, but he couldn't get past his unhappiness with the alterations in his appearance that only he could perceive, and his mind was made up.

He scheduled an appointment with a Memphis-based plastic surgeon, Dr. Asghar Koleyni, and went in for an appointment. The doctor also told Elvis that he was too young to require such a procedure, and he would prefer not to perform a facelift for Elvis. But Elvis was insistent, saying if this doctor wouldn't do it, he'd find someone else who would. And so the doctor finally agreed to perform a minor surgery.

I think he wanted to save Elvis from possibly getting butchered by a less moderate doctor somewhere else.

Elvis checked into the doctor's clinic at the MidSouth Hospital, and once again I stayed with him through the whole experience. Dr. Koleyni did a very subtle facelift, making incisions behind Elvis's ears and pulling the skin back there. Thankfully, the procedure involved an easy recovery of only three or four days at the clinic, but Elvis was outfitted with a drainage tube beneath his chin. When he had recovered, the change to his appearance was indiscernible, but he seemed to feel better when he looked in the mirror. And so I suppose it did serve a positive purpose for him. There has been speculation through the years that Elvis had his eyes done or some other mystery procedure, but that mini facelift was the extent of his plastic surgery.

While Elvis's facelift and recovery were remarkably easy, his overall health noticeably declined again that month. He had put on weight, and he was often short of breath and unable to function at his best. In late January, he was transported from Graceland to the hospital, forcing him to cancel his usual winter engagement in Las Vegas. Among the reasons given in the press for his hospitalization were intestinal blockage and the flu. However, the underlying reason was to stabilize his system and prescription drug use.

I again settled down for my inpatient stay by his side. Since this was our second hospital stay—our third if you counted his recuperation from his recent facelift—I knew what to anticipate. I quickly regained the sense of relief I'd experienced during our previous visit to Baptist Memorial, knowing that I could relax my constant vigil now that medical professionals would control his drug use and monitor his breathing. But it was still a difficult time, and as we were naturally drawn to do, we turned to each other for support.

During this same time, my grandmother, Ninny, was gravely ill at another hospital, St. Joseph's, in Memphis. I spent most days shuttling back and forth between the two hospitals, so I could visit with my grandmother, while also giving Elvis the nurturing he required. Ninny was the closest to my heart, other than my parents, and I felt an urgency to spend as much time as possible with her, especially as we knew the end of her life was growing near. I actually had the great privilege of being with her when she passed away. Holding her hand, I let her know how much she was loved, and that this love was going with her on her journey to eternity.

Afterward I returned to Elvis, climbing up into the bed that he'd had them place right next to his in our shared hospital room, wanting the comfort and safety he could still provide so effortlessly when I was near him.

"I want to take care of her funeral," he said immediately after hearing the news. "Let me take care of it."

Elvis was well aware that my grandmother was poor and had resided in the Lauderdale Courts, the same housing project where he'd lived with his family as a teenager. Not only did Elvis pay for everything, but he also added the kind of special touches that really showed he cared, even getting Sherrill Nielsen and the Voice, who sang backup for him, to perform "Amazing Grace" and "I Come to the Garden Alone" at my grandmother's funeral.

For a time following Elvis's hospital stay, our life together was again filled with energy and positivity. Elvis appeared to be clear and focused, and he appreciated my unwavering devotion to him, proudly boasting to the guys, "Linda was right there in the bed next to me the whole time I was in the hospital, man—that kind of love is hard to find."

Unfortunately, his health turnaround was short-lived. In March, seeming to be fully recovered, he returned to his normal activities with a two-week engagement at the Las Vegas Hilton, but he was battling his weight, and he and one of his regular Vegas doctors decided to try a radical diet plan. We left the Hilton and went to stay at this doctor's house. As soon as we arrived, Elvis changed into his pajamas and climbed into bed in a spare bedroom.

"Let's just put you to sleep now," the doctor said, giving Elvis a shot.

What? I thought, trying to fathom what was unfolding around me. Elvis had told me that his doctor was putting him on a special diet, but this was way beyond anything I'd expected. For the next two weeks, the doctor had Elvis under near-constant sedation. During this time, Elvis was in bed sleeping except for a few brief periods each day when he woke up long enough to go to the bathroom and eat a small portion of food. Then he was sedated again and went back to sleep. Apparently, this really was the diet his doctor had devised for him.

I felt like I'd stumbled into a backward reality where bizarre, unhealthy behavior was considered the norm. I couldn't believe that a doctor was enabling this, but I knew better than to question or contradict Elvis. If he didn't like my reaction, he would have simply sent me away. I was worried about him and wanted to be there to monitor his breathing and overall health. With the doctor gone during the day at his private practice, I stayed close by Elvis's side, watching TV, reading, writing some poetry, for two weeks. Now that's when I *really* went stir crazy. At least when we were sequestered together at the hotel, we could order room service, or go out onto the roof to sunbathe, or see other people at night.

When I'd first stayed awake in the early days of our relationship, happily watching Elvis sleep beside me, I'd had no idea how much of my life this activity would come to occupy. Normally, I was still content to keep myself entertained in order to stay close to him while he dozed, making sure he was not in any danger. But with this situation, I'd found my patience tested to its limit. There was just something so extreme— and to my perspective, unhealthy—about his doctor's decision to purposely render him unconscious for the better part of every day for two weeks. And perhaps I needed to show I wasn't a willing participant to this surreal, fun-house reality.

Finally, after we'd been there nearly the full two weeks, I couldn't stand it anymore, knowing there was a whole world out there I was missing. The limousine came and took me to the Hilton, where I just walked around aimlessly. I didn't even really do anything special when I got there. It wasn't long before I began to worry Elvis might need me while I was away from him, and I returned to his side. Nevertheless, it was exhilarating to be free and have something other than the four walls of that guest room and Elvis's sleeping face to look at. My brief moment of freedom had been sweet, and my decision to take this space for myself was a small step forward for me, even if there was no obvious change in my dealings with Elvis at the time. When Elvis was done with his "diet," he had lost weight, not to mention muscle mass, and he seemed to think the entire experience was completely normal.

As if his medically dubious choices weren't concerning enough, Elvis's dalliances with other women were getting harder to ignore. That spring and summer, Elvis toured quite a bit, and although I almost always accompanied him, it was no longer a given that I'd be traveling to every city with him on the road. On July 24, I joined him in Asheville, North Carolina, where he had given a show the night before as well. We were in our limo on the way to Elvis's show when the driver turned around and handed me a ring.

"Oh, ma'am, I think you dropped this ring last night," he said.

"Ah . . . ah . . . ah," Elvis stammered, clearly unsure how to handle the fact that the limo driver had confused me with whatever woman Elvis had been with the previous evening.

"Oh, thank you," I said, as nicely as I could, feigning innocence as I took the ring and examined it.

Elvis was sweating bullets and tried to explain, "Oh, honey, that's mine. I must have dropped that last night."

"Yours?" I slyly implored, still examining it. "I dare think not," I continued, using my best Eric Idle voice, raising my eyebrow to emphasize the clear connection between the ring and its original bearer. "This ring is a mere cheap imitation."

I couldn't help but be a little amused at my own humor.

Elvis relaxed a little, smiled, and said, "Naw, now honey, I think somebody gave it to me."

"I'll bet she did," I said.

We never mentioned it again.

As much as I tried to have a sense of humor about everything—and I managed to most of the time—I was so caught up in the emotions of the moment that I couldn't see what was really going on. Looking back now, it's clear that our relationship was deteriorating, and Elvis was getting more careless. Maybe he was exhausted from living a double life. Maybe he was reeling from the pills and beginning what we couldn't see then was his final decline to the end of his life. Regardless, it meant an increasing number of messy moments for us.

While Elvis had always preferred that we remain as isolated from the tabloid coverage of our lives as possible, it was harder to avoid seeing the glossy publications when we were on the road. By now, I was used to catching sight of pictures of Elvis and me in Las Vegas and outside other venues where he performed. But it was a terrible shock to my system to see him photographed with another woman he'd apparently been seeing. When I furiously confronted him, his response did nothing to alleviate my heartbreak.

"I don't know why you're so upset by that; that was just a fun fling," he said.

Even worse was when he introduced this woman from onstage at the Hilton, as he'd done with me so many times in the past, leaving me not just heartbroken but humiliated.

As generous as Elvis was, he would sometimes use his generosity to try to manipulate a situation, and me, even when I could see right through it. Once, when I was staying at the Monovale Drive house in Los Angeles, Elvis called me from Las Vegas.

"Honey, I found the most unusual piece of jewelry," he said, sounding excited. "I found the most unusual ring. I can't wait to give it to you."

"Oh, that's sweet, honey," I said.

"Yeah, I can't wait to give it to you. It's just so unusual. I've never seen one like it."

Of course, I didn't need another ring and hadn't been expecting him to give me anything, but he had made such a big fuss about this special ring, so I was curious. And on top of that, I was suspicious because I'd heard he was with this other girl in Vegas, the one he'd introduced from the stage. When he came back from Vegas, the ring was on my mind, but he didn't say anything about it, and I didn't want to be the one to mention it.

The next day, he brought it up.

"Honey, you remember I told you I had an unusual piece of jewelry for you?" he said, only this time he didn't describe it as a ring specifically.

"Oh yeah, I do remember that," I said. "What happened to that?"

"I'm going to get that for you," he said, sounding guilty. "I'm going to send for that."

He dispatched a member of his entourage to pick up a piece of jewelry, and not long after that, he gave me a beautiful diamond bracelet.

"Oh, I thought you said it was like something I'd never seen before?" I said. "Something really highly unusual."

"Well, at the time, I guess, I thought it was unusual," he said evasively.

"Honey, I love you, but I'm not stupid," I said. "You also said it was a ring like you had never seen before. I know you gave that ring to somebody else. Because I heard you were—"

"Well, what can I get you?" he interrupted me, sounding sheepish.

"It's not about that," I said. "It's not about that at all. You can't get me anything to replace that. You didn't have to buy it for me in the first place. It's just knowing that something you got for me, you gave to someone else. That hurts my feelings. Whether it was a ring out of a Cracker Jack box or something that you found unique."

I handed the bracelet back to him.

"Thank you, I appreciate the gesture, but I don't want something you bought out of guilt because you gave away to another girl what you specifically had in mind for me." I got a lot of mileage out of that. He genuinely felt bad, I could tell, and he was on his best behavior for a short time. Well, at least when he was in my sight.

In such moments of clarity, I could stand up for myself. As I began to learn to hold back a part of my heart for safekeeping, even from the man I loved, I found myself growing into a woman who would one day, soon enough, become self-sustainable. His unfaithfulness was now a given in our relationship, even though I'd never overtly agreed to this arrangement.

Once or twice, the guys in his entourage even told me about his liaisons. As loyal as they were to him, I think the guys really loved me. We spent countless hours together because I was like the fourteenth steady guy in the crew. They knew beyond a shadow of a doubt that I took good care of Elvis, and it made their jobs easier. When I was around, they didn't have to check on him every few minutes. And I appreciated when they came to me to talk about something related to his health and well-being because it reminded me that I wasn't totally alone— there were others who were looking out for Elvis, too.

And they knew that if I needed anything, like help after he'd taken too many sleeping pills and lay in a heap on the floor, I'd ask them for assistance in lifting him and getting him safely tucked back into his bed. I always respected their positions, which I think they could sense.

I've often been asked, do you think the guys really cared about Elvis? And the answer to that is yes. They did—to a man. It would have been virtually impossible to spend that kind of time with Elvis without caring deeply about him. They all devoted their lives to Elvis, really. Many of them sacrificed their own marriages. Being on the road all the time, with women following them around, wasn't conducive to a happy home life. And they didn't get paid an exorbitant amount of money, considering what they gave up. Of course Elvis was generous, and they had many Peter Pan–like, fun-filled times when we all traveled together or spent time in Vegas. But they eventually had to go home, where they had missed time with their families and watching their children grow. Looking back, I can see how we were all living under this magical enchantment that caused us to put Elvis's well-being before our own. And since we were kindred spirits in this experience, the guys looked out for me, and let me know they appreciated my caring for Elvis.

Complicating my growing awareness of Elvis's cheating and my ambivalence over what to do was the fact that he seemed to need me now more than ever, because his drug use was intensifying. That August we returned to the Vegas Hilton for another month of shows, and I grew concerned by the attempted interventions of those around him. There were times when the guys in his entourage, or even Elvis's personal physician, Dr. George Nichopoulos, aka Dr. Nick, emptied out the contents of some of Elvis's pills, so they would act like a placebo when he took them. Their hearts were in the right place, but I never wanted to do this. I was afraid if Elvis thought his pills weren't working as they should be, he might take more to make up the difference and accidentally overdose.

Often it wasn't even clear what Elvis was on. On one occasion, Elvis wanted to go see Don Rickles perform—we both loved his acerbic, indiscriminately insulting humor—but Elvis was under the influence of one of his substances of choice that evening. When Don introduced Elvis in the audience, Elvis proceeded to make his way up onto the stage with Don. Don seemed a little taken aback, but honored to have Elvis share his stage. That is, until Elvis began reading from the Bible he had brought with him. For minutes Elvis droned on and on, reading from 1 Corinthians 13 until final everyone had enough.

"Elvis, are we going anywhere with this?" Don finally burst out. "Or are we just jerking off up here?"

Needless to say, that comment broke the reverential tone, and cracked the audience up.

"Naw, man, I-I-I-," Elvis stuttered. "I just wanted to share a little Bible wisdom with you all."

Elvis then left the stage to thunderous applause.

Later on in the show, Elvis leaned into me.

"Honey, I've got to piss like a racehorse," he confided. "I'm not sure what to do. I sure as hell can't hold it much longer, but I can't get up to go to the men's room, because I've already interrupted Don's show, and if I get up, you know every eye in here will follow me and take away from Don. I can't do that to Don. Tell you what—just hand me that empty glass right there."

"What?!" I challenged, knowing he was about to do the unthinkable.

"Honey, hand me the damned glass, I tell you, before I piss my pants!"

I casually slid the glass over to him, whereupon he deftly slipped the glass beneath the table and, out of view, covered his lap with my napkin, unzipped his pants, and peed in the glass until it was brimming with gold. He waited a bit, then casually set the full glass back on the table. I must admit, I was impressed with how easily and surreptitiously Elvis accomplished his goal of emptying his bladder in a full show room of people with only he and I being the wiser.

More often than not, though, when Elvis's prescription pills incapacitated him, the mood was far more frightening than amusing. In fact, one of my most chilling experiences with Elvis came during one of our stays in Vegas that year.

As usual, we had ordered room service—chicken noodle soup and his favorite, honeydew melon. One of the guys spread the food out on a towel on the bed, where Elvis was propped up, eating his soup.

"Honey, I'm going to go wash my face and brush my teeth and get ready for bed," I said. "Have you already taken your sleeping pill?" At the time, he was taking Placidyl, which was a powerful sleeping pill and tranquilizer I'd learned to watch him closely on, and so this routine had become second nature.

"Yeah, I already took my sleeping pill," he said, his voice mellow.

"Okay, all right, I'll be right back then," I said. "I'm just going to wash my face and brush my teeth."

I was gone just long enough to hurry through my bedtime routine, but by the time I came back into the bedroom, he was facedown in his big bowl of chicken noodle soup. Whatever he took besides the Placidyl hit him hard and fast, and he was in real trouble now. I could just see the headline: "Elvis Presley dead, drowns in a bowl of chicken noodle soup in his Las Vegas suite."

I shouted to wake him up, but he was completely passed out in his chicken soup, as if he was dead. Terrified, I jumped onto the bed, moved the soup out of the way, lifted his head, and straddled him. As I held his head up by his hair, he had chicken soup and noodles all over the front of his hair, and all over his face. I started to clean his throat, literally pulling out chunks of food. The whole time, I was yelling at him, trying to wake him up. One of the doctors had left a shot of Ritalin by the bed, in case he ever had too much of one of the sedatives he regularly took. None of my attempts had seemed to make any difference, and so I picked up the Ritalin and administered it to him. Still holding on to his slack torso, I leaned over and called one of his regular Vegas doctors.

"You need to get over here," I said. "He's out, and I don't know if he's aspirated some of his chicken soup, but you need to get over here right away."

I had already cleared out his throat enough that his breathing was no longer compromised, although he had not yet regained consciousness. There was nothing for me to do but sit with him, keeping him in a seated position, and pray. The doctor arrived within a few minutes and gave him another shot, which I believe contained a bit more Ritalin.

Although the doctor told me that Elvis would be fine, I kept a restless vigil in our bed beside him. A few hours later, he awoke, just enough to look up at me in wonderment. When he spoke, he used that same stalled, stilted, laborious speech I'd begun to hear more and more, which he gravitated toward when he was really out of it.

"M-M-M-Mommy," he said.

"What, honey, are you all right?" I asked, leaning down to hear his words.

"I-I-I-I had a-a-a dream," he said, taking an excruciating amount of time to get out these few words.

"What did you dream?" I asked.

"I dreamed that I was dying," he eventually said.

"Well, honey, you fell asleep in your chicken soup, and I had to call the doctor," I said, trying to soothe him with my voice, as a mother would. "I gave you a shot of Ritalin that was here, and then he came and gave you another shot of Ritalin and revived you enough that you're okay now. You're okay."

"I had a dream that . . . I had a dream that you were my twin, and that you let me be born first," he said, taking his time to form each word. "And you didn't get enough air, and you smothered. You let me be born, and I lived, but you died."

"Aw, honey, it's okay," I said. "We're both okay."

But I was thinking, *Wow, I wonder if that's how it really happened, when he was born and his twin brother, Jessie Garon, was born dead. Maybe he had all of that memory lodged deep somewhere in his subconscious, and when he nearly died himself, it rose to the surface of his mind.* While I was moved by the fact that he'd dreamed I was his twin, I also felt the danger implicit in the image he'd described: that I had died while I was trying to save his life. More than just a dream, it was a powerful metaphor. It brought home for me how I was putting aside my whole life to care for him, and just how exhausted I was as a result. In my total devotion to him, I was losing myself.

The hardest truth to accept was that, no matter how selfless I was, my devotion was ultimately in vain. I could only do so much in the face of his self-destruction. I had known enough to assess Elvis's state before leaving him alone to get ready for bed, and even so, I'd nearly lost him. Having witnessed all I had by this point, I knew it was only a matter of time before something catastrophic happened, which made my bottomless love and care feel futile. Especially when his appreciation of my efforts did not stop him from spending time with other women. Even when he knew such behavior was painful for me. His hurtful and disturbing choices involving drug use and his other women were increasingly driving me toward depletion, a state where there would be no more for me to give. Maybe, deep down, I knew this process was inevitable, and necessary for my own self-preservation.

Elvis recovered from his near-death experience, but it was clear he was in no condition to keep up with the rigorous demands of his Las Vegas performance schedule. This was not an easy admission for him to make, to himself or anyone else, but he made the difficult decision to cancel the rest of his two-week engagement, although he had only performed on three days.

Because his breathing was compromised from all the sedatives, we flew back to Memphis on a private plane equipped with oxygen. And so began another stay at Baptist Memorial Hospital to treat what was reported as "exhaustion" when the news was announced in the press on August 22, 1975.

This was when I think people largely began to suspect that something was amiss with Elvis. There were stirrings that he'd been slurring his speech onstage, or that he'd acted like he was drunk, or on drugs, or not fully himself. Up until then, he'd done a remarkably good job of keeping the reality of his drug usage from his adoring fans. Yes, there were a few occurrences when he basically crashed onstage, and maybe he wasn't enunciating clearly, or he forgot the lyrics to a few of his songs—shows at which some audience members realized something wasn't exactly right. But usually he managed to charm the audience members by making light of his shortcomings, and up until this canceled Vegas run, he was mostly able to hide the truth of his dependency on prescription drugs.

As soon as we got home, we checked Elvis into the hospital for a two-and-a-half-week visit. During this particular stay, he received a liver biopsy, which meant he had to lie flat on his back and remain completely motionless for twenty-four hours. And of course, when they did the procedure, he wanted me right there with him in the room, holding his hand the whole time, a unique challenge all its own for me.

While, thankfully, the test came back negative as far as cancer went, this was his second hospitalization in a year, and it was becoming more difficult to deny the problem. Dr. Nick even went so far as to bring in two physicians who were addiction specialists, or at least much more knowledgeable than most health-care professionals were in that day and age. These doctors worked closely with Elvis during his stay. He had apparently been on Demerol, Dilaudid, Percodan, and a variety of other powerful painkillers as well as the sleeping medications. His doctors gave him methadone to assist him in withdrawing from the opiates. This really did help him, allowing him to be drug-free for the first time in years. Two nurses were hired to watch over him in his first few weeks at home. Their names were Mrs. Cocke and Mrs. Seaman. It did not escape Elvis's attention, or his sense of humor, that he was now, once again, surrounded by the inexplicably coincidental, sometimes hysterically funny, circumstances of his life.

Elvis was given a good long time to recuperate and spent much of that fall 1975 and early winter 1976 at home at Graceland, using a new passion project to keep him busy and excited. In April 1975, he'd purchased a twenty-eight-seat Convair 880 airplane for $250,000. We flew together several times to Dallas to oversee the reconfiguration and decoration of the plane. He immediately christened it the *Lisa Marie* and refurbished it to his exact specifications, including a bedroom, conference room and bar, and video system with four screens. Elvis and I had quickly developed a routine when we flew on the *Lisa Marie*, which was to get on the plane and go straight back to the bedroom, where we'd sleep or rest. Sometimes he'd change into pajamas, and I'd change into something casual, and we'd climb into bed and spoon for the duration of the flight.

Elvis had always been known to indulge in his whims. Now, with the *Lisa Marie* at our disposal, we had more wild and spontaneous fun than ever before, flying to Denver to eat peanut butter and jelly sandwiches for dinner or heading to Vail to watch me flail around on skis. Difficult as things had become, Elvis always found ways to remind me of how deeply in love we were.

Still, no amount of travel could hide the fact that these carefree moments were becoming less frequent. In early December, we returned to Las Vegas so Elvis could make up the shows he had been forced to cancel. He clearly seemed to be feeling better, but there was a sense now that the trouble always lurked below, ready to erupt at any time.

While in Vegas, Elvis requested a simple errand, although by this point we all knew what his real intentions were.

"Go get Red," he said to me. "I want to go to the dentist."

When Red followed me into the suite, he was less than enthusiastic about facilitating Elvis's ability to get what he wanted. Elvis was already in one of his moods, and so this attitude set him off.

Elvis didn't like the way Red reacted to him. So he started yelling. And then he actually went into our bedroom and came back out into the suite's living room with a gun. Red has a temper, too, so he got mad. Now Elvis was yelling at Red, and Red was yelling back at Elvis. When Red's cousin Sonny came in, he watched the proceedings uneasily.

Like an idiot, I stood between Elvis and Red, facing Elvis, trying to talk some sense into him.

"Please stop," I said between tears. "Stop. Just please stop."

The situation cooled down soon after that, and Sonny pulled me aside.

"Don't ever do that again," he said. "Don't you ever stand between Elvis and Red, or anybody else, if anybody's got a gun. I know you were just trying to stop the situation, and you knew if you stood there, Elvis was not going to use the gun. But the gun could've gone off."

"It could've gone off on Red, too," I said.

"I know, but it's not your battle," Sonny said. "I know you were trying to defuse the situation, but don't ever do that again."

"Must Have Been Angels"

Sometimes
I think about the hearts of angels
Perfect light
To guide their flight away from
   danger
With their halos of gold
Their wisdom of old
And feathered wings that unfold

It must have been angels that
   carried me
When I was too weak to lift my feet
When I was too blind to clearly see
Heavenly light shone down on me
It must have been angels
Watching over me

Time is cruel
To youth and grace and flawless
   beauty
Life is hard
Do unto others—that's our duty
When my soul was in pain
With more loss than gain
I heard an angel speak my name

It must have been angels that
   carried me
When I was too weak to lift my feet
When I was too blind to clearly see
Heavenly light shone down on me
It must have been angels
Watching over me

Every day I feel the touch of an
   angel
With the wind and the rain in my
   hair
The warmth of the sun will soon
   appear

It must have been angels that
   carried me
When I was too weak to lift my feet
When I was too blind to clearly see
Heavenly light shone down on me
Love came and set me free
It must have been angels
It must have been angels
Watching over me

LYRIC: LINDA THOMPSON

Chapter Ten

The Pain of Too Much Tenderness

As 1976 wore on, I came to realize with increasing awareness that I had to leave Elvis. What had been untenable for years had finally become impossible.

One night when we were home at Graceland, I woke up, and Elvis wasn't in bed beside me. Knowing he was under the strong influence of his sleeping medication, I was immediately concerned, and so I went on a search-and-rescue mission. I walked all around the upstairs of Graceland, but I couldn't find him anywhere. Finally, I peeked my head into Lisa Marie's room, although I couldn't imagine why he'd possibly be in there, as she wasn't staying with us at the time. But there he was, lying on the little daybed in Lisa's room that had once been used by the baby nurse and nanny. He was sprawled across the sofa, completely out of it, with his pajamas' fly open, while a woman who was temporarily working at Graceland kissed him. I could see the back of her head moving, but it looked like he was asleep, or barely clinging to the edge of consciousness.

I cleared my throat, loudly. "Ahem!"

The girl jumped away from him, falling abruptly to the floor beside the daybed.

"Oh dear, Linda, this isn't what it looks like," she said.

Elvis struggled to open his eyes enough to look up and focus on me with great effort.

"You should've knocked," he slurred.

"Should've knocked?" I sputtered. "I should have knocked?" I repeated incredulously. "I live here. I shouldn't have to knock. Or walk in to find you kissing another girl."

"I wasn't kissing her," he said. "She was kissing me."

"Either way, I'm out," I said.

The female employee slunk out as quickly as possible. I went to my dressing room and started packing. After Elvis had slept off most of the effects of his medications, he came ambling back into our bedroom suite area, where he spotted my suitcase. He seemed surprised.

"Where are you going?" he asked.

"I'm going to my house," I said.

"That's not why I bought you that house, so you could just leave me whenever you want," he said.

"Well, I'm not going to walk in and see you kissing another girl, and have you tell me I should've knocked, when I live here," I said. "I either live here, or I don't live here."

"You can't leave," he said.

"Watch me," I said.

My clothes were packed. My suitcase was at the ready. Now I just had to muster all of my strength and self-possession and leave the man I loved.

"I told you, you can't leave," he said, growing agitated. "You can't leave me. I love you. I didn't kiss her, she kissed me."

When I didn't immediately capitulate, and he realized from my demeanor that I might really leave him, he snapped. He pushed me in the direction away from the door. My suitcase was behind me, and I tripped over it onto the floor, landing on my backside. I wasn't physically hurt, but I started crying, my sobbing audible and cathartic. Elvis stood there, momentarily stunned that he had pushed me down, I think. Then he began studying me. A bemused look overtook his expression, and then he started laughing.

"Why are you laughing?" I choked out through my tears. "I'm really mad. I'm crying here! Why are you laughing at me?"

"Honey, you just don't have a face meant for crying," he said. "Your beautiful face is always smiling, so when you cry, your little eyes get all red and swollen."

"That just hurts my feelings even more," I said.

"Look at your little face," he said. "Go look in the mirror when you're crying. You look comical. Your little eyes get swollen and red like little pitiful pig eyes, and you get this red runny nose. C'mere, baby."

He sat right down on the floor with me and started petting me, teasingly, and loving me. Even though I didn't want to be won over so easily, I couldn't help myself. He snapped me right out of my anger. Just like that, I almost forgot why I was mad in the first place. Almost.

"Look, I was half-asleep," he said, his voice gentle now. "More than half-asleep—hell, I was out of it. I didn't even realize what was going on, honey. She was kissing me. I'm sorry. Honey, I'm so sorry. Keep your bag packed. We're leaving for tour in the afternoon, and I want you with me."

When we got on the plane later that day, I remember going straight back to our queen-sized bed in the back of the plane, getting undressed to rest, and Elvis holding me, spooning, and repeating, "I'm so sorry, Ariadne. I love you so much." That is a particularly sweet memory. One thing I can say about Elvis is that he never hesitated to apologize to me when he felt he was wrong. Not everyone finds apologizing so easy to do.

Still, the painful realization that had been growing within me for more than a year had finally arrived: My fairy tale was ending. (I'd even encouraged Elvis to perform and record the Pointer Sisters' song "Fairytale" in 1975 because it perfectly captured my disillusionment.) While I'd been unhappy for quite a while, this transgression showed that I was no longer able to ignore it. No matter how much I loved Elvis, I did not want this existence to be forever. In the beginning, as we all have a tendency to believe, I'd thought that love would conquer all, but now a new thought occurred to me—*maybe we sometimes have to choose ourselves over love.*

I really felt like I was withering; that, like Elvis, I was dying a slow death. While he was destroying his physical body, it was also killing my spirit. I was fighting a losing battle against Elvis's drug use. Time and again, I had seen him go to the hospital and clean up, only to come out and return to his previous level of pill consumption within no time at all.

Much as I had when I'd left Elvis for a few hours during his "sleep" diet, I found myself thinking about who I was away from him, about who that person was and who I wanted her to be. More than anything else, she had her own intuition, intelligence, and clarity of vision that allowed her to make up her own mind, even when it differed from Elvis's drug-distorted reality. She had great strength and resilience. And she had an incredible amount of love to give, enough to not only nurture her future husband, but also her children, and in return for this love, she deserved respect and fidelity. I thought about my four years in college—I knew I was capable of, and honestly deserving of, so much more. I began to crave broader horizons for myself. It dawned on me that I had to *want* more for my own future, rather than allowing my relationship with Elvis to define the parameters of my world.

And when I looked at all the pieces of myself that I had given up on Elvis's behalf, increasingly I saw that staying with him would demand a sacrifice that I was unwilling to make. I'd always known I wanted to be a mother, but I could not bring a baby into my life with Elvis. When I was with him, I had to be up all night, watching Elvis, which meant sleeping during the day. What would happen to my child while I slept? It struck me that, really, *he* was like my baby. His hours, and his attitudes, didn't promote the healthiest situation for marriage, and certainly not for motherhood. As much as I loved him, I knew I wanted more—and motherhood was just the start.

So I consciously began weaning myself off Elvis, figuring out how to leave. He was addicted to drugs, and I was addicted to him. I couldn't bear to rip the Band-Aid away all at once. Not when I still had a heart full of dreams leftover from the beginning of our romance, when we'd spoken often about marrying and having a family together someday. And so I decided to take baby steps away and exert more control over my own life and schedule. I began spending small increments of time away from him. I knew we both needed an opportunity to prepare for life apart.

One night during one of the 1976 tours, I accompanied Elvis back to our hotel suite, as usual, after he was done performing. But rather than wanting to kiss and cuddle or watch TV, he was feeling tired and decided to take his sleeping pills right away. I'd become very accustomed to entertaining myself while Elvis slept, keeping an eye on him while I read or wrote poetry. But on this night, I found myself growing restless. Finally, I approached the bed and leaned down over Elvis's face, perfect in its repose. I reassured myself that he was sleeping peacefully and would not wake up for hours. Then I dared to slip out of the room, telling myself that it would be okay because I would be nearby and would come back to check on him. I actually wandered down to the hotel bar, where some of the guys in the band and entourage were unwinding. The guys were surprised and happy to see me "out of my cage." It felt so strange not to be monitoring Elvis's every breath, so I didn't stay long. I didn't really drink anyway, but that Diet Coke tasted like a little bit of freedom.

On another tour that year, this time in El Paso, Texas, I woke up before Elvis, as usual, but on this swelteringly hot day I did something remarkable: I went down to the hotel pool in the daytime. As I walked around the concrete patio to where the guys sat drinking beer, the sun was hot on my skin. I turned my face up to the sky, luxuriating in the warmth. I was very aware of how alive I felt, with an extraordinary lightness of step. I felt like I was playing hooky from the darkened bedroom where I normally would have been sequestered, even on such an inviting afternoon.

I pulled up a patio chair and joined the band members, whose beer bottles dripped with condensation in the heat-soaked air.

"She's alive in the daytime," David Briggs, Elvis's keyboard player, joked.

"That I am," I said. "And it feels good."

After a while, the temperature became almost too much for me, and I found myself feeling parched, but there was nothing to drink down by the pool but beer.

"I think I'll try one of those," I said, pointing to the bottles in the ice bucket.

"Watch out, she's joining the band," David joked, handing me a beer.

I never drank, but the cold bottle felt good in my hand. I took a curious sip.

"Ugh, it doesn't taste good, but it's cold and wet," I said.

David, bass player Jerry Scheff, and the other guys laughed when they saw the look on my face. I never quite acquired a taste for the bitter brew, but I drank down that entire beer. I do believe it was the only time in my life I've ever had a whole beer.

What a fun afternoon that was in El Paso. I felt so alive and energized, being outside in the sunshine. I realized how much I had missed being able to call my own shots and assert my own independence. It dawned on me that I had missed something as simple as daylight. I actually enjoyed the company of these other guys. Their lifestyle was seemingly more normal than that which I had become accustomed to. I even found myself somewhat inexplicably attracted to David Briggs, with whom I'd forged a friendship. David was the antithesis of Elvis in many ways. I found his laid-back humor and attitude refreshing. He made me laugh, which I needed at the time.

Being out in the sunshine reinforced the decision to leave. *There is life after Elvis Presley*, I thought. It was a bittersweet realization. I wasn't going to fool myself into thinking I could ever feel that same way about anyone ever again in my life, but I'd be able to live life on my terms. Since the day we met, Elvis had occupied every corner of my heart, so it came as something of a relief when it finally dawned on me that I really could go on. For the first time in four years, I began to understand how much in life I had to look forward to.

As I imagined life without Elvis, I knew I needed to start my own career, so I exhumed my longtime dream of being an actress. I'd planted the seed for spending more time in Los Angeles to pursue my own projects the previous year, when Elvis was in the process of selling his Monovale home. Elvis had always been very supportive and appreciative of my talent as a comedic actress, and he was happy to hear that I felt ready to begin going on some auditions.

"I think maybe I'll rent a place in L.A., just for when I'm coming out to read for parts, instead of staying in a hotel," I said.

"Yeah, why don't you do that?" he said. "Rent an apartment, and then when I need to come out, we'll have a little place to stay."

The first place I rented was on Holman Avenue in West Los Angeles, near the Mormons' Los Angeles Temple. It was a fairly spacious two-bedroom apartment, which was quite modest compared to what Elvis was accustomed to, but he had no problem staying there with me and even helped me to make it homey.

"Let me give you some furniture," he said. "I've got all this stuff in storage. Let's put it in your apartment."

So he and I had a variety of items taken out of storage. Of course, the furniture from his luxurious Holmby Hills mansion was too big for my little apartment, but we made it work. And then, when the lease was up after the first year, I rented another place around the corner on Eastborne Avenue. Elvis had me outfit both apartments especially for him and his needs, putting foil and a black velvet bedspread over the bedroom windows and sliding glass door to completely block out any light, and stayed with me at both locations several times.

"I'd really like to start doing some television," I had declared to Elvis as I began to make my bid for independence from him.

"Well, if you want to do that, you should meet Aaron Spelling," Elvis said. "He's producing every good show on TV."

And it was true. At the time, Aaron Spelling was doing *Starsky & Hutch* and was just about to cast *Charlie's Angels* before going on to produce all kinds of hits, from *Love Boat* and *Dynasty* to *Beverly Hills 90210*. Elvis had actually met him taking the train cross-country to L.A. He called about getting me in to see Aaron Spelling, which meant that the meeting happened right away.

I flew out to Los Angeles, staying at my apartment on Eastborne Avenue, to meet with Spelling, who was very encouraging and gracious to me.

"I'm doing this show called *Charlie's Angels*," he said. "Let me set you up for an audition."

Now, I didn't even have a Screen Actors Guild (SAG) card, but I ended up testing for *Charlie's Angels* because Aaron Spelling had recommended me to his casting agents. I was such a novice that I didn't really understand what a significant opportunity this was, and so I didn't have enough sense to be nervous. The day of the audition, I wore this beautiful black leather Gucci pantsuit Elvis had bought for me, which

I still have. It was made up of black leather pants and a black leather jacket, all with red piping along the edges. I was super skinny, so it fit me perfectly. Dressed like a rock star, I strolled in like it was no big deal.

Of course, looking back, I have a good laugh when I imagine the ABC executives catching sight of this Southern bumpkin in her black leather outfit, and them thinking: *What is she doing here? Who is that anyhow? Who's her agent? She doesn't have an agent. What?*

I didn't get the part, of course, because a big network show couldn't take a chance with an unknown actress who didn't even have a union card. But Aaron Spelling sent a message around to all of his casting people that he had a new girl in town, Linda Thompson, and to please consider her in whatever came up next.

Sure enough, Spelling came through and I got my first role on his show *The Rookies*, which was enough to launch me on my way in Hollywood. I got my SAG card and started doing a bit of acting here and there throughout the rest of 1976. This new independence gave me a burst of optimism about my life. For months I'd been exploring what life after Elvis would *feel* like; now, for the first time, I started to understand what life after Elvis would *look* like.

Complicating this newfound sense of optimism was that, as much as I feared to admit it, Elvis's condition appeared to be deteriorating. One day when we were back at Graceland for a few days before leaving on tour again, Elvis was so out of it he could barely speak. I had only a short time at home, so I wanted to take a little break to see my parents. I approached the side of the bed, where Elvis lay heavily sedated.

"I'm going to go see Mama and Daddy for a little while," I said.

It took him what felt like five minutes to muster his reply.

"When . . . are . . . you . . . coming . . . back . . . ?" he slurred.

"I'll be back in around thirty minutes," I said.

"I-I-I n-n-need another sleeping pill," he said, again taking an agonizingly long time to form the words. He tried to lift his head to reach for his pill bottles but was unable to coordinate his movements to do so. He couldn't even lift his head off the pillow. I moved the bottles so they were beyond his reach. I didn't have it in me to watch him poison himself anymore.

"You don't need another sleeping pill, honey," I said. "You're asleep.

All you need to do is close your eyes and put your head back on the pillow. You're straining your neck trying to lift your head. Close your eyes. I'll stay here with you until you fall asleep."

"No," he argued. "I need another sleeping pill, goddamnit."

I hovered by his bed, concerned for him, but also losing my patience. All I wanted was to go see my mom and dad. I could literally be there and back in thirty minutes. It was like having a newborn baby and trying to get it to go back to sleep. But this was a grown man. I wanted to leave, but I didn't want him to try to get up while I was gone and injure himself. I sat there with him as the minutes dragged past. He kept fighting the sleep that was tugging at his consciousness and arguing with me for more pills. Finally, I became so exasperated that I couldn't maintain my composure anymore.

"I'm slowly watching you self-destruct, and I'm helpless," I said. "You're torturing me. You're torturing yourself. You're killing yourself, just as surely as that gun would. You are dying before my eyes. And you are hurting the people who love you."

I was shocked at myself. As soon as the words had left my mouth, I regretted them. I felt nervous and guilty, wondering if I'd hurt his feelings and what he would say.

His eyes were closed, but a big wide grin erupted on his face. Slowly he opened one of his eyes and peeped at me, as if he were thinking, *I finally got her to break.* He was barely conscious, but he was grinning from ear to ear. Looking at me out of the corner of his beautiful eye, he had a mischievous smile on his face. If he could have pulled himself together enough to laugh, he clearly would have.

"Okay, Mommy," he said. "I'll go back to sleep."

He closed his eyes and his breathing deepened as he drifted off. I didn't get up right away. I was rattled, and I sat there for a long moment, watching the face I adored, the man I loved so much. Moments like these were the terrible inverse of how I'd once stayed awake to study him sleeping because I was marveling at his beauty and the sheer wonder of Elvis Presley lying beside me. I still did, and knew I always would, adore Elvis, but now I studied him at night in order to keep him alive. I was tired from being up all the time with him, taking care of him, and making sure he didn't die. All I'd wanted was the simplest thing—to see my mom and dad for thirty minutes—and I couldn't even have that little break for myself.

It was easy to see that his health and control of the situation were unraveling. Even Elvis knew. For someone who lived in such denial, he could be remarkably self-aware.

"What do you think your greatest flaw is?" I once asked him.

"I'll only say this once, probably, but I do know it," he said. "I'm self-destructive. I have a self-destructive streak. But don't you worry about me, honey. I'm going to live to be in my eighties."

There was his delusional way of thinking again; even though he recognized his self-destructive nature, he thought that he could handle things. He could deal with it. He could conquer it. He would outlive us all.

Misplaced as his self-confidence was, his self-destructive impulses were exacerbated by the fact that, after Elvis had rather unceremoniously fired his longtime bodyguards Red and Sonny West, they decided it might be time to write what some described as a vengeful book, containing information about Elvis's drug abuse, which they knew he wouldn't want them to talk about publicly. They've since said they published a tell-all because they thought it would help him. And maybe that's the truth. Maybe they hoped it would encourage him to realize how out of control he'd gotten and inspire him to take care of himself and stop his self-destructive behavior. Instead, knowledge that the book was imminent sent Elvis into a spiral. He was hurt, feeling that they'd betrayed him, humiliated that they'd turned on him, embarrassed by what he knew the book would contain, and fearful of how his fans would react.

By the time the book was released—in the United Kingdom in May 1977 and in the United States in August 1977—I would no longer be in Elvis's life. But I still cared about him deeply, and it was painful for me to know how devastated he must be. It also bothered me that some inaccuracies had been put out into the world. Such as the inclusion of the story of Elvis's midnight trip to the funeral home, but written so that I'd been right there on the eerie tour with the guys. They'd written the scene indicating that I was walking through the funeral home, expressing dismay in the cutest little Southern voice, when in fact, no,

I absolutely was not inside the funeral home, but rather nervously waiting in the car for the whole macabre incident to be over with.

Elvis and I had teeter-tottered through the late summer and fall of 1976 as a couple, but our changing circumstances were undeniable. Up until then, he had always saved his affairs for California, or Vegas, or the road, out of some form of respect, since they wouldn't get back to me as easily (although, of course, they sometimes did). And so when I learned that he'd gone out with another girl in Memphis a few times that fall, I had to admit to myself that we'd moved past the point of no return.

In late November, we were on tour—Elvis was performing two shows at the Cow Palace in San Francisco—when he approached me with a change of plans.

"Honey, I brought the plane in for you, to take you back to Memphis tomorrow," Elvis said after his first show. "I thought you might want to go back to Memphis and see your mom and dad."

"Really?" I asked.

He nodded his head. We had been in San Francisco for a couple of days. There had been nothing in his behavior or manner that suggested anything was out of the ordinary.

"Really?" I asked. "You brought the plane in from Memphis, *just for me?*"

"Yeah," he said.

I was well aware by this time that he was dating a girl in Memphis. And I just knew in my bones that he'd brought in the plane from Memphis with her on it, because he'd wanted to see her. And now he was sending me away, without any further explanation.

"Okay," I said.

Without another word, I went to my own dressing room. I gathered up all my stuff, packing my clothes, and my books, and my cosmetics. By the time I got into bed, Elvis was almost asleep, but turned to kiss me good night.

"I love you, Ari," he said.

I was exhausted. Physically. Emotionally. Psychologically. No matter how much I cared for him, I just couldn't do it anymore, coming and going at his whim, watching him hell bent on his own destruction. No matter how much I sacrificed my own well being for his, there would always be other women. I was heartbroken. But I was ready for it to be over.

The next day, we awoke around noon and had our breakfast. I gathered my luggage, and I prepared to say my farewell. I didn't know it would be the last time I ever saw Elvis alive. I went to where Elvis stood, waiting to say goodbye to me.

"All right, I'll head back to Memphis then," I said.

"Yeah, I'll be home in a couple of days," he said. "You'll enjoy spending some time with your mom and dad. Give you a break. I know you're tired. You're on the road with me all the time."

"So you're telling me that you didn't bring somebody else in from Memphis?" I asked, knowing well what the answer was. "You know you didn't need to bring the plane in just for me. I'm happy to fly commercially. I like to be around other people."

"No, you fly on the plane," he said. "Of course I brought it in just for you."

"Really?" I said. "You're going to stand here and tell me that you didn't bring somebody else in on that plane?"

"Honey, oh my God, are you kidding me?" he said. "I love you. I don't love anybody else. There's nobody else."

He was right, I was tired—of being on the road, of waking up past noon every day, most of all, of his attempts to deceive me, and to deceive himself. I was worn weary trying to always be the understanding, strong, forgiving, loving, self-sacrificing martyr. It no longer fit me. As I'd soon learn, there was another girl, Ginger, whom he'd had put on the floor below us. At that very moment, she was in a holding pattern, waiting for him to bring her up when I left. I didn't have to hear him admit there had been a girl on the plane to *know* there had been a girl on the plane. And *this time* I wasn't going to pretend otherwise.

"You don't have another girl here?" I asked.

"Look at me," he said, while drawing me in as close to him as possible. "Look me in the eye. I love you. I don't love anybody else. There is nobody. But I want you to know, if you ever hear anything, or see anything, or read anything about me with anybody else, I just want you to know I don't love anybody else. I just love you. I don't love anybody else. I will always love you. You're my girl. You're my little Ariadne Pennington, three years old. You're my sweetheart. I love you. You're it for me."

He held my gaze as he spoke, fervently and with great conviction, and tears brimmed from his eyes. He held me longer than usual and kissed me tenderly. I knew he was telling the truth about loving me. And maybe at the time, he hadn't fallen in love with Ginger yet, and what he'd said about loving only me was true as well. But I'm sure he loved Ginger soon enough. He loved Priscilla. He loved me. He probably loved models Ann Pennington and Sheila Ryan, who were two of the steadier women he saw on the side when he and I were living together. Elvis had a tremendous capacity to love. He loved women, and we loved him.

That was the thing about Elvis—when he told you he loved you, you never questioned it. I never felt more deeply loved in my life than in the moments when he spoke of his love for me, even in this bittersweet moment when we were parting. As I've said, he had this way of loving so hard I could actually hear him grinding his teeth. He loved Lisa like that. I had heard him grit his teeth as he put her to bed at night, saying: "Daddy loves you so much. I just want to squeeze the life out of you."

I was well aware that I had a part of his heart that nobody else had, and I would possess it until the day he died. And that knowledge comforted me, even as my heart was breaking at the fact that he'd just looked me in the eye and lied to me before sending me away. But I was past fighting. I let it go.

"Okay, honey," I said. "I love you, too. You know that I love you. I will always love you."

I suppose the moment could aptly be described as a final goodbye without either of us knowing it. It was, in fact, as I said, the very last time I saw Elvis alive. We kissed. We hugged. We loved. We cuddled. I felt sad, but also wise. I felt secure in my certainty that I knew what was really going on between us. I didn't need to confront him with his lie. My personal knowledge was enough for me to make the decisions I needed to make in order to take back my life and my future. All of this enlightenment came to me in a flash. At the same time, I knew that I loved him so deeply and unreservedly that I would never love anybody else in the same way. And I knew my heart would require a long, long time to heal.

I went back to Memphis alone on his JetStar. Now that his womanizing had become so blatant it was too hurtful for me, I didn't want to put up with it anymore. I also knew I had to face the fact that, no matter how diligently I watched over him, I probably would not be able to keep him alive. It would have been even more devastating for me if I had actually been the one to find him no longer breathing. I had been trying for several months to wean myself off him emotionally as much as I could—building my strength, discovering what my life without him could be. He had found another woman to keep him company and take care of him. I figured this was the moment to let him go on with his life, while I went on with mine.

When I arrived back at Graceland, I started slowly gathering up my possessions. I called my daddy and asked him to come over and help me move my belongings from Graceland to my house. Several days went by, and I didn't hear from Elvis at all. I was sure he was with someone else. I figured he must have been a little embarrassed and more than likely afraid to confront the awkward fact that I knew.

It was December and approaching our favorite holiday. I still had my American Express card, and I used it to purchase a few Christmas gifts for people. Most important, I bought a big beautiful diamond ring for Elvis. It was yellow gold, with a concave design backed in black and surrounded in diamonds, so that it looked almost like a volcano set with diamonds.

Soon after I made that purchase, Mr. Presley canceled the card. I knew Elvis would never have done such a thing, but I understood why his dad had acted in this way. It was clear to everyone that I was moving my things out of Graceland and into my home around the corner. I wasn't afraid to leave behind the opulent life, nor the tattered remnants of the fairy-tale façade I'd inhabited for the past four and a half years. I had faith there was a more modest yet normal life that awaited me on the other side of those famous Graceland gates.

I sat down and wrote Elvis a two-page letter that attempted to express everything I was feeling—the sense of loss, the gratitude for having had the privilege of loving him and having that love returned to me. I let him know I was aware that he was with someone else, but I hoped he would be happy. I assured him with these parting words: "You are and will always remain the love of my life. In all honesty, I never want to love that way again. I have already known the 'pain of too much tenderness,' " quoting Khalil Gibran's *The Prophet*. I told him I would I always be just a phone call away, if he ever needed me for anything. I meant each and every word with all of my heart.

It was nearly two weeks before Christmas, and I hadn't spoken to Elvis even once since I'd left San Francisco. It was the longest we'd ever gone without speaking—or seeing each other—since we'd met. I knew that wherever he was, and whomever he was with, he was distracted, which meant that he was distracted enough for me to really leave.

I gave the letter and the ring to Elvis's cousin Billy Smith. Elvis and I had spent a lot of time with him and his wife, Jo, over the years. I trusted Billy to be my messenger.

"Billy, I'm moving out of Graceland," I said. "Please give Elvis this ring and this letter, and tell him I said, 'Merry Christmas and I love you.' "

My daddy came to Graceland and helped me load the last of my belongings into the Cadillac Elvis had given me. I was able to take all that was left in one final load. Before I got into my car, loaded with the clothing I had once worn with Elvis by my side, I paused in our upstairs area. I took one last look at the organ where we once sat and sang together, laughing, as I taught him my silly Alpha Delta Pi sorority songs. I breathed in one long, last breath of the rarefied air in Elvis's most private sanctuary—his bedroom. I picked up his pillow, buried my face in it, and breathed in again. I was struck with a profound sadness as his lingering scent reminded me of the closeness we had shared. It was the right decision to leave, but it was a gut-wrenching one. With no exalted sense of ego on my part, I was sincerely fearful that Elvis would not live long. That made leaving all the more painful.

As we finally drove down the long driveway, just before the gate, my daddy glanced at me.

"How do you feel?" he said.

"Relieved," I said.

We drove around the corner to my house. Since Elvis had bought it for me, I'd probably only spent seven nights there, total. I'd always been at Graceland. So it was a huge adjustment to begin staying there by myself. I missed Elvis terribly. At the same time, I was grateful for every life experience I'd had with him—even in the early, painful days of our split, I was glad for all the love shared and the lessons I'd learned during my time with Elvis. I'm still appreciative today. I also felt thankful for finding the strength I wasn't sure I had to actually leave Elvis, and to do so with sincerely loving wishes, gratitude, kindness, and an open door.

Billy and I later talked about the moment when he gave Elvis my letter and the ring. He was too loyal to Elvis to divulge anything that was more private than Elvis would have wanted me to know, now that I was his ex-girlfriend. I wouldn't have wanted Billy to betray Elvis's confidence anyway. But he did speak honestly to me about Elvis's reaction.

"I gave him the letter, and he read it, and he was very moved by it," Billy said. "He was very quiet and just held on to it. Then, I gave him the ring, and he thought it was beautiful. He was just sad. It was just a sad moment."

Aunt Delta also later told me a story about bringing Elvis something to eat one night after I'd left. She found him upstairs at the organ with my letter spread out across the top. He was crying and singing "Unchained Melody," which goes, "Time goes by so slowly / And time can do so much / Are you still mine?"

"Are you all right, son?" she asked.

"Aunt Delta, you don't forget about someone overnight that you've been with for nearly five years," he said. "It's going to take a long time. I'm really sad."

I missed Elvis and our love for each other, but we only actually spoke on the phone two or three times in the eight months we were apart before he died. And yet, I never really felt like Elvis and I were totally done. And neither did he, apparently. My brother, Sam, who'd left his job as a sheriff's deputy in 1976 and went to work for Elvis full-time as his personal bodyguard and tour advance man, was still working for Elvis after our breakup. In fact, he was there until the end. He told me about how Elvis called him in to see him, maybe four or five months after I'd left.

"Sam, I just wanted to talk to you for a minute," Elvis said. "You know that I've loved your sister for a long time."

"Yes, I know, but life goes on and people move on," Sam said.

"We're not done," Elvis said. "We're not finished. Our story's not over yet. I just wanted you to know that. I just wanted you to know that Linda and I are not finished."

Fate has a way of working itself out, and life unfolds as it is meant to. We will never know what might have been if Elvis had been given the gift of a longer life. I am saddened to this day that he left us far too early. I, like millions of others, would just be happy to know he was still a living presence in our world, no matter what he might now be doing, and no matter who he might choose to be with.

"Every Time You Cross My Mind"

There's a hole in the sky
Where the sun used to shine
Back in the days
When I called you mine
And the stars lost their light
There's no candle that glows
The moon's out of sight
And I just don't know.

I don't have any teardrops left
   to cry
There's no emotion left
Not since we said goodbye
The only time I know I'm still alive
Is by the way that my heart feels
Every time you cross my mind

Empty spaces ahead
Time is something to dread
Whatever you did
Or maybe what I said
Can we forgive and forget
Could we try it again
Or will my life forever be
A memory of what's been?

I don't have any teardrops left to cry
There's no emotion left
Not since you said goodbye

The only time I know I'm still alive
Is by the way that my heart feels
Every time you cross my mind

LYRIC: LINDA THOMPSON

Chapter Eleven

Hee Haw Honey

Literally overnight, I stopped flying on a customized private airplane, staying in presidential suites, and having people pack and unpack for me and cook my meals, all while I was doted on by the world's most famous, gorgeous, and charismatic rock star. Yes, the experience had encouraged me to blossom from an innocent college student into a woman of the world. And Elvis had been generous enough to give me my own house, a collection of gorgeous designer clothes, and great jewelry. But my day-to-day reality was clearly much more modest now. And much more normal and peaceful.

After spending the holidays in Memphis with my family, I flew out to Los Angeles. I was seeking some distance from my old existence at Graceland, and I wanted to fully dedicate myself to pursuing my career and placing myself at the center of this new moment in my life. I'd put the jewelry Elvis had given me in a safe-deposit box in the bank. I now lived alone in my two-bedroom apartment in West L.A., surrounded by vestiges of my former life, including Elvis's furniture, and paintings, and the memories they evoked.

But the disparity between the before and after of my life with Elvis didn't make me feel at all diminished. I had known this more ordinary life until I'd met Elvis, and I was comfortable returning to these circumstances now. It was, after all, what I had finally chosen for myself. Besides, I've always thought we need to be like a rubber ball, bouncing with resiliency. When you hit rock bottom, know that you'll bounce right back up, probably only to plummet again and repeat the process.

I've always been an intrinsically positive person, and that remained true in these days. I was heartbroken, but I was also surprisingly optimistic. I had believed in myself enough to choose my own personal fulfillment and path forward over anyone else's. Given the major moment of self-empowerment I'd just experienced, even the pain of my broken heart could be a source of pride. My philosophy has always been to let life flow through you, while not questioning it too much, or balking at circumstances that aren't ideal. I chose to see the positive in the transition I was undergoing, painful as it might sometimes be. I knew I had to create fresh meaning and opportunities for myself now, opening up all new chapters in my future. My freedom was sweet, even if it came at a price.

Not that it was easy. I felt absolutely depleted. I'd given everything I possibly could have. I think it's wonderful and rare to love unreservedly, maybe once in your life, but through that experience, I also learned to hold something back of myself, for myself. Elvis and I used to talk about this need, actually, in terms of both relationships and spirituality.

"Everybody has within them a hallowed ground, where no one else can go, and that's their own sacred space that they have to hold on to for themselves," Elvis said.

I listened to him say the words, and I agreed, but then, I gave *everything* to Elvis. I was now realizing that I should have held on to that core of my being. This lesson has stuck with me for decades. (I cowrote a song in 2015, "Hallowed Ground," about this way of thinking, and it was on the charts for nearly three months in Scandinavia.) I had completely lost myself, and I vowed that I would never allow that to happen again. I felt like I was an empty shell, and I needed to fill myself up with who I was. I sought to remember who I had been going into my relationship with Elvis. Not Miss Tennessee. Not Elvis's Girlfriend. But Linda Thompson, a young woman who'd put herself through college, who'd aspired to be a wife and mother, an actress, and most of all a good person. No matter where I landed, I didn't need private planes to be happy—I wanted normalcy.

Initially, I went on auditions and started getting some acting jobs, but I also soon had an entrée to a career I'd never imagined for myself: as a songwriter. The opening for this began when I started dating David Briggs, Elvis's keyboard player. Our relationship was never that serious, as I was still healing. It amounted to a long-distance relationship since he lived in Nashville, while I was mostly based in Los Angeles, which kept it casual.

The fact that he was familiar from my days with Elvis was helpful, because it meant I hadn't lost everything from my old world. David was familiar and a comfort of sorts to me. Of course, our relationship created a raised eyebrow or two as well. Apparently, Elvis found out David and I were dating, and he mischievously unplugged David's keyboard onstage one night. But aside from an occasional little prank like that, Elvis didn't make a big deal of the situation. He allowed David to continue working for him because David was very talented, Elvis and I had already broken up, and the music always came first for Elvis. Did it bother him? Maybe. But not so much that he would diminish his band because of it. Also, I think Elvis knew I'd been very good and extraordinarily faithful to him, and down deep, he wanted me to be happy.

More than anything, David was a respite. He was the opposite of Elvis, because he was very easygoing. He also saw something in me that I'd never brought to its fullest potential before, and by doing so, he helped me to make a profound leap forward in my artistic life. I began sharing with him a few little love poems when we were apart, as was my way. He called me on the telephone one day after receiving my latest musing in the mail.

"You should let me put these to music," he said. It was similar to what Elvis had told me, and once again I demurred.

"Oh no, I just write poetry," I said. "Perhaps I'll publish a book of poetry someday, but that's it."

Not long after that, David surprised me by sending me a tape. He'd taken it upon himself to put music to one of the lyrics I'd written. And he'd gotten the lead singer of the Oak Ridge Boys, Steve Sanders, to sing the demo for him. Steve had a great voice, and it sounded incredible. Now it was my turn to call David.

"This is what could happen with your lyrics," he said. "This is the full fruition."

"Oh, wow, that's really pretty," I said, finally getting what he and Elvis saw in my songwriting potential.

While Elvis had told me that my poetry would make good lyrics, I'd never really believed it, or felt entitled to turn the private emotions of our love into a public song. Now that I heard it for myself, however, there was no denying that I had a way with words that translated well into music. David and I began writing songs together occasionally, and I learned a great deal about songwriting and musicality from him.

"This is what you could be doing because you're a lyricist," David said. "You're not just a poet. You're a lyricist and a damn good one. It's something you can do for the rest of your life. You really have a talent."

"Okay, I'm a lyricist now," I said with a laugh.

I'd always believed the poetry I'd written was too personal to be of interest to anyone but my parents or Elvis or David. So it was gratifying to receive this validation, especially at a moment when I was trying to define myself on my own terms.

After Elvis and I had been apart for several months, without any contact, I felt I had healed enough to call him and see how he was doing. I wanted him to know that, even though we didn't live together anymore, he was still in my heart. I was back in Memphis at the time, at the house he'd bought for me. I was a little nervous as I waited for Elvis to come to the phone, and then just like that, I could hear his breathing and sense his presence on the line.

"Hey, Ariadne, how are you doing, baby?" he said.

"I'm doing well," I said. "How are you doing, sweetheart?"

"I'm okay," he said. "I'm good. Everything is good."

"I'm just checking on you," I said. "I just wanted to make sure you're okay."

"Yeah, yeah," he said. "I'm all good."

"I'm mostly living out in L.A. now," I said. "And I'm doing some acting roles. Using my college training for something. I just think about you a lot, you know I love you, and want you to know I'm always here for you. Are you taking good care of yourself?"

"I am, honey. I am."

"Are you eating right? Getting enough exercise?"

"Yeah, I'm playing some racquetball."

"Okay, Buntyn, well, don't overindulge in anything. You know what I mean."

"Naw, naw, I'm good," he said. "Are you okay? Do you need anything?"

"I have just about everything I need," I said. "I've got my house, and I'm doing some acting. I'm doing a lot of Aaron Spelling shows. I'm fine."

"Do you need some money?" he asked. "I can give you a hundred thousand dollars if you want, and you can start a business, or do whatever you want with it."

"Oh my gosh, no, no, thank you, but I'm good, honey," I said. "I want you to know that I don't want anything. I'm so grateful for my house, for everything. You were very good and generous to me. I'm grateful for the time we had together. I love you. I wasn't there for you to give me a buyout or payoff at the end. Please know that."

"Well, I appreciate that, honey," he said. "Just let me know if you ever need anything."

"Of course, thank you. I love you," I said.

"I love you, too, Ariadne."

We hung up. In the way we spoke affectionately to one another, it was if we'd never missed a beat, and no time had passed. It was wonderful but also wrenching.

It never would have occurred to me to take any money from Elvis, simply because I'd once lived with him and now no longer did. But around the same time, a woman named Michelle Triola Marvin made a splash in the media with just such a claim. She'd been the live-in companion of actor Lee Marvin for several years. They'd never married, but she'd legally changed her name to Marvin, and she was very ensconced in his life. When he broke up with her, she sued him for "palimony," a term she and her attorney coined. She won around $100,000, although the decision was later overturned and she never received any money.

Still, it was a high-profile case and got many people talking. Several people had told me I should sue Elvis in the same way. I was incredulous at the suggestion, finding the very idea offensive. But I'm sure Elvis knew about the palimony case, as it was big news. Maybe that's one reason he offered me money like he did. Whatever his motivations, it meant a great deal to me that I'd set him straight. I'd never had an agenda when I was with him and didn't need to be paid for what I considered the privilege of loving him. It had been my decision to be there.

To this day, I derive a great deal of satisfaction from knowing that when Elvis drew his last breath, he had to know who loved him authentically. And in doing so, he knew that I'd always been there with him for the right reasons. When I left, I hadn't asked him for anything. And I wouldn't let him give me anything, even though he wanted to do so. I know he died with the absolute conviction that I loved him truly and purely. You can't buy or manufacture a better feeling than that.

Not long after that first call with Elvis, I ended up dialing his number again. In the spring of 1977, I landed a role on *Hee Haw*. The show, created by Bernie Brillstein, John Aylesworth, and Frank Peppiatt of Yongestreet Productions, was on the air for twenty-five years. Of course, I found it ironic that I had to leave Memphis and come out to California to audition for a show that would take me back to Tennessee. I replaced Barbi Benton, making me the new girl, even though I ended up being a regular cast member for fifteen years. The show was meant to be pure country, and it was a lot of fun to do. I met just about every old school, iconic country music artist in the world. Not only did I work with such incredible stars as Dolly Parton, Merle Haggard, Kenny Rogers, Johnny Cash, Tanya Tucker, Loretta Lynn, George Jones, Tammy Wynette, and too many others to mention, we also had special guest stars like Jonathan Winters, Ed McMahon, and Tommy Lasorda. Admittedly, as *Hee Haw* Honeys, we were clearly objectified in the cornfield, but 98 percent of the time I really didn't mind. It was all in good fun. Elvis and I had watched *Hee Haw* together religiously, so I was familiar with its premise and the full cast of characters. When I was cast, I knew he'd be excited, and I decided to call him again. He came right to the phone.

"How are you doing, honey?" I asked.

"I'm fine, sweetheart," he said. "Are you doing okay?"

"I'm calling to check on you," I said. "I'm going to call and check on you from time to time. Just make sure you're okay."

"Good, honey, you do that," he said. "Even if they say I'm not available, you just call and check on me. Tell them to let me know that you called."

"Okay, I will," I said. "You know, I've got a job. I'm going to be coming back to Nashville to film *Hee Haw*. I'm going to be one of the *Hee Haw* Honeys."

"Oh my God, you're going to be one of the *Hee Haw* girls?" he said, obviously thrilled for me.

"You'll have to start watching in September," I said. "They're going to air the shows then, but we're filming in June and October. I've already filmed some shows, and I'm going to be filming again in October. It'll start airing in September."

"You know I watch it everywhere I go," he said.

"I know you do, honey," I said.

"Okay, I'll watch for you. That's great, sweetheart. I can't wait to see my little Ariadne out in the cornfield on *Hee Haw*. You'll be great."

"Thanks, sweetheart," I said. "I love you."

"I love you, too, honey," he said.

Of course, I didn't know at the time that Elvis wouldn't be alive to see me make my debut on *Hee Haw* that September. Or that this would be the last time I spoke to him. But looking back now with the full knowledge of what was coming, I'm even more grateful that I was able to be that sweet and loving to him, and him to me, although we weren't dating anymore. And I'm also glad that we were able to leave things on such warm, affectionate terms.

I was appearing on *Hee Haw* with Kenny Rogers's wife, Marianne. She and I were great friends, and I was over at their house almost every night. We often had dinner and played Scrabble together, enjoying casual, homey activities like that. I was visiting with them when I brought up my newfound creative endeavor.

"Hey, Kenny, my friend David Briggs sent me this cassette," I said. "Would you listen to it and tell me what you think about it?"

"Oh no, you too?" he said, with a laugh.

"What does that mean?" I asked, genuinely surprised.

"Are you pitching me a song?"

"Oh gosh, no," I said.

I was so naïve at the time, I didn't know people were always pitching him songs.

"No, no, no," I said. "I just wanted you to listen to it and give me a critique, because it's the first one of my poems that's ever been put to music."

"All right, I'll listen to it," he said, somewhat indulgently.

He went back to his dressing room alone, while Marianne and I sat and visited. Not long after that, he rejoined us with an openly astonished look on his face.

"Linda, I'm going to give you a critique," he said.

"That's all I wanted," I said. "I just wanted to hear what you thought."

"My honest thought is that this is one of the most beautiful songs I've ever heard," he said. "I'd like to record it. Do you have any more?"

My heart swelled with pride at the knowledge that I really did have my own talent and was on the verge of finding my own standing and recognition.

"Yes, I do," I said. "I've got plenty more poetry."

Kenny was as good as his word. He recorded that song for his 1985 album *The Heart of the Matter* and released it as the B-side to his album single. He had enjoyed a major success with his 1977 song "Lucille," and was still at the top of his game, not to mention the pinnacle of his career, so this was a confidence booster for me. Kenny also wanted to record more of my songs. To add to the thrill, Sir George Martin, known as the fifth Beatle, was the producer of Kenny's record, and I had the pleasure of working with him. George even asked to read some more of my poetry because he found it compelling, he said. This was a major coup for me—I'd launched myself into a proper songwriting career.

That was my first-ever royalty check. Marianne was selling a pair of her diamond earrings around the same time and decided I needed to get my ears pierced and buy them from her. That's exactly what I did. Our friendship and those diamond earrings were a great investment.

"Love Don't Live Here Anymore"

This is the house
That love built
With memories of you
Built in each wall
Warm tender scenes
Still haunt my dreams
Thought I just heard your voice
In the hall
The mirrors reflect
All the heartache I feel
Smiling photographs
Just don't seem real

Nothing's been moved
But everything's changed
Each chair is in place
Just my life's rearranged
The wind cries your name
Through each window and door
But love don't live here
Love don't live here anymore

The firelight still glows
A pale blue
And the mantle is cruel
To hold pictures of you

Your scent lingers there
In the bed that we shared
The last plant that I sent
Is in bloom
These rooms are unkind
To play tricks on my mind
I can't believe
You'd just leave
Without me

Nothing's been moved
But everything's changed
Each chair is in place
Just my life's rearranged

The wind cries your name
Through each window and door
But love don't live here

Love don't live here anymore

LYRIC: LINDA THOMPSON

Chapter Twelve

A Final Goodbye at Graceland

On Friday, August 12, 1977, I had a strong urge to talk to Elvis. I'd been thinking about him all week, worrying about his health in a way that made me feel uneasy. I just had a sense of foreboding, so I called Graceland and Charlie Hodge answered the phone.

"Charlie, it's me," I said. "I'm just calling to check on Elvis. How's he doing?"

"He's fine," he said. "He's good."

"I have an uneasy feeling about him," I said. "Would you please just go upstairs and check on him?"

"Honey, he's fine," Charlie said. "He's sleeping."

"I have this feeling, just an uneasy feeling," I said. "Please, Charlie, do me a big favor and just do a quick check to make sure he is breathing all right and he's okay. Do you mind? I know it sounds silly, but I've just got a weird feeling about him."

"All right, all right," he said, sounding a little annoyed. "Hold on."

I didn't care if I'd irritated him, though. All I cared about was Elvis. He put down the phone. After a few minutes he came back on the line.

"He's fine, honey," Charlie said. "He's alone and he's sleeping soundly. He's good. His breathing is fine."

Of course, I don't know if he was really alone, or asleep, or even if

Charlie really went up there. It wasn't acceptable for anyone to simply walk into Elvis's room. I was well aware of that. But what more could I do? It wasn't like I could fly in from L.A. to check on him myself.

"He's breathing well and he's all right?" I asked, still unsettled.

"Yeah, yeah," he said. "We're going on tour next week. Everything is fine."

"Okay, Charlie, do me a favor," I said. "Tell him I called, tell him I love him, and just keep an eye on him. I worry about him."

"I know you do, but try not to worry," he said.

I can't explain how I'd known, but I was certain Elvis was in trouble. I guess sometimes there's a kind of energy in the atmosphere that we can pick up on. Just as technology allows us to receive and transmit invisible radio and TV waves, I believe the human mind can sometimes perceive thought waves and energy. And that's what prompted me to call him that Friday.

Just a few days later, on Tuesday morning, August 16, I received the call from Lisa Marie with the terrible, heartbreaking news that her daddy was dead.

A short time after Lisa Marie called me, my phone rang again. It was Vernon Presley, Elvis's father. His voice sounded weak, defeated, and sad beyond description. There can be no greater tragedy than the loss of your child, at any age.

"He's gone, Linda," he said. "My boy is gone. Oh me, Lordy, I don't know what I'm going to do."

"Oh, Mr. Presley, I'm so sorry," I said. "I'm so sorry for your loss. I don't even know what to say. I'm devastated, and I know you must feel the same way. It's just in the wrong order. No one ever expects to lose a child. And no matter how old he was, or how long he'd lived, or how famous he was, he was still your baby. I can only imagine your hurt. I'm so, so sorry. If there's anything that I can do . . ."

"I appreciate that, Linda," he finally replied. "And I appreciate that you were good to him, and he loved you, and we all love you."

As I listened to him sigh heavily on the other end of the line, my heart broke for him. I recalled one of the many occasions on which I'd ridden in an elevator with Mr. Presley. He'd suddenly looked at me.

"Linda, I honestly believe you are the kindest person I have ever known," he said out of nowhere.

I was so taken aback, because Mr. Presley rarely let his defensive guard down.

"Gosh, thank you, Mr. Presley, that means so much to me," I stammered.

And it truly did.

"I once had an aunt back in the day that I always thought was the kindest person on earth, but I believe you've got her beat," he explained.

It was a beautiful compliment to give, and now, listening to the devastation in his voice, I hurt knowing that part of his being was empty.

"The *Lisa Marie* will be out there to pick y'all up for the funeral sometime tonight," he continued, referring to Elvis's private plane. "Have your things ready to come back home. I reckon the plane will take off from L.A. about, oh hell, I don't know. I'll let you know, hon, what time to be there, or better yet, you can just call Priscilla and y'all coordinate it."

"I'll be happy to call her, and I appreciate so much your thinking of me," I said. "I of course was planning to get to Memphis as quickly as I can, so I thank you so much. I'll work it out with Priscilla."

I really did appreciate the fact that Mr. Presley had thought of me when he was trying to orchestrate the logistics of getting loved ones back to Memphis. He was so shaken by Elvis's death, and yet he'd had to plan and organize the unthinkable task of burying his only child. I wrote down Priscilla's number. And then, after we hung up, I resumed my silent grief in my lonely L.A. apartment.

A short time later, I called Priscilla about flying on the *Lisa Marie* as Mr. Presley had instructed me. Before I dialed her number, I gathered my thoughts about what I might say. Because I'd always been respectful of the relationship Priscilla had with Elvis regarding Lisa Marie, I measured my words carefully now.

"I'm so sorry," I said. "I just got a call from Mr. Presley. And Lisa Marie had called me earlier today to let me know about Elvis."

"That's what I understand," Priscilla said.

"I'm so sorry," I said again. "I know it's a tremendous loss for all of us, and I'm so sorry for little Lisa. It's an unthinkable tragedy."

"Yes, it's a terrible thing," she said.

"Mr. Presley said he's sending the *Lisa Marie* for us to come back on," I said. "And he just said to connect with you, and to find out what time."

There was a pause.

"Well, I don't really feel comfortable with that," she said.

"I beg your pardon?" I said.

"Yes, well, I don't want to land in Memphis and get off the plane to a three-ring circus of the press saying 'Linda and Priscilla flew together on the *Lisa Marie*,' " she retorted. "I don't think you and I should arrive together. I should be the only one like that on the plane."

Like what? I thought, flabbergasted. *Like someone Elvis loved?* To my knowledge, the trip to Memphis from Los Angeles on August 16, 1977, would be the first time Priscilla had ever flown on the plane. I was so stunned by her attitude, but I wasn't about to create any discord by just showing up at the airport and barging my way onto the plane.

"You know what, Priscilla, don't worry about it," I said. "I'll make it to Memphis to honor Elvis if I have to scoot on my butt to get there."

I was hurt, to say the least, but there was no way I was going to add to Mr. Presley's anguish by calling him back and making this his problem. I would never have bothered Mr. Presley with something like that in his darkest hour. Instead, I let him grieve in peace, and made other arrangements to get to Memphis in time to pay my respects. Luckily, I was able to book a midnight commercial flight, and thus my backside was spared the wear and tear.

To her credit, Priscilla approached me right away when I arrived at Graceland the next day.

"I just wanted to let you know I'm sorry for not allowing you on the plane," she said. "It was just a crazy time."

I understood—it was a devastating time for all of us. And I truly did accept Priscilla's apology, knowing we are all capable of saying and doing unusual, even inappropriate things, when under duress. Priscilla also surprised me, and made me understand that we'd had more in common than I'd ever known, with the confession she made to me next.

"When you were with Elvis, I didn't hear from him very often at all, only very occasionally when it had to do with Lisa, so I knew that he was happy and well taken care of," she said. "I just want you to know that, that I felt like you took really good care of him. I started to hear more from him since you've been gone, and I was a little worried about him."

It was bittersweet to hear her say so, but then again, those days at Graceland following Elvis's death were alternately painful, humorous, healing, confusing, and deeply cathartic. Just walking up the steps to the front door had been hard enough, observing the stained glass climbing roses on either side of the door, and the monogram above, all of which I'd designed and had installed during the renovation. It was profound to see them there now, a symbol of the life I'd lived there with Elvis. When the door opened, I was welcomed by the familiar smells, and sounds, and energy of people milling about, but there was something profoundly missing: Elvis's laughter, warmth, and boundless energy.

I kept expecting him to come down the stairs and say, "Hey, Mommy, I've missed you." I kept expecting to feel that familiar hug. But instead, I looked around and saw many other faces: Mr. Presley, and the guys, and my family, as well as some not-so-familiar faces, including Priscilla's family, and Elvis's last girlfriend, Ginger Alden, and her family. I felt a kinship with everyone there, even those I didn't know, because everyone was there because they loved Elvis, and he'd loved them, and so they all belonged.

I sat on the landing of the stairs leading up to Elvis's bedroom with Elvis's cousin Billy, Billy's wife, Jo, and another of Elvis's cousins, Patsy Gamble, as his body lay in state at the base of the stairs for public viewing. It was surreal to sit cloistered on the landing, peering down at the open casket, watching the public file through to pay their last respects to their idol.

The four of us, who understood his heart and his humor, sat for hours, laughing and crying hysterically, and remembering the man we'd all loved so very deeply. We talked about all the good times, riding on the golf carts around Graceland, and Elvis's kindness and generosity, and his uniquely irreverent sense of humor.

Later, the body was moved to the living area, and Rev. Rex Humbard led the service. As I sat and listened to his eulogy, I couldn't help but look at the beautiful stained glass peacocks I'd also designed and had installed in this room. Heartbroken as I was in that moment, I felt some degree of comfort knowing I had created some beautiful details for him to enjoy in his home, things that remained, even now that he was gone.

I had some long, private moments with Elvis as he lay in repose. Looking down, I can't say that the body looked a lot like the man I knew in the living years. In no way did death become him. Elvis was such a powerful life force, always in motion, with his knee jiggling, even when he was sitting down, so viewing him, laid to rest, he looked so cold and unnatural. His hair was combed too perfectly. His suit was not something he would have worn, except maybe on a gospel TV special. I studied his hand, still scarred from an infection he sustained due to an overly zealous fan who'd scratched Elvis as he reached down from the stage one night to shake hands. I stared at the perfect face I'd memorized and adored.

Among the family mourners were only a handful of well-known faces. Colonel Tom Parker was, of course, in bombastic attendance, replete with his firmly rooted baseball cap on his head—indoors and out. His short-sleeved, rumpled casual shirt was dotted with Southern summer sweat. The only "celebrities" at Graceland during the funeral events were George Hamilton, Caroline Kennedy, Ann-Margret, and her husband, Roger Smith. Elvis had been deeply in love with Ann-Margret, and at one time even considered marrying her. He had told me several stories about their courtship, and he had seemed to carry a lasting fondness for her.

Eventually the time came for close friends and family to get into the long line of white limousines that were to follow the hearse carrying the King of Rock and Roll to his final resting place. As if to say a final goodbye, inexplicably, a large tree branch fell from one of the trees, nearly hitting one of the cars. As I climbed into the third car with my parents and Sam and Louise, I thought how fitting it was that the limos were white, not black. The string of vehicles trailing down the famous driveway toward Elvis Presley Boulevard looked like a peaceful train of pure white light, carrying one of the brightest and most beautiful stars ever to grace our planet.

Thousands of fans lined both sides of the boulevard as the funeral procession passed. Bouquets of flowers were piled up along the gates of Graceland. (Later, I was not at all surprised to learn that on the day after Elvis died, more flowers were sold than on any other day in history.) People were four, five, and six lines deep, crying, holding their hands over their hearts, and mourning along with those of us who knew Elvis on a personal level. These fans loved him, too, and they stood out in the oppressive heat of August in Memphis to pay their respects to their music idol. The throngs of mourners went on for the entire stretch of highway, all the way up to the Forest Hill Cemetery.

Riding in the limo, I felt comforted by my family's presence. We were all stunned by the sudden loss, even though he'd been in bad shape during the last eight months of his life. In fact, when I watched the special that CBS aired about Elvis after he died, and saw how he had gained something like thirty pounds and looked so puffy and unkempt, and not like the man I'd been with, I just stood there in front of my TV and cried.

During our limo ride, my mama leaned over toward me.

"You know, a lot of people came up to me and said if you had been with him, he'd still be alive," she said. "Do you think that would have made a difference, if you'd been there? Not to make you feel bad."

"Mama," I said. "No, I really don't. I think things happen as they're meant to happen."

I didn't want to say too much to Mama because she didn't yet have any idea about his drug use. I knew there were times when I had cared for him when he could have easily died, and that it was unfair to make me or anyone else responsible for keeping him alive, no matter how much we had loved him. I'm fairly certain that, no matter what any news report indicates to the contrary, Elvis most likely did die in the way his innocent Lisa Marie blurted out to me when she called me on that fateful day. "He smothered in the carpet," she wailed. Whether Elvis ultimately died by suffocation, or of a heart condition that was exacerbated by his prescription excesses, he was certain to have met an untimely end if he didn't give up drugs. And even someone who had practically watched him 24/7, as I had, could only do so much.

Elvis's body was interred in the mausoleum where his beloved mother, Gladys Love Presley, had also been laid to rest years before. That was that. Forty-two years old, and gone.

After Elvis's funeral, Mr. Presley came to my house and sat on the floor at my feet.

"I want you to know that I realize you kept my son alive for nearly five years," he said. "I would have lost my boy years ago if you hadn't been with him, and hadn't cared for him the way you did. I want you to know how much I love and appreciate you for that. Don't think that I wasn't aware of that and that it goes unacknowledged."

"Thank you, Mr. Presley," I said. "I can't tell you how much that means to me."

"I wish you had been with him," he said.

"Well, I don't know," I said. "I did try to take care of him for the time that I was with him, but fate has a way of working itself out. I don't know that I could have saved him if I had been there."

One of the main reasons I left was that I didn't want to be the one to wake up one day and find him no longer breathing. That would have been even more devastating than opting to walk away from him. I always felt bad for Ginger, who did find his body. That had to be a haunting experience for her. We've never met. But I believe she did the best she could, given all the circumstances, which is all that could be expected of anyone.

After Elvis died, in my naïveté and desire to protect him, when I was asked to comment I tried to dispel some of the drug rumors that surfaced. It wasn't that I wanted to put untruths out into the world, but I knew that Elvis would have been very embarrassed by the way he died. I don't think anybody was more surprised than he when his spirit left his body. I could always picture him thinking, *Whoa, wait a second, what just happened? That wasn't supposed to happen. I was going to live to be eighty*.

So, at first when I was asked about his drug use, I always had a strong reply.

"Oh, that's just ridiculous," I said. "He was given a federal narcotics badge by President Nixon."

But it didn't take me long to realize I couldn't live for him anymore.

I had to step away from protecting Elvis's myth and let it develop as it was going to do. It was time for the truth Elvis had created to reveal itself. I had matured into a woman desirous of living my own life of authenticity and credibility. That seemed more important to me than trying to hide Elvis's mistakes from public view.

Even though I feared disappointing his fans who could not conceive of his ever doing anything wrong, my fears were unwarranted. It was so moving to see how fans forgave him when they learned the truth of his prescription drug abuse. It speaks beautifully to the strength of their commitment to his legacy. Even more than that, I think it would have been meaningful and restorative for Elvis to know he was loved, accepted, and allowed to be imperfect, with all that entails. I would offer that this portion of my memoir is dedicated to Elvis's legions of fans who have accepted his shortcomings and revere him still. To those who honor the man who brought us the music.

Within the first week after Elvis passed away, I started dreaming about him. Not every night, but often enough that, strange as this may sound, I came to feel like there was a plane of consciousness on which we could visit. As if I were suspended between life and death when asleep, in a different realm, and there we could be together. And while I realize now that it was probably all in my imagination, I'm grateful that I had those moments with him, even just in my dreams. I think it was what I needed at the time in order to say my final goodbye. In these dreams, I was aware that he was gone, but I still got to cuddle and visit with him, and it felt profoundly comforting to be reunited.

It may have been a comfort to have Elvis visit me in my dreams, but I was well aware that I had to live in the real world. That was a struggle now. When I returned to my apartment after his funeral, I was terribly lonely, and I couldn't sleep.

I wasn't really surprised to hear when Mr. Presley died, on June 27, 1979, destroyed by a broken heart, I'm sure. I was in Memphis at the time, and I went to the funeral to pay my last respects. Elvis was his only child and had been his whole life, his whole world. Saddened as I was by Mr. Presley's passing, I found some solace in the possibility that Elvis and he had finally been reunited with their beloved Gladys in the place we call eternity.

My mama,
Margie White
Thompson,
who taught me
that a parent's
unconditional
love for their
child is the most
important thing
in the world.

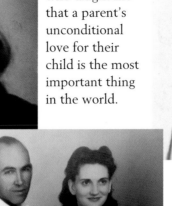

My daddy,
Sanford
Thompson, in
his World War II
army uniform.

An early family photo with my
dad, brother Sam, and mom,
taken in Memphis.

On vacation in Gulf
Shores, Alabama, with
my cousins and aunts
shortly after meeting
Elvis (L to R: cousin
Lori, cousin Brenda,
Aunt Betty Sue, Aunt
Christine, Jeanne
LeMay, cousin Janet,
and me).

Here we are with my friend Jeanne LeMay in 1973 on tour. *(Photograph © Jeanne LeMay)*

I first met Elvis when I was only twenty-two and had just been crowned Miss Tennessee Universe.
(Photograph Peter C. Borsari/© Borsari Images)

During our first Christmas together, Elvis bought me this beautiful floor-length muskrat coat; when I put my hands in the pockets, I found $2,500 in one and a diamond ring he had designed for me in the other.

This photo was taken on one of our many trips to Las Vegas.

Eventually, Elvis bought his own airplane, which he named the *Lisa Marie* after his daughter.

For four and a half years I traveled almost everywhere with Elvis when he was on tour.
(Photograph © Sean Shaver)

(Photograph © Sean Shaver)

On tour in 1974.

(Photograph © Jeanne LeMay)

A family photo with Elvis at the Las Vegas Hilton Hotel, wearing the Suzy Creamcheese dress that impressed Tom Jones.

When we were taking this family photo in Las Vegas, Elvis teased my brother that he was blending in with the wallpaper.

I created a photo book for Elvis with photos of me in Graceland's many rooms. Here's the kitchen where I made my famous peanut butter and banana sandwiches.

The Jungle Room in Graceland; I've always thought the Marc Cohn line "There's a pretty little thing waiting for the King and she's down in the Jungle Room" was written for me.

After Elvis bought the *Lisa Marie*, we had more spontaneous and wild fun than ever before. *(Photographs © Sean Shaver)*

On tour with Elvis and his lifelong friend Red West.
(Photograph Peter C. Borsari/© Borsari Images)

For Christmas in 1973 I designed a Maltese cross for Elvis, which he's wearing here on tour.
(Photograph © Sean Shaver)

Lisa Marie came on part of this tour with us, and I loved being with her.
(Photograph © Jeanne LeMay)

As much as I enjoyed being out on the road with Elvis, we were always our happiest at Graceland.
(Photograph Peter C. Borsari/© Borsari Images)

We separated only eight months before Elvis's death. I take comfort in the knowledge that he died certain of my love and devotion.
(Photograph © Jeanne LeMay)

This was the very first day I met Bruce, at the Playboy Mansion for a celebrity tennis tournament in the spring of 1979.

(Photograph Peter C. Borsari/© Borsari Images)

With Bruce at the Hotel Bora Bora after promoting his movie with the Village People, *Can't Stop the Music*.

On our wedding day, surrounded by the love of my family.

I couldn't hide the joy on my face with a newborn Brandon in 1981. Brandon became the absolute sunshine in my everyday life.

With Brandon in our Lake Tahoe home, where we often went to snow ski, water-ski, and Jet Ski.

Bruce with baby Brody in 1983.

Kenny Rogers and his then wife Marianne, whom I met while appearing on *Hee Haw*. Kenny later recorded my song "Our Perfect Song" on his 1985 album, *The Heart of the Matter*. *(Photograph Peter C. Borsari/© Borsari Images)*

Everybody except Brody seemed to enjoy Disney on Ice (L to R: Brandon, Mickey Mouse, me, Brody, Donald Duck, Burt, and Bruce).
(Photograph Peter C. Borsari/© Borsari Images)

We took these
photos for our
Christmas card
in 1984.
The card read:
"Merry Christmas,
Malibu Style."

I took this photo of Bruce in a wet suit when we lived on Las Flores Beach, known locally as Dog Beach.

This photo was taken after we had separated but still appeared together, and Bruce had begun his transition.

(Photograph Peter C. Borsari/© Borsari Images)

Brandon, Brody, and I looked forward to rare rainy days in Malibu so we could bake cookies together. It was our tradition.

With Brandon and Brody at the Malibu Racquet Club.

(Photograph © Linda Conrad)

Our blended family (L to R: our nanny Allison, Brandon, Erin, Brody, David, Sara, and Jordan; I'm on the bottom).

The boys were only four and six in this photo taken with David and me after Brandon's Little League game. *(Photograph Peter C. Borsari/© Borsari Images)*

David and I got married on June 22, 1991, on a gorgeous bluff overlooking the Pacific Ocean in Hope Ranch.

(Photographs courtesy of Essam and Layla Khashoggi)

Kicking back on David's boat
(L to R: me, Barbra Streisand,
David, Richard Baskin).

Barbra Streisand has always
been a dear friend; here we are
celebrating her birthday together.

With a very young Céline Dion, shortly after
David and I discovered her in Montreal.
(Photograph Peter C. Borsari/© Borsari Images)

Back in 2002 on
the twenty-fifth
anniversary of
Elvis's death, I
did my first-ever
interview about
Elvis with
Larry King.

We shot this family photo for publicity for *The Princes of Malibu*.
(Photograph © Heather O'Quinn)

With Brody on our way to a Halloween party at the Playboy Mansion, the very spot where I'd met his father so many years before.

Here I am with Bruce and his first wife, Chrystie, not long after his separation from Kris.

This photo was taken at Brody's birthday party in 2014, shortly before Bruce came out to the world as Caitlyn.

Having a birthday celebration for Brody at my home in August 2015 (L to R: Kaitlynn Carter, Brody, me, Caitlyn, Brian Rapf, and Brandon).

With David in April 2016 at a Mohammed Ali event in Phoenix.

From the moment I first discovered that Bruce identified as a woman, I made every effort to instill compassion and a broad scope of understanding in my sons. I'm so proud of how they've accepted and supported Caitlyn.

Caitlyn stopped by the house for Thanksgiving 2015, one of the first times we were together.

Here I am with Dad when he was living with me and David.

With my Dad and the boys in 1990; my daddy helped to create and shape the person I still am today. I am forever a daddy's girl.

I am in love with being a grandmother—"LaLa"— to the most beautiful baby girl (L to R: Kaitlynn Carter, Brody, Brandon, Eva James, Leah Jenner, and me).

The two boys who continue to humble and inspire me with everything they do.

"Me Loving You"

When you see
A shooting star above you
That's just a kiss
That I'm throwing down to you
After a storm

I'll paint a rainbow on a sky of blue
Be still, and feel me loving you

When the moon
Is smiling through a halo
Never doubt
When your deepest wish comes true
You'll feel me close
A presence there forever by your side
You'll see, that's just me, loving you

And sometimes when you dream
Does it ever truly seem
I'm lying there beside you while you
  sleep
'Cause I never really left
And you're never by yourself
My love keeps on beating in your
  heart

In the night
The darkness will enfold you
But don't be afraid
Rest assured I'm holding you
Let others say

It's just your imagination—know
  what's true
Be still, and feel me loving you

And sometimes when you dream
Does it ever truly seem
I'm lying there beside you while you
  sleep
'Cause I never really left
And you're never by yourself
My love keeps on beating in your
  heart

When you're tired
And holding on to nothing
Velvet nights
That your tears all melt into
Only love remains
A gentle breeze will whisper out
  your name
Be still . . . and feel me loving you

LYRIC: LINDA THOMSON

Chapter Thirteen

Gold Medal Love

The year before Elvis died, on a hot July Memphis night in 1976, Elvis and I were watching the Summer Olympics, being held in Montreal. We were lying in bed (our usual perch) and had been watching the telecast for days. We were closely following Bruce Jenner, an American who was dominating the decathlon competition. Bruce was on the final lap of his last race, the tenth event, and as he crossed the finish line to win the title of "World's Greatest Athlete" that connotes the Olympic gold medalist in the Decathlon, Elvis and I were exuberant about the win for the United States. We were also commenting on what an amazing specimen of a man Bruce Jenner was.

We watched as Bruce ran the victory lap around the track with his Olympic-size arms stretched gloriously above his handsome head.

"Damn, if that guy is not handsome!" Elvis remarked. "I'm not gay, but damn, he's good looking!"

I quite agreed.

"Wow . . . he *is* gorgeous!" I teasingly said. "I'm going to marry that guy someday!"

"Yeah, honey . . . over my dead body," Elvis replied.

File that conversation under the category of "truth is stranger than fiction," and "words have power."

I first met Bruce Jenner at a celebrity tennis tournament in the spring of 1979. In the years since Elvis's passing, I had split my time between Los Angeles, Memphis, where I maintained my residence, and Nashville, where I'd fly in to tape *Hee Haw* for a month, twice a year. While in Nashville, I'd spent some time with David Briggs, but our bond never deepened beyond a casual relationship that was based more on friendship than romantic passion. I had earnestly begun the process of rebuilding myself on the inside after emerging from my Elvis cocoon, and I was more interested in enjoying my newfound independence than instantly getting into another serious relationship.

Although I inconsequentially dated a few nice men when I was in Los Angeles, simply going out on dinner dates, I spent a great deal of time with my girlfriends, going to the gym, writing, and traveling. I went to Europe for the first time, hitting the highlights of eleven countries while I was there. Traveling was an eye-opening experience for me, since I had never ventured far beyond the United States. I even climbed to the top of the ancient Pyramid of the Sun in Teotihua-can, outside Mexico City. I was finally free to pursue some of my own dreams and aspirations, and to allow myself the luxury of time and self-carved experience to let my priorities and goals evolve. My mind and heart were not on a quest to find romance. It was a time for my broken heart to heal enough to even be receptive to another love.

It was gratifying to find myself thriving as an independent working actress and model, almost as if I were working from the post-college itinerary I'd had planned for myself before I met Elvis. My acting career was as consuming as I wanted it to be at the time, since I was never what could be described as overly ambitious. I wanted enough time to "stop and smell the roses" all along my life's path. I still make that a priority. But the connection Elvis had forged for me with Aaron Spell-ing helped immensely and sometimes made me feel like Elvis was still looking out for me from beyond. Having been true to his promise to assist me, Aaron had seen to it that my next role was on his show, *Starsky & Hutch*, on an episode that aired in September 1977. I would go on to appear several times on his series *Vegas* over the next few years, as well as on his many other productions. I also continued exploring the possibilities of my blossoming songwriting career, finding other composers along the way with whom to collaborate.

But while I loved my life, by the spring of 1979 I was ready for the next chapter to unfold. I'd healed the double heartbreak of losing Elvis to our breakup, and then to his death. I'd learned to stand on my own. I had replenished, restored, and reestablished who I was at my core, and how I wanted to continue to grow as a person in this world. And now I was poised to find a partner with whom to forge a future.

It was in that moment that I met Bruce Jenner. A charity tennis tournament was being held at the Playboy Mansion. I had never been to the mansion before, but as a regular cast member on *Hee Haw* and a fledgling actress of some note, I'd grown comfortable in the L.A. scene. On the day I met Bruce, I'd been invited to the mansion to hand out the trophies to the participants playing tennis. No surprise, Bruce won the tournament, and I presented him with his trophy. That's how we first met—on a tennis court.

Bruce was clad in shorts and a sweaty T-shirt, his well-toned, muscular body still in Olympic form. He was sweet, shy, and very gentlemanly. In fact, I was a little surprised to find him so humble and down-to-earth. The main image of him in my mind up to that point was his triumphant victory lap at the 1976 Summer Olympics—that iconic image indelibly etched in the minds of all those who saw his remarkable triumph. We sometimes have a tendency to attribute qualities to celebrated individuals in a way that is akin to putting them on a pedestal, while not allowing them to exhibit human qualities. I'd never seen Bruce interviewed on TV, and I didn't know much about what he'd been up to since the Olympics, except for having come face-to-face with him on the cover of my Wheaties box. And so, having no knowledge of his vibrant career as a motivational speaker, I had no reason to expect he'd be so articulate, even funny, in an understated, boyish way. Having grown up around Southern gentlemen, with their proper manners and easy charm, I found myself responding to these same qualities in Bruce, even if he wasn't a Southerner himself.

"Do you come to the Playboy Mansion often?" he asked.

"Oh gosh, no!" I said. "I've never even been here before!"

I don't want to give him the wrong impression, I thought. *I don't want him to think I'm an aspiring Playmate!*

His friendliness became a little flirty, until I finally grew uncomfortable.

"Hey, aren't you married?!" I said. "I watched you win the Olympics, and I recall your wife was very present!"

Bruce's whole demeanor changed.

"No, I'm separated, and it's really not a lot of fun," he responded sadly. "I've actually been living part-time here at the mansion."

He seemed so childlike and lost in that moment—my heart went out to him.

"I'm sorry to hear about your separation," I said.

We continued to chat for a while, still on the court.

"Chrystie packed up her things one day while I was away," he said. "When I got home, I found her closet empty. She had taken our eight-month-old son, Burt, with her to San Jose. I was surprised and devastated by her decision to leave."

"I am very sorry to hear that," I said.

Everyone at the event was reconvening for dinner after tennis, and Bruce had planned to go home, shower, and change his clothes before returning. But instead, he just kept hanging around.

"I really don't want to leave you alone here even for a little while," he finally explained. "I've seen how George Peppard and others are looking at you and just waiting for me to leave so they can hit on you."

I thought how charming and gallant that was. Bruce stayed in his shorts and T-shirt, while others were dressed for dinner, and he and I continued to get to know each other. After dinner, he didn't seem quite ready for the night to be over.

"Can I come back with you and just visit for a while?" he asked.

"Sure," I said.

He joined me at my apartment, sitting with me on the sofa to continue our conversation. My high school girlfriend, Eileena Stoval, had moved in with me by then. She walked into the room and stopped short, unable to mask her bewildered expression.

"Can you come back here for a second?" she said.

"Excuse me," I said to Bruce, standing and smoothing my skirt as I followed her out of the room and down the hallway to her bedroom.

"What's Bruce Jenner doing in our living room?" she said.

"I know, right?" I said. "He's separated from his wife."

"Oh my God, he is so hot," she said, as excited as a teenage girl.

Still laughing, I went back into the living room, where Bruce and I visited for a bit longer. But that's all we did. We just talked. There was no making out, nothing improper. He was very bashful, which again made me enjoy his company all the more, as he seemed to be a genuinely nice guy. Finally, after getting to know a little more about each other, we were both growing sleepy, and it was clearly the moment for him to leave.

"I'd love to take you out properly," he said.

"That sounds great," I said.

"Maybe I could take you out to dinner tomorrow night then?" he suggested.

And so, the next night, Bruce arrived precisely on time, walked me out to his white Porsche, opening doors along the way for me. As we arrived at the restaurant and settled into our table, I couldn't help but appreciate the fact that this was exactly the kind of normal dating experience I'd dreamed of when I'd left Elvis. Sure, Bruce was a famous public figure, but he was able to go out to dinner without attracting an impossible amount of attention. And here we were, enjoying the kind of quiet night out that young men and women everywhere shared. After everything I'd been through, this everyday experience felt more special to me than being whisked up to the Presidential Suite or onto a private jet. It was as normal as being out to dinner with the world's greatest athlete can be.

At dinner, after exchanging some pleasantries, I grew a bit serious.

"What do you honestly think the chances are of your getting back together with your wife?" I asked.

"I really don't know . . . maybe fifty-fifty," he said with what I believe was complete transparency. I genuinely respected his integrity in not leading me on with some dishonest answer that he might have assumed I wanted to hear. There was no game playing from the very beginning. At least none that I knew of then.

"I appreciate your honesty," I said, responding in kind. "And I must tell you that if there is a chance you might get back together with your wife, I will be your friend. We can go out to dinner, movies—whatever—but I don't want to confuse the issue by getting involved with you romantically. Until you know for sure there is absolutely no chance of reconciliation, I won't have sex with you."

Bruce was understanding, and he honored that restraint of mine as we began spending time together. During the several months of uncertainty that followed, I even gave him a couple of pro-marriage books. I really tried to help him make a well-thought-out decision as to the fate of his marriage.

One day, Bruce called me.

"Chrystie wants to come back home and try again."

"You should make that effort so you'll never have any regrets," I said.

Bruce and Chrystie did indeed get back together, during which time I did not see or speak to Bruce. I did think of him occasionally and sometimes wistfully. He was such a great guy, a gentleman, a gorgeous man. More than all that, he was refreshingly down-to-earth, even with his elite accomplishments and worldwide fame. He was up front about what he wanted and how he felt, and he made it clear in his words and deeds that he respected where I was at in my own life. When he had something to say, he spoke plainly and from the heart, and when it was his turn to listen, he did so attentively. He seemed like the kind of man I could start a family with, the kind of man who had been quite elusive in my life until then. But I reconciled in my mind and heart that it was truly for the best that he and Chrystie were trying to salvage their marriage.

Several months later, I was in Memphis, having just left Nashville, where I'd finished taping thirteen episodes of *Hee Haw*, when I got a phone call from Bruce.

"Hey!" he whined in that distinct voice of his. "It's Bruce Jenner. How the heck are you?"

"Wow . . . great, Bruce. How have you been? Where are you?"

"I'm in L.A., and I've got some good news and some bad news for you."

"Oh . . . okay," I said. "Better give me the good news first then."

"Well, the good news, for us anyway, is that things didn't work out with Chrystie, so I am separated and gonna get a divorce," Bruce declared. "She left me again!"

"I'm sorry to hear that, Bruce, but you should feel good about the effort you made, and now you know with more certainty."

I respected the fact that Bruce had apparently given his marriage every effort, and I was genuinely under the impression that he had. I have to admit that as sorry as I was to hear of another end to a per-ceived fairy-tale romance, I was a bit grateful that such a good man still existed in the world of dating. I was encouraged that he and I could now resume our friendship and see where it led. *At least they tried*, I thought, *and according to him, it was she who had left him. Again. Twice now.*

"Okay, so what's the bad news?" I asked.

"Chrystie apparently had a plan that I was unaware of. I think the reason she wanted to reconcile was to get pregnant," he said. "She's pregnant."

That's how Bruce explained the situation. At this time, I had not yet met Chrystie, so I only had the very one-sided information Bruce relayed to me.

My heart sank.

I felt a jumble of emotions. The overriding one was a rather power-ful sense of responsibility for encouraging Bruce to reconcile. And now this. Chrystie was pregnant. It was a seemingly huge complication for all of our lives. But Bruce appeared to be quite clear about Chrystie's resolve, and about what he wanted.

"Can I pick you up at the airport when you come back into L.A. from Memphis?" Bruce asked me.

"No, that's not a good idea," I said. "Let me think about all this, and I'll get in touch with you when I'm back in a couple of days."

I spent the next several days contemplating what to do. It was obvi-ously a decision I couldn't take lightly. I knew it would be controversial, even in my own mind. But I felt I had been through so many challenges in my life already, so many unusual circumstances and scenarios—this would be just one more. As far as I could tell, looking on from the out-side, Bruce had fully committed himself to marriage and fatherhood, and he had been a faithful, supportive partner and a present father.

I already knew I could never really understand the inner functioning of his relationship with Chrystie, but from my perspective, he seemed to have done everything in his power to make their union work. During the brief time we'd previously spent together, he'd shown himself to be attentive and reliable, and he didn't seem to have any urge to play the field or avoid commitment now. Even with his complicated family situation, I viewed him as an exceptionally promising potential life partner, especially because our temperaments seemed to be so well matched and we shared the same basic principles. And although we'd never acted on our attraction for each other, it was strong and mutual.

I also felt somewhat responsible for encouraging Bruce to go back to Chrystie—with that reconciliation resulting in the situation in which they now found themselves. It sounds like convoluted reasoning to me now, but with Southern Baptist guilt mixed into the equation, that's how I felt at the time. Ultimately I decided that I would see Bruce again, resolving to be understanding about the strange situation we found ourselves in and to look for the silver lining that is almost always present.

I felt tremendous compassion for Chrystie having to go through a pregnancy without the emotional and physical support of the baby's father. Little did he know that baby would turn out to be a most phenomenal woman, without whom none of us could imagine our lives. But I'm getting ahead of my story.

Bruce and I eventually went out to dinner and discussed the situation. I could see that he was upset by the whole predicament. He couldn't help but wonder how his life and future would be affected by this turn of events. I couldn't help but wonder how my life and future might be affected, too. It was certainly a complex situation, and one that would necessarily impact his next relationship. To his credit, at the time he seemed committed to remain in his children's lives, and I wouldn't have wanted to be with a man who would have chosen otherwise. There was a candor in the way Bruce assessed the situation and stated his emotions that made the complications seem less insurmountable.

Here was a man who was sharing with me the truth of his messy life, and the truth that was in his heart. The easy frankness between us made me feel like we might eventually become real partners. Having left behind the heady romance of my fairy tale with Elvis, I had entered into a much more practical time in my life. Not that love and poetry weren't important to me. I happen to be a natural romantic, and an inborn poet, and I sought out such elevated qualities now as well. But I also wanted to build something tangible, a happy marriage and family. I understood innately that to do so would require communication, mutual respect, and trust, all of which Bruce was in the process of building with me now.

Rather than scaring me away with his openness and his raw emotions, he was demonstrating himself to be just the kind of partner that might be worth navigating the mess for—and with—and I left our conversation that night feeling hopeful. We were still in the early stages of getting to know each other, but we agreed that we both wanted to explore this new relationship, as well as the feelings that were blossoming on both sides.

Against all odds, Bruce and I grew closer and established a committed and loving relationship. We dated, trying to stay respectfully "under the radar" and not be blatant about our romance. We traveled some together, weathering a storm of gossip and conjecture about how and when we met . . . and trying to counter some people's perceived notion that "Bruce left his long-suffering wife for Elvis's ex-love." That's not by any stretch of the imagination how it really unfolded. But there is no denying it was an uncomfortable situation. The only solace I felt was in knowing that Chrystie did in fact leave Bruce, not the other way around. And I hoped she was happy being blessed with another baby in her future. We were all presented with the challenge of getting past the very unorthodox beginnings of our romance and our growing extended family.

The whole ordeal was painful to me because I'd always tried to remain above the fray of drama, but in the end, I just had to reconcile myself to the fact that life is messy. In fact, that could be another title for this memoir—*Life Is Messy*. Through this experience, I learned not to judge people, ever. As I well know from my own personal life, whatever someone may be going through can often be interpreted much differently by others. More important, I learned to simply trust life.

Destiny finds its own path. Looking back, there isn't anything I would change, because the difficult circumstances then brought about the joy we can share today, and the beautiful blended family with whom we are blessed.

Bruce was a romantic, thoughtful guy—the type of man to send flowers and to remember anniversaries with flowers, gifts, and a card. He liked to wine and dine me, although we didn't really drink wine, so mostly he just dined me. Part of Bruce's training had been to eat pasta the night before a big meet to store up all those carbs, and he still loved to go out and eat pasta.

Bruce quickly set me straight about healthy eating habits with an adage he adhered to himself and often repeated to others: "I eat to live," he said. "I don't live to eat." Not only was this a great line that got me thinking about my own relationship to food, but I also witnessed him putting his philosophy into action. I can remember being out to dinner with him one night when I was pushing my way through an oversize portion of pasta, even though I'd already exclaimed how full I was. Like a faithful Southerner, I loved good food, and I had grown up without a lot, so I couldn't bear the thought of wasting anything. I was one of those people who, when they go out to eat, often think, *Oh, should I take this home or should I just finish it here because there's starving people in the world? I feel too guilty to leave this on my plate.* On this night, Bruce had left some of his food uneaten, as he often did.

"Bruce, how can you do that in good conscience?" I said. "There are so many starving people in the world."

"Honey, this is the way you've got to look at it," he said. "That's either going to be garbage in a can somewhere, or it's going to be garbage in your body. If it's garbage in your body, it's going to turn to fat and toxicity and slow you down. It's unhealthy and it's going to make you sluggish. Would you rather throw garbage in your body, or throw it in the can, where it's not going to do you any harm?"

"You're absolutely right," I said.

I put down my fork. It was a revelation to me, and from then on, my relationship with food changed. I'd grown up on country-fried everything, from fried chicken to fried catfish, and then I'd become a bit of a foodie, but I began to frequently think of Bruce's admonishment to not treat the body like a garbage disposal. I started adhering to that approach every time I went out, splitting entrees and dishes as much as I could, something that continues to this day. And if there was food left on my plate, I stopped myself before being stuffed to the point of discomfort. There were many other healthy habits I learned from Bruce. While I already exercised fairly regularly, I had to pick up the pace to stay in step with him, so I began incorporating exercise into my daily routine.

I find it so valuable to be able to look back on a past relationship and acknowledge: I've learned so much from that person, just as I hope that person will be cognizant of lessons I may have imparted to him during our time together. After all, I feel that's why we are here, to help each other grow and learn along the way, as our paths intersect in life. Elvis had already brought a great deal to my existence. And now, here was Bruce, adding even more, inspiring me to tackle each new day with as much exuberance as he applied to every moment of his experience.

In nearly every way our relationship felt like the opposite of my life with Elvis. Instead of staying in and watching TV, Bruce and I were constantly on the move—indeed, there were many thrills and spills dating Bruce. He made a good living from his sponsorships by such brands as Wheaties, London Fog, and Minolta cameras. He did infomercials, had a contract with NBC Sports, and was an in-demand motivational speaker who gave talks all over the world. We even did an exercise video together. As a hobby, he raced cars. Not long into our relationship, he took me to the twenty-four-hour race at Daytona Beach, Florida. I ended up getting sick because I was up all night to be there for him as he completed the course. Even though the race was in the Sunshine State, at that time it was cold outside, and I was freezing and on my feet for hours. I was used to being up all night with Elvis, watching TV, but now I was seeing the dawn with Bruce so he could race cars. During that event, one of the engines exploded and oil went all over his windshield, almost causing him to crash. My heart was in my throat the whole time. It didn't at all alleviate my fear that his racing suit was labeled with his name, Jenner, and his blood type, B positive.

"I'm really worried about this," I often said to Bruce.

"Oh, it's perfectly safe," he responded, casual as could be.

"If it's such a safe sport, then why is your blood type on your suit?" I asked.

He didn't have a good answer for that. But even though I was sometimes worried about Bruce's adrenaline-junky side, he was so highly skilled at everything he did, even at the highest speeds, that it was difficult for me to imagine any real harm befalling him. And I could easily comprehend how someone as driven as he was would constantly need to set the bar higher in all-new attempts to challenge himself. Elvis definitely had a self-destructive side, and I couldn't help but wonder if Bruce's tendency to want to go faster, higher, harder was any indication that he, too, had such a streak. Elvis had often engaged in risky behaviors on the spur of the moment, almost like a little boy who couldn't resist the adventure. Bruce had a remarkable natural athleticism but still pushed the envelope when it came to what most of us would call dangerous activities.

I was seeing the world through the rosy lens of love, as we do when we're really falling for someone we're dating. I wanted to do things for Bruce to show him my appreciation and affection. I decided to plan a whole special evening and have him over.

"I want to cook for you," I said.

I knew that he loved pasta, so I made baked stuffed shells. I filled those giant pasta shells with ricotta cheese and covered them with a sauce I'd made. I even put together a pretty little menu that I wrote out with a flourish describing all of the items I would be serving that night. We ate by candlelight in the living room at a big table I had placed in there, and it was quite a lovely evening.

I went on to cook several special meals for Bruce during our years together, but the truth is, I'm not a great cook.

"Honey, don't worry," he said. "That's not the best thing you do."

Instantly, I felt myself relax. I could be at ease with Bruce, bad cooking and all, and he only seemed to like me more. I was so pleased to find that he wasn't at all thrown by life's little bumps in the road. Rather, he was showing himself to be patient and mild-mannered, just the kind of man I'd want to marry and give my future children as a father.

Like Elvis, Bruce never expected a woman to be the picture of domesticity. The more I got to know and love him, the more at ease

I felt. Having gone through so much pain over the past few years, due to my separation from Elvis and the grief caused by his untimely passing, it was wonderful to be happy and in love again with a man who had so much to offer.

Bruce was world famous, handsome, fun, entertaining, and exciting—all qualities I'd also experienced with Elvis. But he was also a great deal lighter in his demeanor and his temperament than Elvis had been. Although Elvis was certainly lighthearted, and amusing, and wonderful in his own way, he'd had his dark side, of course, with his quick temper and mood swings. Having grown accustomed to anticipating and ameliorating the outbursts of both my mother and Elvis, I was good at staying one step ahead of mercurial personalities. But now I no longer had to be so vigilant and diplomatic. It was a relief to stop expending so much energy being another's emotional nursemaid.

Much as Bruce had been direct and open with me during the complex circumstances of our early days together, he remained communicative and flexible. When he needed to travel for his job as an NBC Sports correspondent, or for a speaking engagement, he preferred to have me with him. And he was an easy companion with whom to make plans and travel. But if I had an acting role booked, or a desire to see my family back in Memphis, he was comfortable with me having a life of my own, too. We made all such decisions together, without fanfare, proving that our union did have the potential to be the respectful partnership I'd hoped. It was as if I could exhale now.

But even beyond his disposition, he was just so much more a regular guy with a more predictable, normal life. Sure, Bruce was famous, but not "Elvis famous." And after Elvis famous, Bruce famous seemed fairly natural to me. Neither of us was extravagant in our tastes or habits, and we didn't need much beyond our casual, active life in Malibu. We were happy doing everyday things like heading to the beach and going out to dinner. He traveled often for his motivational speaking, and when I accompanied him, as I regularly did, it allowed us to explore other destinations, too. It was a nice life.

Knowing I had spent years sleeping all day, and staying up all night, and had continued that pattern after Elvis and I broke up, Bruce was happy to welcome me back to the sunshine. Every morning, Bruce would greet the rising sun with a resounding "Good morning! Today is not just another day—it's another day to excel!"

In some ways, Bruce and Elvis were almost like different incarnations of the ideal man. While Elvis was beautiful to look at and listen to, the reality behind his beguiling façade was another story. On the other hand, Bruce hadn't earned the title of "World's Greatest Athlete" for nothing. He set the world on fire. He was confident, and he was pretty much the perfect physical specimen. He took impeccable care of himself.

Unlike Elvis, who had exhibited a very different persona in public than in private, I never saw a crack in Bruce's high-energy, positive veneer. He was never "off," or cranky, or short-tempered with me, except for a few noticeable times during my second pregnancy.

When Bruce and I had first come together, he was made vulnerable by his divorce, which gave me a chance to take on the caregiver role I relished. But even then, Bruce did not truly need all that much care. This minor vulnerability only brought us closer together. It also humanized Bruce and made me understand that he wasn't impenetrable, even if he sometimes seemed that way.

I never really had a reason to doubt Bruce. Maybe, in part, it was because I was naturally much the same—easygoing, motivated, active, family oriented, and positive. When Bruce was traveling, he was always reliable and thoughtful about calling me every day, sometimes multiple times in a day.

Every morning, Bruce and I would take turns getting each other coffee and bring our cups for a walk on the beach while we talked about our feelings and our future. One of the things I loved most about him was how lighthearted he always seemed, and so impossibly optimistic. He was a delightfully easy person to not only spend time with, but to live with as well. Everything felt so natural with him, from jumping in the shower together after a hard game of tennis, to entertaining friends and family, to just listening to music at home.

Bruce was a great coach, teaching me every sport I now enjoy, as well as teaching my nieces how to dive while they were visiting us one summer. He was patient and encouraging. I would be hard-pressed to find very many things to criticize about Bruce early on in our relationship. He added greatly to my happiness and was my treasured best friend for those years. I thought we were the happiest of young couples, that I had found the "normal" I had been searching for.

Bruce and I enjoyed the process of getting to know each other better, which also meant becoming close to each other's families. Whereas Elvis and I shared a Southern upbringing, Bruce had grown up in Tarrytown, New York, which made him a Yankee. But Bruce and I still had a good deal in common in how we'd been raised. Bruce was also from a solid middle-class background, so we were both imbued with good middle-class values. Both Bruce and I had fathers who had served in the army in World War II—his as an Army Ranger, while mine was in an army engineer combat unit under General Patton that advanced ahead of the troops to pave the way and build bridges. His dad was a hard worker who owned his own tree-trimming service. My dad was a truck driver. Both of our moms were housewives.

One area where Bruce and I did differ was religion. While my faith continued to be extremely important to me, he was basically an agnostic. I think Bruce is a believer now, but during our time together, faith was not a part of who he was. Although he was not what you might term a Christian, or even someone who believed in God, I saw him as a truly spiritual person because he led such an exemplary life.

When Bruce and I were back in Memphis together, someone I knew there brought up Bruce's lack of religious belief, in a conversation with just me. I made sure they knew the real man he was, and the great value I saw in Bruce's way of being.

"Well, you know Bruce says he's not sure he believes in God," this person said.

"Maybe not, but he lives it," I said. "He just lives it. So I think that's more important than professing to believe in Christ's teachings, and in God, when you behave quite the opposite. Because then you're a hypocrite. At least Bruce lives it."

Whether Bruce believed in God or not, in my view he exemplified what godly teachings would instruct us all to do: treat each other with kindness, compassion, and integrity. So, even though we didn't have the same spiritual connection that Elvis and I felt, I still felt like Bruce and I were well matched in this respect.

Bruce and I used to joke that we both got our degrees from Graceland: I earned a PhD in life from Graceland in Memphis, and he got his bachelor's degree at Graceland College in Iowa. So we had those points of reference to entertain our sense of irony. And as for my Southern colloquialisms and Southern way of thinking and being, he adapted quite easily. He came to visit Memphis often and even guest-starred on *Hee Haw* in Nashville with me on many occasions. He could get down and hokey with the best of them. Plus, he liked to sing and dance, and was skilled at both, so he was happy to jump into the cornfield and do jokes or sing a song. He was incredibly supportive of my career and was not at all threatened by it.

As my feelings for Bruce deepened, one of the greatest revelations was how comfortable I was being myself around him. His easygoing attitude and relaxed demeanor put me at ease from an early point in our relationship—he encouraged me to be the person that I'd blossomed into ever since I'd left Elvis. I had learned a thing or two in my years of willing subjugation to a king. I knew I had a tendency to be a little more submissive—make that a lot more submissive—than my mother had been in her marriage to my father. But I'd also discovered that there is great strength in tenderness—as Elvis used to say, "Never mistake my kindness for weakness." I didn't mind playing my part in the background, behind my more famous partners. I never had the ambition or the desire to be the center of attention. That being said, I never took kindly to being casually disregarded, either. There always has to be a healthy balance. Luckily, Bruce was always very respectful and caring, so I didn't have to go out of my way to assert my growing independence and sense of self around him. I could just be that self. It felt safe to love him, and to let him love me, as we embarked on our life together.

Bruce was also great about encouraging my songwriting, which I continued to pursue with David Briggs after we were no longer dating, and with a few other songwriters. Bruce was musical. He played a little bit of guitar and took piano lessons. When I recorded demos of the songs I was writing, Bruce was so sweet that he would take my tapes and play the songs in his car. Even though these demos never went anywhere and were never sold to anyone, Bruce knew all the words to all the songs I'd written. He also enjoyed the poems I sometimes wrote for him to commemorate a special occasion, such as his birthday or our anniversary.

As the months flew by, and Chrystie neared her due date, she and Bruce seemed to be smoothly advancing their divorce proceedings. Although I tried to stay out of their business, I was always checking in to see how Chrystie was getting along. She had great support from her mom, her sisters, and her many friends.

Although Bruce often came to Memphis with me, sometimes I traveled there without him to see my family. I was alone at my home in Memphis one night and was awakened abruptly by a phone call from Bruce's father, Bill.

"Well, Bruce has a healthy little baby girl! Chrystie and the baby are fine," he said.

I can't explain how and why I was so thrilled to hear that news. I jumped up out of bed with goose bumps and tears of joy and excitement flowing. As I hung up the phone, I was actually taken aback by my own response: *Really? Why are you are jumping for joy and so happy about this birth?* I acknowledged to myself. *YOUR boyfriend's ex-wife just had HIS baby and you're celebrating?* But I truly was. I couldn't wait to meet and hold this new precious little being, who would become such a treasured part of my life.

It would have been understandable to feel conflicted by the circumstances that surrounded the beginning of my relationship with Bruce, but I knew in my heart that all babies are blessings. I was happy to welcome this baby girl to the world and to my life. And as time reveals all things worth knowing, that gorgeous baby girl, Cassandra Lynn "Casey" Jenner, is one of the most beautiful, intelligent, kind, wonderful women I've ever had the pleasure of knowing. She is a light of love in our family, and I cannot, nor have I ever been able to, imagine my life without her. I am so very grateful that she was born—circumstances be damned.

There were surprisingly few trying or difficult times with such a complicated family situation. I always felt that Chrystie was generous to share her darling children with us and leave them to my care during their regular times with their dad. She also deserves full credit for never trying to turn her children against their father or me.

It certainly helped that all of us were in a good place in our own lives, and that made it easier to be accepting and loving with each other. Chrystie was very content having her two wonderful children close together in age. I was happy in my relationship with Bruce. Chrystie and I always got along and communicated well. I instantly loved Burt and Casey, as I do to this day. I think we all made the best of a challenging, but blessed, state of affairs. I believe life unfolded as it was meant to for all of us.

After Casey was born, I asked Chrystie if she would have lunch with me so we could talk about our intersecting lives. She agreed it was a spectacular idea and we met at the Sand Castle Restaurant, which is now the Paradise Cove Beach Café. We sat in the corner booth for five hours and talked and talked. We both wanted to clear the air and pave the way for a smooth conjoining of our families. I always wanted to include Burt and Casey in everything Bruce and I did and to make sure they felt like a part of the family Bruce and I were beginning to build. And I wanted Chrystie to feel comfortable and a part of that, too. And as it turned out, Chrystie informed me that day that she would like to remarry. She had met and begun dating a wonderful man named Richard Scott, who would become Burt and Casey's stepfather and who essentially raised them. We had a great lunch, and I really felt like we bonded. Chrystie and I have always enjoyed a good relationship, and I love and value her presence in my life. Today we remain very much a family, jokingly calling ourselves "ex-wives-in-law." We even have family gatherings on Thanksgiving and Christmas, most often at my house.

Things might have been messy at the start of my relationship with Bruce, but it was quickly becoming the best kind of mess I could have imagined.

"You Are My Solid Ground"

When you're lying tenderly
  beside me
And I feel your breath so soft
  against my cheek
All my fears just disappear in
  darkness
And I know for sure
I could never leave

You are the strength that I've found
  to see
You lift me up when I'm down—
  loving me
When I never thought
That I'd feel my heart come around
You are my solid ground

I don't need a fairy tale to save me
I've got all the magic I need in your
  arms
And I won't ever fly away in
  madness
I'll stay close enough to always feel
  your warmth

You are the strength that I've found
  to see
You lift me up when I'm down—
  loving me
When I never thought
That I'd feel my heart come around
You are my solid ground

I'm . . . so in love with you
You're everything faithful and true
I know—I could touch every star
When you're lifting me
And I'm right there where you are

You are the strength that I've found
  to see
You lift me up when I'm down—
  loving me
When I never thought
That I'd feel my heart come around
You are my solid ground

You are my solid ground

LYRIC: LINDA THOMPSON

Chapter Fourteen

A Model Family

With the tensions that had marked the beginning of our love safely passed, Bruce and I were able to enjoy life as we hadn't before. Our love had been tested and we had made it through together.

In the spring of 1980, Bruce and I traveled to Australia to promote *Can't Stop the Music*, a film he'd starred in with the Village People. Allan Carr had produced the movie and we became fast friends. Allan was very flamboyant, funny, creative, and generous. He insisted that on our return trip from Australia, he wanted to treat Bruce and me to a "pre-honeymoon" of four days on the gorgeous Tahitian island of Bora Bora.

Bruce and I had a relaxing, romantic time in that enchanting place. We stayed in one of those thatch-roofed, over-the-water huts, so that we could just step off of our deck into the crystal clear water and be swimming with multicolored fish in an instant. At night we lay under the stars and talked about our future and the magical quality of the universe in which we lived.

Bruce and I made quite an ideal couple in those days. We got along well and enjoyed many of the same activities, that is, once he'd taught me how to play the sports he liked. It's fair to say that Bruce unleashed the natural athlete in me, teaching me how to Jet Ski, water-ski, snow ski, play tennis, work out regularly, and basically to lose my fear of getting my hair wet and opening my eyes underwater. Well, I might be exaggerating about the losing-my-fear part, and opening my eyes underwater. But I was glad to have such a good coach. Under his instruction, I became a pretty good tennis player. Our neighbors Linda and David Caplan had a court they let us use. They even let us have a gate put in so we could go up and use their court whenever they weren't using it. We were also members of the Malibu Racquet Club and played there all the time.

Bruce took me to Alta, Utah, to teach me skiing on the slopes. He was so patient, and so kind. He did push (he *was* Bruce Jenner after all), but in a way that was very encouraging.

"Your ability exceeds your confidence level," he always told me.

That was and wasn't true. I had developed some ability on my skis, but I still didn't know how to stop. One day, early on in our lessons, Bruce and I were out skiing together. I was wearing my little orange fiberfill snowsuit, just flying down the hill.

"Turn! Turn! Turn!" Bruce shouted from where he was skiing close behind me.

I don't know how to turn, I thought.

"Slow down!" he said. "Okay, you need to stop."

Okay, and how would one do that? I thought, fearfully examining the tree I was nearing. *How would a person do that if they did want to stop before they hit that tree up ahead?*

I tried to make the turn and ended up in a big snowbank by the tree. I was lucky I didn't hurt myself, even though I ended up by the tree trunk, my skis sticking up in the air. One of the tree branches had ripped my snowsuit, so I had fiberfill coming out of it. I was a mess. I looked up, and there was Bruce, coming down the hill like the Olympic athlete he was.

Swish, swish, swish.

Perfect form.

Snow flew up in my face as he stopped right beside me.

"You okay?" he asked, looking down at my crumpled body.

"I don't think anything is broken but my pride is terribly hurt,"

I said. "Look at my snowsuit. I've got Bruce Jenner, the amazing athlete, teaching me to ski, and here I am, in a heap on the ground."

He did eventually teach me to ski, and we had fun during our lessons, too. He was the kind of boyfriend who helped me into my ski boots, and he carried my skis for me, too.

"Can you carry the poles?" he'd ask.

"Of course!" I'd reply.

When we were done skiing for the day, he got down on the ground in front of me and helped me out of my boots. And then he rubbed my feet.

He was such a gentleman.

Of course, there were a few occasions when he wasn't entirely patient with me. But it was only because he was so skilled at everything he did.

"Really? You can't do that?" he might ask me during one of our lessons.

Really, Bruce, no one but you can do that, I'd think.

In general though, he was a phenomenal teacher. I'm just sorry that our boys didn't get to experience that side of his personality and athleticism, because by the time they were old enough to start playing tennis and other sports, he had moved on.

Indeed, the Bruce I knew back then was unstudied, casual, and comfortable in his own skin. Or so it seemed. He seemed to excel in every sport he tried—he could have been a professional anything. Just as I had felt that Elvis could fix anything, including me, if I got broken, I felt so safe with Bruce that I never feared getting broken in the first place.

Bruce and I had talked about marriage, family, and our mutual desire to have children together; we knew we shared the same basic values in this area. Bruce was a very decent man who loved the traditional idea of home and hearth. And our relationship was naturally unfolding at a pace we both felt comfortable with. We didn't have to fight about—or even negotiate, really—those issues that sometimes become snafus for other couples: how much time we spent together, how committed we were to each other.

Having enjoyed many hours with Elvis, discussing religion and philosophy and the meaning of love and life, I definitely noticed that Bruce did not seem to engage with these topics in quite the same way. But he wasn't an artist—he was an athlete. And as such, he seemed to be wired differently, to be less meditative and more practical, results oriented, and driven. He did speak very poignantly about all that had gone into his Olympic glory—the irrepressible drive, the years of sacrifice, the constant striving to be better and then, even better still. As well as the immeasurably sweet moment he'd stood on the winner's platform in Montreal, living his dream of gold and basking in the glory he'd earned for himself, taking mental snapshots so he would never forget the experience.

I knew Bruce was capable of deep passion and emotion, but he was more of a doer than a thinker. This is not to say he was in any way shallow, just that he seemed to be most comfortable in motion. We didn't spend a lot of time in the morning, planning our day, or at night, reflecting on what had happened. We simply embarked on the adventure together, and much of the communication we had was about what was happening in the moment. And how it might happen just a little bit better, as Bruce never lost his urge to improve himself.

After years of being sequestered at the Las Vegas Hilton and Graceland, I was happy to feel young and strong in my body, in the sun, on the beach, playing sports, making love, and just sharing everyday life with this beautiful man.

Although I had managed to keep our relationship platonic until after he and Chrystie were clearly finished as a couple, there had been a strong physical attraction between us from the first moment we met. At that time, Bruce was masculine, virile, and strong, no matter what internal battles might have been raging. I never got the sense he was masquerading in any way or hiding a deep secret.

Bruce did so many kind and thoughtful things for me in our years together. He was also generous, at one point buying me a Porsche 928, topped with a big red bow for Christmas. I'm not exactly a car person, but there are a few cars I've really responded to, and as Bruce knew, this was one of them.

That May, I turned thirty just as Bruce and I were returning from traveling to one of his appearances. When we arrived home from the airport and rounded the corner onto the deck outside our beach-front home, I suddenly encountered my mother and father, brother and sister-in-law, and several friends, including motocross racer Jimmy Weinert and his girlfriend at the time, Patty.

"Surprise!" they shouted when they saw me.

Bruce had planned a little surprise birthday for me and flown in my family. He'd hired a caterer that made paella. We had a big party right there on the beach and had a great time.

That was typical of the thoughtful things Bruce did for me. From the start, he was honorable, energetic, patient, and all around . . . well . . . just too good to be true. Yes, just too good to be true indeed! In fact, when I introduced Bruce to my good friends Kenny and Marianne Rogers, wanting their approval of my new love, Kenny spoke more prescient words than any of us could have ever realized at the time.

"Either Bruce Jenner is the nicest person in the world or the biggest phony," he said.

At the time, of course, I just laughed at Kenny, having no way of knowing how true his observation would prove.

It was during this blissful period in our relationship that I found myself pregnant for the first time in my life. When I got the news, I fell to my knees with joy and prayed that I would be worthy to carry that precious life—to be the vessel for this new life that would enter the world. It is a feeling I'll never forget. In that moment I felt as if anything negative that had transpired in my life, any transgression I had ever perpetrated had somehow been cleansed from my being, and that this was a new start. Above all, I was delirious with delight.

Now I just had to tell Bruce. As I've said, he and I had talked openly and often about marriage and children. He knew my strong desire to be a mother and believed I would be a great mom. If he had been somewhat reserved about Chrystie's second pregnancy, it was because of where they were at as a couple, not because he had any resistance to being a father again. In fact, he looked forward to having more kids.

However, his divorce was not yet final, so our timing could have been a bit tidier. But I was confident that Bruce would share my sheer and utter joy at the news—he and I were going to have a baby together.

When were alone together later that day, I couldn't contain my excitement and happiness any longer. I wanted to share our blessing with him. I had been living near the Mormon temple in West L.A., but I had recently moved in with Bruce to a small apartment on Las Flores Beach in Malibu. As we sat on the little love seat in our apartment looking out over the blue Pacific, I said, "I have something to tell you. I'm pregnant!"

"You are? That's great! I'm thrilled," he said, his trademark enthusiasm instantly going full throttle. "I'm so excited. Let's get married then."

"Okay," I said. "We have to work that out, though, because you're still technically, legally married."

So the only negative in the situation was that his divorce could not be finalized until December of that same year. So we would have to wait a few months to get married the following January. Bruce was very loving and reassuring that everything would happen in its appropriate time, and said he was very much looking forward to being a dad again. With Burt and Casey already a joyous addition to our lives, we were going to be the proud parents of three little Jenners.

Not long after I'd given Bruce my baby news in the fall of 1980, we went to pick out my engagement ring. I have always loved estate pieces, and the ring we found was antique from the 1920s. There were three diamonds, two carats each, set in filigree platinum, rather than the customary single-diamond engagement ring configuration.

"You, me, and baby makes three!" I declared, pointing to the three diamonds.

A few days later, Bruce asked me to climb into our Jeep with him, and he drove me up to a beautiful, barren plateau in Malibu accessible only by a dirt road. As the sun set over the ocean, he got down on one knee and pulled out my ring.

"As we look out over Malibu and watch this beautiful sunset together, I'd like to ask you—will you marry me?" he said.

It was a sweet and romantic moment from which to launch our life together.

Bruce and I were married January 5, 1981, when I was just entering my fifth month of pregnancy with our first son, Brandon. We were married at the beautiful home of Allan Carr on the Hawaiian island of Oahu. There were only about thirty-five people in attendance, including our parents. Bruce's son, Burt, served as best man—even though he was only two years old and was constantly interrupting our nuptials with "I want up." It was touching and lent a warm, familial mood to the ceremony. My beloved nieces, Jennifer and Amy Thompson, served as flower girls. It really was quite an exquisitely beautiful wedding. We said our "I dos" at 6 P.M., just as the sun was setting over the placid blue Pacific.

A few months before our wedding, Bruce and I had met the actor Lee Majors. Even though we had not known Lee for very long and only shared a few social dinners with him, he insisted on paying for our wedding. Bruce and I could not believe such a generous and kind gesture. Lee had been heartbroken over Farrah Fawcett's leaving him for Ryan O'Neal in 1979, and he seemed to find comfort in friends at that time. He was, and is, an exceptionally nice man.

I had designed my wedding gown and had it custom made. The gown was off the shoulder with panels of free-flowing vintage cream-colored lace that blew in the tropical breeze. I felt more than a little like Mother Nature herself, with a baby blooming in my belly. Bruce was beyond handsome in his casual suit and was very happy to be celebrating our union, set in paradise and shared with family and a few close friends. Jeannie LeMay, who had been my roommate in the Miss USA pageant, was in attendance with her boyfriend, as well as Bruce's sisters, Pam and Lisa, and brother-in-law, Billy; my brother, Sam, and his wife, Louise, who is my best friend and was my matron of honor.

Bruce was a very secure man, because the music I chose to have playing as I walked down the aisle was Elvis Presley's "Hawaiian Wedding Song." It had always been my dream to get married in Hawaii. It was a dream that had been spawned by Elvis's movie *Blue Hawaii*, which I'd watched over and over as a little girl, and every time I saw it I thought how romantic it would be to get married in that tropical paradise. To Bruce's credit, he went along with my fairy-tale plans for a cinematically inspired wedding at the base of Diamond Head crater on Honolulu's Waikiki Beach, in Allan Carr's Japanese garden at sunset. Only Elvis was missing from my proverbial fairy tale. Still, I had found a new Prince Charming.

When we returned from our wedding trip, we resumed our life by the sea in Southern California, walking on the beach every morning with our coffee, Jet Skiing, playing tennis, or just enjoying each other and many other activities. We lived a pretty idyllic life. He'd take me out sailing on our Hobie Cat, with me flying out on the trapeze, literally hanging out over the ocean. Bruce would sometimes dip the boat down so my butt hit the water, startling me each time.

He knew I was not a great swimmer, and a little more timid than he was, prone to panic, even. He knew me well enough to know and respect my limits, especially during my pregnancy. He didn't want to discourage me from participating in a sport by flipping the boat purposefully, or making me more frightened than necessary. And so I really did trust him, and it was a lot of fun.

Our place had two bedrooms. Sometimes we slept in the bedroom that was right on the water. When the tide came up, I'd lie in bed and watch the waves rise above the deck and kiss the sliding glass door. And then, behind the house, I'd hear the rockslides cascading down toward the beach. It occurred to me that the ocean and the mountains were having a love affair. We were separating them, and they didn't like it much. It was such a romantic time for me that even the elements seemed to be in love. Listening to Bruce sleep beside me, feeling the strength and health exuding from every cell of his body, it was hard not to marvel at how different my life was now, and to feel very happy and lucky to have gotten myself to this moment. I'd drift off to sleep, feeling content, and safe, and very much where I was supposed to be.

We often did laundry and other household chores together. Bruce was not one to define certain tasks as my job because they were "women's work." Instead, he always jumped right in and was happy to help. He never criticized anything I did around the house and was always complimentary and kind.

We never fought, or even argued, really. We only had one small outburst of anger in the six years we were together, and even that was a silly little nonevent. It happened when we were living at the beach, before we bought our house. We were doing laundry together. I was pregnant, and I was walking upstairs with the laundry basket while he came up the stairs behind me. He playfully slapped me on the behind, and although it had been a joke, I was startled and it stung. I had a knee-jerk reaction.

"Don't ever do that!" I yelled.

"Geez, I'm sorry, I was only playing," Bruce said, looking crestfallen.

And that, literally, was just about the only time we ever had the slightest bit of friction between us. We really got along beautifully, and I thought of him as my best friend. I happen to be very even-tempered, and so was Bruce back then. Neither of us was a "drama queen," if you will, and neither of us relished conflict. In that respect, I don't think he was behaving in a way that was contrary to his true nature, in order to keep me from delving deeper and really knowing him. Yes, he had a secret. A big one. And he was pretending to be someone he was not in one major area of his life. But the core of who Bruce was, and is, I believe to be authentically the same.

Yes, I did love Elvis with more abandon. And after Bruce, I did subsequently love David longer. But in some ways, Bruce and I were the most inherently alike (which holds its own irony).

Bruce and I had carved out as a picturesque life together. One of the most rewarding things about the relationship was my ability not to lose myself or give up every part of myself in my relationship. Rather, I now only shared as much of myself as it was healthy to offer. I realized this didn't mean I loved my partner any less; in fact I had come to determine that it was actually a more sustainable way to love. As we are instructed each time we fly, you have to put on your own oxygen mask first, in order to be of any use to yourself or anyone else around you. It's empowering and healthy to know that you can survive without another person. That, for me, is a more mature and healthier way to love another. It takes away nothing from the sheer bliss of romance, or the excitement of embarking on a shared life together, and yet there is no diminishment of your own self-worth and personal power, and no clingy desperation to off-put your beloved.

After our wedding in Hawaii, Bruce and I went house hunting in Malibu. We found a relatively modest home on a small one-acre estate, where I planted roses, fruit trees, and flowers, and where many wonderful, lasting memories were made. My very dear friends Kenny and Marianne Rogers had bought a fourteen-acre estate called "The Knoll" around the same time. So I named our little home "The Knest." Yes, with a *K* for sheer affectation. Bruce and I loved the property because it was so private, and we felt nicely tucked in, as if we were in our own little nest. And so as we settled into our new home, I began setting up my nest in earnest, preparing for the birth of our baby.

While I was pregnant, Bruce made me feel loved and sexy. He was not the kind of man who was turned off by a pregnant woman's body. He thought it was beautiful, and he told me that I was beautiful, caressing me and making me feel that his compliments were based in reality. We continued to make love, and I felt very close to him and supported by him.

Throughout my pregnancy, I felt so healthy and well that I foolishly climbed atop fairly high ladders to hang paintings in the living room. I felt so good I forgot I was pregnant half the time. I played tennis into the ninth month, stopping only a couple of weeks before Brandon was actually born. When I passed a mirror, I was surprised at the image of a pregnant woman I saw. *That's me!*

I think Bruce was a bit blown away by the ease with which my body was preparing itself. When I was pregnant, he even said to me, "This is the most athletic endeavor you will ever undertake. You're going to have to push a baby out, so you want to be in your optimum shape."

He made a point of going to Lamaze classes with me. He did everything the instructor told him to do and was a good sport about it.

"Now, listen, honey," he told me. "When you go through labor, if you want to call me every name in the book, if you want to rip my shirt off, don't even worry about that."

"No, you don't understand," I said. "I don't want to get to that point. If I get to a point where I can get the epidural, I'm going for the epidural. I'm very secure that I'm a woman. I don't need to prove that I can squat in a field and give birth. That's why we have medical science, and fewer fatalities during childbirth in today's more advanced world. But thanks for the offer to call you names and rip your clothes off in anguish. I appreciate that."

I went into labor at four o'clock in the morning. We called my doctor,

Dr. Ed Cohen, and got ready to go the hospital. Around five thirty, Bruce pulled out onto the Pacific Coast Highway to drive us to St. John's Hospital in Santa Monica. I turned my head to look out my window and saw the beautiful gray ocean blending into the gray sky in the early dawn. Every time I see that gray ocean now, I think about our morning drive to the hospital, and the day my darling Brandon was born.

We had a beautiful birthing experience. I was in labor for ten hours and Bruce was in the labor and delivery room with me the whole time. I was able to breathe through some of the major contractions. Bruce was great, very nurturing, kind and gentle, but he was still all guy, and a total jock at that.

"Hey, you're doing good," he said, cheering me on as if he were my coach.

We had a phone available and I frequently called my mother and father, who were in town and waiting in the adjacent waiting room during my labor, to keep them updated on the progress. My mother, in hindsight, was hysterically funny.

"I know you're suffering death right now, aren't you, honey?" she kept saying to me. "You are just praying to die right now, aren't you?"

She was the quintessential Southern drama queen. I must have learned early in life to minimize my reactions, so as not to maximize hers.

Brandon Thompson Jenner was born in the afternoon of June 4, 1981. I thought I knew what love was before giving birth to my baby. But whatever I had experienced in the past paled in comparison to the utter, unconditional love I immediately felt for the little bundle I now held in my arms.

Burt and Casey came to the hospital and got to see and bond with their new little brother, Brandon, born just one year after Casey. Those were very happy days for me. I truly loved Burt and Casey, and Brandon was the absolute sunshine in every day of my life. This newfound motherhood thing seemed to be my natural calling. I recently read that when a mother gives birth, she in actuality gives birth to her own heart. Her heart no longer resides within her being, but is now out there in the world, in the form of her child. That expresses how I felt then and still feel today. My sons are my heart.

I had already practiced mothering on Burt and Casey, since Bruce and I frequently had them stay over at our home, and they were still very young. I knew how to diaper, feed, and lovingly care for little ones, so I felt prepared to be a mommy to Brandon. I loved having this little ready-made family to spend time with and enjoy. When Brandon was born, I planted an avocado seed near our house, and that tree has grown into a fifty-foot giant, bearing delicious fruit.

Just because Bruce and I were now married parents together didn't mean that our lives slowed down any. If anything we were busier than ever.

In many ways our lives followed his job and celebrity. Bruce's contract with NBC Sports meant he had to travel frequently. I had become friends with one of their staffers, Linda Jonsson. I had taken Bruce's last name after we married, so I was Linda Jenner, or LJ West, and she was LJ East. She thought I was great on camera, so she wanted me to travel to Nice, France, to cover the triathlon with Bruce.

Brandon was a year old and I had just stopped nursing him. I wasn't sure about leaving him with a nanny when he was so young, but Bruce really wanted me to go, and it would be a turnaround trip, taking only three days altogether. I always tried to balance being a wife and being a mother the best I could. I wanted to be there for my husband, but motherhood was and still is my number one priority, and the baby came first. It was difficult to be that far away from Brandon, but it was an exciting new challenge that brought Bruce and me closer together. We had a great time, except for my struggle to master French pronunciation on national TV.

"Here we are in the South of France, in Nice," I said. "Where they're better known for their bouill . . . a . . . baisse, not for the triathlon that's about to be held here . . ."

I just could not get the word *bouillabaisse* correct, and we had to do take after take.

Bruce and I also traveled to Toronto to host a show on bodybuilding. I was fascinated by these female athletes, with their ripped muscles, and even subtle beards. I believed some of them were clearly on testosterone. I knew women must have a certain amount of body fat in order to menstruate, and I couldn't resist my urge to ask them if they still had their periods. Most of them didn't have periods because their body fat was so low, something like 5 percent.

As part of the show, Bruce and I had our body fat tested. Although he was good-natured about it, Bruce was being his usual highly competitive self.

"Yeah, just wait and see," he said. "I'm going to kick your butt in this body fat competition."

I smiled good-naturedly, sure he was right. Well, when they did the test, he had something like 20 percent body fat, and I had a mere 16 percent. I couldn't help but indulge in a victory dance all around him because my body fat was actually lower than his.

"Let's see, you're the former world's greatest athlete, is that correct?" I teased him. "And I'm just a wife and mother?"

Much as we had before Brandon's birth, Bruce and I appeared on red carpets regularly and were perceived as a glamour couple, also lending our time to charitable causes. We were the national honorary chairpersons of the Juvenile Diabetes Association and regularly supported the Special Olympics. For several years Bruce and I even hosted our own celebrity tennis tournament benefiting United Cerebral Palsy Children's Foundation. It was called the Bruce and Linda Jenner Love Match.

Bruce's fame opened doors to all kinds of experiences. One day we got a call asking if we would be available to meet President Ronald Reagan in the Oval Office of the White House as the national chairpersons of the Juvenile Diabetes Association. I was still nursing Brandon, and the timetable was "We would need you here in Washington the day after tomorrow." We didn't want to miss the opportunity for an audience with the leader of the free world. I barely had time to find something appropriate to wear, and get on a plane to the White House. It was a quick trip—we were back in Malibu in a matter of hours—but it made for a lasting memory.

With an engaging personality, commanding countenance, and a ready, warm smile, President Reagan immediately put Bruce and me at ease. There is, however, something very daunting about being in the Oval Office, where so much history has transpired, and so many monumental decisions have been made. A keen sense of reverence would certainly not be out of order for anyone who's fortunate enough to enter that room.

And just because we now had Brandon didn't mean that any of Bruce's adventure sports ended, either. He owned a home at Lake Tahoe, and we went there often to snow ski, water-ski, Jet Ski, and participate in other sports and activities. Friends often accompanied us, as well as family. Bruce had an ultralight airplane, which he flew all around Lake Tahoe, until one of his friends crashed it into the lake. Bruce always seemed to be looking for that more highly charged thrill. He was definitely an adrenaline junky. I became something of a jock, too, just by osmosis. I often took the wheel of our boat, so Bruce could water-ski, and there's even video of me piloting our boat while nursing Brandon. Crazy.

Of course, as adept as Bruce was at every sport he attempted, it would have been impossible for such a daredevil not to have a few close calls. As a commentator for NBC *SportsWorld*, Bruce was regularly sent to cover the surfing championships. And so, our family developed an unusual Christmas tradition where we traveled to the north shore of Oahu every December while Bruce did his job. We stayed at the Turtle Bay Hilton and enjoyed wishing each other "Mele Kalikimaka" instead of "Merry Christmas." One time, Bruce took a Jet Ski out in huge surf, and as I stood watching, he suddenly disappeared beneath the epic waves. As I lost sight of him from the beach, I became frantic. Thankfully, someone from the competition jumped on a Jet Ski and rescued him. It turned out that Bruce's Jet Ski had died and sunk. He was fine, but I was rattled by the experience. I trusted Bruce to always be there for our family, and the possibility of him disappearing just like that had terrified me. I was overjoyed to have him back on solid ground with me.

But for all the celebrities and adventure, the red carpets and Oval Offices, it was the quiet moments that I cherished the most—and in truth those are the ones that still resonate all these years later. Bruce was very handy around the house and a skilled builder. He and my daddy very craftily built a storage shed that matched the lines of our home precisely and painted it the same blue as the main house. I still cherish the times when Bruce and I were home together with Brandon, and eventually Brody, being there for each other as a family. I really felt like I had found where I belonged. I looked forward to spending the rest of my life with this man I loved so deeply, who had given me the family that was the purest expression of my heart.

When Brandon was just over a year old, we began discussing how it would be nice for him to have a younger sibling. Bruce had commented that I had gotten myself into great shape, had a good "childbearing body," an easy pregnancy with Brandon, and the timing was right for a second child. I was completely on board for another baby. Bruce was not the most hands-on father, but this was largely because like many new moms, I was happy to bathe and care for my child myself. Mothers immediately respond to an infant, and sometimes fathers want their children to come out at about three or four years old so they can relate to them better. I perhaps became a little overly protective when I saw Bruce unwittingly handle Brandon like a sack of potatoes. Even so, Bruce enjoyed fatherhood and looked forward to the time when the kids were older and could join in our active, outdoorsy lifestyle. As soon as we said, "Let's have another baby," the stars aligned, and within a month or two, I was delighted to be pregnant once more.

Early on in the pregnancy, I was offered a nice part on Spelling's ABC show *The Love Boat*. I'd still been doing some acting, both on *Hee Haw* and other television shows. For a time, I had an old-school talent agent, Meyer Mishkin, who also represented Richard Dreyfuss and Lee Marvin, among others. And I also worked with an agency called the Artists Group. I always preferred comedy. While many people say it's more difficult than drama, I always found it easier and more fun. But I also enjoyed doing Aaron Spelling's shows, my favorite perhaps being *Vegas*. One of my most enjoyable roles involved getting run over by a car. I had to give a dramatic scream. #Emmyconsideration.

Although I again didn't have any morning sickness, I wasn't sure how I'd do on the boat when I was pregnant. But primarily, I didn't want to leave Brandon, who was only eighteen months old. I asked if I could bring him with me, but the producers said he was too young. So I turned down the part. My kids always came before my career.

During the nine months that I was pregnant with Brody, I again enjoyed a model pregnancy, playing tennis into the ninth month and even winning a tennis tournament. Pregnancy agreed with me—I wasn't ever nauseated—not even a single morning, and I gained the recommended textbook twenty-five pounds.

I was two weeks overdue and entering my tenth month of pregnancy when my doctor decided he would induce labor that Sunday morning. Bruce and I went to La Scala restaurant the night before I was to go into the hospital to deliver. There, in the booth next to ours, sat Paul Newman. We had met him on several occasions at different races he and Bruce had participated in. We stopped to say hello, and Paul reached out to rub my round tummy.

"How far along are you?" Paul asked.

"I'm two weeks overdue," I said.

"Are you serious?" he asked, visibly startled.

He quizzed me with his impossibly translucent blue eyes, opened wide.

"You look amazing," he declared, words that would stay with me a lifetime.

It *was* Paul Newman. I joked to Bruce that it would have been like a comedy skit if I had just thrown Paul down in that red leather booth when he touched my stomach and lay on him like a beached whale. We laughed about that imagined scenario.

The next morning, Bruce drove me to St. John's Hospital, and I was given an IV to induce labor. After only a few intense contractions I was sure the baby was in the birth canal. The attendants hurriedly rushed me into the delivery room with me panting and blowing the whole time. They administered an epidural, but not in time for the birth. Sam Brody Jenner entered the world with a loud yelp on the morning of August 21, 1983. He was mighty for his six pounds and seven ounces. I named Brody after my brother, Sam.

They were the most adorable cherubs, from the moment they were born. Every morning, when the boys were small, I'd start their days by addressing them in their cribs, "Good morning, my precious angels."

One morning, when Brandon was only two years old, I was sound asleep on my side of the bed, which was closest to the far wall of our bedroom. I was awakened by something gently touching my cheek.

I opened my eyes and there was Brandon's adorable little face right in front of mine, his eyes staring into mine intently.

"Good morning, my precious angel," he said, mimicking the tone I used with him.

He had climbed out of his crib, walked upstairs, and found me in my bed so he could wake me in the same way I greeted him every morning. Of course, my heart melted at his sweetness. And I was thrilled to see that my boys were absorbing the love and nurturing with which they were showered.

Those were the happiest days of my life. I was married to a wonderful husband, who was a great partner and the most athletic, high-spirited, energetic, easygoing, manly man imaginable. I had two beautiful, healthy baby boys. I had two great stepchildren. Life was just about as good, and as normal, as it gets, which was all I had wanted when I left Graceland and followed my heart out on my own. I had found all I had dreamed of in my life, and I was blissfully happy.

I didn't have a clue what was lurking on the horizon.

"Miracle
Who Could Ever Love You More"

(Every Mother's Lullaby)

You're my life's one miracle
Everything I've done that's good
And you break my heart with
* tenderness*
And I confess it's true
I never knew a love like this 'til you

You're the reason I was born
Now I finally know for sure

And I'm overwhelmed with
* happiness*
So blessed to hold you close
The one that I love most
Though the future has so much for
* you in store*
Who could ever love you more

The nearest thing to heaven
You're my angel from above
Only God creates such perfect love

When you
Smile at me—I cry
And to save your life I'd die
With a romance that is pure in
* heart*
You are my dearest part
Whatever it requires
I'll live for your desires
Forget my own—your needs will
* come before*
Who could ever love you more

There is nothing you could ever do
To make me stop . . . loving you
And every breath I take
Is always for your sake
You'll sleep inside my dreams and
* know for sure*
Who could ever love you more

LYRIC: LINDA THOMPSON

Chapter Fifteen

I Married a Woman

In early 1985, when Brody was about eighteen months old and Brandon was about three and a half, it felt like we had really hit our stride as a family. My first priority was always my boys, and having two little ones now did not afford me as much opportunity to travel with Bruce, as I had before. But he was very understanding about my desire to stay home, and he never gave me the impression that he felt neglected as a husband.

When Bruce was traveling for work, I never worried about our time apart, as I knew he was a faithful and loyal partner. I did miss him, though, and we tried to travel as a family as much as we possibly could. I felt like we had built the foundation for a rich and rewarding shared life, and I couldn't have been happier.

And then Bruce came to me one day with a very somber look on his face.

"There's something about me that I really need to tell you, something you need to know," he said.

I thought he might be about to tell me he'd had an affair while on the road. As it turns out, that would have been the good news. However, his being unfaithful seemed highly unlikely to me, since I truly did trust Bruce implicitly and had always known him to be a devoted, loving husband. But an affair was not what he wanted to confess to me.

"I identify as a woman," he said.

"I'm sorry, what?" I asked. "What do you mean you identify as a woman? What does that even mean?"

"I am a woman trapped in a man's body," Bruce declared.

"Whoa, Bruce, honey, have you looked in a mirror lately?" I protested. "You are not only clearly a man—you are the very epitome of the ideal man!"

"And therein lies my problem," he lamented. "For as long as I can remember, I've looked in the mirror and seen a masculine image staring back at me, where there should have been a feminine reflection. I have lived in the wrong skin, the wrong body, my whole life. It is a living hell for me, and I really feel that I would like to move forward with the process of becoming a woman, the woman I have always been inside."

My immediate, uneducated response was "We have to get into therapy to see if we can fix this!"

Since Bruce publicly transitioned to Caitlyn in 2015, people have asked me, "Were there any signs or clues through the years that Bruce might have had this issue? Any evidence he wore your clothes or exhibited any feminine behavior?"

No. Not a clue. Nothing. Nada. Never.

I would venture to say that thirty years ago, very few of us were adequately educated about the world of gender dysphoria. I certainly wasn't. I was living in my little Malibu cocoon of marital, motherly bliss with my world-champion, muscular, athletic, handsome husband, and my two perfect baby boys. So my reaction to Bruce's shocking declaration was one of utter confusion, even desperation.

Nowhere in our house felt safe. When I looked at Bruce, I had no idea who or what I was seeing anymore. Visually, he was pure man. The man I had planned to spend the rest of my life with, who had fathered my two sons, and whom I still loved. Every fiber of my being rebelled at his words, which echoed in my head like a cruel taunt. How could he be a woman? He was very clearly a man in my eyes and in my heart. In that moment the very foundation of this new life I had built with my family, and my whole world, began to crumble.

When I was with the boys, I felt the excruciating pressure of trying to act cheerful, to create a façade of normalcy, so they'd have no reason to feel upset or scared themselves. At the same time, being with them only made me worry all the more about what our futures might hold. How could I possibly help them to handle a revelation I had no tools to understand myself? I needed help, but I didn't know where to turn. I couldn't tell anyone what was happening in my life and in Bruce's mind.

My suggestion that we go to therapy right away was a sincere and urgent attempt to remain connected to my husband. I resolved to make an effort to understand fully what Bruce's issue was, and then to determine if it was something we could overcome or "fix." I was naïve. As I said, I was pretty ignorant of the fact that being transgender isn't something that can be overcome, fixed, prayed away, exorcised, or obliterated by any other arcane notion. Being transgender, like being gay, tall, short, white, black, male, or female, is another part of the human condition that makes each individual unique, and something over which we have no control. We are who we are in the deepest recesses of our minds, hearts, and identities. But at this moment in time, back in 1985, I still had to learn that life lesson and apply it to my own expectations for my future and the future of my family.

I found a therapist who specialized in gender dysphoria. Her name was Dr. Gertrude Hill, and we began going to her right away. She was a lovely woman who very calmly, and as gently as she could, massacred me with the information that broke my heart into a million pieces. She confronted my denial in one of our first few sessions.

"Linda, this is who Bruce is," she said. "His identity is that of a woman, and that will never, ever go away. You have a choice to make. If Bruce goes through with his gender reassignment, as he is now planning to do, you have the option of staying with him after he becomes she, or you can divorce him and move on with your life."

She told us that 25 percent of transgender people commit suicide because they are so depressed and feel so hopeless. I resolved I couldn't let that happen, even if I had to face some hard truths and make some seemingly impossible decisions in order to help prevent it.

As we tried to work through both of our feelings, Bruce told me he was considering traveling out of the country, possibly to Denmark, to try to have the gender reassignment surgery anonymously and then come back to the United States as female.

"What about our children?" I asked Bruce.

He thought maybe he could reenter their lives as a female relative. He was grasping for a lifeline, and it was a desperately confusing time for both of us. If Bruce wasn't who he had represented himself to be for all the years we were together, to whom was I married? And what did our marriage mean anymore? I didn't doubt that he loved me and felt attracted to me because he'd said he wanted to stay married to me. I desperately yearned to wake from this hideous nightmare that was destroying my perceived reality, and just make it all go away, and return our life to the paradise it had been up until now. Even in light of Bruce's revelation, I still looked back on the time we'd shared together as a little slice of heaven.

I'd been there. I'd lived it. I knew that the feelings we'd had for each other were real, and the intention in starting our family genuine. Without a full understanding of what was going on with him, it was hard not to wish Bruce could have just kept pretending for our sakes, as he'd done for so long. But every time I felt that way for a second, I corrected myself immediately: Living this lie was clearly making Bruce miserable. I wanted to be a good enough partner—at least a good enough friend— and a good enough human being to support him in the brave choice he was making, even if it was painful for me right now.

As utterly devastated as I was, my heart bled for Bruce and what he must have lived with his entire life. It's impossible for those of us who are comfortable living in our own skin to fully grasp what an imprisonment that must feel like to be born into the wrong body. I know it's difficult to understand, to emotionally, or even intellectually, wrap your head around. Believe me, no one understands the complexity of emotion that the concept evokes better than I. It was extremely difficult for me to comprehend, and adjust my life accordingly, to the realization that the man I had married—the very masculine, gorgeous, ideal, wonderful hunk of a man who had fathered my children—would be no more. The human entity was still alive, but it truly was like mourning the death of the person I had grown to know and love, and with whom I had planned to spend the remainder of my life.

Throughout the spring and summer of 1985, we continued to see Dr. Hill, whom we'd begun calling Trudy. She also met with both of us privately. Bruce confessed to having dressed up in his mother's and sister's clothing when no one was around to notice such behavior. He also told me that he still loved me, and after he transitioned, his wish was to stay married to me and continue living together as a family.

For my part, I talked about how I wanted to support my husband, but I was having difficulty digesting his words and their meaning. I still mostly thought of him as the most masculine of men, the man I had married, the man who had given me the greatest gift of my entire life, my two sons.

But with all this new information and even with therapy, I couldn't comprehend how we could move forward together. I'd fallen in love with a perfect male specimen, not simply because he was handsome and fit, but because of all the traits that had made up his stellar character and winning personality. His fierce drive and focus. His indomitable positivity. His simple goodness. I didn't know if the woman he planned to become would possess those qualities as well because I didn't know her. I wasn't even sure if Bruce knew her yet, either. But even if she was the same person he'd been, I wasn't sure I could continue. I had never been sexually attracted to women. I didn't want to be married to a woman, even if she were the same living, breathing entity that was my husband, Bruce.

To say I was brokenhearted with my head spinning would be a gross understatement. His revelation made me wonder who Bruce even was, and what else he might be hiding from me, or even from himself. I couldn't see a way for us to make it to the other side of all this, at least not as a married couple.

I had already begun grieving all that I was about to lose. My supposedly ideal life had become even more surreal than my incomprehensibly exaggerated life with Elvis. I thought I had traded in one fairy tale for another, but now I was going to be forced to let go of the illusion of my lovingly devoted relationship and perfect family as well. I was struggling to adjust to the new actuality that had been presented to me, and it was a confusing, emotional, deeply painful process.

Still, we kept our promise to see where therapy would take our relationship and we kept trying to understand and be there for one another. In the meantime Bruce continued to present himself to the world as the very masculine Bruce Jenner. On one occasion during this time, Bruce had to be in New York City for an appearance. He really wanted me to meet him there.

"Why don't you come and be with your husband in New York?" he implored.

Husband *is the word I've been waiting for*, I thought. *He referred to himself as masculine. That's what I've hoped to hear all along. Okay, I'll give our marriage this last-ditch effort, try to have a romantic weekend, and see if this is something he can bury again.*

I was probably trying to convince myself there was a shred of hope this was all a bad dream, and I might awaken to the very happy life we shared before Bruce's revelation. I so hoped to bring Bruce back to that masculine persona with which I'd fallen in love, I tried to block out everything else he'd told me in the past few months. I always had uneasy feelings about leaving my children for any amount of time when they were so young, but I hoped this brief weekend rendezvous would potentially breathe new romance into our relationship, and allow us to save our family unit.

When I arrived at our hotel room in New York after the long flight from Los Angeles, I knocked on the door with hopeful anticipation that my romance and marriage might be rekindled on this trip. Bruce opened the door dressed as Caitlyn. Full wig. Full makeup. Heels. A nice feminine dress adorning his muscular body. And a big smile on his red lips.

I crumbled right there, and burst into tears. It was a devastating moment for me. All my hopes and dreams came crashing down in that hotel hallway. *I came all this way. I left my two little babies to travel across the continent to be with my husband, to try to make some sense of all of this with him. Then, I'm met at the door by this woman.*

"Oh, I'm sorry," Bruce said, upon seeing my complete and utter devastation. "I feel bad that I surprised you like that. I just wanted you to see who I really am. It's time you saw me as I truly am. This is me!"

At that moment I was able to fully grasp who she really was. This woman had emerged from inside this very masculine man. I had to pick myself up and face what was before me. *This is what she's been trying to reveal to you,* I thought. *This is who she believes she authentically is. Accept it and deal with the reality.* Clearly, as Trudy had told me in therapy, this wasn't going away. It dawned on me with the very greatest irony that Bruce had in fact, left me for another woman: the one who lived inside him.

Up until that point, Bruce and I had continued to share our home in Malibu as man and wife. At least that's how it appeared from the outside. I still loved him and felt like he was my family. But you can't unsee what you've seen. You can't unhear what you've heard. Now he felt more like my best girlfriend to me than my husband. I was not attracted to him anymore, and we didn't have sex again. The few times we traveled together after that, we had twin beds in our hotel room and slept separately.

Despite these differences, we remained, or so I thought anyway, best friends, which was a huge comfort to me. Although I might have been losing my husband, I was relieved to find that the people we were at our cores, regardless of gender or the title by which we referred to each other, were still intact. And we both clearly still felt a tremendous amount of love and respect for each other. At a moment when nothing else was certain, I was sustained by this constant in my life.

I was slowly gaining some new perspective on some unusual behavior Bruce had exhibited during the past few years, which I'd explained away because I was so happy in my marriage to a man I viewed as almost flawless. During my pregnancy with Brody, I had been surprised when Bruce seemed agitated with me once or twice. This may seem very insignificant, but for two people who got along as well as we always did, it was startling.

We were traveling together one day, as we had done without incident on so many previous occasions. While in line to board our aircraft, I asked him a simple question.

"Do you have the tickets?"

He wheeled around and glared at me.

"I told you three times I have the tickets," he snapped.

"Okay, okay, I was just asking," I said, shaken.

Such behavior was so unlike him, I almost couldn't believe it was happening. The same was true on another occasion, when he was driving us somewhere in Malibu. The windshield was smudged, and I was concerned about our limited visibility.

"Can you see?" I asked.

"Yes," he said.

After watching Bruce drive for a few more minutes without making any move to clean the windshield, I couldn't contain my apprehension and spoke up again.

"Are you sure you can see?" I asked.

"I've already told you I can see," he snapped at me.

Okay, I guess I was being kind of annoying, I thought. But, again, this short fuse was so unlike him that it gave me pause.

Not long after that, my sister-in-law, Louise, was visiting us. Bruce acted in the same way in front of her. I didn't snap back at him because I recognized it as a small lapse in our normally congenial relationship and nothing to turn into a major fight. But I was still so shocked by this new side of his personality that I couldn't let it go entirely, either.

When Louise and I next had a chance to speak privately, I brought it up to her.

"Is it just my imagination, because I'm pregnant and overly sensitive, or is Bruce being very difficult?" I asked. "Did you happen to notice him being rude?"

"He's being a real ass," she said, without hesitation.

Louise is a devout Catholic and the nicest person on earth. So for her to speak about her brother-in-law so harshly confirmed I wasn't alone in my perceptions.

"I thought so," I said. "I definitely thought he was being kind of rude."

Thinking back to these moments now, and knowing what he'd revealed to me, I can comprehend the root of this lashing out. These behaviors were not Bruce. I surmised that he was actually jealous of me and that I was living in the body he felt he was meant to have. His emotions had magnified and reached fruition when I was pregnant with our second son, Brody. Here I was—fully embodying all of my powers and my life-giving fullness as a woman—an experience that he would never get to have because nature had made a mistake, in his estimation, by placing him in the wrong body. Because he felt unable to confide in me about any of this, his deep resentment had surfaced in some small moments of frustration and pique.

Although Bruce and I were not living as husband and wife anymore, I still considered him family and my best friend. My mother and daddy loved Bruce, and he visited them in Memphis with me several times during the period when we were figuring out what to do with our marriage. His familiar presence was a comfort to me, as my mother had been diagnosed with emphysema in 1983 and was now gravely ill and had been given six months to live. The room that Bruce and I shared was across the hall from the room in which my mother was bedridden. One day she called me into her room, where she was lying on the bed, wasting away.

"Let me ask you something," she said, through her oxygen tube.

"What is it, Mom?"

"Is Bruce queer?" she asked.

"What, Mom?" I said.

"Is Bruce queer?"

"You mean is he gay?"

"Yeah."

"Why would you ask me that, Mama?" I asked, feeling anxious.

"Well, my door was open, and he left the door to your bedroom open a crack," she said. "I saw him preening and posing in front of the mirror. He just had his underwear on, and he took his genitals, and he tucked them behind, so that he was flat in the front. And then he was posing with his genitals tucked behind."

"Oh, I don't know, Mama," I said. "He's been working out. Maybe he's just full of himself. Or who knows. Maybe he was just being silly."

My mother always used to say that she could have been a detective. Even when she was lying there, dying, she was able to observe Bruce's secret, even if she didn't understand its full implications. I decided not to confide the truth in her before she died because I didn't want to burden her with that information, or the worry it might have caused her on my behalf. And so she passed on never knowing the truth about Bruce.

For about six months in the aftermath of Bruce's revelation, we struggled, going to see Trudy weekly the whole time. Finally, one day in therapy, it was time for me to articulate a decision.

"You have a choice," Trudy said. "Bruce wants to stay married, so you could allow him to go through the transition and stay married to him. Some women do this, and they live together, sometimes just as friends, sometimes as lesbians, but they raise their kids together. That's his first choice. You can also divorce him, and that's your choice, too, because I know you didn't bargain for this. You can either stay married, or you can get a divorce."

"Listen, I love you," I said to Bruce. "I'm so sorry that you feel like this is the hand that nature has dealt you. I would do anything in the world to help you, but I cannot stay married to you. I married a man. Trudy's right, I didn't bargain for this."

I could immediately tell from the expression on Bruce's face that my decision was deeply upsetting. He really wanted to stay married. He wanted to keep his family intact. I did, too, but not under these circumstances. Tears streamed down his face, but he nodded his head as if he understood what I had said and why, and he accepted my choice. I began to cry, too. This was really happening. We were really getting a divorce. We were really breaking up our family.

With a great deal of sadness, Bruce and I separated. Being married to a woman was not what I had envisioned for my life.

I was so heartbroken after this that day and night I would get in my car and aimlessly drive up and down Pacific Coast Highway, crying. I mourned the death of my marriage, my husband, and my dream of enjoying a lifetime of family togetherness. I was also empathetic to the pain that Bruce, who was still my best friend, had experienced every day of his life. As earth-shattering as his confession had been for me, pulling the proverbial rug out from under my entire world, Bruce's struggle seemed to make mine pale in comparison. I now had to "man up," support Bruce and his decisions regarding his own body, take care of my sons, and move on with my life.

Bruce went to see a doctor and began injecting female hormones. Thirty years ago the only hair removal that was permanent was electrolysis. There were no laser hair removal places then, as far as I know. Poor Bruce began the process of having electrolysis performed on his heavily bearded face. He then began having the hair on his chest removed, one single hair at a time. I was horrified at the thought of how excruciating those procedures must have been. I truly hurt for him. But his conviction and determination were more powerful than the torture he was willing to go through to achieve his final goal. Bruce began to grow breasts as a result of the female hormones he was injecting.

My whole life, my psyche, my femininity, my sexuality, my sanity was in a state of upheaval. I panicked about what I would ever tell my two innocent little boys about their former Olympian father, and how I would raise them alone. And then I would experience waves of crippling sorrow, not only for myself, and my sons, but for Bruce as well.

It wasn't that I felt stupid or duped; Bruce had fooled not just me but the whole world. And besides, I've always had a strong enough sense of self to know that it really wasn't incumbent upon me to discover all the truths about everybody else. As openhearted, generous-minded humans, I think we want to take people at face value, and we want to believe they are who they say they are. I'm comfortable with having lived my life this way. Through my experience with Elvis, I'd also learned that it's conceivable to love someone as much as it's humanly possible to love, and yet still not gain access to every corner of their being. Really, such autonomy between partners is beneficial for the health of each person, and for the couple they form. My time with Elvis had given me a greater emotional maturity and broad-mindedness, which served me well with everything I would face in my life with Bruce. Still, I felt devastated that this wonderful man would be no more, at least not in a form that would be recognizable to me, or to his sons.

During this time, my faith was extremely comforting to me. And by this, I mean my belief that we all possess, if we can tap into it, inner strength, self-knowledge, and equanimity within us. There are still waters deeply embedded in my soul, a place I can go to find peace and comfort during my most trying experiences. Some call this our God Self. It doesn't matter what we call it, as long as we know it's there for us. I've always been able to take a deep breath and go to this place.

Whatever's happening on the outside that's beyond our control, we can only work on controlling our perception and reaction. This is a lesson I've attempted to impart to my kids. "Your perspective on life is your own gift to yourself," I'd tell them. "It's as simple as viewing life as either a challenge or a struggle. Glass half empty or half full. Look for the silver lining." Of course, I'm still very human, and sometimes I lost sight of my inner stillness, collapsing into *Oh no, what am I going to do?!* I'm not infallible and my faith wasn't an infallible source of strength, but it was, and is, a constant one.

This sense of being a part of something larger than myself, and acknowledging that we are all different versions of the human experience, also gave me more empathy for Bruce. I think it's why I also hurt for him, instead of just hurting for myself and my boys. It's a mixed blessing to be overly empathetic and sympathetic, because then you feel so much in your life.

Around Brody's second birthday, in August 1985, Bruce moved out. He rented a house in Malibu that was located on six acres, up a long driveway. It was very private, so he could transition and dress as a woman without having to worry about any prying eyes bearing witness to his newly emerging femininity. During this time, he made a confession to me about his behavior during our marriage. Apparently, when I'd taken the kids with me to Nashville to film *Hee Haw*, leaving him home alone, he'd dressed up as a woman and even gone into Beverly Hills and walked around the park.

I felt myself thinking back—suddenly there was an explanation for the time I'd found my favorite silk blouse stretched out and smeared with makeup. I'd been so trusting of the Bruce I knew and loved that I didn't think he was cheating. And, of course, it never would have occurred to me that he'd worn the blouse himself. I'd concluded that maybe my housekeeper had tried it on, but I wasn't concerned enough about the mystery to ever mention it to anyone.

One night when Bruce had been out of the house for a few months,

I was organizing our TV room when I came across a VHS tape I couldn't identify. I was focused completely on my task, which I'd been absorbed in for several hours. We had taken lots of videos of the boys when they were young, and so when I came across an unlabeled tape, I assumed it was another birthday party or Christmas morning. I was prepared to label it, file it, and then move on. I put it into the VCR, and as the image came into focus on the screen, I gasped.

"Oh my God," I said.

Bruce had set up the video camera in our bedroom while I was out of town doing *Hee Haw*, and he'd filmed himself having a fashion show for the camera. I guess he must have had his own wardrobe hidden somewhere in the house, maybe in the attic of the guesthouse. As I watched, I felt such sadness for him. And then I got angry that he'd left such concrete evidence of his secret around the house, where the boys might have found it and required an explanation. But, mostly, I was just stunned.

In the video, which lasted for a few minutes, he was wearing a variety of wigs, full makeup, and a glamorous wardrobe of women's clothes and shoes. He was also wearing my silk blouse that I'd found stretched and smeared. He was thirty-five at the time, and he actually pulled off the cross-dressing convincingly and looked quite pretty. I never would have been capable of such an impartial assessment of his appearance when I first saw him dressed as a woman in our hotel room in New York City. Too much was at stake in that moment—our marriage, our family, our entire future together—and I had been too shell-shocked to do more than sob.

By now, though, I'd accepted the fact that the Bruce who was transitioning was the real person for me to know. And that the masculine jock I'd married had been the costume, rather than the other way around. Maybe it was even constructive for me to see such irrevocable proof with my own eyes, because it suggested to me that there really had been no way for us to suppress this truth and move on as the couple we'd been. This was our reality now, and I simply had to do my best to adjust, as I was in the process of doing. *Poor Bruce*, I thought. *The real person Bruce is has to live in the shadows, hiding the secret self she believes herself to be. That nightmare is worse than the one I'm faced with.*

Still, it was shocking to me, even after I knew his secret and had seen him dressed this way before. He—or perhaps here I should use *she*—was preening, posing, and smiling for the camera, and it was heartbreaking to see her so desperate to be in another visage. Watching the video was almost like reading someone's diary. It occurred to me that Bruce's secret didn't only exist in relation to our marriage. It was his personal struggle, and I was just one part of that journey. I had made a series of decisions that meant I no longer thought of him as my husband, and no longer relied on him for the emotional support of a spouse. But it was a profound loss to my life and my future. As the best friend I was now trying to be for him, I could understand that this video was just one of the many steps he would need to take on his path toward defining his new life in ways that were still revealing themselves.

Now, having the truth confirmed, I was horrified about one thing, though. Not that he dressed like a woman, but that he'd started taking a tremendous risk by dressing as a woman and parading around the park in Beverly Hills.

Again, this was thirty years ago, and simply coming out as gay was often difficult. And I was fairly confident that Bruce Jenner would be met by more than skepticism if he revealed *her*self too soon and in a haphazard fashion.

Whenever I worried about Bruce, as I often did, my thoughts immediately went to Trudy's figure that 25 percent of transgender people committed suicide. And from there, my thoughts leapt to our little boys. They would be scarred by any of these potentially devastating events should they happen to their father, and should the boys inadvertently be exposed to them in the press. I simply wanted to keep all of us safe.

"Please be careful," I said to Bruce after he told me about walking in the park in Beverly Hills, dressed as a woman. "You're Bruce Jenner. People are going to see you."

"No, I look great," he said. "When I dress up, you can't tell that I'm Bruce Jenner. I'm a woman."

"You're six two and you wear a size-twelve shoe," I said. "It might be obvious to a couple of people."

In fact, I received a call that summer from our former neighbor Jeff, whom we'd lived next door to in the beachfront apartment we'd rented before we were married.

"Hey, I ran into Bruce a few nights ago," he said. "He was driving down the street, and he was dressed like a woman. So I said, 'Hey, Bruce what're you doing?' He looked kind of shocked to see me, and he told me that he was going to a Halloween party. I thought, *That's weird, a Halloween party in July?* Okay, whatever."

I laughed nervously and changed the subject. I relaxed a bit as I realized that Jeff wasn't overly concerned by what he'd seen. Bruce was so masculine that his explanation had seemed logical, even if it meant a Halloween party in the middle of the summer. This was Bruce Jenner, after all, and so he must have been telling the truth. He was clearly a man, through and through, and an Olympic American hero at that.

"Pray for Peace"

When you close your eyes to sleep
Pray for peace
And for the ones who've given up
Pray for love

Pray each life will lead the way with
  kindness
Pray that truth and beauty remain
  timeless
Pray for dreams
To fly high on shattered wings

Pray for hearts—broken, strong or
  weak
Let us think before we speak
And pray for peace

To forgive and then forget
Pray for that
That no one must walk alone
Pray for hope

Pray for time—let music play
  forever
In a song that brings the world
  together
For our children can't we please
Pray for peace

Reach for my hand
And open heart

No need for us
To stand so far apart
The universe
Hears every word
And every mother's child
Holds the same worth

Now I close my eyes to sleep
And pray for peace

For the souls trapped by the night
Pray for light
And choosing love to conquer hate
Pray for faith
May we feel compassion as one
  heart now
Unholy wars must end before they
  start now
Pray for trust
To embrace life is a must

And pray to heal—hurting broken
  wills
Pray for smiles on every child
And pray for peace

LYRIC: LINDA THOMPSON

Chapter Sixteen

Music and Lyrics by Us

It was time to pick up the pieces and move on. I was faced with so many decisions about how to best do so, not only for myself, but also for my family. *When kids are this young, how can I even begin to talk to them about an issue this complex?* I wondered.

After much reflection, I decided it was best for the time being not to even try. In fact, I didn't explicitly tell the boys their father had moved out. He traveled so much for work that they weren't accustomed to having him around anyway. I waited for them to ask questions, and didn't burden them with too much information about our very adult situations. I truly think that is a mistake too many parents make when they split up. They drag their children through the mire, and make the divorce about them as well. There is no need to impose that kind of weight on a child.

At any rate, Brandon and Brody didn't seem to notice anything had changed in our lives. Bruce came to visit us sometimes, and they never asked me where he was when he wasn't with us. As I came to understand how little the boys registered his absence around the house, I finally realized just how far apart Bruce and I had already become without any conscious awareness on my part. I now saw how much he had already distanced himself from our family, maybe because he was preparing for what came next, or was just too consumed by his own personal challenges to give us his full presence and attention. I realized I had been the boys' primary parent all along.

Brandon was the first to notice that Bruce wasn't living in the house anymore. Since he's older than Brody, he has more of a memory of our life together with his father. Even at that, he only has one memory of Bruce walking down the hall in our home while he lived there. That's it. That's the only thing he can recall about the time when Bruce was living with us. I've noticed that Brandon has always tried to maintain a connection with Bruce.

"Mom, how come Daddy never sleeps here anymore?" Brandon finally asked me after a few months. "Daddy doesn't live here anymore?"

"Well, you know Daddy travels a lot," I said. "And then, Mommy goes to Nashville a couple of times a year. It's just easier for Daddy to have his own place. We love each other. He is still your daddy. I'm still your mom. But he's going to live in his other house now."

This explanation was enough for the boys. They never questioned me further or created any drama about the separation. If anyone seemed angry at times, it was Bruce. I think he was frustrated by his circumstances, that he had to be alone because of his decision to transition. He sometimes seemed to take his bitterness out on me, as if he thought I should have gone through this life change with him. I was sympathetic to his point of view, but I knew I'd done what was right. I'd followed my heart, as much as he had when he made his confession to me, and I knew that was all any of us can do in this lifetime. I did my best not to react when he was short with me; I would remind myself of everything he was going through and focus on trying to be the best friend to him that I could.

I continued to wear my wedding ring for a while. We were keeping up the pretense that we were still married. I was trying to cover for Bruce and just be there for him in any way that I could. I had an open-door policy for Bruce when it came to visitation, letting him see his sons anytime he wanted to. Brandon and Brody went over to his home occasionally but never spent the night there. Bruce never created a room for them to sleep over at that house. One day, after having spent a little time at Bruce's house, both boys came into the kitchen.

"Mommy, we saw Daddy getting out of the shower naked, and Daddy has boobs!" they said.

That day I began trying to cover for Bruce, to protect him and explain away what was clearly happening to his body.

"Well, boys, you know how your dad was super-muscular and trained very hard for the Olympics?" I said. "He had big muscles, and some of those chest muscles are called 'pectorals.' When you stop training and you stop lifting weights, sometimes the muscle turns to fat. So his pectoral muscles have probably just gotten a little flabby and look like boobs."

I felt such an obligation to keep Bruce's gender dysphoria his secret to reveal, or not, that I did not even tell my sons until they were thirty-one and twenty-nine years old, respectively. I wanted Brandon and Brody to experience enough life and garner enough knowledge, confidence, and compassion to be able to deal with their father's true self. We are not defined by our parents, but we don't know that as young children. I tried to raise my sons to embrace open hearts, forgiveness, kindness, tolerance, and an inclusive spirit. They have been imbued with good values and are remarkably noble, showing great acceptance, understanding, and forgiveness toward Bruce and others.

Although they were under two and four years old at the time Bruce shared his truth with me, I immediately began trying to instill in them an encompassing scope of understanding and tolerance toward all variations of human existence. I made a determination then that it would be incumbent upon me to help cultivate in my sons the deepest facility to understand and accept all races, religions, sexual preferences, and expressions of the human condition in this world. Of course, I always would have wanted them to grow up with openness and a strong sense of humanity. But now, it was even more important for them to have a gracious heart and spirit, and an intelligent, sophisticated understanding that humans are infinitely varied. We need to embrace all people and understand that our differences as well as our commonalities are precisely what make life so interesting.

I knew if Brandon and Brody were eventually going to understand who their dad was and still feel secure within themselves, they would need to be able to call upon all of the strength and flexibility they had been imbued with as little boys. It had been clear from the time both of my sons were born that they were all boy and totally heterosexual. They both loved little girls, even when they were quite young. I sometimes wondered if they would be able to understand their father's need to express himself as the woman he truly felt himself to be. Again, please remember, this was three decades ago, when we knew so much less about the transgender experience, and it was so much more hidden within our culture. I felt so much pressure to get it right, to do what was best for my sons, and also for Bruce, even though it wasn't clear back then how all of this would eventually play out. It was an agonizing experience for me, and I don't think I've ever felt so alone.

In my darkest moments, however, I always returned to my empathy for Bruce and the even darker moments he was facing and had faced for as long as he could remember. The story of our separation began to leak among our friends, and our community in Malibu, in September 1985. But we didn't go public with our separation until the following February. When the story was picked up in such publications as *People* magazine, we attributed the split to the distance that had come between us because of how much Bruce traveled for work. In the *People* interview, I tried to remain upbeat, not ruling out the possibility of reconciliation, even though my own heart had closed that door.

I did everything in my power to support Bruce and make his life easier for him, including not asking for any child support or alimony. I may be the only woman in the state of California to have done so, but when Bruce and I divorced, that's what I did. As confused and sad as I was, I knew that Bruce was also very confused and extremely distraught. His life was far too important to me and to our sons to risk over money.

When Bruce and I went to court so our divorce could be granted, the judge paused the proceedings in order to discuss my choice with me. He seemed genuinely concerned.

"Do you understand what you're doing?" he said. "You've got two little kids to raise, and you're waiving child support and alimony? You can come back for child support, if he decides to be a deadbeat. But you can never come back for alimony, even if he wins the lottery."

"That's fine," I said. "I hope he does win the lottery."

He can live out his dreams and become who he wants to be, I added in my head.

Of course Bruce hadn't gone public with his story yet, and so I couldn't mention the truth of our situation, that Bruce was basically going off to become someone none of us would recognize. She in all likelihood wouldn't be able to come out as her true self. At that time in history, who knew how people would react? Today, thirty years later, she's been able to go on and have a vibrant public life. Back then she would have very likely lost the income from Bruce's public speaking engagements, appearances, and endorsements once the transition was complete. She would have probably ended up living in hiding somewhere, denying any relation to the former Bruce Jenner.

Because I couldn't tell the judge any part of our secret, I simply tried to appear as positive and self-possessed as possible. Plus, I was still appearing on *Hee Haw*, so I naïvely thought I could raise two kids on that meager salary, along with whatever acting jobs I landed. And Kenny Rogers had released "Our Perfect Song," which he'd been smitten with when I'd first played it for him, on his 1985 album, *The Heart of the Matter*. So there was extra income from that, too.

"Well, I'm doing a little TV show," I said, putting on my most upbeat tone. "And I've got a pretty promising songwriting career. So I'll be okay."

The judge didn't look entirely convinced. But he accepted my explanation and granted our divorce with the terms we'd requested. When Bruce and I finalized the division of our assets, we agreed that I would keep our Malibu home and assume the mortgage, and he would be granted our Lake Tahoe home, which was of similar value, maybe worth a little more. In keeping our Malibu home, I at least felt better about not disrupting Brandon's and Brody's lives further by having to move. Bruce assumed our tax debt, and we agreed I'd take our modest retirement fund. The only problem was that I had to pay a significant tax penalty. So I decided to sell a few items of jewelry Elvis had given me, including a lion's head necklace that had been his. This was a difficult decision to make, and I wish I still had that piece today. But I had to take care of my two little boys, and I knew Elvis would have been glad to help me in this way.

When I broke the news of our divorce to our inner circle, I explained the distance between us by saying that he traveled a lot, and we had grown apart.

On top of the complex new reality Bruce and I were attempting to navigate, we also had to learn how to coparent our children, which is challenging even under the best circumstances. I tried to support Bruce and help him to maintain his relationship with the boys, but I was often alarmed by his freewheeling parenting methods. At the time, he had a big station wagon, and when he came to pick up the boys, he didn't put seat belts on them or even make them ride in the seats. He put them in the back of the station wagon, and when he took corners sharply, they slid around. Brody came home with his whole entire back bruised. I called Bruce right away.

"This is unacceptable," I said. "What are you doing?"

"Oh, they had a great time," he said. "I put the seats down in the station wagon, and they were just flying around back there. They had a ball."

"That's not safe," I said. "You can't do that."

On another occasion, when Brandon was seven or eight, Bruce picked him up from school in Calabasas on his motorcycle. He put him on the back, without a helmet, and drove him home via Malibu Canyon Road, which is extremely narrow and winding. I was furious at his irresponsibility.

"Oh, you're overprotective," Bruce said.

"No, that's not overly protective," I said. Returning the focus to what he had done, I said, "That's dangerous."

It was a real struggle for me. I didn't feel completely comfortable when Bruce had the boys, because he clearly wasn't careful with them. But still I wanted them to have a close relationship with their dad. I resigned myself to sounding like the nagging mother. I started taking them over to Bruce's house myself and dropping them off along with a list of guidelines.

"Be careful," I said. "Put seat belts on them. Don't just let them fly around in the back of your car. No motorcycles. Dirt bikes up in the hills, that's fine, but not on the road. And, always, helmets."

I'm sure Bruce heard, "Blah blah blah . . ."

Anyway, they survived, thank God, and Bruce did, too. My house continued to be open to Bruce. He was invited to all of the birthday parties, Christmas and Thanksgiving dinners, and Easter egg hunts, and he was free to drop in and hang out with the boys anytime he wanted. This arrangement seemed to be more comfortable for Bruce than having the boys at his house. And I was happy to do what I could to make sure they got time with him. Of course, this setup would cause friction in my own personal life, soon enough. But the boys came first. Always.

In the beginning, the only people other than Trudy who knew Bruce's secret were the singer Lionel Richie and his wife, Brenda. Bruce had actually confided in Lionel himself. The Richies were great friends and I knew they were trustworthy.

It was such a relief to have one place where I could be honest about all I was going through and receive the compassion and support of true friends. They were wonderful and did so much to help me. Right around the time Bruce left home for good, and I was struggling with my new reality as a divorced single mom, they invited me to Hawaii for a few days. Lionel kept us laughing, which was the best possible therapy, and Brenda was great. She was very kind to the boys. When my world was falling apart, they rose to the occasion and made my existence so much better than it would have otherwise been, and I'll always appreciate that.

Without any of us realizing it at the time, Lionel and Brenda had also opened up the next chapter in my life when they'd invited me to be their guest at the 27th Annual Grammy Awards on February 26, 1985. This was right after Bruce had made his initial confession to me, and I was glad to have a night out with my friends to take my mind off the problems at home.

That year, Lionel was nominated for Producer of the Year, and it was a thrilling experience to be there cheering him on. My seat was across the aisle from Huey Lewis, who was a big star at the time, and the whole show offered me the chance to reconnect with the music world, which in many ways I'd been missing since Elvis's death. After all, this world had been my life during my years with Elvis, and I was happy to find myself revisiting now as a burgeoning songwriter. Of course, at the time, Bruce and I were still officially together, and I was trying to grasp the full implications of what he had confided to me and figure out what course my life would take going forward. So at the time, I was still very much a married woman in my mind and had no interest in anyone other than my husband. And I wasn't at all sure about him anymore, either. It was the Grammys, and I just wanted to relax, hear the music, and have fun.

Lionel won that night, tying with a producer I'd never heard of, named David Foster, so that each received a Grammy for the song he'd produced. Lionel had his after party at Le Dome restaurant, which was a big music industry hangout, and David Foster came by with his then wife and congratulated Lionel on their shared win. This was where David and I first met, although I have no memory of the interaction. I was caught up in celebrating Lionel's victory, and there were a great many people stopping by our table to say hello. And besides, I never looked twice at a married guy.

A few months later, I was in the kitchen of Lionel and Brenda's house when David came in with his wife at the time. Introductions were made all around.

"Nice to meet you," I said, extending my hand to David with a smile.

"Oh, we actually met the night of the Grammys," David said.

I didn't pay any attention to David beyond that. But, as I would soon find out, he already had designs on me. In November 1985, David surprised me by calling me on the phone. I was aware that David was a well-respected songwriter and producer, although he wasn't as well known in the United States as he was in his native Canada. He seemed nice and was extremely charismatic, and charming. I've always been a big believer in being cordial and open to friendliness in others. David said he was calling me as a favor for someone else.

"Do you know of anyone that's renting a guesthouse?" he asked. "I have a friend who's moving here from Canada, and I'm trying to help him out."

We chatted a bit. He was clearly smart and very amusing. I told him I had a guesthouse on my property that I might consider renting to his friend.

David came over to check out the space, taking everything in as I gave him a tour.

"I thought you were married to Bruce Jenner," he said. "I've never met Bruce Jenner. Is he ever even around here?"

"Oh, he travels a lot," I said.

Bruce was already living in his other house by then, and a few people in our inner circle and Malibu community knew about our separation, but we were still keeping everything as quiet as we could. David gave me a quizzical glance, but then he nodded, and we began talking about something else.

The next time David called me, several days later, his tone was even warmer.

"Do you like Malibu?" he asked. "We're thinking of buying a house and moving to Malibu."

He and his then wife did ultimately buy a house together in Malibu. Because he was still obviously married, I didn't think much of our budding friendship beyond the fact that he seemed like a great guy. Anyway, I had much bigger issues than a new neighbor weighing on my mind and captivating my attention.

But soon David called wanting to play tennis. And then he called asking me to meet for a game of racquetball. Our interactions grew increasingly friendly and more intimate. He was obviously "crushing" on me, and I was all too susceptible to his attention. I knew some of David's work, and I was impressed with his talent. I also thought he was a good family man, and I began to like him as a person. He was very funny, in a kind of deviant and irreverent way, not unlike Elvis's sense of humor, which of course I loved.

However, he was still married, and for the time being, at least, I was trying to simply think of him as a new friend. Given the insecurities, sadness, and what could accurately be defined as insane desperation swirling around in my consciousness, this was a moment in my life when I needed all the friends I could find.

Adding to my fragility during this time was the fact that, while I'd been dealing with the whole Bruce situation, my mother had been told by her doctors that she was in the final months of her life. I was not only traveling with my sons to Nashville twice a year to film *Hee Haw*, I was also taking the boys back to Memphis once a month to see their grandmother in an attempt for them to get to know her before she died.

My mother had been in somewhat poor health for as long as I could remember, and following her emphysema diagnosis in 1983, she'd been given six months to live. And while she'd amazed the doctors by defying the odds, she was extremely ill, bedridden, and on oxygen.

I'd long grown accustomed to my mother living with one ailment or another, and it was difficult to believe anything could really fell her, strong as she was. When I was a little girl, she'd had her gallbladder removed, and she'd gotten an infection and almost died. I went to visit her in her hospital room, earnestly clutching the flowers I'd picked for her. The nurses started crying at the sight because she was gravely ill, and they thought it was so sweet that I'd brought her what I'd thought were pretty flowers I'd picked for her myself, and they were actually weeds. But she'd hung on and lived. Probably the only reason she didn't die is that she was such a devoted mom, and she refused to leave her kids.

By the time I'd married Bruce in 1981, she had diverticulitis, an inflammation of the digestive track. When she came to Oahu for our wedding, it was her first time in Hawaii, which was her dream trip. Sadly, she couldn't really enjoy it as much as she wanted to, because she had such terrible abdominal pain. And she couldn't eat many of the local delicacies, like pineapple.

Her health had been on a downward spiral, and then she'd received her "death sentence" in 1983, which is when I'd begun making my monthly trips back to Memphis with the boys. She wasn't a heavy smoker, but she was a resigned smoker. She was sadly addicted to tobacco, as have been far too many others.

"You need to quit smoking," her doctor said.

"Well, honey, you've got to die of something," she said in her inimitable Southern way, having no idea what was coming for her.

"Mrs. Thompson, you don't understand," her doctor went on. "Suffocating is a very horrible death. You can stop smoking now and maybe even live a few more years, but if you continue to smoke, I'm afraid there's no other way to put it, you will die a horrible death."

My mother continued to smoke, but she inexplicably also continued to live. Not that it seemed like any kind of a blessing after a time. It was the most god-awful death imaginable, because she truly was like a fish out of water, gasping for breath, even with help from her oxygen tank.

As soon as I arrived at her house each month, I'd go and sit on her bed.

"Mama, can I do anything for you?" I asked.

"Honey, just breathe for me," she said.

And I would. During my visits, when I went out for a run in the park near their house, I breathed as deeply as I could, knowing that she couldn't. The very act of breathing is something we often take for granted, but not me, not after witnessing what my mother endured. I am grateful for each and every breath I'm fortunate enough to take.

With emphysema, the sacs in your lungs fill up with air and fluid, making it so you can't expel the air. This means you can't take in a good breath because the little air sacs are already full. She didn't want to have food or anything around her face because it further inhibited her breathing. She was five foot ten, but her weight sank to 86 pounds. It was a slow process of suffocating and starving to death, and it was excruciating to witness.

"I don't know what I've ever done in my life that God would punish me this way," she said. "That I would have to suffer so."

Obviously, this was a very difficult time for all of us. But I could tell it lightened my mother's spirits immeasurably to see the boys each month. And as sick as she was, she was still a wonderful, doting grandmother. And as all good grandmothers do, she gleefully ignored all of the parameters I tried to impose at the start of each of our visits.

"Mama, please don't give them candy, because they'll get too wired, and it's not good for them," I always said when we arrived.

"Of course not, honey," she reassured me.

Then, when I was busy helping my father or otherwise occupied elsewhere in the house, the boys knew it was just the right moment to go in and find her in her bed.

"Mammaw, where's the candy?" they asked.

"You just step up there and it's right there in that little box," she said, pointing to where she'd had my daddy hide candy for them on her bureau.

She always had banana kisses and chocolate drops. They knew exactly where she kept her candy, and they knew she would never say no to them. Even though they weren't allowed too much candy at home (but, really, they were), I couldn't be too upset about these lapses in the regular rules. I was so glad to see her smile and felt blessed they got the time with her that they did.

This was a tremendously emotional, stressful period. I was grieving over my mother's horrible demise, taking place right before my helpless eyes. I was concerned about being the best mother I could be for my sons, and worried about whether I'd be able to support us and keep our house. I constantly despaired over the looming probability that my sons would grow up fatherless, and I also had to deal with the uncertainty surrounding Bruce's agonizing struggle and the unpredictable process of his ongoing transition.

In the midst of all this mental and emotional chaos, a Canadian knight in shining armor, named David Foster, seemed to arrive just in the nick of time, on a white steed, galloping to my rescue. I'd continued to see David sporadically that winter and into 1986. After we'd gotten together several times to play tennis and racquetball, he made a confession to me.

"Listen, I think I'm falling in love with you," he said.

"Whoa, wait, what?" I said. But I felt the same way. I was definitely swept away by David.

I had a hard and fast rule against getting involved with married men. I still do. But I was exceedingly vulnerable at that time in my life, and David was very determined to be with me, confessing that he'd seen me sitting across from Huey Lewis at the Grammys and had instantly fallen in love with me.

"I've been in love with you since the first time I saw you at the Grammys in your red dress," he said. "I couldn't take my eyes off you then, and I can't get my mind off you now. I never thought my marriage would be forever. I can help you. I can be a father to your boys."

With everything going on in my life, I wasn't strong enough to resist him. I fell for it, hook, line, and sinker. I don't know how much of what he said was true, or how much was just feigned charm and the lines I needed to hear. I can't deny I found a huge measure of comfort in his reassurances. He made me feel like a desirable woman again after feeling all the insecurities I had experienced after Bruce's revelation. We were helplessly, hopelessly falling in love.

Even so, I tried to fight it, as I'm certain David did, too. I didn't want to be the other woman. I really kept trying to move away from him, and I dated several other people over the next six months, including the actor Christopher Lambert. However, my dating other men just seemed to fuel David's desire to be with me even more. He was insanely jealous, even though he was himself married.

"I don't want to be the reason that you leave your marriage," I told him.

In the summer of 1986, I was in Nashville filming *Hee Haw*. I was attending a small dinner with several friends, including Kenny and Marianne Rogers, Cathy Baker, and the comedian Gailard Sartain. During our meal, the phone rang. Surprisingly, it was for me. My first thought was one of concern. Something had happened to my mother. Why else would someone be calling me here? But it was David Foster.

"I've done it! I've left my wife," David declared.

As is David's way, he has since turned this into a funny, irreverent story that casts him in the hangdog role. In his telling, he called me in the middle of a raucous party where everyone was laughing and having a grand old time to give me his sad, serious news, and I could barely hear him over the frivolity. Of course, that's not how it really happened, but that's part of his sense of humor. In actuality, I went into the other room, leaving the noise of the group behind me, so I could really talk to him.

"You what?" I said.

"I've left my wife," he said. "I want to be with you."

"Listen, please don't make me the reason you're doing this," I said. "If you're unhappy, and you don't want to be there, that's one thing, but I don't want to be the reason you're leaving. I don't want that on my conscience."

"No, no, I've never been happy," he said. "Yes, you're part of it, because I want to be with you. I've fallen in love with you, and I want to be with you." I now know what a tremendous toll that decision took on David. It weighed heavily on both of us for all the years we were together.

I had no reason to doubt him. And I had fallen in love with David, too, no matter how hard I had tried not to. But it did lay heavily on my conscience for many years, and I allowed myself and others to beat me up with guilt for longer than I should have.

I took David at his word and agreed to begin an exploration of our feelings for each other, which developed into a deeper, long-lasting love, resulting in marriage, which kept us together for nineteen years. Considering the length and depth of our union, I hold a deep conviction that David and I were meant to be together. Even so, I'm not proud of how we first came together. But I am no longer embarrassed by it, either. I have allowed myself to be human, and have long since forgiven myself, which is a step in the right direction toward healing.

At that time, after all I'd just been through, and all I was facing on my own, I didn't have the strength to resist the comfort, and love, and affection David offered me. And looking back, I'm glad I didn't. My dad used to tell me that, at the right time, with the right person, under the right circumstances, anything can happen. I've found that to be true in my life. I believe some of that magic was at work when David and I found each other. I am grateful for the years we shared together.

It wasn't just a romantic bond we were forming in those days, either, but also a creative unity that would lay the groundwork for the greatest collaboration I've ever experienced. Not long into our relationship, David came to me with an idea.

"Hey, why don't we try writing together?" he said.

"I'd love that," I said.

I invited David over to my house, and we went out to the guesthouse, which ultimately became his studio. He was always opinionated, bossy but brilliant, and we worked very well together. He wrote incredibly beautiful, intricate melodies, which stirred emotions deep within me, inspiring me to tap into the creative reservoirs of my soul. David was extremely appreciative of my lyrical gifts. We were already becoming a great team. He wrote the music, and I wrote the lyrics. It seemed to be a songwriting marriage made in heaven.

"So in Love with You"

You are to me
What poetry
Tries to say with a word
You are the song
All the music
My heart ever heard
I can't escape
The air that I breathe
Even speaks of you
And I'm not ashamed to say
That I feel this way

I will stand before God
Give you all that I've got
I can promise you
I'll be true
I reveal here and now
As we both take this vow
I am so in love
I am so in love with you
Words can't express
What I confess
With each beat of my heart
I'm overwhelmed
With a passion I felt from the start
I vow this day we'll never part

Our love will grow
As years come and go
I'll remain by your side
There isn't anything
That I would deny

I will stand before God
Give you all that I've got
I can promise you
I'll be true
I reveal here and now
As we both take this vow
I am so in love
I am so in love with you

LYRIC: LINDA THOMPSON

Chapter Seventeen

Navigating Life

As David and I began to explore our relationship, I quickly discovered how intoxicating his personality could be. The first six months were a honeymoon of sorts and he was extremely sweet and devoted. We were newly, madly in love, and in these early months together, we shared many beautiful, poignant moments. Our bond was intense and passionate.

As I had already discovered with my two former loves, with extraordinarily gifted individuals almost always comes complexity. David was a spectacularly multifaceted genius. He still is. The David I have gotten to know over the many years we have shared a relationship of one sort or another is a compassionate, caring, philanthropic, highly charged, passionate, brilliant, and paradoxical man. Not unlike the Elvis I knew and loved. He is a loyal friend and ally, and is that person who would put himself out to help another. He is the one to call to organize entertainment for a charity event. He extends his talent, time, and energy to show up for a good cause. After all these years, I believe him to be, at the very core of his being, a good man.

Early on, David and I compared notes about our hometowns. I was always honored to be from Memphis because of its rich history, including the musical heritage of the rock and roll, rhythm and blues, and country genres. It's always been said that songwriter W. C. Handy pushed the blues through a horn on Beale Street. And because music was David's life, I was excited to share this heritage with him.

I took David to Memphis, the former cotton town on the Mississippi River, steeped in cultural riches and Southern pathos, where I'd come of age. We went to hear blues on Beale Street, a special experience, the music making its way out every door as you walk along. We went to the Rivermont Hotel, where I'd stayed when I was Miss Liberty Bowl.

One day, we ended up at a little park on the bluff overlooking the Mississippi. Admiring the view, we sat on a bench, looking at Mud Island and the barges sliding by. David put his head in my lap, and I ran my fingers through his hair. We never forgot that moment. We were deeply in love.

Shortly after that trip, we went to see his hometown, Victoria, British Columbia. When I got off the plane and first entered Victoria, I noticed all the lampposts were adorned with gorgeous, colorful flowers. Everything was perfect, not a brown spot on anything. The charm of the town was overwhelming. I was enchanted by the city's beautiful Victorian architecture and its famous formal gardens, as well as the harbor.

"I'm so embarrassed," I said, turning to David. "Are you kidding? You were so nice about Memphis, but you grew up in Disneyland. It looks like Main Street in Disneyland."

We laughed about that. We still laugh about that today.

Victoria was beautiful, and the people welcoming. Canadians are a lot like Southerners in that respect. They're very hospitable, down-to-earth, and familial. Even though David grew up in a different country and was from a smaller family than mine, we were raised very much alike. We both grew up humbly and were instilled with the same values. David maintained a deep devotion to hard work, personal improvement, and his family, and these were all qualities I valued in a partner.

Meeting his family in Victoria for the first time, especially his mother, explained a great deal about the man he'd become. As I came to understand, David grew up feeling very special, which he absolutely was and is. When he was about five years old, it was discovered that he has perfect pitch and enormous musical talent, and he became a bit of a child prodigy. He was the only boy in his family, born right in the middle, with three older sisters, and three younger sisters. His mother thought he hung the moon; she nurtured his talent and pampered him. She was a great mom, but I think in some ways she spoiled him because he was the only boy, and because he was undeniably gifted.

David's mother was a fantastic woman. She hand-sewed all of her seven children's clothing, knitted, and darned their socks (which explained where David got the notion that this was something I should be doing for him). She cooked, she baked, she donated her time to philanthropy, she was impossible to live up to, but in the best possible way. She knew it, too, and she was cute about it.

"I ruined him, didn't I?" she used to joke about David.

It was true. She was strong, formidable, personable, caring, just a great lady. After David and I eventually married, I used to always joke that I'd married him for his mother. "A husband you can find, but a great mother-in-law, that's another thing," I often said. "If you find one of those, marry the man." I adored her and would often good-naturedly say, "None of us women could ever compete with you and the kind of woman you set as an example for David."

Of course, her special treatment paid off in the end, as David became wildly successful—he's been nominated for 47 Grammys and won 16—and was always extremely devoted to his mother, taking good care of her, along with the rest of his family.

After that initial visit together, we developed an annual ritual of spending a month in Canada each summer, during which we visited with David's mother and six sisters, as well as his many nieces and nephews, and took all of our young children out on extended boat trips. David's mother often went with us, much to my delight, as I genuinely enjoyed her company.

David's boat was a sixty-three-foot Hatteras yacht with a salon, galley, and three staterooms and three heads (boat talk for bathrooms). We loved being on board together and had a lot of romantic times there, especially in the beginning. When it was docked in California, we took the boat to Catalina Island and Newport Harbor. In the summer, we cruised through the Gulf Islands of British Columbia and the nearby San Juan Islands of Washington State. With a boat like that, it was easy to feel like there was a bit of magic in the world, and after the last few years with Bruce it felt good to be swept off my feet and onto the water.

From the start, being with David required a commitment across nearly every aspect of my life; because we both had children from previous marriages, we couldn't wade tentatively into things. Besides David and his kids, I had the boys, acting, and my songwriting career.

When David and I first got together, between us we had five children ages five and under, including David's daughters, Sara, age five; Erin, age three; and Jordan, age one; and my sons who were four and a half and two and a half. David's older daughter, Amy, from his previous marriage, was a teenager and did not spend time with us as regularly as the little ones, but we did make an effort to always make her feel welcome. Our children scarcely remember anything before about age five, making it hard for them to recognize the good we tried to do for them, or how much we cared for them during their very early years. During those initial months, I think David and I really tried to do our best to unite our family. But of course, as time went on, the reality set in that, often, blended families are less "blended" than they are "curdled," with lumps that are virtually insoluble.

Merging our two very full lives proved a complex process, as it always is in a new romantic partnership. David and I had both been disappointed in our failed previous marriages. We were both healing from sadness, loss, and feelings of accountability in the aftermath of our respective divorces. We related to each other on many levels and frequently leaned on each other.

But not long into our relationship, our differences in parenting style and our sense of responsibility for our children complicated the process of uniting our families. David always wanted to take trips alone, just the two of us; I always wanted to take all the children with us on vacations and even working trips. David thought I was too permissive and affectionate. I thought he was too harsh and irritable. Our family dynamic deteriorated into Daddy's girls against Mama's boys, David against Linda, his against hers, and it spiraled from there. Our history was at least partly to blame. David and I were each dealing with our debilitating guilt about the circumstances of our coming together—an angry ex, a transitioning ex—and the kids quickly sensed the tension beneath the surface of our family life.

We established an understanding between us early in our coparenting: He would discipline his daughters, and I would discipline my sons, when we each saw fit. That way there would be no unnecessary additional discord between us. While I wanted peace in our household, I also stood my ground with David if we ever had a disagreement about how things should be.

At the time I couldn't see how much I'd changed in just ten years, from the sweet, submissive girl who'd followed every direction, subsuming my own feelings in order to keep Elvis placated and happy. I understand now that this newfound ferocity was the result of becoming a mother. When you carry a baby for nine months, and struggle through labor, and nursing, and everything else that goes into mothering, your primary job is to keep your kids safe. It's primal. Even today, they're grown men, and I would stand up to a lion, a bullet, or anything else on their behalf. That's the kind of intense, "mama bear," protective love they've awoken in me, and which they'll always inspire. Having found my power as a mother had also translated into other areas of my life as well, helping me to stand up for what I believed was fair and right, rather than simply going along with whatever was happening in order to keep the peace.

But whereas our differences in childrearing led to some occasional tension between us in our personal life, when we began collaborating on songs in our professional one, the experience instantly brought us closer together. Music became a catharsis for us, helping to complete the circle we needed to close in order to move into our new future as one.

As we started collaborating, I had even more reason to admire some of his best qualities. David was an intelligent man with stratospheric ambitions—better at self-promotion than anybody else I've ever met. Throughout the 1980s, David produced a succession of top-charting albums for the band Chicago, and his continuous accomplishments were leading him to be an even more sought-after producer. Once we began writing together, these aspects of David's personality also benefited me immensely. David was an outspoken advocate and ally when he needed to be, and I appreciated that strength when I was more retiring in my presentations.

And so began a nearly two-decade union in which we alternated between periods of tension and intimacy in our romantic relationship, while always collaborating on a successful and rewarding shared career. I don't think I can overstate how meaningful this aspect of our relationship was to me. While I'd obviously been dabbling in songwriting for years and had enjoyed success at it before I met David, it soon became clear that David could help me uncover new depths of creativity within myself, and in doing so, I was able to bring my talents to full fruition and accomplish so much more.

Our first notable collaboration was in 1987, when we were asked to compose a special song for an event called Rendez-vous '87 to commemorate a very important hockey game between the United States and the Soviet Union. David wrote the music as usual, and I wrote the lyrics to a song called, "Love Lights the World." The plan was for the Red Army choir to record the song, fly to Quebec City, where the event was being held, and perform it on a television special for the Canadian national network, CBC. David and I flew to Moscow, via quite a circuitous route, arriving in Moscow after about thirty hours in transit. When our Aeroflot plane arrived, because of significant tailwinds we were approximately fifteen minutes early. The Russian soldiers who met the flight would not allow us off the airplane until our appointed time of arrival, saying, "If we allow you to disembark the aircraft before its appointed time it would be a sign of insurrection." Remember, in 1987, this was pre-Glasnost, pre-Perestroika Russia, and they were still living under hard-line communist rule.

We finally got off the airplane, made it to our hotel, rested for a bit, then were transported to a military facility. We sat with Russian generals, and I had to explain through an interpreter what each word of my lyric meant and indicated. They scrutinized the lyric very carefully to make sure there was nothing derogatory or incendiary. It was quite an intimidating experience, and yet strangely humanized for me a people who had been very mysterious to me. Once the ice was broken, I found the Russian soldiers to be warm and welcoming to David and me. We toured Red Square, which was breathtaking. We were in Moscow in January, and it was brutally cold. It was fascinating to see the looks on the faces we passed on the street as people glanced at us in wonder, or just stared blankly at us. There was a bleakness in the air and in the people we encountered that went well beyond the frigid air. It was a remarkable experience.

When we finally did shoot the CBC special with the Red Army choir, we brought all our children along. Brody was just under four years old and when he saw the imposing uniformed Russian soldier before him, he broke into a big smile and ran toward the soldier with open arms. This big, burly, decorated man lifted Brody high in the air with tremendous warmth. It felt like such a unifying moment. In the hearts of children, there's so much trust and love. If only we could all cling throughout our lives to the wonder and innocence that are always present in a child.

Our next big job was for the film *Stealing Home*, starring Mark Harmon and Jodie Foster, which was due to be released in August 1988. David came up with a beautiful melody, which inspired me profoundly, and the lyrics seemed to just flow out of me. We called our song "And When She Danced." My lyrics went like this:

"And when she danced, I lost my innocence. I loved her then, I always will."

The first time I sang these words for David, he stopped me right there.

"You can't write 'innocence,' " he said.

"Why not?"

"Just because it won't sing well," he said.

"But it does sing well," I said, singing the line again. " 'And when she danced, I lost my innocence.' It fits perfectly. It flows beautifully."

"No, it doesn't," he argued. "You can't do that. You've got to listen to me. I'm the one with the experience."

I couldn't argue about the fact that he was the more practiced songwriter than I was. But I was also fully confident that I knew my way around a lyric, and that in this instance I was right about my use of the word *innocence*. Having found my strength and my voice, I was determined to make good use of both.

"Yes, 'innocence' sings," I said.

We were at an impasse. Neither one of us is a singer, so we hired a vocalist to come into the home studio David had built in our guest-house. She was going to record vocals for our demo, so we could send it to the film's producer. After she ran through the song, her first reaction made me smile.

"Oh, I love how 'innocence' sings," she said. "What a beautiful word."

David just looked at me like: *Well, all right, I guess you won that one.* I didn't rub it in, but of course, I was pleased. Relatively green as I was, I felt justifiably confident in my lyrical talents, but every little bit of fortification helped when dealing with a strong personality like David's.

Admittedly, it was sometimes a challenge to hold my ground, because he was so undeniably accomplished. I knew I had to defer to him when it came to his knowledge of production and song composition. But I thought some aspects of his approach amounted to casual dismissal, and in these instances, I had to stand up for what I knew to be fair and right. The unexpected upside to all the loss, disruption, and profound transformation I'd experienced in the past decade was that I was somewhat emotionally fearless by this point.

While David sometimes created such moments where he down-played my expertise, he also gave me glowing accolades for my abilities, and the longer we worked together, the more my confidence grew. It was yin and yang in our songwriting and in our life together. The good and bad, the up and down. And it worked for a very long time.

"I Cry Real Tears"

You ought to be ashamed of yourself
The way you talk down to me
Oh baby
And didn't anybody ever teach you
To act more respectfully
I'm telling you
I'm only human too
Don't you realize
Look at my face
What do you see in my eyes
When a part of me just dies

I cry real tears
I have real fears
I've got a heart that's beating inside
Sometimes it breaks
And when it aches
My eyes cry real tears

You treat me like you think I'm
   made of stone
Like when I'm cut I don't bleed
Oh baby, don't you know I'm just
   flesh and bone
So what do you want from me
I'm telling you
That I'm only human too
Don't you realize
Look at my face
What do you see in my eyes
When a part of me just dies

I cry real tears
I have real fears
I've got a heart that's beating inside
Sometimes it breaks
And when it aches
My eyes cry real tears

There's something called the golden
   rule
Someday you'll wish you'd followed
   it more
You've been a fool
My love is truer than any love you'll
   find
But I'm worth more, and so is my
   time

I cry real tears
I have real fears
I've got a heart that's beating inside
Sometimes it breaks
And when it aches
My eyes cry real tears

LYRIC: LINDA THOMPSON

Chapter Eighteen

No Filter

Throughout the rest of our many years together, David and I would remain passionately—sometimes tumultuously—in love and our musical partnership would extend to heights more fulfilling than I could have imagined. But the joy of our early days did not last, unfortunately. Just as Elvis and my mama had been riddled with paradoxes, so too was my new love, David. As our relationship stretched from its first months to its early years, David revealed another aspect to his complex personality: he could be difficult. I tried to hold my ground, and as a result, we argued a great deal.

One of the clearest manifestations of David's intensity and most common sources of conflict between us came from his tendency to become jealous as well as controlling—even when it came to my past. In April 1987, at a U2 concert, I had the happy surprise of running into Lisa Marie, who was now a very mature and poised young woman of nineteen. Since Elvis had passed away, I hadn't had any way to get in touch with Lisa or maintain our relationship, so we'd fallen out of touch. As we each absorbed this emotional moment, it was apparent she had a lot of Presley in her, not just in the eyes, but also in the wariness and dark humor. Just as Mr. Presley was not won over very easily, Lisa seemed cautious, which was totally understandable given the circumstances of her young life.

Seeing Lisa brought my past back to me in a visceral way, reminding me how deeply I had loved her and her father and how his family and world had been mine for four and a half years. I felt the urge to reconnect with her if possible, and to be a friend. I gave her my phone number, and we reunited from time to time in the years to come.

David was gracious to Lisa Marie at that encounter, but I soon came to see that he did not like to be reminded of the fact that Elvis had been my first love. That summer, David and I were alone on his boat on what happened to be the tenth anniversary of Elvis's death. There was a news story on TV about how the date was being commemorated. David came in, took one look at the TV I was watching, and turned it off.

"What are you doing?" I asked. "I was watching that."

"I don't want you watching a show about your ex-boyfriend."

"Oh my God, he's been dead ten years," I said. "He's not coming back to claim me. This was a part of my life, a part of my history, and it's a part of history, period. You're in the music industry. You don't want to watch this?"

"Hell no, and I don't want you watching it, either."

Okay, he is not going to want to ever hear about Elvis, I thought. *So I guess if I'm attempting to make a life with this person, I'll need to respect that.* David was clearly threatened by Elvis's ghost and never wanted me to mention him.

But whereas avoiding the topic of Elvis was relatively easy given that he was no longer alive, David also had to contend with the fact that my ex-husband happened to be the world's greatest athlete, Bruce Jenner. As most red-blooded American men would be, David was a bit resentful that my ex was Bruce Jenner, but for him, these feelings were complicated by the fact that not only were we living in the house that Bruce and I had shared, but Bruce was still coming by the house to visit the boys. And while these visits didn't happen every day, nor did Bruce commit himself to a regular schedule, he stopped by more frequently than David would have liked. Bruce had the gate code, and he was free to come and go as he pleased. Once or twice a week, he stopped by to swim or play with the boys for very brief increments of time. Bruce was also invited to, and usually attended, every holiday celebration and kids' birthday party. He always had his video recorder in hand, and he was very much in the mix at such events. I tried to do everything I could to make David feel at ease, while also making Bruce feel comfortable, but my primary concern was always that Brandon and Brody felt secure in their young lives. I wanted my boys to feel that everyone was there for them, and that we could all coparent together.

I did tell Bruce on several occasions that he also needed to set up a dedicated room for the boys at his new house, so that if they ever wanted to sleep over, they would feel like they were welcome to do so. Bruce acknowledged what I said but he never created such a bedroom. I got it. As one of the only people in the world who knew Bruce's secret, I was also one of his only confidants. Although we did not engage in lengthy conversations about his state of mind, now that we were separated, when I asked him how he was doing, I could see in his face and hear in his voice that he was really struggling. He was in the midst of his own deeply personal, deeply confusing and emotional metamorphosis, which required him to have his own private sanctuary. I stopped pressing the matter with Bruce. But David, not immediately knowing the full story, remained adamant.

"Why is Bruce always coming over here?" David used to ask. "Why doesn't Bruce take the boys to his house?"

Very early on in our relationship, I knew I had to confide in David about Bruce, so he would stop seeing him as a threat. Furthermore, because David also resented that Bruce did not in any way provide for the boys, I wanted David to understand why I'd agreed to this arrangement. I needed David to see why I did not want to burden Bruce with financial concerns, but cared rather about him seeing the boys.

"Listen, I need to tell you the truth about Bruce," I said one afternoon. "He's really a woman, and he's in the middle of transitioning."

Of course, this concept was hard for David to grasp at first. He had much the same initial reaction that I'd had when Bruce told me.

"What?" he asked incredulously. "What do you mean?"

And then he glared at me suspiciously.

"Are you just telling me that because you don't want me to be jealous or threatened?" David asked.

"No, this is the truth, David," I said. "This is really what's going on."

I went on to explain my rationale for refusing child support from

Bruce and why I remained so encouraging of any efforts Bruce had made to be in the boys' lives. Unfortunately, the knowledge of Bruce's secret, even coupled with the visible signs of Bruce's ongoing transition, couldn't sway David. He simply didn't like Bruce being at the house as much as he was, even though his visits were brief.

For his part, Bruce had his own issues with the situation. Bruce didn't like the fact that David had moved into the house that he had bought with me, and in many ways he still seemed bitter about the choice I'd made to end our marriage. We were dealing with all the tensions and resentments that couples experience in a normal divorce, plus we had our own unique baggage. I might not have been as cognizant of Bruce's turmoil then as I am now, because I had plenty of my own inner turmoil to contend with, but I could see a few things clearly. Bruce was angry at David for taking his place, and understandably so. And he was angry at me because I was able to move on with a new love and find another life for myself. Bruce still loved me, and he still loved the idea of having a family with me. He'd wanted to transition to be a woman and then stay married to me, as a woman. But I'd already moved on. Meanwhile, he was wrestling with his transition and feeling very much alone. And so it was painful for him to be reminded of all that he'd lost. It was gut-wrenching for me to witness Bruce's agony and his attempts to navigate uncharted waters on his way to transitioning. To have another man live at the house he'd given up to me and our sons in the divorce chagrinned the part left inside of him that was masculine and territorial. The two continued to have some obvious rancor between them.

One day David and I were standing at the kitchen sink. Bruce had come to see the boys, and then quickly left in a huff when he found David at home. Bruce was getting into his car when he looked up, saw David in the window, and flipped him off.

"He just gave me the bird," David said.

"You guys, stop being children," I said.

As these and other issues began to loom larger for us, I suggested David and I go to see Trudy so she could fully explain Bruce's circumstances and counsel us about the problems we were having in our own relationship. After Trudy, we saw a therapist named Brandy, and then we saw a man who looked like my dad. None of it went well.

It was obvious there were no easy answers for the things we needed to work through. Beyond Bruce, one of the most frequent sources of our disagreements came from David's antiquated view of women. At times, he had an expectation that I was there to serve and take care of him, to make beds and do housework. He used to say things to me like, "You don't do anything for me. You don't iron my shirts. You don't darn my socks."

"Yeah, I don't do that much darning, since I don't even know how to darn and have no interest in learning!" I answered, incredulous.

I almost felt bad for David, that he had such an unrealistic view of a woman's role in the world. At that time he didn't believe that women should have careers. He found ambition in a woman to be unattractive. (Today, I'm happy to note, David seems to be much more enlightened on these issues.)

This narrow-mindedness made things difficult—especially when it came to my acting work. During our first year together, I was still paying the mortgage on my home, which meant not only was I taking care of David—I had to earn a living. Much as I always had, I continued pursuing acting jobs, in addition to the songwriting work David and I were doing. One day I was called to read for a pilot, being written and produced by Dan Aykroyd, called *Mars: Base One*, depicting the first colonization of the red planet. I was to play the resident dim-witted bombshell, thanks to typecasting from my days on *Hee Haw*.

I was on my way to my audition, driving through Hollywood, when my phone rang. It was one of those big, chunky car phones located in the middle of the center console. This was back when you could still talk on a handheld phone in your car without breaking California law, and so I answered while I was driving along. It was David, calling from our house.

"Hey," I said.

"Where are you going?" he asked.

"Oh, I'm going to my audition," I said. "I have an audition."

"This is not working for me," he said.

"What do you mean this is not working for you?"

"I don't want you to act," he said. "I don't want you to be an actress. I don't want you to work like that."

"David, I have two little boys to raise," I said. "I don't get alimony or child support. You're not paying anything for the upkeep of my house. I have a mortgage. What do you mean you don't want me to work? I have to work."

But of course, it wasn't just about me working—he was supportive of my career as a lyricist and was never threatened by my stint on *Hee Haw*. He simply didn't want me to be an actress who might ever have to do a love scene.

"I don't want you being an actress because you might have to kiss somebody, and if you do, it's not going to work for me."

"I'm sorry you feel that way, but I'm going to this audition, and I hope I get it. There aren't any kissing scenes anyway in this part. The contract for the role is for sixteen thousand dollars a week. That's substantial money. I can't turn it down."

In spite of David's protests, I got the part I'd auditioned for on *Mars: Base One*, and we shot the pilot. As fate would have it, the pilot didn't sell. We really thought it would, too, because the very brilliant Dan Aykroyd wrote the show, and it was hilarious. It was, in fact, ahead of its time.

Even before we were in therapy, it crossed my mind to leave the relationship when I first saw these early signs of David's sometimes controlling nature. At this point in my life, I was no longer a complete pushover and felt the call to defend myself. Still, I didn't like the rush of anger and indignity that arguments with David stirred up in me. That defensive person was not who I wanted to be or how I wanted to live. But I was so conflicted about the genesis of our relationship that I actually blamed myself for his behavior and the complications of our relationship. I believed that whatever came my way as a result of how we'd united was most likely my karma. *I probably deserve that*, I thought when he yelled and cursed and lost his temper. This was God's punishment for my transgression, I stupidly resolved.

I have to make this work at any cost, I thought. *This man says he left his wife, to be with me. Even though he expressed to me he wasn't happy in that marriage. I owe it to everyone involved to stick it out.* Like anyone who resigns him- or herself to being in a compromised relationship, it was an insidious and dangerous conclusion that hemmed me in for years.

But guilt was only part of what kept me there. Through my mom and Elvis, I'd developed the skill of defusing bombastic personalities, leaving me adept at compartmentalizing and making excuses for bad behavior. I had been too respectful of my mama to question her authority, even when she was in a rage that did not feel entirely justified. And I'd been too devoted to Elvis to do more than try to sweet-talk him out of his foul tempers. Those relationships, though, made it possible for me to reconcile the fact that funny, charming, talented, and otherwise wonderful David also came along with another David, who could be full of anger and controlling. I remained adept at handling this kind of unpredictable personality type, if for no other reason than I'd been there before. It was never comfortable for me, but it was familiar.

I found myself thinking back to the first time my mother met David. She was lying there in her bed, on oxygen, clearly studying him very closely.

"I bet you've got a bad temper, don't you?" she said to him.

David held her gaze, not in the least bit embarrassed or intimidated.

"I bet it takes one to know one, doesn't it?" he said.

I couldn't help but think: *Boy, do they really have each other's number, or what? Pot meet kettle, kettle meet pot.* And of course, looking at them, grinning at each other in mutual recognition, I could understand why I loved them both as I did. Two big, passionate hearts, who sometimes let their anger rule their actions.

My phone rang in the middle of the night, which was never good. It was my sister-in-law, Louise, calling from Memphis.

"Linda, you need to get a flight home," she said.

"Oh no, is it Mama?" I asked, fearing the worst.

"No, it's actually your daddy."

"What?"

"Yeah, Sam is at the hospital with him," she said. "He collapsed on the floor. He had a bleeding ulcer and nearly bled to death."

It sounded critical, and it was. I caught the next flight to Memphis, taking both Brandon and Brody with me, and hoped I would get there in time. Thankfully by that point the boys were quite used to the trip, as I'd still been bringing them with me to visit my parents once a month for the last few years.

My dad had been a selfless saint when it came to caring for my mother. He was always patient and loving, even when her suffering caused her to be difficult and demanding. He never complained, instead internalizing all of his own fears and problems, without ever taking a moment to care for himself. And he'd developed a bleeding ulcer without realizing it. One night he went to the sink to get a drink of water and began expelling blood from his mouth. He was able to reach the phone before collapsing, but instead of calling 911, he called my brother.

"Sam, help, I fell. I'm on the floor . . ." Daddy said before his voice trailed off.

Sam rushed over there and he found our dad, his face pale white, lying in a pool of blood. Sam called the paramedics, and then, he went back to check on our mother, who was bedridden and on oxygen. Now, our mama didn't like our daddy's name, Sanford, and she never had. And so, for the whole of their nearly fifty-year relationship, she called him Thompson.

"Sam, where's Thompson?" she asked when she saw Sam.

"Oh, Daddy, he's just in there," Sam said.

"Well, what's all that commotion?" she asked.

"Oh, I just have some friends in there visiting," Sam said.

"What do you mean friends?" she asked, knowing this would have been out of the ordinary, to say the least. Sam later described to me how he felt like he was caught in a black comedy as he tried to appear casual while frantically rushing back and forth between her room and the living room, where the paramedics were trying to stabilize our dad so they could get him to the hospital. Finally, my brother had to tell our mother what was really happening, because he had to have someone else come to the house to take care of her in Daddy's place.

I helped as much as I could during my days in Memphis. I stayed there until Daddy was out of the hospital and things had settled down to their normal routine.

After my father's scare, I continued to bring the boys back to see my ailing mother once a month. It was tiring to make that journey with two small children in tow, but I'm still thankful we had that time. Brandon and Brody were able to bring the biggest smile to their Mammaw's face, even as I struggled with the pain of watching her waste away to a skeletal remnant of her once-beautiful self. I'm grateful that my sons still have memories of their grandmother and how much she adored them.

It was a difficult time for everyone and took its toll on my relationship with David. Coupled with how raw I felt while dealing with my mother's long, excruciating demise, I also felt like David didn't treat me with the respect and sensitivity I deserved during these emotional times. After the problems that we'd been having, which had already landed us in therapy, this perceived lack of empathy from him felt like a sign that we weren't meant to be. I think watching my mother's life slowly and painfully come to an end made me more conscious of my own life and circumstances. Perhaps our differences and problems—his temper and controlling ways—were too great to overcome the good in our relationship, even considering his charm and our musical symbiosis. And so I asked for us to take a break in our relationship and see other people. We were both saddened that our relationship had gotten to this point, but he concurred that a break was probably a good idea.

During that period, one of the men I went out with a couple of times was Dodi Fayed. I had met Dodi in London when I was there with Christopher Lambert during one of my attempts to pull away from David. Dodi was a perfect gentleman, and even though I'd only gone to dinner with him—nothing more—he invited me to his family's yacht. Dodi called me from London and said he was sending his private jet for me and would meet me on his yacht, where I would have my own stateroom; we would cruise the Mediterranean. It sounded like a welcome respite from my problems at home. I agreed to go, and on a Tuesday, Dodi called me and said all of the arrangements had been made.

"My jet is at the airport and waiting for you to board," he said.

"Dodi, I am so sorry, but I have changed my mind," I said. "I have a bad feeling about my mother. She is back in the hospital, and I don't want to be so far away in case I am needed."

"But I sent the jet for you all the way from Europe, and everything is all set up on the yacht for us to go," he protested.

I felt terrible about canceling, but I didn't want to take a chance on not being there for my family if I was needed. And in truth, I wasn't comfortable about making such a potentially big move away from David. I still loved him, after all. I spoke with my mother every day that week, and she seemed to be improving day by day. She said the doctors told her she might even be going home over the weekend. Then that Thursday night, I got a call from Sam that Mama had experienced a setback, and it didn't look good. I scooped Brandon and Brody out of bed, and we caught a red-eye to Memphis. When we arrived there on Friday, I went immediately to the hospital, and I never left my mother's side.

For the last two days of Mama's life, I sat by her bedside, holding her hand, with a treasured crucifix between her palm and mine. I felt her consciousness ebb and flow, and I cherished the warmth in the body that had conceived mine. Hers was the first warmth I had ever known, and I wanted so desperately to cling to her last bit of life and energy. I studied the face that, for all of my life, had looked at me with unconditional love.

Mama had a single teardrop that kept forming in the corner of her weary eye. As I kept my bedside vigil, I pondered how each of us will have cried one last teardrop when we finally depart this existence. I wondered what a person's last tear would signify. I felt that if Mama could speak through me (and I feel that she did), she would have indicated that she was crying for more time. More time to be with the people she had so generously loved here. And I know I was crying for more time to be with my beloved mother. I held her hand tightly with my left hand, while I wrote "The Last Tear I Cried" with my right.

> *And the last tear I cried was for time*
> *For the years I spent believing time was mine*
> *There seemed time enough to do*
> *All the things I wanted to*
> *Thought there was time enough to say*
> *Words to take the pain away*
> *Now I close my eyes to sleep*
> *Knowing time's not ours to keep*

If I could say one thing to you
That might help see you through
I'd say listen to your heart
And you'll know we're not apart
Don't let your precious breath be spent
Forming words of detriment
Build long bridges—not high walls
And think of me when raindrops fall
I'll be kissing you with sunshine
A part of you will always be mine
And when you're in your darkest night
I'll be waiting in the light.

I was able to tell Mama in her last moments that I finally understood what she meant when she'd said to me over the years, "There's no love like a mother's love." She took her last breath on Saturday, September 5, 1987, looking straight at me as she passed on. It was wrenching to be with her when she died, but it would have been more painful not to be.

David flew in to be with me, and Bruce flew in as well. David left before the funeral but Bruce stayed on and served as one of my mother's pallbearers, which seemed appropriate, given that he still felt like an integral part of our family and always would. Although he was enduring deep troubles in his personal life, Bruce was still Bruce. He remained the same reliable, thoughtful, trustworthy person he'd always been, just the type of kind soul I'd want by my side during a time of loss and sorrow. My mother had loved Bruce dearly and trusted him to take good care of our family. The days in which we'd stood together as husband and wife were long gone, but his kindness and steadfastness to me during my grief was a huge reason he remained my trusted best friend. He was, and she still is, after all is said and done, the father of my beloved sons, and a person with whom I shared meaningful years of personal history. I was grateful for how the people in my life stepped up to show their support for me during my time of grief. Even though Dodi had every right not to speak to me again, he sent three dozen red roses to me upon hearing of my mother's passing.

After my mother died, I felt more at a loss than ever. Bruce was becoming a woman. I had two little boys to raise, knowing that someday I'd be faced with the task of explaining the unexplainable. So I reached for the lifeline that was present for me. David and I reunited and recommitted ourselves to each other. I still had reservations about many aspects of our relationship, but I was shattered and he was ready to resume being the man in my life. He was, of all things, a man who could take charge, and that's what I needed. David was loving and comforting during this time for me. There was then, and probably will always be, a deeply felt love for David no matter our differences.

Brandon and Brody were my ultimate comfort, though, as I grieved for my mother. Not long after she had passed away, I was with the boys and we had just finished a shower. We all had towels wrapped around our heads, turban-style.

"Mommy, who taught you to put the towel around your head like that?" Brody asked.

"My mom," I replied.

"But who is your mommy?" he countered.

"Well, Mammaw," I said. "You remember Mammaw."

Brody looked at me for a moment.

"But Mammaw is dead," he finally replied.

Brandon jumped in, sensitively admonishing his little brother, "Brody, Brody! Let's not say that Mammaw is dead. Let's just say she's not alive right now. For instance, if the phone rings, and I answer, and I say, 'Hello,' and someone says, 'Is your mammaw there?' I'll just say, 'I'm sorry, my mammaw is not alive right now, would you like to leave a message?' Then when I get to heaven, I'll give her the message."

Brandon gained the nickname "Gandhi" a long time ago for always exhibiting such wisdom and kindness. And I'm sure my mother was up in heaven, flapping her angel wings with delight and love at Brandon's declaration.

"Heaven Holds the Ones I Love"

I've spent my life
Building castles of dreams
Reaching for
Each distant star
As tears clear my eyes
I finally realize
Happiness is where you are
And I'm still a part of you
And you're still a part of me
I swear I'll always celebrate
Your memory
You'll live inside of me

Heaven holds the ones I love
I see your eyes twinkle in the skies
    above
My hopes are floating in the clouds
The wind repeats your name out
    loud
Ohhh
Heaven holds the ones I love

At times I'm unsure
Why our hearts must endure
All the pain
And such great loss
But look what I've gained
I feel your kiss in the rain
It's your smile I miss the most

But I'm still a part of you
And you're still the biggest part of me
And I swear I'll always celebrate
Your memory
And trust what's meant to be

Heaven holds the ones I love
I see your eyes twinkle in the skies
    above
My hopes are floating in the clouds
The wind repeats your name out
    loud
Ohhh
Heaven holds the ones I love

And in my grief and disbelief
One thing I know is true
Every breath I take
Brings me that much closer to you

Heaven holds the ones I love
I see your eyes twinkle in the skies
    above
My hopes are floating in the clouds
The wind repeats your name out
    loud
Ohhh
Heaven holds the ones I love

LYRIC: LINDA THOMPSON

Chapter Nineteen

Voices that Care

After David and I got back together, it didn't make any of the problems that we'd been having go away, but we both seemed to understand much more clearly that we wanted to be together, wanted an incredible life as one, and so we got to work making that vision a reality.

One of the things that always brought us all together was traveling. In addition to our annual trips to Canada to visit David's family, we took our children just about everywhere. Ski vacations to Whistler, Banff Springs, Lake Louise, Lake Tahoe, and tennis camp in Florida. Trips to Disneyland, Disney World, Knott's Berry Farm, Medieval Times dinner theater. We traveled all over Europe, went to Japan, and explored Africa. We toured the White House and saw Broadway musicals; we hired private yachts to cruise the Greek Islands and St. Bart's; we went to Hawaii many times. David and I both wanted to widen our children's horizons.

Everywhere we went, and whatever we did, we tried to lead by example for all our children, and I aimed to instill positive values in my sons. I felt a very strong responsibility to raise my boys to be understanding and accepting of other people and cultures, our similarities and our differences. Through all this travel, they got to see firsthand that the world is a very diverse place, with different cultures, religions, languages, values, histories, ideas, and even definitions of beauty. These teachings were especially critical, I believed, because my sons would no doubt one day find it necessary to try to understand the truth about their dad and his gender issues.

They also came back to Tennessee with me quite often, and actually lived there with me for a month at a time when I filmed *Hee Haw* twice a year. Not only did I want them with me, but I also wanted to imbue them with at least some of the culture in which I'd been raised. They got to eat fried catfish and turnip greens. They were exposed to generous helpings of country music and the blues. They got to absorb at least some of Southern gentility and sensibility. We caught fireflies in the summer months and even released them in our hotel room and watched them light up as they flew free. I'll never forget one day when Pappaw said, "Let's go over yonder directly." Brandon asked, "Mommy, just where is Yonder and when exactly is 'directly'?"

Sometimes that open-mindedness they learned while traveling even had to extend to David who brought his own peccadillos to each trip. David is terribly claustrophobic, and I was protective of him, trying to avoid situations that might make him feel closed in. He hasn't taken an elevator in well over thirty years because of his claustrophobia. He has been known to climb forty flights of stairs to avoid getting on one.

One year we went on a grand tour of Europe with a huge group of people. We took my brother and sister-in-law, five of David's sisters, their husbands, some of their kids, and all of our children; plus each of our kids was allowed to bring a friend. We had so many people with us that we had taken over most of an entire charter bus. On one leg of the journey, our whole group had gotten off the bus to go see the Eiffel Tower.

It was raining and David and I had seen the tower before, so when David decided to stay on the bus, I agreed to keep him company.

"We have to lock up the bus," the driver informed us. "You can stay on if you want, but we're going to lock it."

David agreed, not thinking about the fact that he wouldn't be able to get off the bus until our group came back from their tour. The driver locked the bus and walked away.

"Do you think they left the door open?" he asked, looking around.

"No, he said they were going to lock the bus," I said.

He quickly began to panic, having heart palpitations and pacing the aisle.

"Come and sit here, and I'll scratch your scalp," I said. "I'll rub your shoulders. I'll try to relax you." Thank God I stayed with him. He would likely have broken the windows otherwise. I loved the times when David and I connected for each other like that.

The highlight on our travel calendar each year was our summer trips to British Columbia. And it was on one of those trips, in 1990, that David and I had a chance encounter with someone who would become an important part of our lives for years to come.

Usually the whole family—the boys and I, David, and his daughters— would spend weeks out on the boat together, but this particular year we were in a bit of a tiff, and we mutually decided that David would stay on land with his daughters and visit with his family, while I'd head out to Desolation Sound with the boys and the captain for a week.

Then David received a call from his friend, Richard Baskin, who was a composer and producer, and around this time, Barbra Streisand's live-in love.

He asked if a friend and his wife could go out on David's boat with us.

"Linda is taking the boat out with her kids, but I suppose they could go out with them," David said. "Who is it?"

"It's Kevin Costner and his wife," Richard said.

"The hell I'll let Kevin Costner get on that boat with my girl," David said, recalling, I'm sure, that I always commented on how handsome the actor was. "No way."

When I arrived at the boat with Brandon and Brody in tow, ready to embark, I was shocked and confused to see David there, waiting for me, clearly ready to go out with us. The girls were not with him.

"I've decided to come on the boat with you," he said.

"I thought we had agreed that the boys and I would go alone," I said. "Why are you coming with us?"

"Because Kevin Costner is coming with his wife," he said.

"Oh, okay," I said, knowing just how David thought and how jealous he could be. I had to smile, and then he and I both broke into a giggle.

"Yeah, I've got a Polaroid picture of me letting you go out into the open sea with Kevin Costner," David howled.

The truth is that I was so happy and relieved to see David. I was always anguished when we would argue because I wanted nothing more than to just be loving together. When we were in that loving frame of mind nothing was better.

Later that day Kevin and his then wife, Cindy, arrived. They were darling, the most down-to-earth people imaginable. They even showed up with their own candy bars, in case we didn't have any sweets on the boat. *Anybody that shows up with a little brown paper bag of candy bars, just to be safe, is my kind of people*, I thought.

"I just finished making this film," Kevin told us when we got to talking.

"Oh, really, what's it called?" I asked.

"*Dances with Wolves*," he said.

"Oh, okay," I said. "I think I've heard about that."

"Yeah?" he said. "It's a long film, and I directed it, and I starred in it. And I'm exhausted. I'm just depleted."

As was his way, Kevin understated the significance of his film, displaying his characteristic humility. *Dances with Wolves* was not only a blockbuster film, but also one of the most beautiful cinematic experiences any movie enthusiast could ever have.

Kevin was a guy who loved to be in the water, loved to be out on the dingy, loved to fish. He was a real guy's guy, but also very suave and charming. Cindy was a doll, too. As I remember, when they met in college, she played Snow White at Disneyland as her summer job, which seemed appropriate. We got to be good friends and stayed in touch after our boat trip.

In fact, Kevin invited David and me to the *Dances with Wolves* premiere in November 1990. And while neither David nor I realized it at the time, this idle boat trip with Kevin and the friendship that it formed would end up spurring one of our most satisfying and successful collaborations ever.

The longer that David and I were together, the more we came to understand that part of achieving the vision of what our relationship could be came from the fact that we were both such social creatures.

Gone were the days of staying home and watching TV with Elvis or going to bed early so I could rise with Bruce and the sun. Instead, David and I enjoyed a vibrant and invigorating social life, and over time that became one of our most rewarding ways to spend time together.

David and I always enjoyed ourselves when we went out together, and became known as something of an "it" couple, with abundant invitations to all kinds of parties.

"As soon as you and David got here, the party started," people always said afterward.

David was, and still is, quite charming and very entertaining. He had a fantastic sense of humor to go along with his incomparable talent. That's the David I fell in love with, and that's the David who made me fall in love with him again and again. When we were socializing, I could tap back into that original feeling of love he'd inspired in me, even though we experienced so many contentious moments in our private life. Our natural, affectionate rapport in public did a great deal to repair our private rifts and hold us together as a couple.

David loved being the center of attention. He didn't like to just blend. When we arrived, he started snapping his fingers.

"You got a piano?" he almost always asked the host.

He sat down and started playing, people sang along, and the crowd loved it. Many times hosts even asked him to bring in singers to entertain their party guests. David was kind of like the go-to party entertainer. He and I even had this little routine we did a lot. David brought me into his act like, "Let's tell the joke about the couple from Pensacola," and given my fifteen years on *Hee Haw*, I could certainly deliver a punch line. I used to joke that David was the dancing chicken at these festivities, and I was his sidekick. Over time, it became a running joke: *Oh, I'm with the piano player.* But, of course, David was not just any piano player. He is a musical genius, and he was the man who held my heart in his talented hands for many years. I appreciated his talents and enjoyed his showmanship as much as anybody. I was always proud of him when we went out, and he was the center of it all.

During these years, Hollywood mogul Marvin Davis and his wife, Barbara, often hosted lavish, glamorous parties, and through them we met many people who became dear friends. I reconnected with Don Rickles, whom I still remembered so fondly from my time in Las Vegas with Elvis. We met Sidney Poitier, Jackie Collins, and Michael Caine, all of whom we would vacation with many times over the years. That was one of the best things about my relationship with David, other than our symbiotic creativity: all the friendships that we both shared and loved, and the many good times we had with them.

We must have been highly entertaining, because David often didn't seem to have a clue about propriety, which could lead to awkwardness at many of these elevated social functions but made him all the more lovable. He was completely unbridled and unfiltered. He was so funny and talented that he almost always got away with it, and his irreverence became a part of his appeal. Even in the most extreme cases, like the time we met Nancy Reagan.

We were at a party and Nancy was with us when David started telling the most profane, off-color joke imaginable. As soon as I knew where he was going, I was practically kicking him under the table.

"No, don't tell that joke," I warned. "That's so inappropriate."

When he got to the part about licking a goat's penis, no one laughed and everyone just looked at each other. Then there was a slight, polite murmur.

"That's quite the joke," Nancy Reagan then said, always her gracious self.

David the party guest was great. If I could have had that David all the time, I'd probably still be married to him. But the David that I brought home with me was not always the same person who had performed for the crowd.

I'm sure David had his own complaints about me, too, but it felt to me like David only cared about impressing others and had no concern for how his everyday behavior impacted me. The prospect of marriage seemed uncertain. I didn't care that he was inappropriate—God knows Elvis had that same instinct in spades. It was more that I felt David seldom seemed to afford me the kindnesses that he showed others, especially when we were alone and there was no one for him to impress.

In fact, the subject of marriage had become ammunition of sorts during our regular confrontations. I was genuinely torn. I knew he was difficult. He was the most difficult man I'd ever loved. And, needless to say, I've loved some complicated, difficult men. I didn't like how he treated me. I consistently felt like he didn't show me the respect I deserved. But I was also deeply in love with him, so we always made up. It was a tumultuous, complicated, and yet enduring love affair.

Fortunately, whenever there was doubt and tension between us, there was also music. And perhaps in the end, that was the real glue that kept us together; for every temporary rift we experienced, we had a creative collaboration to reunite us.

In 1991, we joined forces for one of the proudest moments of my career. When the Gulf War broke out, my sons were seven and nine. I looked at them and thought: *Oh my God, if they were draft age, and the draft was implemented, my kids would have to go. I'd move to Canada. I'd move to Australia. I'd take them anywhere to keep them from having to go over and fight in this war.* Even thought I am a proud patriot, I found the Gulf War a difficult one to stand behind. And every patriot's heart has to be challenged when your child is involved in conflict and exposed to danger. I felt such sadness for the parents of the kids who did have to go into battle. I wanted to do something to reach out to our soldiers in the Persian Gulf to extend our best thoughts and love to them during what must have been the most difficult time in their lives. I conceived the idea to create a song and an event that would be completely apolitical. It wasn't for the war. It wasn't against the war. It was meant to comfort those the war impacted most directly.

"I want to do a song for the soldiers," I said to David.

"Okay, I'm on board," David said.

David enlisted Peter Cetera, one of the founding members of the band Chicago, and together they wrote the music for our ambitious undertaking. And then I wrote the lyrics, titling our song "Voices That Care." The whole idea was to let our soldiers know that though they may be far from home, they were far from forgotten. We were all reaching out to them through our voices.

David and I agreed that if we could get Kevin Costner on board, it would help the project immensely in terms of publicity.

"I'm in," Kevin said, when I called to ask him if he'd participate.

"Can we use your name?" I excitedly asked.

"Absolutely," he said.

With Kevin on board, David and I both started making phone calls to PR people, managers, and some of the major stars of the day. From there, the project instantly built momentum. There was a wonderful feeling of energy and positivity in our house during that whole time. Once I got the inspiration to reach out with this ambitious project, I was obsessed with making it happen. Having Kevin involved inspired all these other major stars to participate, and we soon had more than one hundred lined up to sing, including Meryl Streep, Michelle Pfeiffer, Mike Tyson, Magic Johnson, Billy Crystal, and Brooke Shields.

On the appointed day, all of the celebrity participants gathered on the Warner Bros. lot. Robert Daly was running Warner at the time, and he and Terry Semel opened up the studios for us. Irving Azoff agreed to put out the single on Giant Records. Everybody involved was generous with their time, their expertise, their devotion, and their love. We recorded a television special, too. All the money from the sale of the single went to the USO and the Red Cross. With our record sales, we raised several million dollars for both organizations.

I had so many soldiers reach out to me in the wake of the song. Even now, twenty-five years later, every once in a while I'll hear from former military personnel.

"That video, and that record, really sustained us when we were over there," they'll say. "Because when you feel all alone, to know that people are thinking of you back home, and reaching out like that, really means the world. It was incredible to know that everybody from John Doe to the biggest star in the world was thinking of me."

Not only was it the biggest project I'd done with David until that point, it was also significant for me because I landed a publishing deal with Warner/Chappell Music, and I've been with them ever since. It was one of those times in our marriage when everything—our careers, our family, and our love for each other—converged into one project. All I could do is hope that we'd have many more moments of such harmony.

"Voices That Care"

Lonely fear lights up the sky
Can't help but wonder why
You're so far away

There, you had to take a stand
In someone else's land;
Life can be so strange

I wish we didn't have to choose
To always win or lose
That we could compromise

But I won't turn my back again
Your honor I'll defend
So hurry home, and till then . . .

Stand tall; stand proud!
Voices that care are crying out loud
And when you close your eyes
     tonight
Feel in your heart how our love
     burns bright

I'm not here to justify the cause
Or to count up all the loss
That's all been done before

I just can't let you feel alone
When there's so much love at home
We're sending out to you

All the courage that you've known
The bravery you've shown
Clearly lights the way

We pray! To make the future bright
With no more wars to fight
For this we'll sing your praise

Stand tall; stand proud!
Voices that care are crying out loud
And when you close your eyes
     tonight
Feel in your heart how our love
     burns bright

You are the voice
You are the light

Stand tall; stand proud!
Voices that care are crying out loud
And when you close your eyes
     tonight
Feel in your heart how our love
     burns bright

LYRIC: LINDA THOMPSON

Chapter Twenty

No Hallmark Memories

In 1990, Bruce had shared with me that he'd started dating Kris Kardashian, soon to be divorced from her husband, attorney Robert Kardashian, who a few years later would be one of O. J. Simpson's defense lawyers in the famous murder trial. They quickly began spending a great deal of time together, and he told me that he really liked her. I had been with David for almost five years at this point, and was thrilled that Bruce might have also found someone new to care about. I knew it had been painful for Bruce that I'd moved on so quickly after our breakup, especially because the complicated situation he was in made it much more difficult for him to date. And it was clear that he was in a delicate emotional state that left him feeling isolated and confused, and he really could have used the support of a loving, devoted partner. I'd done the best I could to be there for him as a friend, but given all that I was dealing with in my own life, I knew Bruce was feeling the loss of our marriage, maybe even more than I.

The years since my divorce from Bruce hadn't been easy for him. Rather than presenting the triumphant demeanor of someone prepared to live his true life in the open, as Caitlyn now does, he often appeared to be worried, distraught, and distracted. I think he was usually eager to hurry back to his home, where he felt safe to be himself in private. Bruce and I had always communicated well, and this continued to be true, even if we had less chance to do so. I watched his subtle transmutation from the muscular jock to a more feminized version of the Bruce I had known and fallen in love with. He was undergoing painful electrolysis, hormone injections, and feminizing surgeries, and morphing before my eyes into someone I no longer recognized. He was struggling with presenting Bruce Jenner to the public while undergoing physical changes toward becoming who he felt she authentically was.

During his weekly or biweekly visits with the boys, he gave me updates on his personal life, and we sometimes spoke at length on the phone when I called to invite him to holidays and birthdays. Although he was not directly involved in day-to-day care for the boys, I tried to involve him in their lives without making him feel any more pressure than he had already.

Bruce always told me when he was seeing someone and he dated several women, even though he had begun his transition and showed visible signs of it. He had no facial hair, no chest hair, but he did have boobs, and he had gotten a nose job, a facelift, and trimmed his Adam's apple. When Bruce had his most complex surgery, a facelift, I offered to come over and take care of him, but as usual, he said he was fine and could manage on his own. As Bruce struggled with his back-and-forth commitment to transition, in the not so understanding or forgiving 1980s, I felt the pain of his conflicted mind right along with him. It seemed to me like he was still confused as to how completely he was ready to commit to transitioning, and it was causing him a great deal of frustration, anger, and deep distress. I imagined that he was experiencing an ongoing inner monologue along the lines of: *If do this, can I get away with it? How will the public react? Will I be accepted? Will I ever work again? I've got two ex-wives and four kids, and I'd like to find a new partner. How am I going to pull this off? What if I can't?*

Bruce may not have told me all that he was feeling at the time, but I was one of the few confidants who knew the extent of his secret, and he did share stories of his dating life with me. One of the women he'd dated, we can call her Jenny, was lovely, and Bruce clearly liked her a great deal. As he revealed to me after they had dated for a few weeks, he felt close enough to her to tell her about his transition process. She was so stunned she began slapping her own face, hard.

"Why does this have to happen to me?!" she yelled again and again.

Bruce also went out socially with a prominent entertainment reporter and seemed to enjoy her company. Again, he decided to tell her everything about what he was going through. Bruce also confided in a few of his close friends. To their credit, all of these people kept Bruce's secret and let him be the first to reveal it publicly.

All of this made me very nervous for him, though. I knew he was still going to sessions with Trudy, as there was a law that he had to complete a certain amount of therapy before he could transition. I was glad he had that support in his life, but his perspective sometimes seemed to be less than completely clear. I was concerned about what would happen if he was outed before he was ready to reveal his true self to the world.

"I'm not telling anybody what you're going through," I said to him. "I think you should keep this to yourself until you've actually made your transition. Unless you're getting married or something, you don't need to tell every woman you're dating."

"No, I want to be honest right off the bat because I feel bad that I wasn't honest with you," he said. "I feel like I caused you a lot of pain."

I couldn't argue with that line of reasoning. I appreciated knowing that Bruce was still the nice person he'd always been, that he felt accountable for not having told me his secret and for having upset my life the way he had.

Bruce seemed to think I was overreacting, and I hoped he was right. I was extremely discreet, determined to keep Bruce's secret until he was ready to share his true self with the world. I didn't even tell my best friend.

Even though Bruce had struggled for the five years since we'd separated, he still tried to be present for his sons. Brandon and Brody clearly loved their daddy, and I think they still felt a connection with him and looked up to him. Admittedly, Bruce was painfully self-involved and could only muster a weekly visit or an outing for a movie or ice cream. But he was still a presence in their lives, even if his participation was limited.

As much as I'd encouraged him to be actively involved in the boys' lives, I'd always given him a lot of leeway to take care of himself first, simply trying to make him feel welcome, so he'd at least continue his somewhat regular visits with the boys. My primary goal was for them to have as much of a relationship with their father as possible for as long as he was around to do so.

Because Bruce was so optimistic about things with Kris, I also approached his new relationship with a great deal of positivity and respect, hoping it would prove to be healing and helpful to the person I still cared for so deeply.

In early 1991, Bruce came to me one day.

"We need to talk," he said.

"Well, I remember how our last 'We need to talk' session turned out," I said.

He gave me a rueful smile, and we both laughed a little, acknowledging all that we'd been through together and separately in these past years.

"I am getting married," Bruce informed me.

I was over the moon with delight. I had watched Bruce struggle and suffer for the past five years. I had read the discomfort and fear on his face. I had listened to him confide in me about how difficult it had been for him to find a woman to spend time with, let alone share his life with. And in those five long years, he had not been able to bring himself to take the final step and complete his transition.

I'd been fully prepared to back Bruce completely, no matter what he chose to do, and even welcome him back into the boys' lives as their female relative, or whoever he wished to present himself as, if that's how he decided to live. But my support was in no way the same thing as having a truly educated understanding of what it meant for him to be transgender. When he decided not to complete his transition, I was relieved, thinking that this decision to remain a man would result in his being much happier and better off. I didn't want him to endure prejudice, rejection, or unkindness. I was afraid that his secret would be revealed in the press in a sensational way. Because of our therapy sessions with Trudy, I knew Bruce would always feel like a woman inside, but I assumed he would be okay with this compromise, as he had lived this way for so long, so successfully.

Though his decision to remain Bruce would eventually take a huge toll on his psyche and well-being, I assumed he was making the right choice. As far as I could tell, he had found a woman with whom he felt ready to take the next step in his life. Most important to me, his decision meant he was going to be around to be a father to his children. Kris had four children of her own with Robert Kardashian, so I assumed she would be a good partner for Bruce, and a woman who understood the important role of parenting.

Bruce told me that he was stopping the hormones and that Kris was okay with everything. Keep in mind that Bruce had no hair left on his face, neck, or chest, and no hope of ever growing hair there again due to the painful electrolysis he had undergone. In addition, he had already had "feminizing" surgeries to his face, and as a result of the female hormones he had been taking for five years, he had substantial breasts, noticeable even to his four- and six-year-old sons. The point is that he would have had a tough time hiding his partial transition from someone with whom he had become intimate. But it was heartening to know Bruce had found someone with whom to share his life. I was elated that perhaps now he finally had found some resolve in his painful predicament.

I did not in any way think that he was choosing to live in the closet or deny himself true happiness. He had created the space in his life to become a woman, at the cost of our marriage, and yet he had not gone ahead and done so. Because he did not express any conflicted emotions or confusion to me about his decision to remarry, I had no reason to be anything but happy for him.

Before they were married, I met Kris once or twice, only briefly, and I thought she was pleasant. She was polite, and I was cordial. When they were married in April 1991, I had high hopes for the blended family we were building and I saw the possibility for ongoing love and support for all of our children. And since we parents can only be as happy as our least content child is, I hoped for some happiness for us adults, too.

With Bruce taking his trip down the aisle, and nicely settled in his new life, as I surmised, I began to consider with more seriousness the possibility of married life with David. I knew it was time for us to take our relationship to the next level. Once Bruce was remarried and I knew he was going to be okay, I started to feel like it was time for me to remarry, too. It was as if I'd wanted to wait until Bruce went on with his life before I did the same. That's how much I cared about him and still felt partially responsible for him. I always wanted to be there for him, much to David's chagrin.

By most definitions, David and I practically *were* married. I was certainly in love with and committed to him and our relationship. David had been living in my home with my children and me for five years. His kids came over most weekends, and we did many things as a family already. We worked together at times and had all the same friends. Our lives were as entangled as two people's can be without saying "I do." And yet in many ways that was the problem. Although he was temperamental, and I came with my own unique baggage, we were in deep together. There was still a part of me that thought: *Oh, I've got to make this work. I'm deeply entrenched in this relationship. My kids and his kids are in this with us now. They've already gone through the pain of divorce. There are too many people involved for us not to make this work.*

Looking back, I think we were both kind of dragging our heels because we were still recovering from divorces. Our baby steps, our one forward, two back, were all done in increments, as much because of my hesitancy as David's.

For their part, the boys really wanted us to get married. Both my sons considered David their true father and loved him. They still do. He was a constant presence in their lives, serving as their paternal figure. Brandon, being our resident little Gandhi, even developed a ritual. Every time we went somewhere, whether it was the Trevi Fountain in Rome or a little fountain in Victoria where people tossed in coins, Brandon always made the same wish.

"You know what I wish, Mommy and David?" Brandon said. "I wish that you would get married."

And Brandon certainly had company. Many of our friends were intent on seeing us get married, too. We were in Philadelphia for a Philadelphia Flyers game with the hockey team's owner, Ed Snider, and his then wife, Martha Snider, as well as our dear friends Ashley and John Lewis and Jelinda and Barry De Vorzon. When we were relaxing in our hotel suite, they began putting the pressure on us.

"Well, when are you guys getting married?" someone said.

"You've been living together, fighting together, raising kids together for four and a half years now," someone else chimed in. "When are you going to get married?"

"Well, first you have to get engaged," someone added.

"Fine, we'll get engaged then," we said.

Ed, Martha, David and I went to a jeweler in Philadelphia and found a beautiful six-carat yellow diamond. Of course, it had to be a yellow stone because that's my favorite color; it's so happy, like sunshine. It wasn't a perfect stone, but it was beautiful, and we bought it on the spot. That was our first step toward matrimony.

"Okay, we've got the stone now," we said. "That means we're on the right path."

We all celebrated, toasting and drinking champagne in our hotel suite.

When we returned to Los Angeles, David and I went to XIV Karats in Beverly Hills. We brought in the stone and told them the kind of setting we wanted. After XIV Karats put the ring together, David picked it up and unceremoniously placed it on my finger. We had already made the determination we would go ahead, so we were engaged now, but we didn't set a date. I wore the ring and we went out to dinner to celebrate our engagement. There was never even an "on one knee" traditional proposal.

David and I were married that June 22. Our dear friends Essam and Layla Khashoggi invited us to have the ceremony on a bluff overlooking the Pacific Ocean at their fifty-acre estate in Hope Ranch. Layla and Essam, along with all our other friends, wanted us to get married so badly that they offered to plan and pay for the wedding, and do everything to ensure it actually happened.

There was just one caveat. Essam turned to David, a twinkle in his eye.

"If you ever get divorced, I'm going to know it's your fault, and you're going to owe me the money back," Essam said.

He never did reclaim the cost of our wedding, of course, but we've made many jokes about it over the years.

David and I were married in a beautiful ceremony at six o'clock in the evening in front of around 150 guests, including our families and dearest friends, Barbra Streisand and Richard Baskin, Kenny and Marianne Rogers, and many of our friends from the Malibu Racquet Club. My daddy walked me down the aisle to the incredibly romantic "*St. Elmo's Fire* Theme Song," which David had written. Kenny sang "Lady" and "You Decorated My Life" for us at the reception. David wrote a song for me expressly for our wedding, "The Color of My Love," which Celine Dion eventually recorded. It was the kind of moment when David really did shine. We honestly did have a great love affair, tempestuous as the best ones so often are. Reference Taylor and Burton, Tracy and Hepburn, and even, sometimes, Edith and Archie. Think the heroes and heroines in the film soundtrack songs we penned together. I felt like I was finally able to exhale. We had all made it to the other side of what had been an extremely tumultuous and emotional time in our lives. I had a partner, and my boys had a father, and together with David's daughters and Bruce's new family, we could all form one big, loving collective.

Unfortunately, the vision I'd had of our happy, blended family was not what came to pass. After Bruce and Kris married, things definitely changed in his relationship with the boys. Having put a great deal of love and thought and energy into trying to build a blended family with David, I had just hoped that we would have some realistic version of this same experience with Bruce's new family. In the immediate aftermath of their wedding, I assumed his distance was just due to the fact that he was busy. And then I tried to tell myself that he was caught up in his newfound happiness after so many years of loneliness.

However, in truth, the union marked a turning point during which periods of several years would go by without Bruce attempting to contact or visit his sons. No birthday cards, or phone calls, no "Merry Christmas," no "Everything okay?" after several Malibu wildfires threatened our home and safety. Having been present at almost all of the birthday parties and holidays in the five years between our separation and his marriage to Kris, with his trusty video recorder in hand, Bruce was a noticeable absence now. At first, when we planned a party, the boys asked if their dad was coming. And when he didn't show up, they asked why he hadn't been there. Their excitement at the possibility of seeing their father on these special occasions, and the disappointment in their sweet little faces when he let them down, broke my heart even more than our divorce had. But after a few years, when they seemed quietly resigned to the fact he was not coming, and they stopped asking, that broke my heart even more.

Bruce quickly assumed an angry attitude toward me, and to this day I do not understand why. I had been his ally, his friend, and genuinely loved him as my forever family. He suddenly became bitter toward me and seemed to perceive me as the enemy, which was extremely painful for me. Maybe he was trying to prove to his new wife how devoted he was to her and their family by essentially discarding his prior relationships. Maybe he'd been bitter all along, but he'd hidden his true feelings because he'd needed my friendship as some form of a sanctuary. I could intellectualize his actions, but there was no reasoning away the pain I felt at this change in his behavior toward me, and even more important, toward his sons. Even when he'd begun transitioning into a woman, he'd still remained the person I loved deeply and was my best friend. I had been eviscerated by the loss of our marriage and the dissolution of our idealized family life, so this closeness had meant a great deal to me. I had been extremely grateful that Bruce had felt able to confide in me as much as he had, and that we were able to remain best friends, if not husband and wife.

Of course, I knew Bruce had a new partner now, and I had no desire to compete with her, in the same way I never tried to overreach my stepparent role by acting like David's daughters' real mother. But I'd been determined to incorporate Bruce into my new life with David, even when it had created tension for me at home. And I'd assumed that Bruce would also attempt to make room, if not for me, at least with the boys, and especially when it came to major holidays and birthdays. How could a parent not even pick up the phone to call their child on his birthday and say "Happy birthday"? I witnessed firsthand how

Brandon and Brody had their feelings hurt, time after time, at such oversights from Bruce. I couldn't understand then, nor do I now, that kind of parental disregard.

That New Year's Eve, David and I celebrated at Essam and Layla's Lake Tahoe home. We were among just a few couples having a New Year's Eve dinner down in their wine cellar, when we were asked to go around the table and say what our biggest thrill and our greatest disappointment of the year had been.

When it was my turn to survey the year that had been, and where I now found myself in life, I became very emotional.

"The greatest sorrow for me was that I felt like I lost my best friend," I said. My eyes fogged with tears. I thought privately and protectively of how my special bond with Bruce, which, in my perception, had only been strengthened during the difficult trials we'd undergone, including the revelation of his gender dysphoria, had been severed for no apparent reason.

After marrying Kris, Bruce not only dismissed me from his life and limited his involvement with his children. He also let go of his PR representative, his personal manager (who had been with him since before the Olympics), and his business manager. Apparently, according to Bruce, Kris wanted to take control of his career and affairs. To her credit, around this time Bruce did enjoy a resurgence in his career. I'm sure this was a huge relief for him after all the anxiety he'd endured about how he would make his way in the world if he transitioned. And perhaps it afforded him a different kind of empowerment and a fresh start that then necessitated him pulling away from the life he had known before. Given how much he'd struggled since our divorce, I'm sure Kris was a lifeline for Bruce. And having needed my own lifeline in the wake of his revelation to me, I did not fault him for turning to his new marriage as a source of solace. I only wished his distancing himself from his old life had not been so resolute and profound, given the pain it caused our sons.

Now, before you begin thinking I blame Kris for Bruce's shortcomings as a father, let me assure you, that's not really the case. While I could not personally respect or love a man who didn't take care of all his children, the responsibility was always Bruce's. That was ultimately on his shoulders.

After a few years it had become abundantly clear that Bruce had checked out of his kids' lives, so I filed for sole physical custody. Bruce didn't contest it, because he wasn't actively involved in their lives anyway. Of course, I made it clear that he was very welcome to visit anytime he wanted. But he never made much of an effort to see them. Since Bruce wasn't around as much as I had trusted he would be and had not provided any money for the care of our sons, ten years after we separated, I went back to court for child support. David insisted I do so, as he was paying generous support for his children and felt Bruce should be, too. David was not wrong about that. Bruce and Kris were chagrined, but it was granted, and Bruce did subsequently pay a small sum each month for a few years.

Anytime I would feel resentment welling within me for Bruce's lack of caring or participation in his children's lives, I'd remind myself that his was a struggle none would envy, and that I needed to call upon my innermost reservoir of kindness and forgiveness to not harbor anger toward him. He was probably doing the best he could at the time given his circumstances.

Ever since David and I had started dating, I'd always been thankful for the fatherly role he'd played for my sons. My sons truly loved him, and do to this day. Even while Bruce was still in the picture, David had played a paternal role for them, but after Bruce disappeared, he was the only father figure they had present. It meant a great deal to me anytime David stepped in and acted like a dad to the boys. Like all of us, David did a few things wrong, but a greater number of things right when it came to helping to raise my sons.

One day not long after we were married, the three of them were busy doing something in the garage together. I went out to investigate.

"What are you guys doing?" I asked.

"We're building a doghouse, Mom," the boys said, excitement in their voices.

I smiled, knowing that David doesn't even like dogs, despite the fact that we had several. Of course, maybe it was his way of expressing his subliminal wish that the dogs would be relegated to the doghouse *outside*. Not that they were. I watched the planning process unfold over several days. And then they got out the hammers, nails, wood, and paint and got to work.

It was a sweet moment, which all of them still remember as very meaningful. David was so busy with his career and doing girly things with his daughters. But this was a moment when he gave the boys his time and attention and did one of the boyish things with them that I often wished their father were around to do.

He taught them how to look people in the eye when giving a handshake. I believe David tried his best to be a good parent to my sons and his daughters. With so many children from different circumstances it had to be challenging.

Another time, David helped the boys and me with a science project.

"Let's build a maze and put a piece of cheese at the end," I said. "We'll time the mouse and see how long it takes him to get to the cheese."

I came up with the idea, but I'm not very good at construction, and so David helped us to build the maze. He was a very smart, industrious guy, and he could be quite handy. He was being present for the boys, which of course mattered the most.

David also got them into hockey. As a Canadian, David was rabid about the sport. Wayne Gretzky, who played for the Los Angeles Kings from 1988 to 1996 and is without doubt one of the greatest players of all time, was one of David's good friends, and David was also friendly with many other hockey players. We had season tickets for the Kings, and we all loved to go to all of the games together. We only had four seats together, but we also had four kids, including David's daughters, Sara and Erin. So we'd pile the extra kids onto our laps, and we'd end up with nachos and cheese on our clothes and shoes and popcorn everywhere. We were a loud, messy group, but it was a family thing that we enjoyed doing together. Those outings meant so much to me, and to the kids, too. I hope it is a great memory for our children.

Every year for the Stanley Cup playoffs, David put together a big cardboard chart of all the teams, and he and the boys checked off the teams as they were eliminated. David and Brandon and Brody got really into it, and I loved nothing more than to come upon the three of them working on their chart together, laughing and talking about something that had happened in the latest game. Even in the midst of our chaotic lives, and with so many demands on his time, David gave the boys and me his attention in these moments, and they definitely remain some of my favorite memories. I will always appreciate the involvement and support of David in Brandon's and Brody's growth and development.

Still, no amount of David's efforts could make up for Bruce's absence. As the years went on, there were scattered, fragmented occasions on which Brandon and Brody spent time with Bruce. Sometimes the boys went to a big social party at Bruce and Kris's on Christmas Eve. Sometimes they were invited, or pressured, into posing for the annual over-the-top Christmas card the Kardashian/Jenner clan was notorious for. Once they went to Lake Tahoe with them. But they never felt they got to know their father very well when they were growing up.

The boys got to know their paternal grandparents a little bit only because of my rather covert efforts. Their grandfather Bill Jenner had a home in Lake Tahoe, and whenever we took the boys with us to visit the Khashoggis at their house in Lake Tahoe, I always made the effort to drive around the lake to Bill's place, so the boys could spend time with him. We were always instructed not to tell Bruce that we had visited.

I also did everything within reason to make it possible for the boys to spend time with Bruce's mother. She called me one day, a few years after Bruce had remarried.

"I'm in town, and I have seen Bruce and some of the kids," she said. "I would like to see Brandon and Brody, but I know Bruce doesn't see them. Could I please come over and see them? But you mustn't tell Bruce."

I was disappointed that apparently Bruce didn't want his mother to even visit with his sons in our home, but I didn't say anything and simply let her know she was always welcome.

"Of course," I said. "You should come over for dinner. We'd love to see you." She did come to the house for dinner. While she was visiting with us, the phone rang and Brandon answered. Surprisingly, it was Bruce.

"Is my mother at your house?" Bruce said. "Let me talk to her."

When she got on the phone, I could hear Bruce yelling at her. I guess we were perceived to be the enemy camp. It was tragic, and grossly unfair to the children and their grandparents.

To be fair, there was one occasion that Bruce and Kris invited the boys to go skiing at Deer Valley, Utah. I was happy for the boys that they were going to be able to spend time with their dad, doing something they loved. Unfortunately, they both got sick, and developed ear infections and were advised against flying, so they had to cancel their trip. That situation seemed to be flipped into a defense for Bruce, the assertion that I somehow kept the kids from him. Bruce and Kris wore that one out. I think they were influenced by the ongoing drama of baseball player Steve Garvey and his wife, Cyndy. During this high-profile, very bitter divorce, Cyndy allegedly kept Steve's daughters from him. I felt like Bruce and Kris were trying to suggest that I must be another Cyndy Garvey. For the record, I never made any attempt to keep my children from their father.

The truth is, as a loving, responsible parent, you want what is best for your child. That is for them to feel loved and wanted by both parents. That's what I always longed for regarding my sons. And taking it a step further, there is nothing or no one who could ever keep me from being there for my children. If I had to go to court, slay dragons, or walk over burning coals barefoot, I could not be kept away from my kids. That falls under the category of being inexcusable. Forgivable, but inexcusable. I've had to remind myself of that philosophy often in my life.

While Bruce was not present in the boys' lives, they bore his name. When they were out and people heard their last name, they often asked the boys if they were any relation to Bruce Jenner, the Olympic hero. The boys were always proud of any association with their father and always excitedly answered that, yes, Bruce Jenner was their dad. While they almost never got to interact with Bruce as a person, his perfect Olympic-sized image loomed large in their imaginations. This would have been enough pressure for them to contend with as young men, but they never got the upside to having him be a constant in their growth and development.

I was forever cognizant of the fact that one day they were going to discover the truth about who Bruce Jenner really was. Even though he wasn't a consistent presence in their lives, by virtue of the fact he was their biological father that truth would have an impact. Eventually they were going have to be able to assimilate the challenging reality about their father and to rebound psychologically and emotionally. I continued to do my best to give them all of the tools they would need, so they would be able to go on with their lives and feel confident and secure in themselves, no matter what. All of those concerns fed into my parenting, and I felt like I needed to do my best to be their mother, father, and psychologist all rolled into one.

One day I was driving Brandon home from a Little League game where he had pitched a no-hitter and we saw Bruce on the lawn at Pepperdine University, hitting golf balls.

"Mommy, look . . . that's Dad," Brandon said. "He was right here! Why didn't he come to my game instead of hitting golf balls?"

"Well, Brandon, when you have a disappointment like that in your life, you can either get mad and act out in a destructive way, or you can determine to just be the very best you can be, and show your dad just what he missed by not being there!" I said.

"Mommy!" Brandon said, an incredulous look on his little, innocent face. "I was just thinking that very same thing! I'm going to be the best I can be, and show Dad what he missed!"

At those words, I was deeply moved that Brandon was such an evolved indomitable spirit, but my heart broke more than a little that he was put in a position to have to rise above such emotional pain.

"What I Wish for You"

That God will hear your prayer
When you reach out in need
That every cloud will disappear
Where angels lead
Someone to love
Who loves you, too
This is what I wish for you

A pearl of wisdom
From a single grain of sand
The miracle of life
To try and understand
A road that's smooth
A sky that's blue
This is what I wish for you

A world that sleeps in peace
Yours to keep
And hold forever in your heart
A living faith that's always true
A perfect universe is what I wish
   for you

That simple truth
Will always hold your heart on
   course
And kindness will survive to live
Without remorse
That time's not fast
And love will last
This is what I wish for you

A living faith that's always true
A perfect universe is what I wish
   for you

The knowledge way down deep
That you are truly loved
The courage to believe
Sometimes that is enough
Sweet memories
Of you and me
This is what I wish for you
This is what I wish for you

LYRIC: LINDA THOMPSON

Chapter Twenty-one

Academy Award–Nominated Songwriter

While I was grateful to David for his presence in the boys' lives and I was unquestionably in love with him, if I'd held out hope that our marriage would suddenly cause him to treat our relationship with greater respect, it was soon revealed that I was mistaken.

During our first year of marriage, David would often get angry at me over something inconsequential and then leave in a fit of anger and not let me know where he was or when he would be returning. He would simply disappear for days or weeks at a time. I was accustomed to David's temper and the dramatic behavior it could sometimes cause, but the first time or two he went missing in action, I feverishly called friends and family trying to determine his whereabouts. I didn't know if I should call the authorities to report him missing or not.

Well, do I call the police? I wondered. *Is he lying in a ditch somewhere? What do I do?*

"Do you know where David is?" I asked when I finally reached a friend in the know.

"Oh yeah, he called me; he's staying on his boat. He's just taking a break."

David's boat was moored in Marina del Rey. He was gone that time for a week.

When David eventually came home, he was totally nonchalant. This was new for me. While Elvis and David both had fiery tempers, here was a big distinction between them. Elvis was always profusely apologetic and reconciliatory when he allowed his anger to get the best of him. David would get angry, disappear, unaccounted for, then come back acting like nothing had happened and expecting me to go along with him. Elvis was difficult, but never *this* difficult.

Had I been stronger, maybe I would have left him the first time he pulled that shenanigan, no matter that we'd just gotten married and I loved him deeply. But I had two little boys to raise, and not only did I want them to have a present father: I also didn't want them to experience another loss in their lives so close to the unavailability of their biological father. Without Bruce, suddenly the stakes of leaving David felt even higher. Though aspects of David's personality were unpredictable, at least he was a fairly constant presence in their daily lives. Given all of this, I felt like I needed to toughen up and muscle through the hurtful moments of my marriage. If that meant suffering indignities occasionally, so be it. I wasn't the first parent to sacrifice a portion of happiness for their children's sake, and I won't be the last, either. Since I was always the primary parent in my sons' lives anyway, they were most often not even aware that David had inexplicably gone missing. When it was possible, I covered for him by lamely blaming his schedule or travel for his absence, so they wouldn't be upset, too, if they noticed he wasn't home.

I made excuses for the worst of his behavior and tried not dwell on it, rather choosing to focus on the positives. I tried my best to blame his absences on his being a temperamental, artistic, mad musical genius, but in truth, it was an emotionally and psychologically damaging thing to do. After a few of these episodes with the same outcome, I knew not to call the police to report a missing person. Not missing—just unconscionably inconsiderate.

It was in the midst of the turbulent months following our wedding that David and I had embarked on a new project together, one that would in many ways be the commercial pinnacle of our joined efforts. And as was often the case with our musical endeavors, it also served to bring us back together.

David had gotten a call from our friend Kevin Costner about a new movie he was doing, *The Bodyguard*, which starred him and Whitney Houston and would come out on November 25, 1992. At this moment in time, Kevin was so revered for his creative accomplishments and talents that he was given a remarkable amount of control over this movie, including production of its music as well.

"I'd like you to produce a song for my new movie," Kevin said to David. "I found this song I already knew of, 'I Will Always Love You,' which was written by Dolly Parton. I want this song in the movie."

"That's a big mistake," David said. "That's a country song. You can do something better than that."

"No, I want this song," Kevin said. "I've got a whole vision for it."

At first, David argued with Kevin about the song and its inclusion in the film, but then, once he listened to it and played around with it, he realized he could produce it in such a way that it would be monumentally important in the film, which, of course, it was.

"We need a couple of original songs," Kevin said. "Can you and Linda write something?"

"Yeah, sure," David and I said. "We'll give it a go."

David was soon inspired.

"I've got this musical idea that's kind of a big, Shirley Bassey, James Bond–ish sound," David said. "I'll play it for you. Mick wants to talk to you about the lyric and what it's meant to say."

By this, David meant the director, Mick Jackson, who wanted to talk to me about the lyric for our song. We were sitting in a parking lot at Warner Bros. when Mick got on the phone and explained the film's premise to me. It was centered around this gorgeous megastar. She's petulant. She's a diva. And she has this bodyguard. He's protecting her, but she's difficult. And then she starts to fall in love with him. And the song has to be called "I Have Nothing."

"Really?" I said. "That's the title?"

"Yeah because she receives all of these menacing notes that always say, 'I have nothing. You have everything.' And it turns out they're from her sister, who ends up being the one who's threatening her because she's jealous of her."

"Okay," I said.

So I had to write the song's lyrics around the title "I Have Nothing," and the description of the star's character, since it was sung from her perspective. Knowing she was a difficult diva, I came up with the line "Stay in my arms if you dare, or must I imagine you there? Don't walk away from me."

Having lived with the very biggest rock star of all time, I had a good deal of experience to draw on while creating that lyric.

There was something magical about my collaboration with David on that song. When he first heard my lyrics, he beamed at me, building me up, as he sometimes could.

"When you get it right as a lyricist, there's nobody that can touch you," he said. "You're the best lyricist that I have ever been around when you get it right."

I took a great deal of pride in receiving such a strong compliment from a man whose talent I admired as much as I did. The song became a huge hit and was nominated for an Academy Award and a Grammy. To this day, it's still being performed. It's such a big song that contestants often performed it on *The Voice* and the now-defunct *American Idol*. Kelly Clarkson even performed it at one time.

Attending the Academy Awards as a nominee was a thrill, of course. But I don't do glam squads, even though I know it's long been the norm. When we went to the Academy Awards, I borrowed a red sequined dress by the designer Pamela Dennis. As always, I did my own hair and makeup. David and I each got to bring a guest, so I invited my daddy and David invited his mother. We all went together.

It was nice to be able to take our parents to the Academy Awards because we'd been nominated. I had had plenty of experience being in the public eye, but this night felt different. I was very nervous. When it was announced that "A Whole New World" from the Disney film *Aladdin* had won, I was almost relieved. I was so anxious just being there, I couldn't imagine having to walk up to the podium and accept my award. We'd been up against "Run to You," which was also a song from *The Bodyguard*. "I Will Always Love You" wasn't eligible because it was a remake, and to be nominated, the song had to have been written for the movie and have been used to propel the story forward. It was said afterward that the vote was split because of these two competing songs from the same movie. But nothing could diminish the thrill of having been recognized with a nomination. David had already been nominated for "Glory of Love," from the film *The Karate Kid, Part II*, but he knew how significant this moment was for me.

"You realize, don't you, that you're always going to be known as an Academy Award–nominated lyricist from now on?" he said.

The Bodyguard soundtrack was one of the high points in our collaborative life, but as had become routine for us, the joy it brought was short-lived.

In January 1994, David ended one of our frequent arguments in accordance with his usual pattern: He stormed out of the room, got into his car, and drove away. I knew from past experience that he might come home later in the day, or he might come home two days later. But this time, he didn't come home or call for an extended period. A week went by, and then another.

Since it was just the boys and me in the house, one night we decided to make a fun night of it and have a slumber party in my bedroom. I made up a little pallet on the floor for them, where they were sleeping, while I was alone in my bed. In the early morning, around four thirty, the house started shaking. I jumped up, my first thought being to protect them.

"It's an earthquake, boys!" I shouted. "It's an earthquake! Get up! Let's go downstairs!"

We did everything wrong, because I was the leader, and even though I was aware of proper earthquake procedure, my half-asleep instincts took over my better judgment. Instead of staying in one place like we should have, we went down the staircase into the kitchen, where things could've been falling out of the shelves and cupboards. Luckily, they weren't. As we got down to the kitchen, the shaking subsided, but we were still shaken up. This was the Northridge earthquake, which registered at a 6.7 magnitude, resulted in fifty-seven deaths, and was felt as far away as Las Vegas. We stood there in pitch black darkness with no power.

"I have some candles here, but I don't know where matches are," I said.

"Mommy, don't get mad, but I have lots of matches in my room," Brody piped up.

Like the three blind mice, we held on to each other, navigating our way into Brody's room, and sure enough, he had a big stash of matches hidden deep in a bottom drawer.

"You little pyro," I teased him, but he saved the night.

Not too much time passed before the phone rang. When I answered, I was pleasantly surprised to find that David was on the other end of the line.

"Are you guys okay?" he asked.

The earthquake had clearly shaken David up, and he ended up coming home later that day. It was moments like these when I felt glad to have a partner. This was especially true because the boys had by now become increasingly aware of Bruce's unreliability and indifference as a father.

The day after the Northridge earthquake, I was outside and stepped back into our TV room, where Brandon and Brody were sitting on the sofa.

"Mom . . . Dad called and asked if we were okay after the big earthquake," Brandon announced. "He was just checking on us."

"Oh, that was really sweet and thoughtful of your dad," I said, truly touched. "How nice!"

"Mom . . . I was just kidding . . ." Brandon said, looking up. "He never called . . ."

And he never did.

"Dream On"

Your heart is young and oh so
    tender
Open to the pain
And once it breaks in sad surrender
It won't be the same
It's part of life to taste your own
    tears

If I could spare you pain and
    heartache
I'd take it on myself
But you can't live protected
On a shelf
One thing you must never lose
. . . yourself

Dream on
Let imagination take you
Dream on
Don't you ever let life break you
There's a part of you
That harm cannot touch
Dream on

When you're down & feeling lonely
Like there's only you
Just look around I'll be there with
    you, too
Don't you ever let go of your dream

Dream on
Let imagination take you
Dream on
Don't you ever let life break you
There's a part of you
That harm cannot touch

Dream on
Let imagination take you
Dream on
Don't ever let life break you
Dream, dream on
Know I'll be there with you
There's a part of you that harm
    cannot touch
Dream on
And always remember that I love
    you so much
Dream on

LYRIC: LINDA THOMPSON

Chapter Twenty-two

Villa Casablanca

In the aftermath of our success with *The Bodyguard*, David and I embarked on a series of collaborations that rivaled anything I could have ever dreamed of professionally. And perhaps the best symbol of our success, and the success yet to come, was the home that we bought together in Malibu in late 1994, a twenty-two-acre estate called Villa Casablanca.

It was far and away the most lavish home I'd ever owned. It included a five-bedroom main house and an eight-car garage. There were two large guest apartments that were connected to the main house by a 150-foot tunnel than ran under the motor court. It was an epic home on majestic, fabulously landscaped grounds. Moving into that manor felt like a culmination and celebration of all the hard work David and I had done over the past decade. It was a place not only to grow our songwriting career and host many charity benefits with hundreds in attendance, but to enjoy a haven for our extended family.

Around the same time, our friend Celine Dion was getting married in an elaborate ceremony in Montreal in mid-December. We had already set our moving date, and the trucks filled with our furniture were set to arrive during her marital celebration, so I opted to stay home and oversee the unpacking. David, who enjoyed a long and fruitful creative relationship with Celine, attended the festivities without me.

I was sorry to miss being there to celebrate Celine's marriage to her longtime love and manager, René Angélil, as David and I had discovered her together in the early days of our romance, and I'd been a huge fan of her artistically and personally, ever since. Back in 1986, David had received a tip about Celine, who was still unknown outside her native Canada, from a friend of his in the Canadian recording industry. Intrigued, David and I flew to Montreal together to see her perform. We braved a downpour to watch the then teenage chanteuse sing beneath a tent in a field. Although she still performed mostly in French and struggled with her English, it was obvious she was a rare talent.

"If you have piece of paper and a pen, sign this girl tonight," I said to David. "Don't let her get away."

David recognized her gift as well and signed her immediately. Not long after that, she came to Los Angeles, and we met with her at his studio. Celine barely spoke English, but she was just like a little colt, bursting out of the gate, ready to show everyone the racehorse she could become. She clearly possessed so much energy and drive that she could not be contained.

From then on, she'd had a special role in our creative life, and our personal life, recording many songs David and I wrote, including the wedding song David penned for me. And she'd recently recorded a song David and I had written together, "Love Lights Up the World," along with Peabo Bryson and Color Me Bad, for an album David released in Japan in April 1994. Our collaborations were always gratifying, and I always thought the world of her.

I had always desired to have a close relationship with David's daughters, and in truth, my inability to break through the barriers was a deep source of sadness for me. I would also have to define it as a failure on my part. I always loved children and tried very hard for many years to be a nurturing presence when David's daughters were with us, either in my home or when traveling. Still, being a stepmother is a very tricky proposition—especially when the children's mother is already hurt and angry because of your presence in their lives. I remember a line from the movie *Stepmom*, when the child of divorced parents says to her mother about her stepmother, "Mom, I'll hate her if you want me to."

I'm sure I must have seemed like an overly attentive mother with my sons, because I probably was. I felt it incumbent upon me to be two parents in one, both mother and father, most of the time. Additionally, I harbored a secret I hoped would not damage Brandon's and Brody's spirits one day, more than their absentee father already had.

I wanted to be the person in David's daughters' lives that I believe I am in the life of Bruce's daughter, Casey. Not the mother of course, but another trusted adult to turn to. Because I was acutely sensitive to the complexity of our family situation, I never tried to overstep that under-stood boundary, to be unctuously solicitous of their affection, or take the place of their mother in any way. I felt damned if I did and damned if I didn't. I pretty much gave up and retreated, waving a white flag.

But, if there is blame to be placed for the dysfunction of our rela-tionship when it came to our children, it lies not with the children, but with the grown-ups. David, his ex, and I should have been able to make adjustments to our post-divorce life in a more civil manner. We all failed to that end.

I have finally come to a place in my life where I can look back, see my mistakes, acknowledge them, and forgive myself, while hoping that others have forgiven me my shortcomings as well. I, like all of us, am merely human. I have made my share of errors and missteps. I'm quite certain I'll make many more. But just as I do not judge others because I have not walked in their shoes, others have no right to judge me accordingly.

In many ways, buying Villa Casablanca and moving out of the Knest meant that David's need to be the head of household became even more pronounced. He wanted to maintain absolute rule, as if he really were a king and we were all his loyal subjects, who owed him complete and constant deference. I don't think I'd ever realized how much it must have galled him to live with me and my sons for all of those years in the house I had acquired with my ex-husband. And to live there with my dogs.

I love animals, especially dogs. I can't remember a time in my entire life that I haven't owned a dog. When David moved in with me, he had to learn to accept my dogs and cats, as well as my children. David simply does not relate to animals.

"I don't necessarily mind dogs. I just don't want to live with them," David often said. "I don't think they should live with people."

"Well, then where do you think they are supposed to live?" I asked. "Do you think they should just run wild on the streets, fending for themselves?"

He thought at the very least they should be relegated to the outdoors. My insistence upon having pets for my children to grow up with was a sore point with David. Even today I have a sign in my kitchen that states, "Every little boy should have two things: a dog, and a mother who is willing to let him have one."

Now, in David's defense, even though Villa Casablanca was on twenty-two acres, I admit I took the rescue thing a little too far, at one time having six dogs. That was not much of a compromise on my part, I know. And the puppies made their share of you-know-what, sometimes in the house. If you are not a dog person, you don't understand that that's part of what you have to do—clean up poop. David never had to, but it was an unsavory sight for him anyway. I get it and give him credit. "I don't love dogs," he said. "But I love a woman who loves dogs." That was a sweet concession and I appreciate his effort more today than I did then.

And now that we had a new address without any prior associations, David was insistent on upsetting what he'd apparently experienced as an unfair power balance and establishing what he saw as his rightful regime.

"This is my house now," he said. "I'm not living in your house anymore."

He went so far as to dictate all of these very specific rules of behavior for our new home. "Nobody sits in my chair in the kitchen," he told us again and again.

Now, around this same time, David became obsessed by what he saw as a possible threat to his dominion in the household, specifically regarding the sanctity of his kitchen chair. My dad lived with me off and on for the twenty-odd years after my mother died, until the time of his death. I brought him to live with me full-time when he turned eighty, and he was with me for the last ten years of his life. This was after he'd had to give up his driver's license, and he was not doing well at his house. I didn't want him to fall and hurt himself.

By the time we'd moved to Villa Casablanca, my dad had limited mobility and needed to use a walker. Because of our vast grounds and enormous house, it was quite an undertaking for him to get anywhere. He would amble through our living room and then had to get up the two steps to the kitchen. He was soon out of breath and he had to sit down in the first chair he could reach in order to regain his composure before continuing. Well, this chair at the end of the table was the one David had designated as *his* chair, which no one else was allowed to sit in, not ever. Not even when David was not home, he had dictated.

I wanted to point out to David how ludicrous all of this was. It was a kitchen table chair. My dad was in his eighties. It was as laughable as any *Monty Python* sketch, except that David was serious.

There was no reasoning with David on this matter and so I couldn't resist at least making a (humorous) statement of protest. Down in the tunnel, we had this prop that was a big, oversize chair with a high back that looked like a king's throne. So I got the boys to help me move it, and we put it at the end of the table in the place where David's chair normally sat. As a joke, we placed a goblet and a crown at his setting and a sign that said "King David," because he'd made such a big stink about my dad having sat in his chair.

When David walked in, he stopped short and examined our hand-iwork.

"Now that's what I'm talking about," he said, without a hint of irony.

"Really?" I said, unsure whether to laugh or scream.

"Yes," he said.

He really and truly wanted to be treated like a king, not like a husband or father, which speaks volumes about what he was like to live with, as lovable as he could also be. His next wife, who was his fourth, has often remarked very publicly in the context of the show in which she is a regular cast member, *The Real Housewives of Beverly Hills*, that David was her king. He subsequently asked me, "Why couldn't you have treated me like a king?"

"Because I want a partnership, not a dictatorship," I answered with conviction.

I guess his current monarchy failed, and he is now going through his fourth divorce. Maybe it's time to just let go of that king thing?

David was very protective of his space and his belongings, and he watched over them jealously. Once we moved into Villa Casablanca, David didn't like us having the boys' friends over. I wanted to be the pizza mom with the house where the kids felt comfortable coming in, hanging out, watching TV, and playing video games. David did not agree with me.

"What are all these kids doing here?" David used to grouse when he got home.

All of David's most challenging behavior seemed to come to a head every year at Christmas. His mood soured as the holiday approached, and when I tried to ask him about my ideas for gifts for the children, including his girls, he was likely to snipe at me. It was as if we were in competition about who was going to spend more, or do more, or buy the better present. I couldn't believe he was getting so worked up about such silly, trivial matters, especially when we were doing quite well financially.

"We are both from modest means," I said. "We have plenty of money to do for our family, and to do for our kids. Money is the last thing in the world we should argue about. And especially at Christmastime."

And yet after usually acting out David was generous and thoughtful in his gift-giving to everyone.

The irony about the money was that it was not all his. I really enjoyed feeling like I brought something in, money-wise, to our relationship, so I made a point of continuing to work. I remained a regular cast member on *Hee Haw* until it was canceled in 1992. "I Have Nothing" from *The Bodyguard* earned us quite a bit over the years, as well as other collaborations, and the much-recorded and performed song "Grown-Up Christmas List."

The bottom line, though, was that David didn't enjoy the holidays, and he begrudged everyone the money that was spent, even on gifts for him, which took away from the pleasure of giving the gift in the first place. It wasn't enough for David to hate Christmas. He seemed determined to ruin the holiday for everyone by pulling his disappearing act nearly every year. *What kind of husband leaves on Christmas Eve?* I thought more than once or twice.

Finally, one year, I bought him a Grinch suit and put it under the tree because it was so David at Christmas. To his credit, he exhibited his customary great sense of humor about the gift.

Villa Casablanca may have been a place that could produce tension between us but it also never failed to bring us back together through music. Thank God for the music. It was the language that David and I could always speak to each other, even when we were finding it challenging to reach accord in other areas. David had a home studio at Villa Casablanca and some of our happiest hours together were spent there.

All kinds of incredible stars came over to record with him. It was always a treat for me to interact with the singers and musicians, but perhaps my favorite musical guest was Whitney Houston, who sometimes came over with her then husband, Bobby Brown.

I was very fond of Whitney from our experience working together on the set of *The Bodyguard*. What struck me most about Whitney during filming was the fact that she was so sweet to my daddy. Even when she was pregnant with Bobbi Kristina, she went out of her way to go over and talk to him, and to give him a big hug, and make him feel very welcome on the set. Believe me, after decades of meeting people at all levels of fame, you notice things like that about people, how human they are, even in their stardom. Whitney always maintained her humility and humanity; her natural graciousness was a lovely thing to experience.

Bobby was always kind to my daddy, too. And when Whitney was pregnant, Bobby was very chivalrous with her. He was very protective of Whitney at all times. He would walk in front of her through the crowd, shielding her body with his own. Their connection clearly ran strong and deep. However dysfunctional their relationship may have been at times, they definitely loved each other. Looking at them together, you knew that she loved him, and he loved her.

And so, whenever I knew Whitney was coming over to record with David in the years that followed, I'd try to be around. And I'd go down to say hello when they took a break from working and went out to lounge in the studio's living area. Bobby was usually with Whitney, and when they were relaxing together, their favorite activity was to watch *The Jerry Springer Show*. And they didn't just watch it. They'd both be up in the middle of the floor, waving their arms, gesticulating, and yelling at the TV.

"What?! You can't say that."

"Don't go back with him. Are you crazy?"

"What?! She's pregnant with your best friend's child?"

They got very passionate about repeating all of the crazy dialogue and trying to predict the show's outcome.

It was the funniest thing imaginable to see this beautiful, elegant woman in the middle of the floor, waving her arms and yelling at the TV set.

"You're crazy!" she shouted. "You can't be with a man that would cheat on you with your own sister's husband's mother's child."

This was the earthy side of Whitney's personality that many people didn't know. There was the Whitney Houston onstage, who was stunning and composed, regal even. And then there was New Jersey Whitney Houston, who could get down and dirty and have a good laugh. I think that often such extremes come hand in hand with greatness. Sometimes the most brilliant people are just a jumble of conflicting impulses, paradoxical, unpredictable, and mercurial.

David and I continued to be asked to write high-profile songs, which allowed us to remain connected as collaborators and partners. In 1996, we were approached with an incredibly exciting opportunity: writing the theme for the Summer Olympics in Atlanta. David collaborated with Babyface on the music, and then it was time for me to pen the words to the song that became "Power of the Dream."

In composing those lyrics, I drew heavily for inspiration from what Bruce had told me about his Olympic experience, including his quest to win the gold and how it felt the moment he was awarded his medal. And how he'd stood on the victory stand, elevated above everyone else.

There was a line in our song that said, "Stand apart from all the rest," which he did. He'd also told me how he'd looked around and taken mental snapshots. All of these details became lyrics.

David and I had the honor of attending the opening ceremony in Atlanta, where Celine Dion performed our song live. My sweet moment was short-lived, however, since when the ceremony was telecast, David and Babyface were given writing credit for the song, with no mention of my name.

"I'm really sorry about that," David said.

I knew that neither David nor Babyface had intentionally tried to steal credit from me, but it was hard not to feel terribly slighted, since I was responsible for the lyrics that had clearly moved and uplifted a huge audience.

Olympic fever was in the air that summer, and David and I were invited to several events related to the games, including one where we found ourselves sitting across the aisle from Bruce and Kris. By this point, Bruce and I weren't really talking anymore; in fact we hadn't been for five years, as Bruce had fully descended into the Kardashian rabbit hole by then. But when I looked over during the event, I could see that Bruce knew and was singing along to every word. I was honestly touched that he had listened to and derived some enjoyment from a song I had written, in part inspired by his own Olympic recollections.

Unfortunately, crossing paths with Bruce at that Olympic event did nothing to inspire him to reconnect with the boys. And, to my dismay, they continued to have much to forgive in their father's continued distant behavior in the years to come.

When Bruce didn't even respond to my invitation to attend Brandon's high school graduation, Brandon understandably took it hard.

"Mom, what kind of a father doesn't come to his son's graduation?" he asked me.

"Honey, your dad may have been the world's greatest athlete, physically, but emotionally, you have to view him in a wheelchair," I meekly replied. "If he had emotional legs, he'd get up and walk to you, but he just doesn't right now. Just try to understand him, love him, and forgive him."

When Brody graduated from high school, Bruce and Kris finally

responded to an invitation I sent them by actually coming. The graduating seniors had to stand and say something about their parents as they
graduated. Brody only found out that Bruce and Kris were coming the
night before the ceremony and he panicked.

"Mom . . . Dad and Kris are coming to my graduation," he said.

"That's wonderful." I exclaimed.

"But I'm not at all comfortable with them coming, Mom," Brody
protested.

"Honey, I will kiss their butts," I assured him. "I'll be so nice to them
to make everyone comfortable."

"No, it's not that at all, mom. I don't want them to come. I have to
say something about my parents, and I don't even know Bruce well
enough to say anything about him. What do I do?"

"Just do what you're comfortable with, honey," I said, my heart going
out my son. "Speak about those you know well enough to comment on.
It's your day to celebrate, and you shouldn't have to feel pressured to
do anything you're not comfortable with."

Brody ended up thanking me for always being there for him and
showing him unconditional love, and he thanked David for inspiring
him. He kept it brief and sat back down. Those are the times you never
forget.

Brandon and Brody will never have those "Hallmark memories" of
father-and-son moments. They were saddened by Bruce's lack of participation in their lives, and my heart ached for them. But I never spoke
an unkind word about Bruce to the boys, and I always counseled them
to forgive their father for his limitations. One analogy I love is that
staying angry with someone is like drinking poison and expecting the
object of your anger to die. And so I cling to the belief that everything
is forgivable; some things are inexcusable, but everything is forgivable.

For the record, I saved letters to Bruce imploring him to call his
sons, see them, come to their sporting games, and just be involved in
their lives. I know how hurtful it must have been for Brandon and
Brody to have to view, later on TV, the notoriously public participation
of Bruce fathering the four Kardashian children, and the two daughters
that he and Kris had together. (Of course, it was through no fault of
the children themselves.) He publicly boasted about driving car pool

for them, preparing lunches, having fatherly advice sessions on camera for all to see, while Brandon and Brody were left to wonder why Bruce wasn't there for them.

Though I commend Bruce for being a good stepfather and a good father to the children with whom he lived, he had four other children who would have loved to have him participate in their lives, too. Forgivable, but inexcusable, behavior.

In 1997, I had the honor of penning words to be sung by two of the premier female singers of our time, Barbra Streisand, who was a dear friend, and Celine Dion. The two dulcet divas had decided to sing a duet together and David and Walter Afanasieff had been approached to write the music and produce. When they tapped me to handle lyrical duties, I had a creative brainstorm of which I remain extremely proud. Rather than pitting the two greats against each other with a "You stole my man"–themed song, I decided to put Barbra in the role of the more experienced mentor to the younger Celine, who approaches her for romantic advice in the first verse. I knew both women well enough to know they would not wish to be singing about competition or rancor, but rather about the strength of female friendships. They both demonstrate their dedication to cultivating a community of strong women in their everyday lives.

Together, the two women joined voices and forces in a triumphant celebration of the power to be found in daring to be vulnerable and emotive, even when the man in the relationship is not being demonstrative of his affection. It was a thrill to hear my lyrics to "Tell Him" delivered by such incredible talents, and then to take part in filming a video for the song, which became an international sensation, going gold and platinum across Europe, and earning a Grammy nomination for Best Pop Collaboration with Vocals.

I continued to write a number of songs with collaborators other than David, and in 1995, I heard from our friend Kevin Costner that he was working on a new movie, *Tin Cup*, a love story involving a down-on-his-luck golf pro. I penned lyrics to go with a melody written by Steve Dorff, which ultimately became "This Could Take All Night," a very sultry song that playfully alludes to sex. That same year, I cowrote a song, "Where Do We Go from Here?" for the Arnold Schwarzenegger movie *Eraser*, also starring Vanessa Williams, who recorded the song for the soundtrack.

At the same time, David and I continued our work together as well. In 1998, he was introduced to a brilliant young singer, Josh Groban, by his then vocal coach. David and I were both struck by Josh's immense talent, and I immediately liked him as a person, too. I was a little surprised at the kismet of life to learn that he'd been in Brandon's class at Malibu Presbyterian Sunday school, and his mother even turned up a photo of the boys at Sunday school together, both wearing little Superman capes. Such is the remarkable serendipity in life's ebbs and flows.

David asked Josh to be his rehearsal singer when he was preparing to play at the 1999 Grammy Awards. Josh sang a duet with Celine in place of Andrea Bocelli, who was not able to be present for the practice performance. Although Josh did not perform on the televised ceremony that night, the show's host, Rosie O'Donnell, caught him during the rehearsal and was so impressed with his voice that she asked him to be a guest on her show. This performance in turn caused him to be discovered by television producer David E. Kelley, who had a major hit at the time with *Ally McBeal*. David wrote a part specifically for Josh that allowed him to perform on the show. Josh did so well that he returned for a second episode, again written around my song. Josh performed, "To Where You Are," which I'd penned with Richard Marx. This was a 9/11-themed episode that attempted to express even a modicum of the stunned grief we were all feeling in the wake of that national tragedy.

Watching this young man David and I had admired and believed in try to salve the aggrieved hearts of millions of people I'd never met was powerful for me. I'd actually written the song as an expression of my own grief, after being inspired to do so by Richard's haunting melody. When he'd originally sent me a tape of his music, I was lying out by my pool, feeling my way into the song and the lyrics I would write. As I usually did, I was listening for the message the melody was trying to impart, so I could structure the lyrics accordingly, whether that ended up being a love song, a song about heartbreak, or a song about familial joy. As I heard the notes, I began thinking about the loss of Elvis and my mother, and the extreme, engulfing grief I'd felt on both occasions. That's what the music was telling me to write about.

When I spoke to Richard, he told me to go for it. His father had just passed away, and perhaps I had felt his heartache in his melody. I wrote the lyrics from the source of those deeply personal emotions, and I felt honored when my words were used to convey a cultural moment of grief on a much larger scale.

Josh not only recorded a version of my song for his debut album; it was also his first big hit, topping the *Billboard* Hot Adult Contemporary Chart for two weeks in August 2002. All in all, it went on to spend a total of thirty-six weeks on the chart.

I resolved to continue writing songs, often inspired by the most important moments in my life, and by doing so, to hopefully resonate with others in their significantly poignant moments as well. I can't think of a more perfect example of this phenomenon than my song, "Who Could Ever Love You More?" which I wrote with Steve Dorff. Steve composed the music, and when he first played me the melody while we were seated together at his piano, I knew immediately what the song was about.

"I'm going to write this about my sons," I said.

The lyric I wrote could easily be called "Every Mother's Lullaby" and is a tribute to the power of parental love and devotion. In 2001, our dear friend and frequent collaborator Celine Dion and her husband, René, had their first son, René-Charles. In celebration of their own miraculous experience, and upon hearing "Who Could Ever Love You More," Celine and René were inspired and conceived a multimedia project that included an album of lullabies, a calendar, and a book celebrating babies, with images by the Australian photographer Anne Geddes. Celine and René wanted to title their project *Miracle* and asked me if they could call the song "Miracle—Who Could Ever Love You More."

Through Celine's exquisite vocals, it would go on to touch millions of other mothers and fathers. The album went platinum in the United States and was nominated for several Canadian music awards, including the Juno.

Though I continued to branch out and have repeated success, writing songs with Richard Marx, Steve Dorff, and many others, David and I continued to have a special gift for writing together. Such was the case in 2002, when we were approached to pen a number for a Ronald McDonald Children's House Special that was being filmed for television. As always, David and I were keen to do work on behalf of a worthwhile charitable organization, especially one that benefited children. He wrote the music, and I the lyrics, for a song that would be called "Aren't They All Our Children?"

When it came time to tape the television special, an incredible group of talents honored us by performing our song: Celine Dion, Enrique Iglesias, Josh Groban, and Nick Carter. It was thrilling to hear their remarkable voices harmonizing together on my words, and I felt grateful that I'd received such a profound opportunity to give back.

Remarkably, we were nominated for an Emmy for "Best Original Song" for our collaboration, and we won. As I was well aware from my years in television, there are actually two Emmy ceremonies. The technical awards are given out the first weekend, and then the big stars come out for the televised, Primetime Emmys ceremony, held the second weekend. Because ours was a songwriting honor, which was considered one of the technical categories, we received our award at the first ceremony. Of course, it was an incredible sensation to be honored, after a few nominations over the years, and for a song so close to my heart. Holding my statuette in my hand with my longtime partner beside me was a wonderful moment during which I was able to pause, and breathe, and appreciate all that I'd accomplished in the past twenty years.

But the fun was far from over yet. The following weekend, we were invited to several parties following the Primetime Emmys, so we sheepishly decided to bring our Emmys from home, even though they'd already been in our possession for a week.

"That's our calling card," we joked, indicating the Emmys in our hands as we gained access to the exclusive parties and celebrated our victory with the other winners. Hey, an Emmy's an Emmy, no matter when you win it.

It wasn't all a bed of roses. Yes, we were thriving professionally. But something had happened between us a few years earlier that always remained in the back of my mind. We'd been hosting one of our many charity events at our home, this time to raise money to fund the Malibu Boys and Girls Club, which we'd founded, along with our friends Mel Gibson, his then wife, Robyn, and Danny Stern and his wife, Laure Mattos. Our property included an approximately six-acre lawn, which we tented in order to host hundreds of people while they enjoyed stellar entertainment and Jay Leno as the emcee. David was rehearsing on our lawn, leading up to the huge show. My brother, Sam, Louise, Jennifer, and Amy were all in town to participate. At the same, I was driving them down Pacific Coast Highway, I nonchalantly looked up into the rearview mirror and saw an extended-cab, long-bed pickup truck barreling toward us. All I had time to say was "Oh my God!"

The truck rear-ended us, knocking our SUV a hundred feet forward, into the car in front of me, and that car into the one in front of him. It ended up being a five-car pileup on the highway and several people were hurt. The Suburban I was driving was disabled, and we were all to go to the hospital to get checked out for concussions and other injuries. My first phone call was, of course, to David.

I was standing in the middle of the highway with emergency vehicles all around, including fire trucks, paramedics, police, and an ambulance.

"David, we've just been in an accident on Pacific Coast Highway and we have to go to the hospital," I said. "It was a five-car collision."

"Well, what do you want me to do about it?" David replied.

I stood there on the highway, in the heat, with my head throbbing, in shock, thinking about the night earlier in our relationship when David had called me around 4 a.m., hysterical. He told me that he'd struck the actor Ben Vereen, who'd been disoriented by an earlier car accident and was in the middle of the Pacific Coast Highway. I jumped out of bed, rushed to David's side, and dealt with the paramedics and police officers at the scene. When David was bereft following the accident, I'd traded in the vehicle he'd been driving at the time and used my own separate money to buy him a new Suburban. Yet another time, when a landslide had hit David's car, and he had called me in a panic, I'd again rushed to his side to care for him and comfort him. That's not heroic. That's nothing more than even a friend should do for another friend. And it's certainly something that any husband or wife should have the right to expect of the other. And yet, when I'd had my accident, David had snapped at me.

What kind of response is that from the person who is my "first phone call" in my moment of need?

I was stunned.

"I'm in the middle of rehearsals," David continued. "I'll just send Kofi." Kofi was a young man from Ghana who was my "nanny" for Brandon and Brody for many years. I'd hired him years earlier when I was working in Nashville on *Hee Haw*. I'd met him while he was working as a waiter in a restaurant there.

"Well, David, the Suburban is disabled," I said. "We have to go to the hospital and will need a ride home."

"I told you I'll just send Kofi," he said.

No other incident was more telling of the disparate dysfunction in our relationship. David's blatant disregard for me made me feel very much alone; I could not count on David to truly be there for me. Of course, he later apologized—and I know he was genuinely sorry—but irreparable damage had been done to my psyche and to the very foundational fiber of our marriage.

When a violation of intrinsic trust like that occurs, resentment and bitterness build up. As a result, I became more and more withdrawn, defensive, and protective of my heart. I became less than I wanted and needed to be in our marriage, and I'm pretty certain less than David wanted and needed as well. As a romantic, one who writes lyrically about love, hope, and promise, I was feeling cheated out of being all that I had the capability of being in a loving relationship, because I didn't feel I could entrust my whole heart to David for safekeeping. That accident and David's callous response were the beginning of the end of our marriage.

Chapter Twenty-three

Party of One

While David and I had more than a few rocky moments in these years, we continued to form a unified front when it came to our career, and we still enjoyed entertaining at Villa Casablanca. In 2002 we held a dinner party that included a very special guest, Lisa Marie, and her new love, actor Nicolas Cage.

Several years earlier, in the early spring of 1994, I had actually reunited with Lisa Marie when David began working with Michael Jackson, who had asked him to produce a song for his upcoming album. Michael was the King of Pop, a consummate musical talent and major artistic force, and to collaborate on a song with him was a huge honor and testament to David's ascendant reputation as a producer.

Michael had flown a group of us to New York City, including David and me, Brandon and Brody, David's daughters, and my niece Amy, who helped us out as a babysitter. Once there, Michael very generously put our large family group up in a beautiful suite at the Plaza. On our first day in the city, Michael invited us all to visit his office, which showed off his boyish, playful side with its abundant Mickey Mouse paraphernalia. But when we arrived, I got a surprise: Lisa Marie was there with Michael.

Of course, I was overjoyed to see her. We hugged and eagerly began catching up. There was an obvious intimacy and affection between

Michael and Lisa, and they seemed to really enjoy each other's company. As far as I knew, they were just dating, but it was soon revealed they had gone down to the Dominican Republic and gotten married in secret. Lisa appeared quite happy, and so I was happy for her.

We all had a memorably fun time on that trip, and I felt like I'd stumbled into yet another incarnation of the extended family of my heart. It meant so much for me to give my sons an opportunity to spend time with the first child I had enjoyed caring for and loving, all those many years ago.

During one of our days together in the city, Brandon, who was about twelve at the time, was wearing a pair of blue khakis.

"I like those pants you're wearing," Michael said to Brandon.

"You can borrow them," Brandon joked.

"Okay, I'll wear those tonight," Michael said. "Let's go to the movies."

Michael generously rented a van to take us to the movies together that evening. When we arrived at Trump Tower, where Michael was renting a suite on the sixty-fourth floor, Michael and Lisa greeted us warmly. As promised, Brandon loaned Michael the pants he'd been wearing that day and changed into another pair we'd brought along. It was just a quirky, odd thing, one of the ways in which Michael displayed much the same winsome playfulness of a child. Now might be a good time to let it be known that Michael acted in a completely appropriate manner with all of our kids.

Michael put on one of those little scarves across his nose and mouth, appearing like a robber. He often wore masks to conceal his identity in public during that time. He was still easily recognizable as Michael Jackson, but we were able to have a nice time at the movies without being mobbed by his fans. He was soft-spoken and shy but also sweet and fun. Lisa was vibrant and full of personality, as she'd always been. They held hands, and it was easy to see that they were close and shared a warm chemistry. Watching her, a beautiful, grown-up mother of two who was in love with one of the greatest entertainers of our day, brought me back to our time together with her daddy. I looked at my own two children and marveled at how far we had all come.

I truly felt for Lisa when her marriage to Michael dissolved. I knew firsthand how it was possible to love a person very much and yet no longer be able to accept the way of life that goes along with being with him. I believe she truly loved Michael and she was involved in their relationship for all the right reasons. In fact, I don't believe Lisa ever really did anything that went against her heart. But I do think that their love story was more complicated than your average straightforward union. Maybe Michael represented an enigma similar to the one her father presented to her—the King of Rock and the King of Pop. In many ways, Michael was the only artist who has ever really come close to Elvis on so many levels.

After this reunion with Lisa in 1994, she and I had managed to stay in touch. The next time I saw her, a few years later, she and Michael had already divorced, but we reminisced pleasantly about those days we'd spent together in New York. Over the next several years, we'd both attended parties at each other's homes. I'd been to a Christmas celebration at Lisa's Hidden Hills property, which she'd decorated beautifully, much as her daddy used to decorate Graceland, warming my heart at the way his traditions lived on through the next generation. (As a side note, Kim Kardashian and Kanye West now own that home, revealing the myriad, unexpected ways—small and large, monumental and inconsequential—in which our lives connect with others'.)

When I invited Lisa to dinner at Villa Casablanca in 2002, she'd wanted me to meet her new love and share my impressions of him with her. Even if she hadn't asked me to assume that role, I would have quietly taken it on myself. I still felt protective of Lisa in that special way of adults who have once loved and cared for someone as a child, and I wanted to get to know Nicolas. And so I worked out the seating arrangement so we flanked him at dinner, with Lisa and me sitting on either side of him.

I had long admired Nicolas's acting talent, and I'd been particularly amused by his brilliant *Saturday Night Live* skit, "Tiny Elvis." As we sat together at dinner, I took the opportunity to compliment him as one who'd spent a great deal of time with Elvis and happened to think Nicolas had managed a quite good rendering of the King.

"I loved your bit on Elvis," I said to Nicolas.

"What bit on Elvis?" Lisa Marie asked.

It dawned on me that she didn't seem to realize what a huge Elvis fan Nicolas was.

"Haven't you ever seen that?" I asked.

"No," she said, fixing Nicolas with that unmistakable Presley gaze.

Nicolas squirmed a little, looking slightly uncomfortable.

"You've got to be kidding me," I said. "Tiny Elvis! Oh my God. It's brilliant. He's shrunk into this little minuscule Elvis, and he's got the suit on, and he's got the nuance down, and the whole thing. He'll sit next to a lamp and say, 'Hey, Sonny, Red, look how big that lamp is, man. That's huge, that's all I'm saying man, it's just huge.'"

I couldn't help but laugh as I recounted the skit.

"You did that?" Lisa asked Nicolas, not sounding entirely sure if she was pleased to find her daddy's shadow seemingly everywhere in her world, even her love life.

"Yeah, it was a character on *Saturday Night Live*," Nicolas said, trying to downplay any significance the skit might have had for him, or might have for them in their shared life.

The awkward moment passed, and we all enjoyed ourselves and laughed a great deal over dinner. Nicolas proved to be an incredibly nice guy. And Lisa revealed herself to be the same darling, charismatic force she'd always been and very much her father's daughter. She had a mouth like Elvis, and I don't just mean her physical resemblance to him, either. I mean she swore *a lot*. At one point in one of her expletive-peppered narrations, Nicolas looked at me, eyebrow raised.

"Has she always been like this?" he asked. "Does she always talk like this?"

"Her daddy was worse," I said, laughing. "She gets it very honestly."

Lisa and I saw each other more frequently for a few years after that.

It wasn't just having Lisa Marie back in my life for a time that had brought her daddy so much to mind around then. As difficult as it was for me to believe, August 16, 2002, was the twenty-fifth anniversary of Elvis's passing. During the intervening years, I had been offered many opportunities to tell the story of my time with Elvis, including some book deals that would have come with substantial payment. But I'd always demurred, being turned off by the idea of capitalizing on my relationship with Elvis, or exploiting his memory in any way. I was always protective of Elvis's tender foibles, unlike some of the unsavory characters who professed to know him well and who had exploited his memory since his untimely death. And I'd been determined that any recounting of my life, when it finally happened, was going to contain my own accomplishments, and not just details of my time as Elvis's girlfriend.

Now it had been twenty-five years, and I had gone on to have other relationships and my own triumphs of a personal and professional nature. And, even more important, I felt like I was beginning to have the necessary perspective to speak with greater temperance and compassion than I might have before. Leading up to the anniversary, CNN talk show host Larry King called me at home.

"I'm doing a program for the twenty-fifth anniversary of Elvis's death, and I want you to do the entire show," he said. "We're friends, and you should know that I'll treat you with the utmost respect. I just think you're the person that knew him best."

I did consider Larry a friend, and I admired him and his show. The way he presented his case, it was hard to say no. *Okay, if I'm going to do it, I want to do it well,* I thought. *Here's an opportunity to say some loving things about Elvis to honor his memory, and give a little more insight into who he was for his legions of fans.*

When I told David about Larry requesting an interview from me, he absolutely did not want me to do Larry's show; I had suspected he wouldn't. My decision to go ahead and be interviewed without his blessing created a sizable rift between David and me. Years earlier, I might have succumbed to his pressure, if for no other reason than to keep the peace. But I was also growing exhausted from his attempts to control what was an integral part of me and my personal history, and I couldn't allow that to happen here. I wasn't about to follow his unfair dictates anymore when it came to a decision that should have been mine alone to make.

Larry interviewed me for a full hour, and while I didn't find anything inappropriate or distasteful about his questions, he did ask me about losing my virginity to Elvis. Mind you, it had happened a long time ago, so it wasn't like the anecdote was emotionally charged for me anymore. And by the early 2000s, social mores had loosened to the point where a little polite conversation of a slightly sexual nature between two adults was hardly shocking. Of course, David and I had both grown up a little more cloistered than what might have been the cultural average at the time. And he did have that jealous nature that was particularly triggered by any and all references to Elvis. Needless to say, he was furious. But I did not believe I had anything to apologize for, and as long as our conflict on the subject was relegated to our private lives, I was not terribly upset by his reaction.

That is, until we were at a party at the home of our dear friends the Davises. This was one of their lovely, sophisticated dinner parties attended by some of the top tastemakers in business and entertainment. We happened to be enjoying the cocktail hour before dinner, with everyone dressed in fine eveningwear, making civilized conversation.

Larry King approached David and me with his wife, Shawn.

"Linda, you were one of the best interviews I've ever had," he said. "You were awesome. David, did you watch the interview? She was incredible."

"Fuck you," David said.

"What?" Larry said.

"How would you like me to ask you about all the women you've been with in front of your wife here? I didn't want to watch it. I can't believe you asked my wife about a man that she was with before me."

It was so shockingly inappropriate that we all stood there for a beat in silence. Larry was just stupified and clearly needed a moment to recover.

"I think you've just insulted me," Larry finally managed to say to David.

Just then, Barbara Davis swooped in, ever the perfect hostess.

"Larry, there's someone over here I'd like you to meet," she said, pulling him away. That incident represented David at his most unfiltered. Sometimes his lack of tact was shocking, as in this instance. But just as many, probably more times, his extreme candor was highly amusing and very endearing. But not this time.

I was very embarrassed, but I was not going to crack in front of our friends and the night's other guests, not when Barbara had gone to all the trouble to put together such a delightful evening. I held my head high, a big smile on my face, until the tension faded. Of course, David and Larry have seen each other many times since then and fully reconciled. It was just one of those moments everyone was anxious to forget and move on from.

Despite our having been together more than a decade by this point, David clearly still possessed a jealous streak. He had a habit of calling me to check on my whereabouts all the time. It was a running joke in Malibu. When I went to get my legs waxed at the Malibu salon Faces & Legs by Vicki, we'd inevitably hear a knock on the door.

Vicki looked at me, a knowing smile on her face.

"It's got to be David," she said.

And, yes, it was David. He'd just wanted to make sure I was where I'd said I was going to be. Suspicious by nature, he couldn't help but check up on me. Of course, there was never anything unseemly for him to discover. I was always where I'd said I was going to be. I was always doing what I was supposed to be doing. I loved the man. No matter our problems, I was in love with David. I was able to understand his complex nature as well as anyone, and I believed in his intrinsic goodness, as I still do to this day—even after all we've been through.

One day, in the summer of 2004, I made a run to Costco, and I happened to be driving through the Los Angeles suburb of Westlake. As I drove along, I was struck by what a sweet little community it was, and I craned my neck to check out one of the adorable stores I'd just passed. As had become my habit, I wanted to check in with David, to let him know I'd left Costco and was on my way home, so I called him from my car.

He wasn't answering, so I left a message: "I just left Costco, and I'm in Westlake," I said. "I may stop into this store on the way home because this is such a cute little community." I sort of babbled on about Westlake and how charming I thought it was. Little did I realize then the significance Westlake would have in my life and the future of my marriage.

Despite David's obsessiveness when it came to my whereabouts, he continued to feel wholly justified in checking in and out of our marriage whenever there was tension between us.

One night, there was a big function we'd RSVP'd to and were supposed to attend together. As the day of the gala dawned, I was extremely conflicted and uncertain about what to do because David was not living at home at the moment. I didn't know where he was, and we weren't communicating. Either I'd go alone, or I'd risk being rude to the hosts. I knew that, whatever I decided, I wasn't going to call David and ask him if he was still planning to be there.

After much internal debate, I got dressed and went out to the party. I still remember what I wore because I felt so sad and strange about being there without David, and about where we had ended up in our marriage. Everything felt deeply unsettled. *Is he just acting out again, or is this disappearance the final time, meaning he's going away for good?* He'd never skipped an event like this before.

I was seated next to iconic TV producer Larry David, and I did my best to appear upbeat and make small talk with him. And then I looked across the giant ballroom, where this elaborate affair was being held, and I saw David sitting at another table on the other side of the room. He was present, but we hadn't been seated together, which was perplexing to me as we had been invited and RSVP'd together. Looking across the crowded room, with dozens of people in between us, my heart broke at the sight of my distant husband, who suddenly felt like a stranger to me.

Over the next few hours, David never came over to where I was sitting, and I never went over to his table, either. If I'd had too much personal pride to call him, I certainly wasn't going to cave now. We never spoke at all that night, and mind you, we were still married. We were not separated. We had not even had a particularly bad fight. As far as I knew, he was just gone for a spell, and he'd be back again sometime soon. I went home alone that night, feeling confused and bereft. He was away for several more days, and then he called me as if nothing had happened.

"Well, did you have fun at the party?" he asked.

"Well, are you coming home?" I asked.

"Yeah, I'll be there," he said.

David did return to our home in the next few days, but so many unexplained disappearances, so many absences had eroded the foundation of our marriage. It was becoming clearer that the reasons for staying with David and tolerating his behavior were beginning to dissipate. With my sons launching into their adult lives, I didn't have to protect them anymore or worry about how my marriage, or lack of one, might impact them. I began to think about myself and my own happiness in a way I hadn't felt able to do before.

By this point in my life the strength of my resolve and emotional intelligence had increased dramatically from when I was with Elvis, or even with Bruce. I was a more seasoned, learned person, and while I hadn't become jaded enough to stop believing in the possibilities of love and life, I was becoming much more realistic and emotionally mature. I was coming into my own, and I liked how it gave me strength.

On another occasion that same year, my good friend Esther was having a big beautiful fiftieth birthday party and David had gone MIA in the days leading up to her soiree. As with other events, we had told her that we would be attending, and I wasn't sure how to approach the situation. I ultimately decided to go alone because we'd said we'd be there. After what had occurred at the previous event, I didn't know if David was going to show up or not, so I didn't cancel for him. *He's a grown man*, I thought. *He can make his apologies for himself if he chooses not to attend.*

Unlike the last time, I hadn't fretted about being on my own this time. For years I'd been scared about being on my own at events like these—after nearly two decades of having David's company and being at the social heart of every party, being on my own had felt uncomfortable, and left me feeling vulnerable. But after the experience of seeing him across the room at the previous party, I determined that I needed to embrace this solitude and the freedom it afforded me. I was on my own, but able to walk in with supreme confidence, knowing I was surrounded by caring friends.

When I walked in, I actually felt completely comfortable, maybe even empowered. With a high-wattage smile on my face I was determined to be there without telegraphing my private dramas to the room.

When Esther asked about David, I simply responded, "He's MIA, missing in action," I said, being sure to keep smiling.

By this point in my relationship with David, my closest friends knew that David's pattern was to be MIA, and so she laughed at my joke, gave me an encouraging squeeze, and did her best to make sure I had a wonderful time that night. David didn't even make an appearance, which I considered very rude, but I went ahead and stayed at the party, even though it meant sitting by myself for some of the festivities.

While the new strength I was finding to be inherent in myself was born of sometimes painful circumstances, it felt good to exhibit my personal power. I became more and more comfortable asserting myself on my own terms. *I am perfectly capable of getting in my car and going to an event alone,* I thought. *I am not going to cower. I am not going to cover for him anymore by claiming he's working when I have no idea where he is.*

By the middle of 2004 my relationship with David had become so contentious that he'd not only left home once again, but he'd actually written up a list of fifteen demands that I needed to meet in order for him to return to the house and me. These included everything from, yes, the rule that nobody would ever sit in his kitchen chair, to no one should ever park in his space in our oversized motor court, to the decree that his word was the final word, and the demand that I sign a postnuptial agreement.

I could laugh at his need to be the king in his house, but there was no way I was going to sign a postnup. I'd had no problem walking away from my first marriage with a modest settlement and no alimony or child support, but this was different. David and I had been together for eighteen years at this point. I'd been working the whole time. And we'd built our profiles and careers together.

Overall, I found the list to be highly insulting. If I had signed it, I would have had no power in my life, and that feeling was all too familiar to me. It would have been like I'd reverted to when I was a twenty-two-year-old beauty queen and Elvis dictated my day-to-day reality. I had fought too hard and grown too much to go backward.

I told him where he could put the list, and I think David could tell how serious I was, and how close to the breaking point, because instead of exploding at me in return, as he usually did, he was subdued. At this point, he'd been MIA for nearly two weeks, but his tone was reconcil-iatory.

"Let's meet on Sunday," he said. "Let's sit down and see if we can work things out."

Well, the night before we were due to meet, I had a strange feeling and decided to call a girlfriend of mine around midnight. We hadn't talked for at least six months, and I knew it was late to be calling her, but I felt such a strong urge to do so that I couldn't ignore it.

"Oh my God, Linda, I'm so glad you called me," she said. "Are you sitting down? I've been waiting for you to call me."

"Why am I calling you?" I asked. "Something just told me to call you."

"Do you want to know who David's girlfriend is?" she asked.

"David has a girlfriend?" I said, genuinely shocked.

She went on to tell me that David had been having an affair for the past six months with a single mother from Westlake with two sons, whom he'd met at an event he'd attended without me. He'd been seated at a table with some friends from Westlake, and they'd intro-duced him to her. They'd been an item ever since, and many in our circle knew about it. My friend hadn't wanted to be the one to call and tell me the bad news, and so she'd been hoping I would call her with my suspicions. And now I had called, and I knew everything.

I looked at our phone records. I found a single number that David had called many, many times, from both his cell phone and our home phone, for the past six months. So now I knew the girl's name. I knew her phone number. I knew their history. The fact that she was from Westlake made me sad when I thought back to how I'd been so charmed by the area I'd even commented on it to David, having no idea that he'd been engaged in an affair with her there at the time. Well, I had all the information I needed now, and I was determined to take charge of the conversation when I sat down with David.

In the morning, David called me.

"Are you ready to have that meeting?" he asked.

"Yes, I am, absolutely," I said. "It has changed a little, though. I have something I want to talk to you about."

He came home, and we went into his studio. As soon as we were settled, I spoke.

"David, do you want to tell me about her, or should I tell you?" I said, using his mistress's full name.

He went ashy, his eyes big, and he remained silent, a rare occurrence for him.

"This meeting is about your affair," I said. "Would you like to tell me, or should I tell you what I know?"

"That's a nonevent," he said.

"Really? It doesn't sound like a nonevent. It sounds like you have been having an affair while I have been struggling to make this marriage work."

"No, no, I haven't even kissed her."

"Really?" I said. "Okay, I have phone records here. I have her phone number. I know you've been calling her. I haven't figured it all out yet. This is all preliminary, but I know you have been having a relationship."

"No, it is just a friendship," he said. "I just needed somebody to talk to, and I haven't even kissed her. It's not a big deal. I've just talked to her on the phone a few times in the last month or two."

"Really?" I said. "I checked the phone records, and they say you've been talking to her for six months."

"Those are wrong," he said.

Now I was incensed. He'd been caught, and he was really going to lie to my face?

"Oh, really, the phone records lie, but you don't?" I asked.

He continued to make excuses. I'd had enough.

"Okay, if I go up to the house and call her, she'll concur that friendship is all it is?"

"Oh, absolutely, it's a nonevent," he said. "This is about you and me. It's not about somebody else. I want to work things out. I'm still in love with you. I want us to be together."

I still loved David, too, and there was meaning for me in his words. And yet this news wasn't over for me. He didn't think I'd do it, but I went up to the house, and I called her. Let's refer to her as Jezebel to protect the guilty. "May I speak to Jezebel please?" I politely asked.

"Who is this?" replied the voice at the other end of the line.

"This is Linda Thompson," I said. "I'm David Foster's wife."

There was a charged silence.

"Why are you calling me?" she asked.

"I'm not calling to judge you or to interrogate you. Honestly, I'm calling you woman to woman for your edification and for mine. I wanted to let you know that my husband is telling me that he's still in love with me, and he would like to work things out. He is asserting that his relationship with you—I know it has been going on for a while, I have seen his phone records—as he puts it, is a nonevent. He says he hasn't even kissed you." I had conjured up my best Grace Kelly demeanor to confront her with dignity. I'm sure my graciousness threw her off.

She laughed a little nervously.

"Well, that is not exactly true," she said. "We have definitely kissed, and it has been more romantic than that, but we are just friends. He just needed someone to talk to, and so I have been there for him."

"I assumed as much," I said. "Listen, I'm not judging or condemning you. I have made a lot of mistakes in my life, too. This is a mistake, clearly, that you have made. My advice to you, woman to woman, would be take care of your two sons. I know that you have two sons. Concentrate on them, and get on with your life, because David is trying to work things out here, and I would appreciate if you would respect that."

"David's friends told me that you are the nicest person in the world," she said.

"No, I'm not that nice," I said. "I just believe in honesty and transparency, so I wanted to reach out to you to clear the air for both of us."

After my call with her, David and I had a long and painful discussion, with him reassuring me over and over she meant nothing to him. I said, "I need you to call her in front of me and tell her that it's done, if you really want to be with me."

He did as I asked, which was a step in the right direction, but I knew that wasn't going to repair the damage. If we were going to stay together, we had to rebuild not only our marriage, but also my ability to trust him. After finding out about this one affair, it had made every other disappearance in our nearly two decades together suspect.

I've read and heard about every possible act of retribution, when an affair is involved, from shredding the offender's clothes, to torching a car, to cutting off the offending penis. Let me just say David got off light. I didn't punish him with any overt act of rage. But I didn't let him forget any too soon how he had damaged our marriage.

We decided to return to therapy in order to receive some support to begin healing. In the early sessions, we discussed David's affair, and I learned that of course there had been sexual activity. It took all my restraint not to call Jezebel back, but I was not going to reduce myself to that.

Therapy can be very helpful, but as I've found, most of the answers you discover in therapy are ones you already have inside yourself. And so the therapist really becomes more like a sounding board as you're excavating your personal truth, from the inside out. And by this point in my life and in my relationship with David, I knew the truth.

During one session with our therapist, David said something really hurtful to me. I can't remember exactly what it was, but as the old adage says, "You may forget what someone says, but you never forget how it made you feel."

I expressed my hurt, and instead of acknowledging my feelings, the therapist tried to ameliorate the situation.

"Well, Linda, what David meant was—"

"You know what?" I said. "I've known David for nearly twenty years. You've known him for what? Twenty minutes in the scheme of things. You just met him, so with all due respect, I've got this, and I don't need you to tell me what he meant. I know what he meant."

I was done with our joint therapy. We had a few more sessions after that, but my heart wasn't really in it, and I wasn't feeling much more optimistic about our relationship in general. But I still loved David, and I believed that he still loved me. And if he said he wanted to continue to work on our marriage, I wasn't going to be the one to give up. So I dug in, attempting to forgive and to rebuild while trying to remain strong yet hopeful. I even got a good lyric out of my pain with a song I wrote with him called "Go On and Cry," recorded by *American Idol*'s Diana Degarmo. At least there was that positive. But broken trust in a relationship is like a broken china plate. You can glue it back together, but the cracks will always be evident, and it will never have the same integrity or strength it once had before it was broken.

"Go On and Cry"

What goes around
Comes back around
Seems that's just the way
Heartache falls
I learned to live without you by my
   side
But I prayed for the day that you'd
   call

So why don't you lie down beside me
Open your heart
And confide in me

Go on and cry
Here's my shoulder
Why don't you try
To imagine that I'd even care
Go on and cry
On my cold shoulder
You left me so sad
And you hurt me so bad
It's your turn to
Cry cry cry
Over me

You say you made
A big mistake
When you threw away
The love I gave
I always knew you'd come around
   again
Looking for the love we made

Go on and cry
Here's my shoulder
Why don't you try
To imagine that I'd even care
Go on and cry
On my cold shoulder
You left me so sad
And you hurt me so bad
It's your turn to
Cry cry cry

Sometimes love is overrated
It can be so hard to find a cure
And when a heartbreak is
   understated
It comes back around, I'm sure
Oh, oh, oh

Go on and cry
On my shoulder
Why don't you try
To imagine that I'd even care
Go on and cry
On my cold shoulder
You left me so sad
And you hurt me so bad
It's your turn to
Cry cry cry
Over me

LYRIC: LINDA THOMPSON

Chapter Twenty-four

Princes of Malibu

While it was clear to both of us that our marriage was unraveling, neither of us were at a point where we were fully prepared, or even able to admit it. Of all things, it took a reality television show to convince us that, once and for all, we were truly done.

It all began when Brandon and Brody made the decision to return home from college. They had both been studying at the University of Colorado at Boulder, with Brandon initially deciding to study music there. A year and a half later, Brody followed in his footsteps, as he often did.

Although I missed them deeply, as other "empty-nesters" can relate, I was elated to see them setting off on their own path and relieved that they had each other. Brody always was that little brother who shadowed his big brother in actions both significant and minor. Thank God that Brandon is such an exemplary human being and has almost always made wise decisions, because he's played such an important role in Brody's life and growth.

"You know who my dad was?" Brody often says, pointing to Brandon. "He was. Brandon taught me how to throw a baseball, ride a two-wheeled bike, gave me advice, and he really raised me like he was my father."

They had always been best friends as well as brothers, and it comforted me to know they had each other at Boulder for support. My own comfort was found in visiting their closets and gazing at their clothes, sniffing their pillows, and sending them care packages. Typical mother.

But then, after he'd finished two years of school, Brandon called to tell me that he'd made an important decision about his future: He was moving back home. He knew that music was what he wanted to do, but the program at Colorado was limited to classical music and his interests were broader. Brandon was never one to make a spontaneous, knee-jerk move. He was always thoughtful and deliberate, so I trusted his judgment in all matters and agreed with his choice. Once Brody heard about his brother's choice, though, he decided he was coming home, too.

And so just like that, they both moved home. Brandon worked diligently on his music. Meanwhile, Brody began carving his creative path toward where he was meant to be in the world as well. Brody and his friend Spencer Pratt decided to create their own reality show and began brainstorming ideas and preparing to pitch them. *Laguna Beach* had been a big hit for MTV, and Brody and Spencer were looking to carve out something similar but about their lives. They were hanging around Villa Casablanca one day when Spencer looked around and had a breakthrough.

"What about you guys?" Spencer said. "This is a show right here. You guys are like the princes of Malibu. It's like Brandon and Brody kind of rule Malibu. Everybody loves you guys. You're living the life here at Villa Casablanca."

Brody quickly warmed to the concept, but then he took it one step further.

"Well, Mom, you and David have to be a part of the show," he said.

"No," I said.

Having my life on TV didn't appeal to me in the first place. And with my marriage under serious strain, I didn't relish the idea of having cameras around all the time.

"Yes, it should be about the family," Brody said.

Brody, Spencer, and Brandon moved forward and created a show called *The Princes of Malibu*. ABC, NBC, and Fox all bid on the show, and so the boys essentially had succeeded with all three networks. They went with Fox in what was a multimillion-dollar deal for them.

I was incredibly proud of the boys' accomplishment and the leadership role Brody had taken in making it happen. But, by this point, the show was the bane of my existence because of my increasingly despairing perspective on my marriage.

"Mom, you have to be part of this show," Brody kept telling me. "It's about living at Villa Casablanca."

"No, Brody, I don't want to be a part of it."

"Mom, you have to," he said. "It's part of the deal."

I was never 100 percent on board. But I wanted to agree for Brody and Brandon and Spencer, because I knew it was a huge opportunity for them, being the creators and producers of the show. As any parent understands, you do what you have to for your kids, even when it's outside your comfort zone. Of course, then the situation worsened, when not long after they'd created and sold the show, I learned of David's affair.

"Brody, I can't do this," I said. "I can't."

"Mom, you have to."

"Well, I can't go on camera and pretend everything is okay when it's not. I'm having a really hard time dealing with this."

"You're an actress, so act. Please, Mom, you've got to do this for me," Brody said. "It's my start."

I'd never been able to say no to that face, and I wasn't about to begin now. Of course, I sucked it up and acted like the happy wife, but it was all for the camera.

I might have kept up appearances, but the relationship was obviously crumbling. I'd learned how to walk on eggshells at a very early age. I'd done it very well for my most of my adult life, in my relationship with Elvis, and then around the secret of Bruce's true identity, and in my relationship with David. And by this point, my feet were tired of eggshells.

More than the changes David and I were experiencing, the real change was going on inside me. I'd been dealing with David's whims for almost twenty years, but despite all of it, I'd always stayed true to myself and to my optimistic outlook. Now, though, I'd finally reached a breaking point. I felt myself becoming a person I didn't like being. I was sad, stressed, distracted, hurt, and withdrawn from the life I had always loved. Being with David had finally taken its toll—I might not have crumbled but I was no longer the person that I wanted to be. I needed to get back to being me.

As I went through the list of reasons I'd found over the years to stay with him—our mutual love, his being a father to the boys, our shared musical careers, our invigorating social life—none of them, alone or together, could overcome the way I felt now. I'd been internally suffering for too long. Something had to change.

And then there was the straw that broke the camel's back—David got involved in the production of *Princes of Malibu*, creating yet another fissure. From its inception, the show was supposed to be about Brandon, Brody, and Spencer, and their vitality and adventurousness, with abundant footage of Brandon playing his music, Brody drumming in his band, and the three of them surfing and doing all the things that young, good-looking kids in Malibu do. According to their vision, it would have been somewhat analogous to *Laguna Beach*, only the Malibu Beach Life. Very youthful, funny, sweet, and authentic.

That is, until David talked them into bringing in an old friend of his from Canada, who worked as a showrunner for a production company, and the boys let him be the producer and showrunner. I thought the guy had stardust in his eyes when it came to David, and would have done anything David bid him to do. They got together and came up with the idea that the show would center around David. And how Brandon, Brody, and Spencer were spoiled brats who abused him and squandered his hard-earned money while they did nothing more than play around, have wild parties, and just generally exploit David's generosity and good nature. This spin was offensive to me, and not only because those were my sons I had so carefully raised to be the opposite of how they were depicted; more important, it was a completely manufactured premise. I didn't want my sons portrayed in such an unflattering light. They didn't deserve to be the brunt of David's dissatisfaction.

David even admitted in his book, *Hitman*, that he turned the show into his own catharsis of sorts, a vehicle for his bitterness at having been put in a situation where he was a stepfather and had felt taken advantage of for many years. His decades of bitterness toward Bruce for his absenteeism, and how David had been forced to raise Brandon and Brody, and be financially responsible, finally found an outlet on the show.

It was too painful for me to watch my kids depicted as entitled terrors, with David as the victim of their excesses. That's not at all how our lives had really played out. Rather, the actual circumstances behind the TV reality found the boys being mature and thoughtful while David was the one who acted out.

The situation became too uncomfortable to bear, especially when coupled with David's absences and the multiple affairs I now suspected. On top of that, David began accusing *me* of having affairs, even claiming to know details of the who, when, and where. Of course, this was as far from the truth as it was possible for David to be, and I defended my innocence vehemently. But David would not be convinced. The therapist we were seeing in the wake of his affair explained that, because David had been caught behaving badly, he was projecting his guilt onto me. This explanation made sense to me, but it didn't make it any easier for me to live with a jealous, accusatory husband.

I finally felt so driven to redeem my reputation in David's eyes that I made a bold decision. Of my own volition, I set up a lie detector test. I drove downtown to the building alone on the appointed day, unable to believe this surreal existence was my life.

To feel criminalized like that, having to face a blank wall, hooked up to this machine I'd only seen in movies, with my heart racing, was the ultimate testament to how far we had strayed from what I believed a marriage could and should be.

What if I fail this because I'm nervous? I worried as the administrator asked me a series of questions to prove that I'd never cheated on David.

Of course, I passed with flying colors. I took the papers saying I'd never been unfaithful back to David, but I didn't really feel any lighter inside. He couldn't deny the facts when they were right in front of him. But I was overwhelmed with sadness that this was where we'd ended up.

No matter how loving and devoted I was—now reduced to taking a lie detector test to try to make him feel better—I could never do enough to show him that I loved him. And I truly did love David very devotedly.

At least I now felt able to walk away clean and have it on record that I was, even with all my faults, at the very least true to him. That meant a great deal to me. I was left feeling like David never really knew me, or the content of my character. He never saw or understood me for who I really was—someone who would have always been there for him, who was faithful to him and our marriage—a woman who loved him with her whole heart. Maybe because of how we got together, or because he'd had affairs, he couldn't see the loyal, trustworthy person I honestly was. And after nineteen years, I was done trying to prove myself.

Finally, we finished shooting the show, and we had about a month until it debuted on Fox in July. My goal was to keep the peace until the show aired, so the boys could have their moment, and then I'd assess where David and I were at in our marriage. My thought was that I'd try to stay at Villa Casablanca until the show aired, and if things hadn't improved considerably in our marriage, then David and I could separate.

Life became strangely normal for a time, and David and I were actually getting along well. I think we were both exhausted from our efforts to continue on in our marriage and as I would later find out, during this time David was also distracted by another relationship with a woman in Las Vegas. Our fourteenth wedding anniversary was on June 22, and we decided to try to have a nice, romantic evening together, in spite of all we'd been through. We got a suite at the Peninsula Beverly Hills. We enjoyed the spa and got massages together. We were getting along well, and there was still enough love and such a long history between us that it even felt romantic.

Later, we were having dinner at Koi restaurant and a mutual friend joined us at our table.

"I've got your dinner," he said. "Happy anniversary."

"Oh, thanks," we said.

We started chatting a bit about one of David's coworkers, a man who had recently charged fifteen thousand dollars' worth of calls on our phone. Now, that's a *really* big phone bill. Upon learning this, I had intuited the story immediately, telling David his friend was having an affair with a woman in another country and had used our phone to communicate with her so his wife wouldn't know.

"No, no, it's not that," David had said. "Those are business calls."

"This is not business," I said. "Fifteen thousand dollars in charges, with calls at three in the morning, four in the morning? You are supposed to be reestablishing trust with me after your affair. We are supposed to be communicating honestly with each other, and I have no interest in being complicit in his deceit. If you are helping to facilitate your friend's affair, that's not doing anything to reestablish trust with me."

"No, no, it's just business," David kept insisting.

It was clear he wasn't going to tell me the truth.

Now, while we were at Koi celebrating our anniversary, our friend buying us dinner, who happened to know the man who'd made expensive calls, got sort of chatty. He asked us what the man was going to do about his girlfriend.

David turned white, knowing his attempt to hide the affair of his coworker was being outed right then and there, despite the lies David had told trying to cover for him.

Our friend looked from David to me.

"You know the guy's got a girlfriend, right?" he said to me.

"Yeah, I did know that when I saw our fifteen-thousand-dollar phone bill," I said. "But David's been trying to deny it."

David stood up from the table right then and there.

"I'm never going to hear the end of this now," he said. And the truth is, he probably wouldn't have.

In any case, neither of us ever found out what would have happened next if we'd tried to stay together. He literally left our table, got a taxi back to Villa Casablanca, and moved into one of the guesthouses. And that was basically the end of our marriage. He knew it was over because he had been lying to me, even if it had been on someone else's behalf.

I have to say, I was devastated. We had a long, tumultuous, but deeply passionate, loving relationship for nearly two decades. It was not easy to walk away from someone I still loved afer all we'd been through. But it was the right move.

The Princes of Malibu aired on July 10, 2005. On Monday morning, July 11, I filed for a divorce. It took two years for us to complete the divorce proceedings, with David keeping his separate musical compositions, and me keeping mine. We divided our community property equally, and I once again did not ask for alimony. We were separated from that night of our fourteenth wedding anniversary on.

Eventually I moved back into the Knest, glad I had never succumbed to David's vehement wishes that I sell it when we moved into Villa Casablanca. All of the kids who grew up playing in this house, from my nieces, to my kids, to Casey and Burt, have expressed pleasure at being able to experience a sense of homecoming when they visit me there. For example, Casey brings her little girls over sometimes and points out all of the places she remembers fondly from her own girlhood.

"This is the pool we all played in when we were little," she'll tell them.

It really is special to have that continuity between generations, and especially for the boys, who have so many formative memories at the house.

It was a big adjustment to be alone again after nineteen years with David, but I felt no other recourse than to meet the challenge. And besides, I wasn't alone. When I walked around the grounds where I had raised my boys during most of their childhoods, I was awash in wonderful memories of all of the family parties, and holidays, and happy afternoons we'd experienced there. When I looked at the majestic avocado tree I'd planted from a single avocado pit when Brandon was just a newborn baby, I was reminded of how my boys had grown up to be strong, noble young men as well. It was very comforting for me to be surrounded by such a verdant sanctuary as I healed. And I had my many caring friends, and my sons, to comfort me and to keep me company. I had also taken on the responsibility, and the privilege, I might add, of caring for my senescent father, who was living with me full-time and required 24/7 care.

When I told Brody that I'd split up with David, he gave me a knowing look.

"Mom, you're going to be very needy now, aren't you?" he said.

"Yeah, I probably will be for a little while," I said, smiling. "Just a heads-up."

Both boys were very attentive, looking after me in their own, unique manner. Brandon, being our family's resident Gandhi, spent his time playing music and meditating at the Self-Realization Fellowship, so we had meals together and walked on the beach. Meanwhile, Brody was a lot more social than Brandon, so he began inviting me out.

One night, Brody and Spencer Pratt took me to the Spider Room, above the Avalon bar. Paris Hilton was there, and we stood on a booth together, dancing.

Who am I? What am I doing here? I wondered while maintaining a wide smile.

Brody came by and looked up at us, giving me an encouraging grin.

"Mom, go dance with Spencer and break out some of those eighties moves," he said.

Okay, I'm in the wrong place here, I thought with a laugh, taking my reality check when it came for me.

That fall, in 2005, there was going to be a big Halloween party at the Playboy Mansion. So Brody invited me to go to along with them.

Or perhaps I invited myself.

I also invited my girlfriend, Wendy Burch, who was living with me at that time. She dressed up as Wonder Woman. I was an old-school Playboy Bunny with pink ears, a little white bunny tail, and fishnet hose. I knocked on the door of Brody's condo in my outfit.

"Brody, is this too risqué?" I asked him.

"Mom, where the hell do you think you're going?" he said. "You're going to the Playboy Mansion. Those girls will be naked. You're like Mother Teresa dressed like that."

"I am?" I said. "This is modest?"

"Yeah, when we get there, you'll see," he said. "You're dressed very modestly. It's okay. You look like a mom."

"Oh, thank you," I said. *I think?*

Brody wore a tux and a rubber mask of one of the presidents like the characters in the movie *Point Break*. We all went together, and sure enough, when we walked in, I noticed there were about fifteen girls in body paint. Of course, being the curiosity seeker I am, I had to get right up there and look at their bodies. *Wait, that looks like a bra and panties, and a little garter belt and hose,* I thought, looking closer. *But that's* just *paint.*

But of course, being the resident mom, I couldn't stop worrying about them.

"Honey, are you cold?" I asked one of the girls. "Aren't you freezing? Can I get you a sweater? Are there blankets here for you?"

They were laughing at me because here I was, dressed like a vintage bunny, and I was being the total mom on duty that night. Well, let's just say it had been a long time since I'd met my husband, and the father of my boys, at the Playboy Mansion.

All this was a fun distraction because even though I had zero regrets that divorce had been the right choice, it was still very much a struggle. I wasn't so much worried about our divorce settlement—my bigger concern had to do with rebuilding myself emotionally. And as far as I could tell, the first step was to figure out how I'd gotten here when I'd fully intended to enter into a loving, respectful partnership that would last "until death do us part," as we said in our vows.

As I looked back over the years, I realized that the kind of emotional sabotage I'd experienced in my marriage was insidious. It starts off small—an insult here, a slight there—and you almost don't notice it. When you do, you make excuses because you're in love. But the problem grows, and it grows. And before you know it, you've become acclimated to the discord, and so you've begun to think it's normal.

On top of that, when you love someone, you make excuses for them, and you can't help but love them anyway. That's okay, I think, at least up to a point. But when you start loving yourself less, losing your self-respect, finding yourself hurt and angry too much of the time, you must eventually acknowledge that destructive behavior has been chipping away little chinks of your personal armor on a daily basis. When that realization hits you between the eyes, it's time to make your exit and save yourself. Once I took this healing step, I was able to love David again and wish him well. Only it was from a distance now.

Making peace with my divorce meant moving on to a new stage of my growth. I had to learn to be alone, because I'd always had a boyfriend or partner, since I was a teenager. But I do believe the real gift, and the point, of life, really, is that in every relationship and every situation, we receive an opportunity to grow. Sometimes you've got to really dig, and ask yourself: *How am I going to grow from this? Because it just pruned the heck out of me.* As Khalil Gibran wrote, "Even though love is for your growth, it's also for your pruning."

I am now reminded every day of life and love and what it teaches us as we make our way through this maze of existence. Rebirth, renewal, and the promise of the continuity of life itself can reshape every human soul. I've taken up the rather painful practice of pruning my lovely rosebushes every year at the Knest, and as a result of cutting them down to "bare root" they've always come back fuller, healthier, and more vibrantly beautiful than before.

"Blessed"

In each heart
There's a space for love
So many faces there
Yet it's never full enough

In each life
People come and go
Some you never touch
And some you'll always know

In this world of everchanging winds
On yourself you must depend
No matter how life may test you
You'll have love inside your heart
To bless you

Blessed . . .
Blessed from the moment you first
    breathe
Your heart's the key to every need
You'll ever face
It's life you will embrace
Full of love . . .
You are blessed

Just look around
The sky show's always free
And the clouds are dancing there
For the stars, for you and for me

Blessed . . .
Blessed when you first open your
    eyes
You're past the pain . . . into the
    light
Of every day
You'll always find your way
Follow love . . .
You are blessed

If you reach inside—down to your
    soul
There's a special gift that's yours
    alone
Oh, there isn't anyone who is quite
    like you
No one to do what you do best

Blessed . . .
Blessed just because you are alive
And every test you will survive
Because you're strong
With love you can't go wrong
Sing your song . . .
You are blessed

LYRIC: LINDA THOMPSON

Chapter Twenty-five

Caitlyn Coming Out

Life really does come full circle, even if it often takes many years for us to see how events that once troubled us will eventually play out in the most positive way imaginable. Maybe I am kind of a Pollyanna, and it's all right if it is sometimes to my own detriment. I'd simply rather view my world through rose-colored glasses than through pessimism. I guess it would be fair to say I create my own happy reality. I begin each day with my affirmations of gratitude and good health, and I pray for those I love, sometimes for those I don't, and for our world to be a kinder place in which to live for all living beings.

After the television show *Keeping Up with the Kardashians* had been on the air for several years, Bruce approached the boys about appearing on the show with him and their stepfamily. This was not the first time Bruce had talked to the boys about the show, in fact he'd asked Brody to be on the show back when it first began.

Around *The Princes of Malibu* time frame, Brody met Kristin Cavallari and Lauren Conrad, who were on the hit MTV reality show *The Hills* when he was out at the popular clubs in Hollywood. They got to be friends, and the girls thought he should be featured on the show, too. So the producers started filming him and incorporating him into the story line. He quickly became the resident heartthrob, and a regular on the show from 2007 to 2010.

Because of Brody's popularity on *The Hills*, he had actually been enlisted by Bruce to appear in the first episode of *Keeping Up with the Kardashians* to heighten the show's exposure. The show was the one where the script called for him to pretend to be babysitting his little sisters, Kendall and Kylie. When Brody agreed to help his father's new family show, little did he know the empire he was helping to establish.

When Bruce reapproached Brandon and Brody years later about joining the show, they had some trepidation about the undertaking, but they both agreed to appear occasionally. I think their primary motivation in saying yes was the hope that they'd at least get to know their dad a little better, even if it was with cameras around and in the context of that show.

They were grown men, and it was their decision, but that didn't stop me from having my own reservations as well. The truth is, even though the popular conception seems to be that the Kardashians and Jenners were raised as one big united family, they really never were. Our families were very separate. There was no malice or hostility, as far as I was concerned, just distinctly different upbringings, to say the least, and very limited contact for all those formative years and beyond.

After Bruce's years of disregard, I was very protective of my sons, and I didn't want to see them hurt again. But as I witnessed them begin to form the first underpinnings of a relationship with Bruce in that season, I was relieved for them.

I had tried to talk to Brandon once about Bruce's gender dysphoria, when Brandon was in his early twenties, but it was clear he wasn't quite ready to grasp what I was telling him. I dropped the subject before I said anything that might have made him uncomfortable around his father and left it alone for the time being. Now they were older, and I was almost ready to discuss the situation with them, but I wanted to find just the right opportunity, and I was still searching my heart for just the right words. In the meantime, I had other caregiving duties that were occupying my time and my heart.

When I moved back to the Knest from Villa Casablanca in 2007,

I also relocated my daddy, who was in his late eighties at the time. Caring for my father in my home with me until the end of his life was one of the greatest privileges and most important decisions I ever made. I am fortunate that I was able to provide for him in this way as his caregiver, along with the angel of a woman, Lillian Rodriguez, who has worked for me for more than twenty-two years. My daddy always referred to Lillian as his angel, and she was unfailing in her love and patience while caring for him. I was always happy to be on duty with him, too, as he had once devoted himself so lovingly to my care.

"Did you ever think you'd be changing my diapers?" he asked me ruefully one day.

"You did it for me," I said. "And I'm happy to do it for you."

I've always admired Asian cultures for how they respect their elders and keep them at home, caring for them there until the end. Here in the West, we live in such a disposable society, with our disposable batteries, disposable diapers, disposable everything. It seems that far too often, when something or someone outlives its usefulness, they are thrown away. Daddy shared his faith in God with me. And I got to witness his belief in the intrinsic goodness of humankind, accountability, and the quiet introspection and evolution of his heart and soul over those last years with him.

Daddy and I always talked about his living to be one hundred, and that was his goal. Every week a lovely woman, Hind, would come to my house and give him a massage, manicure, and pedicure. One September day, two days after my niece Jennifer and her new husband, Sebastian, had been married at my home, Hind had just finished giving my father a massage when I walked into his room to check on him.

"I was just about to come out to the gym and get you, because your dad is not responsive to me," Hind said.

Daddy, who was about to turn ninety, had slipped into a coma, so I rushed to call the paramedics. I followed the ambulance when they took him to the hospital. I had the great privilege of being with my father when he passed. I told him over and over how much I loved him, as he slowly and quietly slipped away. I was a daddy's girl up until the end, and I still am, as he lives on in my heart.

• • •

One perfect Southern California day in 2012, my then twenty-nine-year-old son, Brody, unexpectedly asked me if I would like to take a cruise on his newly purchased, thirty-five-foot Cabo boat to Catalina to spend the night. He had named his boat the *Charlie White* in honor of a wonderful professional fisherman we had gotten to know and be friends with in British Columbia. I was thrilled at the prospect of being on Brody's boat with only him, no distractions, and the opportunity to actually have meaningful conversations with him.

I had never told Brody or Brandon about their father's gender dysphoria, or the real reason Bruce and I divorced many years ago. Brody and Bruce never had a close relationship. As I have mentioned before, Bruce was hardly in the picture at all while Brody was growing up. So I decided that this would be the perfect opportunity to reveal the truth.

We were cruising along the beautiful blue Pacific with dolphins dancing all around the boat, leaping out of the water as they played and frolicked.

"Brody, there's something I'd like to tell you about your father," I said. "I tell you now, because it is my hope that with this knowledge you may find it easier to understand, and even forgive him, for some of his shortcomings as a parent."

Brody looked at me quizzically.

"What the hell are you talking about, Mom?" he asked, in his usual straightforward way.

I paused to try to formulate just the right words to help him understand.

"Well, your dad has something called gender dysphoria," I tentatively said. "Which means he feels he is actually a woman and has been trapped inside the wrong body for all his life."

Brody looked at me as if I were an alien.

"What the fuck?" he said.

"Well, you see, that's the real reason we divorced," I continued, breathlessly letting out a truth so long kept inside me. "Because your daddy came to me one day when you were about eighteen months old and told me that he wanted to begin the transition and become a woman. We went to therapy for six months, but the therapist told me that his condition was not something that would go away, and that twenty-five percent of all transgenders commit suicide. I was devastated, but my heart went out to him then, and still goes out to him today, because fate dealt him such an unfair blow. But I didn't bargain to be married to a woman, and he was determined to begin his transition. So I didn't see any other choice but to divorce him. Bruce feels that he is truly a woman and that nature made a terrible mistake by putting his spirit in man's body."

Brody looked at me with his eyes wide open.

"What the fuck?" he again exclaimed.

Well, that went well, I thought to myself.

"Does Brandon know about this, Mom?" Brody asked.

"No, honey, he does not," I said. "I have never talked to Brandon about this, so please don't say anything to him until we get back to the mainland. Then you and I will sit down with Brandon, and as a family, we will discuss it, okay?"

"Okay, sure, yeah," Brody said. "I won't talk to him until then."

We continued on to Catalina, discussing more about transgender issues in general, and Bruce in particular. I told Brody that Bruce had begun hormone treatments and had gone through the painful process of electrolysis on his face, neck, and chest, and had feminizing surgeries all those years ago.

"Mom, that explains so much," Brody said. "You remember when Brandon and I were little boys, and we went to visit dad, and we came home and said, 'Mommy, Daddy has boobs'? Now I know why. Think about that, Mom. I was just a little kid, and I could tell something was different about him."

Brody stared out at the ocean for a bit before continuing to speak.

"I'm really glad you didn't tell me when I might have been too young to understand," he said. "And knowing this information now does help me to understand Bruce better, and to feel better about why he was such an absentee father. I guess he was really struggling. I feel really bad for him. The poor guy must have struggled, and I just hope he can find happiness."

Brody and I continued on to Catalina, conversing, enjoying nature and each other, and I felt as close to Brody as I have ever felt. He handled the shocking information I imparted to him with such grace, intelligence, empathy, forgiveness, and understanding. I was very proud of my son that day.

We spent the night on Brody's boat, and the next morning headed back to the mainland. When we arrived back at my house, Brandon was in the kitchen waiting for us.

"Mom, Brody told me about Dad," Brandon blurted out as we walked in the kitchen door. "Man, that's trippy!"

"Hey, Brody, you weren't supposed to tell Brandon like that," I said. "You were supposed to wait until we came back, then sit down as a family, and discuss this together."

"Mom, are you kidding me?" Brody said with an incredulous look on his face. "Brandon's my brother! You should have known I couldn't wait to tell him."

I truly believe the knowledge of Bruce's gender dysphoria helped to assuage some of the boys' pain and confusion about why their father had been missing in previous years. Brandon and Brody now had a deeper understanding of their father and the condition that was out of anyone's control, upon which to blame what could have been the biggest reason for Bruce's dysfunction paternally. They handled this newfound knowledge with aplomb, sensitivity, acceptance, and love. They have never wavered.

As a mother, I always felt an acute sense of responsibility to measure my words, and to love and respect my sons unconditionally, and do my best to raise my two little boys into fine young men. Many years ago, when I first discovered that Bruce was really Caitlyn, I determined I would have to make a valiant effort to instill in my sons an openness, a broad scope of acceptance, and a deep understanding of differences not only of race, gender, and religion, but of all variations in the human condition. I wanted to prepare them for the knowledge they would no doubt someday have to absorb about their dad, so they could come to terms with it in a healthy way.

Brandon and Brody seem to have forgiven Bruce's absence in their lives while they were growing up. That does not mean they can ever get those lost years back or that damage was not done. They have exhibited nothing but acceptance, understanding, support, and love for Bruce's transition into Caitlyn. I am extremely proud of the remarkable young men they are. And if I played any part in their graceful reception of their father, I truly consider it one of the greatest accomplishments of my life.

After I made my revelation to the boys about Bruce, life continued as normal for a time. Neither of them spoke to their father about what I'd told them, and they continued to make a tentative foray into building a healthier father-son dynamic with him. I can't tell you what a tremendous relief this was for me, having so long carried my anxiety about what would happen when they found out Bruce's truth. It was as if I could finally stretch myself out in the warmth of the sun, after having lived in the shadow of my fear for so many years.

Over the course of the next year, when I saw the boys after they'd filmed an episode of *Keeping Up with the Kardashians*, they might give me some general news of their father. But I still did not have any direct contact with Bruce by this point in time. My primary concern continued to be my sons and the benefit to them of their fledgling relationship with their dad. It had been decades since my divorce from Bruce, and I was quite happy to love Bruce and wish him well from a distance.

In 2013, Bruce and Kris publicly separated, and the boys began seeing much more of him, I suppose because he was by himself, and it was probably lonesome. During these more frequent visits, they were able to start becoming a little better acquainted with their father, in private, without the cameras rolling. And then, just as they were getting to know Bruce Jenner as their dad, finally, after all these years, he had his own announcement for them. He apparently sat all his children down individually and told them of his issue, then declared, "I'm going to go through the transition."

Now, of course, they already knew about Bruce's gender dysphoria, and had been afforded plenty of time to come to terms with it, but I can't help but think this was still another loss for them, as I well knew from my own experience thirty years earlier. Just as they got their father, Bruce, back, he went away again to become Caitlyn. It was as if they had lost their father twice. I do believe Caitlyn has the same spirit as Bruce, and is essentially the same person, but the transition can't have been without some emotional adjustment for the boys. I know it's been an emotional process for me, even all of these years after I first prepared myself for this eventuality.

I have to admit that I was nervous on Caitlyn's behalf when she made her public debut. I knew times had changed immensely since Bruce first made his confession to me, but I didn't know what the popular reception would be. And I didn't want Caitlyn to have any reason to feel hurt, or ashamed, or scared.

I have been gratefully astonished at the level of acceptance people have shown toward Caitlyn. I know there are those who don't understand. I recognize that gender transition is not an easy road for anyone involved. I have found in my life experience that we need not fully understand something to accept it. Life itself is, after all, a mystery. Caitlyn and I have both agreed since she went public that, had she continued with her transition that she started thirty years ago, there would not have been nearly the same level of understanding and acceptance that has been afforded her today. I believe that Caitlyn is sincere in her efforts to try to make good use of the platform she has been given by creating a positive difference in the world, particularly for those disenfranchised souls in pain. God knows she was one of them for the better part of her life.

I have already described in pretty good detail what a fantastic guy I found Bruce Jenner to be when I was married to him. Now I am getting to know Caitlyn Jenner. Before Bruce announced his plans to transition, I had the occasion to be in his company at Brody's thirtieth birthday party, and again at Casey's daughter's birthday party. Better late than never. We had a chance to visit and catch up a little.

Caitlyn then called me just after the Diane Sawyer interview when I wrote a piece for the *Huffington Post*. Caitlyn had not read my article but took issue with it to a degree.

The *Huffington Post* had agreed to publish the article with my firm directive they do so only after Bruce had publicly made his declaration about his experience of transitioning. I would have never presumed to tell his story; I believe his truth is his to tell, but his truth had a lifelong impact on my own truth, and that of my children. My story is mine to tell as well.

My primary intention in writing that article was to soften Caitlyn's startling revelation and hopefully help others to understand and accept the new Bruce. I knew some people would think Bruce's announcement was all just a publicity stunt for TV ratings, but I wanted to help her with the credibility of her story. I was still trying to protect her, but in another way now. I truly wanted Caitlyn to be understood and accepted.

Caitlyn seems so much happier and freer in her feminine self than she was toward the end of the time I knew her as Bruce. Caitlyn seems to derive extreme pleasure in trying out new fashions, makeup, and all the innocent distractions a young girl coming into her own might experience.

And of course, the perfect family for the job has schooled her in hair and makeup. And if those were her role models, she's emerged as the ultimate example of all they inspired her to emulate and be. I do believe that Caitlyn has imaged herself according to the Kardashian ideal of womanhood, where everything is gorgeous and glam-squad groomed. And while this metamorphosis makes perfect sense to me, I do think it will be interesting to see who Caitlyn becomes as she matures into her own, unique version of that model. A newly transgendered person is sometimes described as being in the "pink cloud," and I believe it might be accurate to say that Caitlyn is in that "pink cloud" at the moment. Brandon, in his sage wisdom, summed up her growth process well.

"Mom, it's like dad is an adolescent girl," he said. "Her body is changing into a woman's, just like an adolescent girl would start to get hormonal and grow breasts and experience every change that comes and goes with that adolescence."

I thought it was a great description of the changes that Caitlyn has been going through. Since then, I have heard, but not yet gotten used to, "Dad," "She," and "Her," used in the same sentence in reference to the same person. Recently I was at Brandon and his wife, Leah's, house to babysit, and Brandon came into the kitchen.

"Mom, Dad just called and said she was going to stop by," he announced. "She should be here in about five minutes. I just wanted to let you know."

I find that, with each day that passes, these jarring pronoun inconsistencies are becoming less noticeable to me, even reaching the point where they're becoming the new normal.

In much the same way, I've found that time can heal even that which seemed irreparably marred. It certainly has done wonders for my relationship with David.

About a year into David's fourth marriage, to Yolanda Hadid, one of the "Real Housewives of Beverly Hills," he called me to ask if he could stop by my house and talk for a few minutes.

"Of course," I said.

As we settled onto my sofa in the old familiar TV room, he asked me about our relationship in years past. He wanted to know if he had inexplicably disappeared during our marriage a few times.

"How many times did I just take off and leave like that?" David asked. "Four or five?"

I had to laugh.

"David, try nineteen or twenty times in the nearly twenty years you and I were together," I answered honestly.

"Wow, that's really terrible," David said contritely. "I'm really sorry. That's awful. That must have been very hurtful for you."

"Yes, it was extremely damaging," I said. "But you need to know, as much as I appreciate your apology, David, I already forgave you a long time ago."

And I truly had forgiven David, just as I hope he had learned to forgive me for any part I played in the destruction of our relationship, or any time I had ever hurt him.

In more recent years, I could not be happier, not only with where he and I are at, but also with the generous overtures David has been inspired to make toward the boys. Not long after his fourth divorce became public, he called Brandon and Brody and asked if he could take them out to lunch.

"I just want you to know that your mom and I are on really good terms," he said. "When you go through a divorce, things are tough for a time, but we're really good friends now. And if you need me, I just want you to know, I'm here. Since I did live with you for all of your formative years."

I appreciated this gesture from David, and especially when he backed up the offer by being true to his word. Brandon has been working on a new record, and it's really accomplished. Brandon played some of an early recording for David.

"Oh, man, this is beautiful," David said. "Let me write some strings for that song."

Like any parent, I appreciate anyone who's good to my kids. And in this particular circumstance, David's generosity has extra poignancy for me.

In the spring, I decided to travel to Phoenix for Muhammad Ali's Celebrity Fight Night charity event. As I was well aware, David volunteers his time to do the music for this evening special every year, but I'd been busy in the days before my trip and didn't get the chance to text him. The event is a two-night charity event, and before the first night I ran into David in the lobby. He offered me a ticket for the first night as well.

While the main event on Saturday night is a huge extravaganza, this was a much more intimate happening in a smaller ballroom. When I walked in around nine o'clock, they were about to get the show started, and David was standing onstage with Larry King and Larry's wife, Shawn. Larry asked David a question, which I couldn't hear, but I did hear David's response: "Well, I don't know about that, but I've been in a few bad marriages."

Those audience members who could see me and knew who I was started to laugh.

"Ahem, I'm right here," I said to David. "I can hear you."

"Oh my God, there's, there's . . ." David said, pointing at me.

David and I knew many of these people from the years David had coordinated the music at this event, and I'd attended as his wife. The place went crazy with laughter.

"There's my ex-wife now," David said. "Come over here, Linda."

I joined Larry and David where they were standing together, and the spotlight landed on me just as Larry turned to me with the microphone.

"So, Linda, why did you leave David?" he asked.

"Well . . ." I said, followed by a dramatic pause. I couldn't help but think of their unpleasant exchange years prior, and how time can heal hurt feelings.

David made a face that showed he knew exactly why I'd left him.

Everybody laughed even harder, and I let the hilarity die down before I responded.

"David's a great guy, Larry," I said.

"I know he's a great guy," Larry said. "So why'd you leave him?"

"Well, you'll just have to read about it in my book," I said.

David looked as if I'd just ordered him to walk the plank, then laughed along with everyone else.

After that, I took my seat and David led the wonderful musical program, as always. But all people could talk about for the rest of the weekend was the moment when I'd walked in on his complaint about his bad marriages and we'd mined the opportunity for comedic gold. I was happy for the moment because of what it meant for David and me, and how far we'd come in our healing process. It really felt like the good old days, when we'd entertained our friends by telling jokes at parties. Only now, with no cause for enmity, and only affection between us, the good cheer onstage was no show.

David feels like extended family to me now, and I feel pretty much the same way about Caitlyn. It's also the same deep emotionality that allows me to speak so fondly about Elvis after all these years. The romantic love we shared may have transmuted into a different kind of love, but the love's still there. David's like my brother. And Caitlyn, well, I guess she's more like my sister now. And I feel grateful to have connections with both of them, especially for the sake of my sons. The fact that both of my ex-husbands are still occasionally in my life—and I have no doubt that Elvis would be, too, if he were still alive—tells me that I might be doing something right, and that my former partners are good souls with their hearts in the right place, and that I chose my partners wisely after all.

As do the many moments in which my life keeps circling back on itself, with all of its unique chapters linking together in new and surprising ways, I've been gratified by how warmly the Elvis fan community has continued to embrace me and consider me one of their own. I have begun to try to accept every invitation I can to take part in events around the world. I happened to be in Vienna for an Elvis cruise with my brother, Sam, my sister-in-law, Louise, and my niece Jennifer. We arrived in Vienna early, only to discover that Josh Groban was in town, performing at the Vienna Opera House.

We all attended his show as his guests, during which he made me feel like a proud mama by singing, "To Where You Are." As a means of introducing the song, he said, "There's someone in the audience I'd like to acknowledge tonight. Linda Thompson, would you please stand?"

I felt so validated as I stood up and received his acknowledgment and the audience's applause, not because of the attention itself, of course, but because it points to evidence of what I've been seeking my whole life, to live in a way that, in the final analysis, has made even a modicum of difference to others. When I look on the walls of my office and see some of the gold records for songs I've written hanging there, I don't think of the record sales they represent. I think of having done something that's hopefully made a difference in people's lives, when they've played those songs at their weddings, or have been inspired to carry on, or had a broken heart soothed by listening. Having put my poetry out into the world in the form of my lyrics gives me the same feeling of continuity and connectivity that I get when I consider the fact that my sons, and their children, will live beyond my time in this world.

And nothing is a better example for me of all that I've tried to accomplish in my life than the fact that my family—in all of its unique loveliness—continues to gather at my home for the major holidays each year.

In the days leading up to Thanksgiving in 2015, I contacted my boys, as well as Chrystie, and Casey, and Burt, and let them know they were invited over for dinner, as always. Once again, Brandon and Brody had a few friends with nowhere else to go, and so I made sure they knew they were welcome, too, as I've always had a policy of accepting everyone at my table.

When Brandon called me, I assumed it was to finalize some detail about the menu or arrival times. But he surprised me with the purpose of his call.

"Mom, Dad wants to know if she's invited," he said.

"Of course," I said. "Of course she can come. I thought she was out of town on her trans-road trip. Otherwise, I would have asked her myself. She's always invited." Caitlyn had been to my house one other time that August for a birthday celebration for Brody. That was the first time I had seen the new version of her feminine self.

We're all there for Caitlyn now, just as we've all been there for each other all along. I never would have predicted that my family unit would look quite like this someday. Of course, it's not without its thorns. We all share a great deal of history, not all of it easy or pleasant. But this is the true family of my heart, which means being honest about both the dark and light.

When Caitlyn arrived at my house on Thanksgiving, she was wearing a red silk blouse with black pants. I happened to have on a red cashmere sweater with black tights. When we saw each other, we paused for a portentous beat before breaking into laughter.

"Did you get the dress memo or something?" I said. "What were we thinking?"

"Well, it is almost Christmas, you know," Caitlyn said.

Having everyone there, around my table, sharing food and laughs and stories of their day made me feel like everything had turned out as it was supposed to in the end. If I'm honest, though, and I am making every effort to be perfectly honest at all times, I sometimes find it surreal to look into the perfectly made-up, beautiful brown eyes of Caitlyn, while remembering the phenomenally masculine, gorgeous man I married years ago, and who fathered my two sons. That admission is just me being real. I completely accept, respect, and support Caitlyn, but I must admit, I sometimes miss Bruce. However, I've seen more of Caitlyn in recent months than I ever saw of Bruce over all those many years when he chose not to be connected to the boys, or to me. And so maybe it was really Bruce who had become the stranger, and it's Caitlyn who feels almost more familiar than Bruce did at the end.

I am probably like many honest people out there who are willing to admit that they miss the Bruce Jenner on the Wheaties box, the one who crossed the finish line of the 1976 Olympics as the world's greatest athlete and served in our culture for a time as the epitome of manhood. Millions learned to embrace Bruce in their hearts and minds as the perfect specimen of athleticism and boyish good looks housed in the body of a Greek god, albeit one that was secretly a prison for Caitlyn for those many years. You have to give her credit—Caitlyn, as Bruce Jenner, did that manhood thing proud. SHE was the best HE could possibly be.

"When you think about it, you were the ultimate man," I've had occasion to tell her recently. "You conquered manhood. You kicked manhood's ass. You were the greatest athlete in the world. You were a six-foot-two, muscular, gorgeous guy that women loved and men wanted to be. You conquered that. You did that. Against all of your internal input about who you were. And now you're working on being the best woman you can be."

After having harbored Caitlyn's secret, and feeling in my heart and mind that I have protected her through these years, I can now breathe a little easier, knowing she has found the strength and the courage to fulfill her dream. She can finally realize her need to be who she authentically is, who she feels she was born to be. That takes tremendous courage. For that I commend her.

Caitlyn has already "gone through the fire," suffering unfathomable discomfort and pain, held prisoner in her own flesh. It is certainly not our place to judge her or others who may feel trapped, ostracized, or alone. As relieved and happy as I am for Caitlyn, I know that her journey is not over. And her battle is not won. I can see she's trying to fight for other people now in whatever ways she can, and I know her attempts have had their rocky moments.

"You know, when I was a little kid, I didn't know my dad very well," Brandon said to me not long ago. "I didn't really know him, but people would go, 'Oh, Brandon Jenner, are you related to Bruce Jenner?' 'Yes, that's my dad,' I always said. I was always so proud of the Jenner name because people would see the Olympic hero and the American icon associated with the name. I still want to be proud of our name, only now, as the son of someone who is a trailblazer for the transgender world, to inspire compassion and understanding and tolerance. Someone that can be an example of all of that."

• • •

Several years ago, Brandon started playing music with a young woman, Leah Felder, who had grown up in Malibu, too. Her father, Don Felder, was a founding member of the Eagles, so I knew him from the music world and our local Malibu community. She'd even gone to the same school as the boys, but she'd been in the grade between them. She always had long, gorgeous, naturally blond hair that was thick like a horse's mane. And she always looked like a beautiful wildflower, just totally free.

Brandon and Leah with some other homegrown Malibu musicians formed a band, Big Dume, together. She and Brandon kind of looked at each other one day and that was it. They've been together for twelve years, married for four. Their anniversary is September 5, which is the day my mother died, as well as Leah's mother's birthday. And their beautiful baby girl, Eva, my pride and joy, is soon to be a spirited one-year-old with the most winsome, infectious smile imaginable. Leah is drop-dead gorgeous, an exemplary mother, nurturing, spiritually aware, and loving. Brandon has turned out to be a very present, amazing, devoted, loving father, and a perfect example of the true meaning of fatherhood. I couldn't be more blessed with how my family has grown over the years.

I loved being the mother of boys, and I am equally as thrilled to be the mother-in-law of two beautiful young women, whom I consider more like daughters than daughters-in-law. As a matter of fact, I love them so much, I've decided to call them my daughters-in-love rather than law. As well as the beautiful Leah that Brandon brought into my life, Brody has blessed me with his gorgeous fiancée, Kaitlynn Carter. Kaitlynn is a very intelligent, down-to-earth, exquisitely beautiful, industrious girl from New Hampshire. I love her so much that I jokingly said to Brody, "If you don't ask this girl to marry you, I'm going to ask her for you."

Oh, and yes, we all get the irony of the two Caitlin/Kaitlynn Jenners looming. Do I wish the former Bruce had chosen another name? Well, it would have been easier for all of us when referring to which Caitlin/Kaitlynn we are trying to reference. But in the scheme of things, that's a very small problem.

Brandon has just finished a new EP of five original songs and I am humbled and thrilled at how incredible every note and lyric of his music is. It's truly inspirational. He's a helicopter pilot, a fixed-wing pilot, and just your typical Renaissance man. Brody is one of the hardest-working people I have ever known and has toured the world deejaying. He is writing original music as well and is always creating new ventures. He has created, produced, and starred in three more TV shows since his days as a standout performer on *The Hills*. Brody continues to be fiercely loyal, while Brandon is our family diplomat. I could not be more proud of the noble, remarkable men they have grown into. They are the solid ground on which I stand.

Sometimes what we have to give is the gift of our resilience and our perspective. If I've accomplished anything on this front, it's the success with which I've imparted these lessons to my sons. And they have rewarded me by becoming my own greatest teachers. I would venture to say I have probably learned more from Brandon and Brody than they have learned from me. Brandon and Brody have continually humbled and inspired me with everything they've had to accept, forgive, understand, and tolerate in their lives. Throughout all these challenges, I'm grateful for how they've managed to remain so honorable, loving, and open. They're really present for everyone in their lives, and their positive attitude is an incredible example for all of us.

In the eleven years since I have been separated, and finally divorced, from David, I have learned how to be alone, and enjoy my own company. I have found it liberating, to be quite honest.

That is not to say that I don't still feel that life is much better shared. But I have discovered so many different kinds of love and people with whom to share that love. I have found those relationships equally as fulfilling as romantic love, which I still experience, but am not consumed by.

I have traveled all over the world, sometimes with my sons and their loves, sometimes with my brother, Sam, and sister-in-law, Louise, with my nieces, with friends, and sometimes with a boyfriend. I can make my own decisions about how many dogs I wish to have, as silly as that may sound. After all, my senescent dogs have been my most faithful and devoted companions for many years, giving me great joy and gratification. I have fifty fruit trees on my property, and I make apricot and plum jam as well as citrus marmalade every year to give out as Christmas presents and on other occasions for my friends and family. It is a gift made with love, time, and energy. Those are the best gifts we can give or receive.

Perhaps part of my greater comfort living in my own space now is due to the fact that the three men with whom I lived, and to whom I gave my heart so completely, were such alpha males, and type-A, driven personalities. I played my own willing part in adapting my life primarily around theirs, with no residual regret. As my son, Brandon, wrote in one of his musical compositions, "Regret is such a waste of energy, you can't go back in time."

It is my hope and humble prayer that sharing my life's extraordinary journey and my heart's deepest emotions in these pages might result in a sense of connectivity for all of us who live and breathe. For no matter how rarified our experiences, as human beings, we share more commonalities than differences.

I have cultivated a blind faith in life, trusting that it does unfold as it is meant to. As much as we may try to guide its course, life has a way of working itself out in its own way, and in its own time. Our mission is simply to try to incorporate honesty, integrity, accountability, kindness, tolerance, generosity, gratitude, patience, love, and forgiveness in our daily lives.

Along with the failures, the triumphs, the pain, the pleasure, the good, the bad, the highs, the lows, the happy, and the sad, we must not lose the lessons we are challenged to receive and to pass on to others . . . What a beautiful gift we have been given—a little thing called life.

Acknowledgments

There are so many wonderful, inspirational people worth mentioning in my acknowledgments. I'm sure I may leave out some who deserve to be recognized, and my hope is that you will know who you are, forgive my brain lapse, and understand how much you have meant to my life and remembrances.

Brandon, your love for your gorgeous wife, Leah, is inspirational. Leah, you amaze me with your talents, beauty, and humility. You are what every woman aspires to be on so many levels. I love you. You are an incredible mother to my precious first grandchild, the incomparable Eva James Jenner! Every time I see Eva smile, my faith in life is renewed and my heart melts. Brandon, you are everything that a father should be, just as you are exemplary in so many ways. Eva is a very lucky little girl to have you both as her parents! I love you.

Brody, your deep love for your beautiful fiancée, Kaitlynn, makes my heart happy. Kaitlynn, thank you for always being so present, thoughtful, and inclusive. I adore spending time with you and the freedom of sharing our feelings. I love you. You have a special place in my heart. Brody, thank you for consistently being such a fierce and loyal ally. Your honesty and integrity are outstanding in a world not always so transparent. I love you.

My brother, Sam, you have always been my most constant friend, and we have a bond of shared history that can never be broken. I admire your intelligence and integrity more than you may ever realize. You are that rare man who can effectively communicate his feelings with truth and compassion. I love you. And to my other best friend, Louise, you are the dearest, most solid, authentic, reliable friend I've ever known. I respect your faith in God and your efforts to be the best person you can. I'm so lucky to call you my sister in law for all these years. You are, in truth, my sister. I love you.

My darling nieces, Jennifer and Amy, you have been so deeply ensconced in my heart from the first moment I saw your baby faces! I'm so very proud of how you have both worked exceedingly hard to help others in your professional lives! You have never been superficially motivated, but remain down-to-earth and focused with your natural beauty always shining through. You, like your mom, Louise, make me proud of my gender. I love you both as if you were my own children, and I love your significant others as well, Sebastian and Murat. I also love your babies as if they were my own grandchildren! Mason, born on Elvis's birthday, is so affectionate, intelligent, and playful; he and I have always had a special closeness. And baby Ayla is on her way to being a great girl like her mommy, Amy, and her Aunt Jennifer!

Aunt Betty, Aunt Dorothy, Aunt Marie, Aunt Christine, cousins Helen, Janet, Shelly, Brenda, Lori, David, Daphne, Wally, Jackie, Scott, Steve, Ninny, Pappaw, Grandma, and all—please know that I love my family, and I thank you all for being who you are individually, and for being such an integral part of my life.

I am so lucky to have someone I call my "ex-wife-in-law," Chrystie Scott. I love you, and I thank you for being a part of my family for so many years. I adore you, Cassandra, and your beautiful family, Michael, Frankie, and Bella. Burt and Valerie, your baby boy on the way is sure to be a precious addition to our family! I love you, Burt and Casey. I always have and I always will. You are so dear to me and a big part of my best memories.

Sarah Tomlinson, I could not have done this without your help. Your patience, lack of ego, kindness, intelligence, and empathy inspired me to write from my heart. Your willingness to let me "take the reins" says everything about how gracious, professional, and competent you are. You are a truly lovely spirit, and you have become a most cherished friend during this intense process. Thank you.

Matt Harper, you are every writer's dream editor! Thank you for your expertise, sensitivity, knowledge, time, and commitment to this project. You are a credit to your profession! Lisa Sharkey, thank you for your belief in me and the encouragement you gave me. Heidi Richter and Michael Barrs, thank you for all of your efforts to help me promote this book.

Jan Miller, I am so grateful for your friendship and your support during this process. You are a remarkable woman and I treasure our relationship, both professional and personal.

I have been inordinately blessed with the most loyal of friends. You are too numerous to mention, but I'll try to acknowledge some of you here. I want you to know by this acknowledgment, that any kindness you have shown me is not unrecognized or forgotten. You may or may not even be aware that you made a difference in my life, but you all have:

Michael Woods, Jorge and Kindra Vivo, Steve Dorff, Teresa McLeod, Ryan Clarkson, Jeanne LeMay, Susan Walden, Ashley and John Lewis, Kelly Wade, Susan Yeagley and Kevin Nealon, Pam and Greg Evigan, Anne and Steve Stodghill, Donna and Dan Aykroyd, Denise Martell, Megan and Peter Chernin, Betty and Bill Cacciatore, Dennis Ivans, Jane and Howard Smith, Jelinda and Barry Devorzon, Layla and Essam Khashoggi, Cheryl and Haim Saban, Carole and Bob Daly, Phyllis and Dennis Washington, Ghada and Ray Irani, Kofi, Irena and Mike Medavoy, Barbra Streisand and Jim Brolin, Tania and Eric Idle, Pam and Ed McMahon, Karen and George Rosenthal, Greta Detrick, Marty Allen, Jane and Tim Allen, Julie and Rick Dees, Alison Miller, Julie Araskog, BJ Cook, Lynn Palmer, Donna Antebi, Arianna Huffington, Brian Avnet, Alison Azer, Catherine Bach, Nancy Moonves, Edie and Skip Bronson, Marianne Rogers, Kenny Rogers, Keely and Pierce Brosnan, Linda and Jerry Bruckheimer, Roma Downey and Mark Burnett, Sharon and Christopher Cain, Shakira and Michael Caine, Jackie Collins, Gia and Anthony Carides, Andreas Carlsson, Linda and Don Ohlmeyer, Michelle and Mark Carter, Kari Clark, Suzanne and Alan Hamel, Natalie Cole, Kevin Costner, Meir and Katya Teper, Tracy and Tony Danza, Chris Earthy, Anita and Nathan East, Greg Philinganes, Nita Whitaker, Barbara and Marvin Davis, Nancy and Kenny Rickle, Suzanne DePasse, Esther and Rick Rosenfield, Eloise and John Paul DeJoria, Danielle Del,

Wendy Burch, Dorothy Lucy, Pam Temmen, Celine Dion and Rene Angelil, Wenda Fong, Cheryl Wheeler, Alexandra Dwek, Margie and Jerry Perenchio, Joe Esposito, Evelyn Heyward, Marie Ferro, Corrina Fields, Bui and Herb Simon, Frances Fisher, Margo Jones Fitzgerald, Joan and Larry Flax, Dee Dee and Rob Frank, Dorothy Torresi, Larry Ellison, Gary Hudson, Robyn Moore, Mel Gibson, Laure and Danny Stern, Dean Graham, Lisa Gregorish, Mary Hart, Brenda and Lionel Richie, Brooke Shields and Chris Henchy, Bill McGee, Tina and Brad Hillstrom, Lisa and Dustin Hoffman, Cindy and Alan Horn, Joanne Horowitz, Diane Warren, Risa Shapiro, Jane Seymour, James Keach, France and Art Janov, Gail Evertz, Pat Kerr Tigrett, Jena and Michael King, Jane and Jerry Weintraub, Shawn and Larry King, Michael Klein, Leslie klinger, Lester Knispel, Anne and Arnold Kopelson, Kelly Sutherland, Lyn and Norman Lear, Avril Lavigne, Mavis and Jay Leno, Julie and Les Moonves, Sam Lovullo, Jon Lovitz, Sheryl and Rob Lowe, Shirley MacLaine, Lee Majors, Tamar and Bob Manoukian, Sandy and Wink Martindale, Richard Marx, Suzie Greene, Wanda McDaniel, Mike Meldman, Vicki and Rafi Mense, Arnon Milchan, Maureen O'Connor, Evelyn and Mo Austin, Jackie and Trevor Rahn, Barbara and Don Rickles, Caroline and Mike Cusamano, Cindy and Jerry Schilling, Martha Snider, Kathy Spanberger, Paula Kent Mehan, Shelly and Donald Sterling, Bobi Leonard, Eileena Stovall, Alan Nierob, Craig Susser, Judy Swartz, Tonya York Dees, Tammy York, Donna and Richard Chesterfield, Robin and Alfredo Trento, Tricia and George Tunic, Donna and Ronnie Tutt, Steve Tyrell, Julia Van Hees, Thereza Verboon, Ruth Vowels, Vicki Walters, Sela Ward, Patricia Waters, Hind Selah, Pat and Red West, Charlie White, Vanna White, Arda and Alex Yemenidjian, Helen and Sam Zell, Josh Trabulous, Lillian, Walter and Wendy Rodriguez, Hilda and Naylin Jarquin, Christie Renteria, Jacque Lookofsky, and too many others to fill these pages! Thank you! God bless you all!

Song Credits

"I'm Only Here for a While"
Words and music by David Foster, Linda Thompson, and Cedric Carl Dent. © Linda's Boys Music (BMI), Warner-Tamerlane Publishing Corp. (BMI), and Cedbev Music (BMI). All rights on behalf of Linda's Boys Music itself and Cedbev Music administered by Warner-Tamerlane Publishing Corp. Copyright © 1995 by Peermusic III, Ltd. Used by permission. All rights reserved.

"And When She Danced"
Words and music by David Foster and Linda Thompson. © Warner-Tamerlane Publishing Corp. (BMI) and Linda's Boys Music (BMI). All rights on behalf of itself and Linda's Boys Music administered by Warner-Tamerlane Publishing Corp. Copyright © 1988 by Peermusic III, Ltd. Used by permission. All rights reserved.

"Must Have Been Angels"
Words and music by Wayne Tester and Linda Thompson. Copyright © 1999 by Universal Music Corp., No Wayne No Gain Music, Warner-Tamerlane Publishing Corp. and Brandon Brody Music. Rights for No Wayne No Gain Music controlled and administered by Universal Music Corp. All rights for Brandon Brody Music administered by Warner-Tamerlane Publishing Corp. All rights reserved. Used by permission. Reprinted by permission of Hal Leonard Corporation.

"Every Time You Cross My Mind"
Words and music by Linda Thompson and Steve Dorff. © 1995 Brandon Brody Music (BMI). All rights on behalf of Brandon Brody Music administered by Warner-Tamerlane Publishing Corp. Used by permission © Dorffmeister Music and Calkait Music.

"Love Don't Live Here Anymore"
Words and music by Linda Thompson and Eric Kaz. © 1999 Brandon Brody Music (BMI). All rights on behalf of Brandon Brody Music administered by Warner-Tamerlane Publishing Corp. © 1998 Seven Summits Music. Kozemoto Music and co-publisher. All rights reserved. Used by permission. Reprinted by permission of Hal Leonard Corporation.

"Me Loving You"
Words and music by Linda Thompson, Bobby Tomberlin, and Steve Dorff. © 2004 Brandon Brody Music (BMI). All Rights on behalf of Brandon Brody Music administered by Warner-Tamerlane Publishing Corp. Dorffmeister Music and Calkait Music. Used by permission.

"You Are My Solid Ground"
Words and music by Linda Thompson and David Foster. © 1997 Brandon Brody Music (BMI). All rights on behalf of Brandon Brody Music administered by Warner-Tamerlane Publishing Corp. Copyright © 1994 by Peermusic III, Ltd. Used by permission. All rights reserved.

"Who Could Ever Love You More"
Words and music by Linda Thompson and Steve Dorff. © 2003 Brandon Brody Music (BMI). All rights on behalf of Brandon Brody Music administered by Warner-Tamerlane Publishing Corp. Used by permission © Dorffmeister Music and Calkait music. All rights reserved. Used by permission.

"Pray for Peace"
Words by Linda Thompson and music by Bernie Herm. Copyright © Brandon Brody Music (BMI). All rights on behalf of Brandon Brody Music administered by Warner-Tamerlane Publishing Corp. © G650 Music/Pure Note Music/Songs of Universal, Inc. (BMI). All rights reserved. Used by permission.

About the Author

LINDA THOMPSON has been nominated for an Academy Award and a Grammy Award, and won an Emmy Award for writing some of the most recognized songs of a generation. She starred on the long-running hit television series *Hee Haw* for fifteen years, as well as the reality show *Princes of Malibu* with her sons, Brandon and Brody Jenner. She lives in Malibu, California.